APPROPRIATING ANCIENT AUTHORITIES

TOWARD UNDERSTANDING HOW SECOND TEMPLE AUTHORS ESTABLISHED AUTHORITY IN APOCALYPTIC LITERATURE

GLOSSAHOUSE DISSERTATION SERIES VOLUME 9
GDS 9

APPROPRIATING ANCIENT AUTHORITIES

TOWARD UNDERSTANDING HOW SECOND TEMPLE AUTHORS ESTABLISHED AUTHORITY IN APOCALYPTIC LITERATURE

Christian A. Wilder

GlossaHouse
Wilmore, KY
www.GlossaHouse.com

Appropriating Ancient Authorities:
Toward Understanding How Second Temple Authors
Established Authority in Apocalyptic Literature

GlossaHouse, LLC
110 Callis Circle
Wilmore, KY 40309
www.GlossaHouse.com

Wilder, Christian A.
Appropriating ancient authorities: toward understanding how second temple authors established authority in apocalyptic literature / Christian A. Wilder. – Wilmore, KY: GlossaHouse, © 2019

xviii, 309 pages, 23cm. — (GlossaHouse Dissertation Series Volume 9)

A revision of the author's Ph.D. dissertation, Gateway Baptist Seminary, 2017.
Includes bibliographical references and indices.

ISBN-13: 9781942697954

Library of Congress Control Number: 2019953911

The fonts used to create this work are available from
www.linguistsoftware.com/lgku.htm

Cover design by T. Michael W. Halcomb

Text layout and book design by Carl S. Sweatman

To my wife, Susan
for believing in me and sacrificing so much
during my academic journey.

GLOSSAHOUSE DISSERTATION SERIES

GlossaHouse Dissertation Series

The purpose and goal of the GlossaHouse Dissertation Series is to facilitate the creation and publication of innovative, affordable, and accessible scholarly resources—whether print or digital—that advance research in the areas of both ancient and modern texts and languages.

TABLE OF CONTENTS

Table of Illustrations

Abbreviations

The abbreviations used throughout this work follow the standard established by the *SBL Handbook of Style*, 2nd edition (2014). Those employed in this work that do not appear in the *Handbook* are (listed according to abbreviation):

ATS	*Acta Terrae Septemcastrensis*
BFOB	*Biblical figures outside the Bible*
EDEJ	*The Eerdmans Dictionary of Early Judaism*
JAJSup	Journal of Ancient Judaism, Supplements
OHAL	*Oxford Handbook of Apocalyptic Literature*
OHS	Oxford Handbook Series
SJSJ	*Supplements to the Journal for the Study of Judaism*
TLC 1	*Treaty, Law, and Covenant, Part 1, The Texts.*

Glossary

Authoritative topoi (category). The largest grouping of topoi, consisting of two subcategories: Literary authority and referential authority.

Authoritative topoi (subcategory). A second-level division of topoi created by grouping the types of topoi based on whether the authority derived from an idea, written language, personhood, or on physical elements, such as the authoritative topoi type, "tablets," which is a reference to tablets upon which a person would write.

Authoritative topoi (subtype). The grouping of individual instances of a topos type by similarities, such as referencing the Tablets of the Heavens, or the Tablets of the Law, both of which are of the authoritative topoi type, "Tablets."

Authoritative topoi (type). The division of topoi based on the method by which that topoi is used, such as calling on cosmology, or basing authority on a tablet.

Authoritative topos (individual instance). A text-specific place (topos) or places (topoi) where an author manipulates the reader's response by using available literary techniques, concepts, or references depending on earlier writing or external knowledge.

Authoritative topos of Cosmology. References to a celestial or terrestrial body or element invoking an authority either through or by the body or element. For example, a reference to Mt. Sinai invoking the authority of the Torah, or a reference to the order of the movement of the stars invoking the authority of God's wisdom.

Authoritative topos of Pseudepigraphy. Authority derived from the process of writing under a name that carries authority as it pertains to apocalyptic literature.

Authoritative topos of Righteousness. A topos of authority by which a person is authorized to act or speak because of their ethical or cultic status as righteous.

Divinely Ordained Journeys. A topos of authority in which a person is either forced to take a journey, or accompanied on a journey by a heavenly being; such journeys include heavenly ascents, descents into Hades, journeys across lands, and astral journeys.

Literary Authority by Idea. A concept used in a text to invoke authority, thereby altering a reader's thoughts or beliefs through the authority granted to it by the reader or the reader's community. This authority lays not within the text but in the idea the text references. Examples include a Revelation of Secrets or Righteousness. Literary authority by idea is one of the three main divisions for authoritative topoi presented in this present work.

Literary Authority through Written Language. A written text that either is an authoritative text or references another authoritative text. Such texts include pseudepigraphy, treaties, and references to narratives held as common knowledge. Literary authority through written language is one of the three main divisions for authoritative topoi presented in this present work.

Parent-child relationship. The relationship between two texts in which a Second Temple apocalyptic text depends directly upon another text for its authoritative material.

Reference to Common Knowledge authoritative topos. A reference in a text to a commonly known narrative that carries authority, such as the Noahic flood and its purpose of judgment.

Referential Authority through Physical Elements. A reference in literature to a literal person, place, or thing (as believed in Second Temple Judaism). The referents are diverse, such as the Tablets of the Law, specific mountains, or even celestial bodies. Referential authority through physical elements is one of the three main divisions for authoritative topoi presented in this present work.

Revelation of Secrets authoritative topos. A topos of authority in which an entity (usually an angel or a god) reveals a previously held secret to humanity often resulting in salvation.

Scriptural Authority. An authority an author invokes by referencing texts in what later became known as the Tanakh.

Short Quotation. Similar to "scriptural authority"; however, the reference is made by inserting a phrase or short passage of the Tanakh, as seen in 1 Enoch, or through interpretation as at Qumran, rather than through weaving an author's work into the text of the Tanakh, such as seen in Jubilees or the Testimony of Levi.

Topos of Covenant Authority. Either a covenant (or treaty) or the reference to a covenant or treaty for the sake of the authority derived from it.

Topos of Tablet Authority. A place within written literature whereby an author references tablets for the sake of using the authority represented by those tablets. An example of authoritative tablets is the Tablets of the Law, which reference the tablets on which God wrote the law according to the authors of the Pentateuch.

PREFACE

This study provides an understanding of how Second Temple authors established authority in apocalyptic literature. This understanding begins by recognizing these authors "borrowed" authority from other sources to legitimize their own works. This insight provides an essential window into reading Jewish apocalyptic literature. The research thus seeks the loci of the sources of authority by comparing authoritative topoi utilized in over two thousand ancient Near East (ANE) documents—including the Tanakh—with similar topoi found in the Jewish apocalyptic material. Possible sources of authority in the Jewish apocalyptic literature are located through a highly structured, modified postmodern methodology. An overview of the process occurs in the chapter 1, followed methodological consideratiosn in chapter 2.

Chapter 3 presents the preliminary research and findings which were then used to delimit all but the texts with the strongest likelihood of a parent-child relationship to the authority co-opted in Jewish apocalyptic material. Chapters 4–6 is a further investigation of the nine topos types most likely to evidence such a relationship.

The research concludes in chapter 7 by determining that while Jewish apocalyptic authors drew broadly from the literary milieu of their day, they did not rely on texts from a specific culture or ancient literary genre, nor did they rely on ancient specific Hebraic movements for authority. Instead, their sources of authority were based in contemporaneous Jewish historical and cultic realities. This conclusion holds significant implications for future research focused on analyzing apocalyptic literature, arguing for less of an emphasis on literary antecedents and more attention paid to the concurrent historical and theological realities of the Second Temple Period.

There are so many to thank that I fear I may forget someone if I begin to list names. However, not doing so feels as though it is a slight against all who have invested in me. At the top of that list is my wife, Susan Wilder, who endured a husband undertaking a DMin degree and then, a month after graduating, beginning a PhD. Without her love, support, patience, and proof-reading, I would not have made it to this point. Close behind her is my late mother, Florence Wilder, who believed in me from day one. Those long nights at the kitchen table forcing an unwilling teenage boy to do homework has finally paid off. Also, the late Lillian Wilder, a grandmother that taught a young boy what it meant to be godly. A lesson I am still learning.

Beyond them, there are so many to name on a personal level. From the late Walt Clouse who loved on and guided a teenager who had lost his father, to Dan Riffle and Leroy Miller, both of whom invested in me as youth ministers and later, as friends. And, how could I ever leave out a family who treated me as a second son? Barbara Roberts and her late husband, Bill (Mommy and Daddy II as I called them in my youth) were influential in ways they will never know. And, if you are reading this, it is time to confess. I broke the brand-new fan, not Steven. Speaking of which, I also owe much to Steven Roberts, my best friend and brother by love if not genetics.

On an academic level, where do I start? Perhaps with Dale Bruner from Whitworth College who taught a young, arrogant kid the humbleness of Christ by demonstrating it in the classroom. It is a lesson I will always remember. At the other end, I owe much to Gary Arbino who served as my Old Testament professor at Gateway Seminary, officiated my wedding, and a few years later, advised me in the PhD program. His influence on me as an advisor, and as a friend, cannot be overstated.

There are many others who should be named here as well. Professors such as Gregg Watson, John Shouse, and going back further, John Lawrence, who was my first Old Testament professor at Multnomah University. My love of the Old Testament was born in his class (but not from his exams). On the personal side, friends such as Gary and Aelyese Mauk, Claire Roberts, Mike Feeney (two great friends from college), my mother- and late father-in-law, Phyllis and David Curland, and so many others all deserve mention here. Each of you has helped me get to this place in my life. So, for those reasons and others, I dedicate this work to all of you.

Chapter 1
UNDERSTANDING AND STUDYING ANCIENT AUTHORITY

The new members…from House Minerva find it perfectly reasonable to accept my authority. I don't fool myself…. It's only because Mustang trusts me that they obey.

–Pierce Brown *Red Rising*

1.1. Introduction

Authority, borrowed or earned, is a currency of influence that purchases the power to provoke cognitive shifts or physical action. Darrow—the "I" in Pierce Brown's dystopian tale of stratified culture and revolt—acknowledged he borrowed authority from Mustang, the leader of a rival house. Inherent in this acknowledgment, however, was his submission—to borrow authority from another person is to submit to that person's authority. Consequently, straying from the bounds of borrowed authority negates that authority. This model, called a "complex authority structure," begins when someone borrows authority, then holds that authority over a third person (or party).[1]

Understanding this structure is essential to studying Jewish apocalyptic authors and authority. Did they borrow authority from the Hebraic movements or the Tanakh? Is it possible they borrowed authority from documents originating in cultures outside of Judaism? These ponderings led to the following research question for this work: how did Second Temple authors establish authority in apocalyptic literature?

1.2. Expanding on the Basic Research Question

At the core of this research question was a concern for sources.[2] Traditionally, this question focused on the Hebraic movements or external cultures from which scholars believed Second Temple

[1] James S. Coleman, *Foundations of Social Theory* (Cambridge: Harvard University Press, 1994), 164–65.

[2] "Sources" as used here signified a text from which an author directly borrowed concepts that were formative to apocalyptic material.

apocalyptic authors borrowed material. However, as determined in stage 1 of this study (presented in the next section), the traditional question introduced correlation fallacies as scholars argued for a source based on similarity alone. To avoid correlation fallacies in this work, stage 2 began with a search for uses of authority in the Jewish apocalyptic material, the Tanakh, and in material from the external ancient world (EAW).[3] Then, like authorities were compared to determine if topoi in the Tanakh or EAW literature were in parent-child relationships with corresponding topoi in the Jewish apocalyptic works.[4]

1.3. Stages of the Study

The first stage focused on developing the study. It included a literary review and conclusions on a method based on observations of previous research. The second stage focused on process. This stage was divided into four main steps. These two stages are presented below, followed by a summary of the steps as organized in the following chapters.

1.3.1. Stage 1: Development of the Study

The study began with research into previous scholarship. In it, two problems were observed that has affected scholarship in the area of apocalytpic studies. The first problem was the a priori acceptance of sources, and the second problem was that no one focused on how authority was used across a broad spectrum. These problems produced two main observations. The first observation was an a priori acceptance of sources in apocalyptic studies. This acceptance came through the

---

[3] In this study, the term, "external ancient world" (EAW) designated all non-Hebraic cultures in the ANE, Egypt, and Greece. "EAW literature" designated literature dated at least one century prior to the Second Temple apocalyptic material to which it was being compared. Finally, Second Temple apocalyptic material did not include any material considered canonical in Protestant Christianity. The reason for this delimitation is provided in §2.4.3.2.3 "Meta-research and Bias Correction" (below).

[4] According to the glossary, a parent-child relationship was defined as the relationship between two texts in which a Second Temple apocalyptic text depended directly upon another text for its authoritative material. Note, the goal in this work is not to follow normal comparative literary studies of whole texts, but to compare the texts *only* as it concerned the topos.

History of Religions School.[5] The second observation was that scholars in apocalyptic studies used a broad-based literary comparison without focusing on the specifics of individual texts. More specifically, there was little to no focus on uses of authority concerning a parent-child relationship. These observations led to two conclusions. First, any methodology used in this study had to incorporate a continued questioning of assumptions and biases. Second, the methodology had to be based on literary criticism and historical studies as the research was focused on literature and its development within a specific historical period. These conclusions led to choosing a methodology derived from postmodern historiography.[6]

Two key elements of this methodology should be kept in mind. First, scientific objectivity is difficult to achieve in subjective studies such as literary comparison.[7] To counter this problem, "loops" were introduced to control for human error and bias.[8] The second element was a text-first approach that incorporates no a priori acceptance of sources between Second Temple apocalyptic literature and the Tanakh or EAW literature. These observations, conclusions, and key elements led to stage 2, conducted in four steps.

1.3.2. Stage 2: Process of the Study

The first step consisted of reading the Second Temple apocalyptic literature, Tanakh, and EAW material independently.[9] The goal of this strategy was to find authoritative topoi in all texts without concern for

---

[5] As presented in chapter 2 (below).

[6] The justification for this methodology is provided in chapter 2 below—see §2.4.3. Defining a Modified Postmodern Methodology.

[7] According to Eric Hayot, "Any comparison shapes what it compares; and it shapes the theory of comparison that makes what it compares comparable" (Eric Hayot, "Vanishing Horizons: Problems in Comparison of China and the West," in *A Companion to Comparative Literature*, ed. Ali Behdad and Dominic Thomas [Chichester: John Wiley and Sons, 2011], 88). Thus, the act of comparative studies is a subjective act molded by the very act and rules by which it is accomplished. Cf., several other authors in the same volume, who make similar points.

[8] "Loops" are defined as temporary returns to earlier parts of the study. This method was used to check bias stemming from better familiarity with the Hebraic texts. The loops provided a broader knowledge base of EAW material, which then allowed interaction with a larger cross section of topos types and topos type occurrences.

[9] A "reading strategy" is defined as the orientation a reader takes when approaching a text. In this case, a focus on the text itself.

possible relationships with other texts. In the second step, the reading strategy shifted toward reading for context. This strategy resulted in culling topoi no longer seen as authoritative. The third step comprised a cross-text reading strategy. In this strategy, EAW passages holding similar topos types to apocalyptic literature were compared and then quantified based on the findings (the comparisons pertained *solely* to authoritative topoi).[10] These three steps completed the preliminary research for this study. The fourth step was an in-depth assessment of the conclusions from the preliminary research. However, each of these four steps subdivided into several more steps.

1.3.2.1. Step 1: Text—Identifying Authoritative Topoi

The first step contained four substeps (steps 1a–d) and one loop.[11] In step 1a, the work concerned identifying and labeling possible authoritative topoi in Second Temple apocalyptic literature. In step 1b, possible Tanakh sources for topos types were listed. Then, step 1c comprised a search through EAW literature for possible sources of each topos type.

After completing step 1c, a predilection was identified for finding topos types in apocalyptic literature with a stronger possible parent-child relationship to the Tanakh than EAW material. A loop was therefore introduced to control this predilection. In the loop, step 1a (apocalyptic texts) was again explored, this time with a focus on topos types identified in step 1c (which was a search of EAW material). This loop controlled for bias stemming from familiarity with the Tanakh and resulted in identifying additional authoritative topos types in the apocalyptic material.[12] These results were compared in the next step (1d).

In step 1d, some authoritative topos types found in EAW or Hebraic material were removed because they were not found in the apocalyptic

[10] The comparisons in this study concerned only authoritative topoi and how they were used in the various materials. Larger textual comparisons were only considered here if it helped to explain the context, and therefore the use, of the authoritative topoi.

[11] To reiterate, this step held a text-first reading strategy.

[12] This loop was necessary due to a familiarity with the Tanakh and, by comparison, an unfamiliarity with EAW material. The result of this familiarity was a study predisposed toward topos types heavy with similarities to the Tanakh. To correct for that disposition, the loop was introduced after step 1c. In the loop, the Second Temple apocalyptic literature and subsequent possible topos types were reexamined for similarities with EAW material.

literature. Several other topoi were also culled to form a new list.[13] This list was then delineated and simplified to prepare for the second step.

1.3.2.2. Step 2: Context–Striking Passages and Delineating Authoritative Topoi

Step 2 also contained four substeps (steps 2a–d). Step 2a was an inspection of the context of possible topoi in both EAW and Second Temple apocalyptic literature.[14] Several passages were struck because context determined the topoi were not authoritative.[15] In step 2b, subtypes were assessed based on the work in step 2a. In step 2c, the topos-type delineation was revised in preparation for the third step.[16]

1.3.2.3. Step 3: Cross-Text–Quantification

The third step was determining possible relationships between the apocalyptic material and the Tanakh or EAW literature.[17] This step began with a loop to step 1c (the search of EAW texts) using a keyword search through the material already explored plus another one thousand EAW texts.[18] The search in this loop included the topos type name (if applicable), synonyms (if applicable), and major elements included within the topos type that might signify an occurrence.[19] This loop was introduced to control for human error and unintentional bias by identifying and then forcing a focus on all possible occurrences of

---

[13] The reasoning for culling each topos was provided in §3.1. and 3.2. (below).

[14] To reiterate, the context reading strategy focused on the context only as it pertained to authority.

[15] There were several places (topoi) that held a reference, but such references were not authoritative. For instance, a reference such as "In the days of Enoch" may have been included because of the reference to Enoch (Authority by Name). However, once context was studied, it was determined "In the days of Enoch" was not authoritative because the author was not borrowing authority from the name. Instead, the phrase was used to establish the setting for the story.

[16] Certain topos types were also demoted to subtypes.

[17] The cross-text reading strategy, like the context reading strategy, was based on comparisons as they pertained to authority. Thus, genre, linguistics, and so on were compared only if it added to or detracted from the authoritative topos in the passage being studied.

[18] See Appendix B (below) for the list of texts used in this loop. Note, however, that some texts were included more than once based on differing translations.

[19] For example, a Boolean search string for the Cosmos topos type might be "cosmos OR universe OR sun OR moon OR planet OR stars [and so on]."

each topos type returned by the keyword search. This method provided consistent consideration of each occurrence across EAW material and deepened the authoritative topoi pool from which occurrences were quantified. The results of this search were examined in step 3a.

In step 3a, the focus was a comparison of contexts between Second Temple apocalyptic material and EAW material.[20] Similarly, in step 3b, the focus was a comparison of the word picture or literary structures in each of the passages between Second Temple apocalyptic literature and EAW literature. Then, in step 3c, the last comparative category concerned the strength of the appeal to authority in the Second Temple apocalyptic material. In these steps (3a–c), the researcher assigned a score to each comparison, ranging from zero to three. Step 3d involved totaling the scores to identify the passages most likely to be in a parent-child relationship with Second Temple apocalyptic literature. Scores were also produced for each authoritative topos type and subtype. After the comparisons of contexts, word pictures and literature structures, and appeal to authority were completed, four topos types looked as though they derived from EAW literature. Four other topos types looked as though they derived equally from the EAW literature or the Tanakh. A ninth topos type, Short Quotation, looked as though it derived solely from the Tanakh. These nine topos types were further investigated in step 4.

1.3.2.4. Step 4: A Focused Return to Text, Context, and Cross-Text

The fourth step (see chapters 3–5) was a closer examination of the remaining topos types to discern if a parent-child relationship existed. The reading strategy from steps 1–3 (the primary work) was reused in step 4 (the primary work). As a result, step 4 was repeated nine times, once for each topos type.[21] Step 4a began with presentations of a topos type, its use as an authority, and where it was employed in Second

---

20 Specifically, the comparison focused on similarities of context, words, and literary structures found in the Second Temple apocalyptic literature and the Tanakh or EAW texts with the same or similar topos types.

21 Only the highest scoring occurrences from step 3 were reexamined in step 4. This re-examination included a focus on the number and strength of the points of verbal contact between an occurrence in the Second Temple apocalyptic literature and the EAW or the Tanakh material. "Points of verbal contact" is explained in the following paragraphs.

Temple apocalyptic literature.[22] The topos type occurrences were selected by strength of subtype, or, in cases were no subtype existed, the strength of each occurrence based on the quantification scores of each subtype in step 3. In Step 4b, the context of each occurrence was examined. Step 4c turned to modern scholarship concerning the passage or topos type. Thus, the first three substeps focused on the occurrence in the apocalyptic material. The following two steps, however, focused on similar occurrences in the EAW or Tanakh material.

In Step 4d the highest scoring EAW texts were reexamined, paying specific attention to word pictures and context as it concerned points of verbal contact. Step 4e followed a similar pattern with the Tanakh material, highlighting possible associations with one of the three Hebraic movements to which scholars often attribute apocalyptic roots. Finally, step 4f held the evaluation and conclusions for each topos type concerning a possible parent-child relationship.

The standard for a parent-child relationship between an EAW or Tanakh text and Second Temple apocalyptic literature was three points of verbal contact.[23] A point of verbal contact may be one of three types. The first type was the presence of the same word(s), cognate(s) or synonym(s) located within similar topos types promoted by the author.[24] The second type of verbal contact was word pictures an author used to verbally paint an overall similar conceptual picture related to the topos type. However, word pictures must have occurred within similar overarching themes concerning the authority under study, and without

---

[22] Step 4a represented a return to the beginning of the text, context, cross-text structure, but focused solely on individual occurrences of a topos type.

[23] A single verbal contact may occur due to similar cultural or linguistic backgrounds or similar experiences. Two verbal contacts may occur due to shared narratives or commonly told tales. As such, two verbal contacts may indicate influence, but it did not necessitate a parent-child relationship. Therefore, three points of verbal contact is the minimum number to indicate a parent-child relationship.

[24] The presence of similar articles, pronouns, or words used to hold together a sentence but not further its meaning (also known as "glue words") was not evidence for a parent-child relationship, nor was the lack of similarity evidence for denying a relationship. A parent-child relationship had to have included more than just synonyms as points of contact. Furthermore, context was not significant for this point of contact except in the Short Quotation topos type, as explained in chapter 6.

meaningful differences in the Second Temple material.[25] The third type of verbal contact was the context of the topos type under consideration between the two texts that were compared. The context must have been complementary. "Complementary" meant two or more distinct similarities were present without accompanying detracting dissimilarities.[26]

However, any of the following conditions ruled out a parent-child relationship, even if three points of verbal contact were present: A meaningful difference to the overall narrative, the word picture, or concepts; the presence of inverted concepts,[27] ideas, or word pictures if the author used the inversion to argue Jewish cultic or cultural superiority;[28] or the presence of similar verbal contacts across several

---

[25] "Meaningful differences" is defined as change that affected the overall message of the text, the role of the characters in the text (if the role is important to the topos type occurrence), or directly affected the teleological purpose of the text.

[26] For instance, if two narratives incorporated an astral journey to the moon and then the sun, the context was complementary. If one narrative had only an astral journey to the moon, but the reason for the astral journey was the same in both texts, it was still complementary as two distinct similarities still existed (journey to the moon and the reasoning behind it). However, if both narratives had an astral journey to the moon, but one journey was forced and the other, willingly taken, then the context was not complementary because of detracting dissimilarities and therefore was not counted as a verbal contact.

[27] The issue concerning inversions is the lack of borrowed authority. As already argued, authority borrowed from one person by a second is negated if the second person strayed too far from the narrative of the borrowed authority. In the case of inversion, the author not only strayed from the authority, but also attacked that authority outright, which negated any kind of borrowed authority.

For this study, an inversion occurred wherever an element of a story changes roles with the same or similar element in a comparative from Second Temple literature. For instance, in an inversion between Prometheus and the Watchers, both Prometheus and the Watchers were punished for giving secrets to humans, but the role of Prometheus (kind, caring, and standing in the way of Zeus's desire to hurt humanity) was inverted in the Second Temple apocalyptic story. There, the Watchers caused all types of problems for humanity. As a result, the good (Prometheus) became bad (Watchers), the main deity who was bad (Zeus) became good (YHWH), and the secret that was good (fire, which saves humans) became bad (heavenly secrets that cause all types of evil in the Watcher narratives). As such, while inversions do not negate a relationship between the two texts (*Prometheus Bound* may have influenced the Watcher narratives) they do rule out the possibility of a Jewish author depending on the authority of the EAW text to confirm the message to the reader.

[28] Inversions that display cultic or cultural superiority occurred when elements of a narrative form or plot were changed to the detriment of the cult or culture

cultures or books of the Tanakh. However, if this third condition existed in the text, it indicated a possible parent-child relationship between the topos types in apocalyptic texts and the overall concept in the EAW or Tanakh (but lacked a link to a specific movement or culture). Finally, if the development of a concept or idea was traced through succeeding texts in the EAW material or Tanakh until it was concluded in Second Temple apocalyptic literature, that set of passages in the EAW or Tanakh material is labeled, "trajectory." Trajectories indicated a parent-child relationship between the apocalyptic text(s) and the overall culture or cultures from which the texts derived.[29] The presentation of this work is presented in the following six chapters.

1.4. Order of Presentation

Chapter 2 is the report of the development of the study, which includes the two key observations resulting from the literature review: a brief history of the Second Temple period, and the development of the methodology. Chapter 3 is a short chapter presenting the preliminary work accomplished in steps 1–3. Chapters 4–6 comprise step 4, which is the investigation into

---

from which the EAW text derived. To use an example from the NT, Dennis MacDonald summarized his argument on an inversion from Mark. In the introduction to his work, here he argued that the "Gerasene demoniac resembles Homer's Polyphemus. In the epic, when the ogre asks Odysseus his name, he responds by saying 'Nobody is my name,' a ruse that later allows him to escape. A similar motif appears in Mark, but now it is Jesus who asks for the name, and the demoniac responds, 'Legion is my name.' Both works use the motif of requesting a name, but Mark transforms it: the hero asks for the name of the caveman, who replies with a name indicating multiplicity. 'Nobody' has become 'Legion'" (*Does the New Testament Imitate Homer? Four Cases from the Acts of the Apostles* [New Haven: Yale University Press, 2003], 5). If MacDonald is correct, this passage represents an inversion and promoted superiority of Jesus over the Greek Hero because Luke wrote Jesus overcoming Legion, a number far superior to that represented by Nobody. Moreover, Jesus overcame Legion by a simple command contra Odysseus, who had to trick the ogre into letting him go. Therefore Jesus, the Jewish cultic hero (for those following him) was far superior to the Greek Hero.

[29] Trajectories were concepts that began their development in ancient times (either the EAW world or the Tanakh), but their use in the apocalyptic literature seemed to be further developed. One such example is the Tablets topos type. In this study, references to this topos type occurred throughout biblical literature, however, only in the Second Temple material do the tablets take on names that carry the authority of the tablet. Subsequently, the mere mention of the tablet name carried authority in the Second Temple texts.

possible parent-child relationships of topos types found in Second Temple apocalyptic literature and the EAW material or the Tanakh.[30] Chapter 7 begins with conclusions, then moves to poststudy methodological assessments and a discussion of future avenues of research.

[30] Step four is repeated nine times, once for each topos type as noted above under the subheading "Step 4—a Focused Return to Text, Context, and Cross-text." It should also be noted again that Second Temple apocalyptic literature or Jewish apocalyptic literature did not include texts found in the Tanakh.

Chapter 2
DEVELOPING THE STUDY: SCHOLARSHIP, HISTORY, AND METHODS

2.1. Introduction

As mentioned, this study began with research into scholarship concerning Second Temple apocalyptic literature. This research culminated with two observations. The first observation was an a priori acceptance of sources introduced into apocalyptic studies through the History of Religions School, as shown in the Babel-Bible controversy that began in 1903. Second, scholars in apocalyptic studies used a broad-based literary comparison without focusing on the specifics of individual texts or the uses of authority that evidenced a parent-child relationship. The following history of scholarship exemplifies these observations.

2.2. Scholarship

In 1832, Gottfried Lücke coined the term "apocalyptic literature" as part of the title to his book, *Versuch einer vollständigen Einleitung in die Offenbarung Johannis und die gesamte apokalyptische Literatur.*[1] Soon thereafter, the early modern period of apocalyptic scholarship (1832–1955) began with a focus on origins, and thus, a drive for sources. The earliest studies located these sources in Zoroastrianism.

2.2.1. Early Scholars and the Drive for Sources

At the close of the nineteenth century, Richard Reitzenstein and Wilhelm Bousset worked out of the History of Religions School. They identified the Zoroastrian *Baham Yast* as the root of apocalyptic

[1] *An Attempt at a Complete Introduction to the Revelation of John and the entire Apocalyptic Literature*. Gottfried Lücke, *Versuch einer vollständigen Einleitung in die Offenbarung Johannis und in die gesamte apokalyptische Literatur* (Bonn: Weber, 1832). According to John Collins: "The word, *apocalyptic*...was introduced into scholarly discussion by Gottfried Christian Friedrich Lücke in 1832" ("What Is Apocalyptic Literature?" in *OHAL*, ed. John J. Collins, OHS [Oxford: Oxford University Press], 2014), 1).

works, claiming it "most closely resembles the Jewish apocalypses in form."[2] Around the same time (1892–93), James Moulton published a three-part article in *The Thinker*. His article, "Zoroaster and Israel" was followed by two more articles concerning Zoroastrian influences. Just over a decade later, in 1905–6, Lawrence Mills published his work in which he zealously pushed parallels between Zoroastrianism and Jewish Apocalypticism.[3] These four scholars represent the beginning of the a priori push for sources in the earliest days of Jewish apocalyptic studies. Perhaps, the best exemplar of this push was found in the Babel-Bible controversy.

2.2.2. Babel-Bible Controversy

Friedrich Delitzsch, an early Assyriologist, brought the Babel-Bible controversy to prominence in a January 1903 speech in which he argued for Babylonian origins of the Hebraic material.[4] Delitzsch claimed the Amarna Letters, found just fifteen years earlier, identified Babylonian influence extending across the Levant.[5] Thus, he argued

---

[2] John J. Collins, "Apocalyptic Eschatology in the Ancient World," in *The Oxford Handbook of Eschatology*, ed. Jerry L. Walls, OHS (Oxford: Oxford University Press, 2008), 41–42. In this study, "apocalyptic literature" referred to noncanonical Second Temple apocalyptic material traditionally grouped by scholars under the genre "Apocalyptic."

[3] Jason M. Silverman, *Persepolis and Jerusalem: Iranian Influence on the Apocalyptic Hermeneutic*, LHBOTS 558 (London: T&T Clark, 2014), 2.

[4] The Babel-Bible controversy illustrated the degree to which scholars strove to link Jewish material to older ANE sources. This proclivity affected not only studies in Genesis, but apocalyptic literature as well, as seen throughout Hermann Gunkel's *Israel und Babylonien* (Göttingen: Vandenhoeck und Ruprecht, 1903).

[5] Friedrich Delitzsch, *Babel und Bibel*; *ein Vortrag* (Leipzig: J. C. Hinrichs'sche Buchhandlung, 1902), 28. Delitzsch wrote, "Als die zwölf Israels in Kanaan einfielen, kamen sie hiernach in ein land, welches vollstandig ein Domäne der babylonischen kultur war." Those items he believed originated in Babylon included weights and measures; various laws; comparable antediluvian people; creation, flood, and other myths; and even monotheism and the Sabbath. Later in life, he concluded that German mythology, heroes, and folktales should replace the OT canon. In his second lecture, he rejected OT revelation and thus by connection, the Israelite cult, proclaiming all had descended from Babylonian myths, which themselves possibly derived from Indo-Germanic roots. These conclusions flowed from his studies in Assyriology and his nationalistic and anti-Semitic tendencies. Along with these biases, Bill Arnold and David Weisberg argued that Delitzsch's reaction to critics of his first lecture drove him to reject the OT—see Bill T. Arnold and David B. Weisberg, "Centennial Review of Delitzsch's 'Babel und Bibel' Lectures," *JBL* 121.3 (Autumn, 2002): 445–47. As an example of his detractors, J. A.

Babylonian influence extended across the Levant, which he then used to help legitimize his arguments for Babylonian roots Hermann Gunkel responded with *Israel und Babylonien: Der Einfluss Babyloniens auf die Israelitische Religion* (1903).[6] Although arguing with Delitzsch, he also proposed Babylonian roots for the biblical material, identifying many places in which he and Delitzsch agreed. In doing so, however, Gunkel provided the seeds for deconstructing his assumptions on Babylonian roots for Hebraic material.[7]

Selbie wrote, "Nothing we have read sets the position of matters in a clearer light, or shows more conclusively that even, whatever may be the claims of Delitzsch as an Assyriologist, as a biblical theologian he is the veriest [sic] blunderer" (J. A. Selbie, "Recent Foreign Theology," *ExpTim* 14.12 (1903): 546–47).

[6] His first book, *Schöpfung und Chaos* (1895), concerned creation, chaos, and their interplay in both primeval and eschatological settings found in Revelation—see Hermann Gunkel, *Schöpfung und Chaos in Urzeit und Endzeit: Eine religionsgeschichtliche Untersuchung über Gen 1 und Ap Joh 12* (Göttingen: Vandenhoeck und Ruprecht, 1895), 239–40. According to Gunkel, scholars often envisioned apocalyptic authors writing a manuscript side-by-side with the OT; however, Gunkel believed the authors possibly wrote from memory, and thus he cast doubt on the role of included material (specifically, texts in which direct dependence was clear). What was the quoted text, then? Was it a direct quote, a gloss, a reference, or something else? For Gunkel, these questions opened the door for form critical analysis, and Richard Clifford and others have attributed the first move in assigning roots to apocalyptic literature to Gunkel: "The first modern scholar to have seriously attempted to trace the roots of apocalyptic literature in ancient texts was Hermann Gunkel" (Richard J. Clifford, "The Roots of Apocalypticism in Near Eastern Myth," in *The Continuum History of Apocalypticism*, ed. Bernard McGinn, John J. Collins, and Stephen J. Stein [New York: Continuum, 2003], 3).

In all fairness, however, Gunkel was not alone in his quest. For instance, Heinrich Zimmern and Hugo Winckler both published essays in 1903, but neither had Gunkel's apocalyptic focus—see Heinrich Zimmern, *Biblische und Babylonische Urgeschichte*, Der Alte Orient: Gemeinverständliche Darstellungen Herausgegeben 2.3 (Leipzig: J. C. Hinrichs'sche Buchhandlung, 1903); Hugo Winckler, *Himmels- und Weltenbild der Babylonier: Grundlage der Weltanschauung und Mythologie aller Völker*, Der Alte Orient: Gemeinverständliche Darstellungen Herausgegeben 3.2/3 (Leipzig: J. C. Hinrichs'sche Buchhandlung, 1903). Contrary to Gunkel, Gerhard von Rad argued the newer texts did not compel a direct link to the OT, but possibly depended on later tradition. In such a case, the scholar needed to consider how well the writings coincided and the likelihood in which the later text depends upon the earlier. Applied to this study, von Rad's method protected against importing unnecessary roots.

[7] Throughout *Israel und Babylonien*, which was originally a pamphlet, Gunkel alluded to scientific theological investigation in reference to the History of Religions School, but in doing so, he exposed his own cyclical reasoning by assuming what must be, because it already was. For instance, he wrote concerning the flood: "diese

In the end, Gunkel understood the relationship between Israelite and Babylonian literature as embedded myths of Babylonian tales within the biblical and later apocalyptic material.[8] He indulged in what Richard Clifford called his "romanticist tendency to overstress origins as an explanation and [thus, he] undervalue[d] reception and particular usage."[9] His method, known as "myth and ritual," attracted many followers

---

babylonische Geschichte ist hier so asführlich geschildert worden, damit der Leser selber ihre merkwürdige abnlichkeit mit der biblischen, zugleich aber auch ihre ebenso grosse abweichung erkennen möge" (*Israel und Babylonien*, 18; "this Babylonian story has been portrayed here so well that the reader may recognize its remarkable affinity with the biblical story, but also its equally great deviations"—translation mine). After listing the similarities, he concluded, "Demnach muss eine Beziehung zwischen beiden Erzählungen bestehen" (ibid., 19; "thus, a relationship between the two narratives must exist"—translation mine). But why? What was this relationship? Gunkel provided a brief geographical synopsis of waterways and then determined the story was Babylonian in origin, furthering his argument by stating, "Den für jeden Sagenkenner ist es ganz unzweifelhaft, dass beide Erzälungen die in nebensächlichen Einzelzügen so sehr übereinstimmen, als erzächlichen Einzelzügen so sehr übereinstimmen, also Erzählungen verwandt sein müssen" (ibid.; "it is then quite clear for every Sayings-Expert the two narratives, which match so closely in the individual details, must be related as narratives"—translation mine). Again, why? The answer was not in the narratives themselves, but in Gunkel's History of Religions and Form bias whereby he believed later writers used older narratives but stripped the original meaning from the form and applied their own.

Gunkel asserted (rather than argued) two forms of the flood story may have existed, but they were not two separate accounts. Instead, the Hebraic story was dependent upon the Babylonian story (another assertion). Yet, this method was exactly what he accused Delitzsch of doing—assigning truth statements based on his own area of expertise to truths that were much larger than his area. The History of Religions School and Gunkel's Form criticism created a narrow window from which to view the vast interaction of the ancient world. Thus, Gunkel discredited the idea of staying within a singular discipline and school of thought within that discipline; yet in the same book, he also assessed canonical material and assumed narrative relationships solely from his Form-Critical approach. The deconstruction of Gunkel here was not to assert no similarities existed between the Babylonian and biblical narratives or to privilege biblical narratives as roots for later Apocalypticism, but to investigate and lay open the assumptions that pervaded research into those similarities.

[8] Note, however, in 1895 Gunkel wrote concerning the book of Revelation, the "Entstehung des apokalyptischen Bildes aus Nachahmung des OT innerlich wahrscheinlich erscheint" (*Schöpfung und Chaos*, 240; "emergence of the apocalyptic image from imitation of the OT appears inwardly probable"—translation mine).

[9] Clifford, "Roots," 4.

studying apocalyptic writing. Despite Gunkel's great contributions, his method was based on the same History of Religions School and the same a priori assignment of external cultural roots to apocalyptic literature.[10] Moreover, his comparisons were broad-based rather than focused on the way in which Second Temple apocalyptic authors used other material in an authoritative manner.

The same held true for Isidor Scheftelowitz who published *Die altpersische Religion und das Judentum* (1920), seventeen years after the *Babel und Bibel* controversy. In it, he proposed Zoroastrianism strongly influencing Judaism only in the Sassanian period (224–651 CE):

> At a time when the principles of monotheism and an absolute dearth of images had become the common property of the Jewish people, [Zoroastrianism], because of its polytheistic character and its images of gods, did not influence the Jewish religion in its essentials. It was only since the first century BC...[that] the influence of Parsiism on Judaism is asserted in the sense that parallel representations of Satan and the future world were provided with a few new Persian views, but only a small part of which was firmly rooted in Jewish faith, while the other part was merely incorporated into the Jewish literature as an individual view of a scholar.[11]

---

[10] Interestingly, Collins wrote on Gunkel and the influence of Ugaritic discoveries: "Ugaritic parallels now appear more adequate at some points.... [But] Gunkel was not wrong to appeal to Babylonian material, since the issue is not the exact derivation but the kinds of allusions involved" (John J. Collins, *The Apocalyptic Imagination: An Introduction to Jewish Apocalyptic Literature* [Grand Rapids: Eerdmans, 1998], 18–19). This derivation-allusion caveat was important, as allusion introduced several variables that made parent-child authoritative textual relationships less likely.

[11] Translation mine. The German reads: "Zu einer Zeit, wo die Prinzipien des Monotheismus und der absoluten Bildlosigfeit endgiltig Gemeingut des jüdischen Volkes geworden waren, hat der Parsismus wegen seines polytheistischen Charakters und seiner Götterbilder die jüdische Religion in ihren Grundzügen nicht beeinflussen tönnen. Erst seit dem ersten Jahrhundert v. Chr, als die Juden infolge ihrer propagandistischen Tätigkeit angeregt wurden, die Religionen derer, die sie zu betehren suchten, in wenig näher in Auge zu fassen, und die Proselyten an manchen dem Judentum ähnlichen Gedanten ihrer angestammten persischen Religion festhielten, macht sich der Einfluss des Parsismus auf das Judentum insofern geltend,

Jason Silverman, in his 2012 work on Persian influence, wrote that Scheftelowitz understood the connection to be "cosmetic borrowings" of Zoroastrian and Persian literature and culture. Thus, in 1920, Scheftelowitz was possibly the first to propose Jewish and Persian apocalyptic themes (such as eschatology, as Silverman notes) were not in a parent-child relationship. However, he acknowledged Babylonian influence upon Jewish Apocalypticism and Zoroastrianism based on similarities.[12]

In England, eighteen years after Gunkel published his first book, Robert H. Charles (1918) published a set of translations in which he assigned Greek and Persian influence to several apocalyptic works.[13] In the twilight of Charles' career, H. H. Rowley emerged, but he also focused on cosmic myths and Persian influence.[14] Rowley's career spanned a waning period of apocalyptic scholarship from the close of World War II until the discovery of the Dead Sea Scrolls.

Thus, for the early part of Jewish apocalyptic scholarship, the early German work (and to a lesser degree, English work) relied heavily on the History of Religions School and a need for sources to explain Second Temple Jewish apocalyptic material. At the same time, dialectical philosophy penetrated both the hard and soft sciences, and

---

als parallele Vorstellungen von dem Satan und der Tünftighen Welt mit einigen neuen persischen Ansässen versehen wurden, von denen aber nur ein kleiner Teil in dem jüdischen Voltsglauben feste Wurzeln schlug, während der andere Teil bloss als individuelle Anschauung eines Gelehrten in das jüdische Schrifttum hineingetragen wurde." Although often considered monotheistic, Scheftelowitz correctly labeled Zoroastrianism "polytheistic" because it included Ahura Mazda and his dualistic opposite, Aura Mainyu, alongside six lesser gods known as the Amesha Spenta, who were worshipped by name: Vohu Manah, Asha Vahistah, Khshatra-Vairya, Spenta Armaiti, Haurvatat, and Ameretat, according to Yas. 16:3 (a *yasna* in the Zoroastrian holy writings)—see Isidor Scheftelowitz, *Die altpersische religion und das Judentum: Unterschiede, Übereinstimmungen und gegenseitige Beeinflussungen* (Giessen: Töpelmann, 1920), 6.

[12] Silverman, *Persepolis and Jerusalem*, 2–3.

[13] Robert H. Charles, *APOP*, vol. 2, *Pseudepigrapha* (Oxford: Clarendon Press, 1913), 164, 58, 531 (shortcited as *Pseudepigrapha* 2); and a contributing author, L. S. A. Wells, did so as well (131).

[14] H. H. Rowley, *The Relevance of Apocalyptic: A Study of Jewish and Christian Apocalypses from Daniel to the Revelation* (New York: Harper and Bros., 1943), 40. He further wrote the "hierarchy of angels" in Dan 10:13 was "reflecting the influence of Persian ideas" but specified, "These ideas were working on a basis of Hebrew ideas" (54).

archaeologists were discovering literary texts from cultures throughout the EAW. This concatenation drove scholars to assign external roots for Jewish literature, making it nearly impossible to study apocalyptic material without attempting to identify sources.[15] These assignments occurred through comparative literary studies focused on similarities without regard for whether authors of the later material engaged an earlier text to borrow authority. Unfortunately, these two observations also hold true for scholarship after the discovery of the Dead Sea Scrolls.

2.2.3. After Qumran: External Influences

Beginning in 1947, the discoveries from Qumran led to stronger interests in Hellenistic roots.[16] This new interest began in the late 1950s with thematic affinities.[17] Soon thereafter, the arguments multiplied to include eschatological and more general influences. For instance, Thomas Glasson began his 1961 book, *Greek Influence in Jewish Eschatology*, with the following passage:

> It is generally agreed that a new development in eschatology took place in Jewish thought about two hundred years before Christ.... When we consider antecedent probabilities Greece, or rather the Hellenistic world, appear to have a strong claim to consideration as providing at least one element in this new orientation.[18]

---

[15] These assumptions were at the heart of Gunkel's work refuting Delitzsch. He argued an old form of Babylonian stories existed into which authors poured new material from narratives and experiences concerning the Hebraic people. The result was a new form, called apocalyptic writing. According to this method, a parent-child relationship existed, but since authors had taken an old form and filled it with new meaning, Babylonian stories could not replace the biblical narratives.

[16] Along with continued Eastern influence, as noted in the previous paragraph.

[17] Examples of authors include: M. Delcor, "L'immortalité de l'âme dans le livre de la Sagesse et dans les documents de Qumrân," *NRTh* 77 (1955): 627; and Paul Beauchamp, "Le salut corporel des justes et la conclusion du livre de la Sagesse," *Bib* 45.4 (1964): 491. The structure of the above paragraph and the following corresponds with John J. Collins, *Seers, Sibyls, and Sages in Hellenistic-Roman Judaism* (Boston: Brill Academic, 2001), 93.

[18] Thomas Glasson, *Greek Influence in Jewish Eschatology: With Special Reference to the Apocalypses and Pseudepigraphs*, Biblical Monographs 1 (London: SPCK, 1961), 1.

Likewise, H. D. Betz ended his 1969 article with an even more definite conclusion: "One thing…must be kept clearly in mind: Jewish and, subsequently, Christian Apocalypticism as well cannot be understood from themselves or from the Old Testament alone, but must be seen and presented as peculiar expressions within the entire development of Hellenistic syncretism."[19] These ideas and others like them are still debated by scholars such as Klaus Koch, Julio Trebolle Barrera, Stefan Beyerle, and Stephen Bedard.[20] A broad approach to comparative studies backed their arguments, but a literary comparison focused on use of authority lays bare an inherent problem: authority in apocalyptic literature does not derive from Greek sources.[21]

This problem concerning general literary comparisons and a lack of investigation into how Jewish authors used the supposed sources repeated over the next few decades. For instance, concerning Akkadian influence, A. K. Grayson and Wilfred Lambert produced an edited text in 1964. They and others (e.g. W. W. Hallo) identified the narratives within the text as "Akkadian Apocalypses" and forerunners of Jewish apocalyptic material.[22] In 1988, Gerhard Hasel argued for Akkadian influence based on festivals in prophetic writings. Recently, Matthew Neujahr produced an article highlighting Assyriologists pushing Danielic dependence on Akkadian writings based on five Akkadian *ex eventu* prophecies.[23] A few scholars have even sought roots in Egyptian

[19] H. D. Betz, "On the Problem of the Religio-Historical Understanding of Apocalypticism," *JTC* 6 (1969): 155.

[20] Klaus Koch, "Daniel und Henoch: Apokalyptik im antiken Judentum," in *Apokalyptic und kein Ende?* ed. Bernd U. Schipper and Georg Plasger, Biblische-Theologische Schwerpunkte 29 (Göttingen: Vandenhoeck und Ruprecht, 2007), 31–50; Julio Trebolle Barrera, "Antiguo Testamento y helenismo: los últimos escritos del Antiguo Testamento y la influencia del helenismo," *EstBib* 61.2 (2003): 277–94; Stefan Beyerle, "'If You Preserve Carefully Faith': Hellenistic Attitudes Towards Religion in Pre-Maccabean Times," *ZAW* 118.2 (2006): 250–63; and Stephan J. Bedard, "Hellenistic Influence on the Idea of Resurrection in Jewish Apocalyptic Literature," *JGRChJ* 5 (2008): 174–89.

[21] As was later identified in this study in chapters 3, 4, and the conclusion.

[22] Robert R. Wilson, *Prophecy and Society in Ancient Israel* (Philadelphia: Fortress, 2011), 120; see also Wilfred G. Lambert, *The Background of Jewish Apocalyptic*, Ethel M. Wood Lecture Series (London: Athlone, 1978). Lambert identified numerous Jewish works that borrowed from or added to Babylonian narratives.

[23] Gerhard Hasel, "'New Moon and Sabbath' in Eighth Century Israelite Prophetic Writings," in *Wunschet Jerusalem Frieden: Collected Communications to the 12th Congress of the International Organization for the Study of the Old*

material.[24] Through all the research represented here, the a priori drive for roots and a lack of concern for how sources worked as an authority within Second Temple material remained, and the same held true for those scholars who turned to Hebraic influences.

2.2.4. After Qumran: Hebraic Influences

Many scholars have argued for prophetic, wisdom, or priestly roots in the apocalyptic material. Other scholars have suggested concurrent roots from two or all three Hebraic movements. Regardless of their positions, these scholars continued the pattern of assigning roots to the apocalyptic material through broad-based literary comparisons. The following subsections present several authors who argue for these positions.[25]

2.2.4.1. Prophetic Movement

Scholars espousing links to the Hebraic prophetic movement included George Eldon Ladd in 1957 and Otto Plöger in 1968, but in 1979, Paul Hanson authored a watershed monograph titled, *The Dawn of the Apocalyptic Age*.[26] In it, he argued Trito-Isaiah bore apocalyptic elements resulting from a rupture between Zadokite priests and marginalized prophets. The latter then redirected older patterns and myths against the priesthood. From this redirection, the apocalyptic genre developed from prophetic writing as "the prophets no longer ha[d] the events of a nation's history into which they [could] translate the terms of Yahweh's cosmic will."[27] However, other scholars noted a

---

Testament, BEATAJ 13 (Frankfurt: Peter Lang, 1988), 37; Neujahr, "Predicting the Past in the Ancient Near East: From Akkadian Ex Eventu Prophecies to Judean Historical Apocalypses" (PhD diss., Yale University, 2001).

[24] See, for instance, Bernd Ulrich Schipper and Andreas Blasius, eds. *Apokalyptik und Ägypten: Eine kritische Analyse der relevanten Texte aus dem griechisch-römischen Ägypten*, OLA 107 (Leuven: Peeters, 2002).

[25] Note, however, these arguments may not have been representative of a scholar's complete thinking concerning apocalyptic sources.

[26] George E. Ladd, "Why Not Prophetic-Apocalyptic?" *JBL* 76.3 (1957): 192–200; Plöger, *Theokratie und Eschatologie* (Niedernberg: ReproPfeffer, 1990).

[27] Paul Hanson, *The Dawn of Apocalyptic: The Historical and Sociological Roots of Jewish Apocalyptic Eschatology*, revised ed. (Philadelphia: Fortress, 1975), 16. The "events of the nation's history" ended due to the Babylonian captivity. Also, note Hanson's general similarities in method to that of Gunkel.

link between the prophetic and wisdom material in apocalyptic literature.

In 1981, Robert Wilson wrote of the trouble separating prophetic and wisdom roots within apocalyptic writing. He proposed multiple sources for the Second Temple authors,[28] but his shift to multiple sources was not unique. Three-quarters of a century earlier, Gunkel identified a mixture of prophetic and Babylonian roots in his book, *Israel and Babylon*. Stephen Cook also linked canonical apocalyptic writing to the prophets in his 1992 dissertation. In 2003, Cook wrote that Apocalypticism was "influenced by foreign cultural traditions," but he kept the locus of the movement in postexilic Israel.[29]

Eight years after Cook's dissertation, Lester Grabbe argued apocalyptic writing was a subset of prophetic literature based on a deconstruction of alleged differences between the two genres. He proposed Zech 1–8 was both prophetic and apocalyptic and therefore evidenced a tacit apocalyptic-wisdom link based on the relationship of prophecy with mantic wisdom. Grabbe furthered this link by highlighting scholarly discussion of mantic wisdom in apocalyptic works. However, he also argued mantic wisdom in apocalyptic writing had no bearing on the genre as a prophetic subset.[30]

These scholars used a combination of social sciences and literary analysis to focus their studies on the prophetic movement. Their arguments, however, assumed sources existed for apocalyptic material, and their goal was to identify these sources. The same assumptions held true for those scholars focused solely on the wisdom movement.

2.2.4.2. Wisdom Movement

Ludwig Noack originally proposed wisdom as the backdrop for apocalyptic writing in 1857. Gerhard von Rad championed this connection as a reaction against rooting apocalyptic writing in prophecy.[31] Von Rad argued apocalyptic writing had no self-designation deriving from the prophetic movement and, unlike prophecy, no link to salvation history. He wrote: "the decisive factor, as I see it, is the incompatibility

[28] Robert R. Wilson, "From Prophecy to Apocalypticism," *Semeia* 21 (1981): 79–95.

[29] Stephen L. Cook, *The Apocalyptic Literature*, Interpreting Biblical Texts (Nashville: Abingdon, 2003), 33–34.

[30] Lester L. Grabbe, *Judaic Religion in the Second Temple Period: Belief and Practice from the Exile to Yavneh* (London: Routledge, 2000), 235–36.

[31] Matthew Goff, "Wisdom and Apocalypticism," in Collins, *OHAL*, 52.

between apocalyptic literature's view of history and that of the prophets."[32] His later thoughts grew even stronger on this connection. Michael Knibb commented on these thoughts in his book on Enoch:

> von Rad thinks it important that the apocalyptic seers are called wise men and scribes, and he maintains that the relationship between apocalyptic and wisdom is evident in the fact that the apocalyptic books are concerned not only with history, but also with nature. He argues that the concept of the divine determination of the times, which is central in apocalyptic thought, is a fundamental presupposition of wisdom, and that the understanding of the times…is the task of the wise man.[33]

Despite von Rad's great contributions to scholarship, his work was another instance of broad comparative literary studies in which correlation constituted causation based on an assumption of sources. He made this correlation through an identification of themes: self-designation and salvation history in the prophetic writing, and the concepts of nature and divine determination in the wisdom texts. His argument hinged on the continuation of these themes in apocalyptic works rather than whether these themes were used authoritatively in such works.[34]

Scholarship on wisdom and the roots of apocalyptic literature has been quite active in the last twenty-five years, including studies by a Society of Biblical Literature consultation group. In 1994, George Nickelsburg wrote, "The entities usually defined as sapiential and apocalyptic often cannot be cleanly separated from one another…. Apocalyptic texts contain elements that are at home in wisdom literature."[35] Since then, several scholars have sought the connection between wisdom and apocalyptic writing, especially as it concerned

---

[32] Gerhard von Rad, *The Theology of Israel's Prophetic Traditions*, vol. 2 of *Old Testament Theology*, trans. D. M. G. Stalker (New York: Harper and Row, 1965), 303.

[33] Michael A. Knibb, "Apocalyptic and Wisdom in 4 Ezra," in *Essays on the Book of Enoch and Other Early Jewish Texts and Traditions*, SVTP (Boston: Brill, 2008), 272.

[34] Instead, von Rad was left to argue correlating themes of nature and history, but such themes also emerged in the prophetic movement, such as Isaiah's calling on creation as a witness against Israel and her history in Isa 1.

[35] George W. E. Nickelsburg, "Wisdom and Apocalypticism in Early Judaism: Some Points for Discussion," in *Conflicted Boundaries in Wisdom and Apocalypticism*, ed. Christopher Matthews, SBLSS 35 (Leiden: Brill, 2003), 269–70.

Qumran texts.[36] Other scholars writing on wisdom and apocalyptic literature have focused on 4 Ezra because of its intertwined dialogues and apocalyptic material. Karina Hogan, for instance, identified the wisdom in 4 Ezra as Jewish wisdom, rather than Greek wisdom.[37] In doing so, she unintentionally hinted that identifying apocalyptic writing with the wisdom tradition called for further research to prove Hebraic roots—a call that again exhibited the predominant push for sources among apocalyptic studies.

2.2.5. Roots of Apocalypticism and Canonical Dependence

Other scholars have sought direct reliance on the Tanakh, but they still worked within the framework of sources. This method originated with a search for dependency among biblical texts. According to Richard Schultz, Heinrich Ewald (1840) was the first to introduce a study on this topic. Later, Augustus Küper (1870) focused on quotes of earlier canonical material in the prophets. For Küper, the prophetic material consisted not of individual books but a single unit. He placed "Isaiah's oracles [as] foundational for all subsequent prophecy."[38]

---

[36] See e.g., Matthew Goff, "Recent Trends in the Study of Early Jewish Wisdom Literature: The Contribution of 4Qinstruction and Other Qumran Texts," *CurBR* 7.3 (2009): 376–416; Kasper Larsen, "Visdom og apokalyptik i Musar leMevin (1Q/4Qinstruction)," *DTT* 65.1 (2002): 1–14; Émile Puech, "Apports des textes apocalyptiques et sapientiels de Qumrân à l'eschatologie du Judaïsme ancien," in *Wisdom and Apocalypticism in the Dead Sea Scrolls and in the Biblical Tradition*, ed. Florentino García Martínez, BETL 168 (Leuven: University, 2003), 133–70.

[37] "The author of 4 Ezra had either no knowledge of or no use for Jewish wisdom that was heavily influenced by Greek philosophy.... On the other hand, the arguments of Uriel in the dialogues suggest that the author was familiar with the type of wisdom that is represented by the wisdom texts discovered at Qumran" (Karina M. Hogan, *Theologies in Conflict in 4 Ezra: Wisdom Debate and Apocalyptic Solution*, SJSJ 130 [Boston: Brill, 2008], 43). Hogan also listed scholars and their contribution to the work of wisdom and apocalyptic, based on 4 Ezra, some of whom were Michael Stone, whom Hogan argued, often mentioned "wisdom terminology" in his work on 4 Ezra, but failed to develop any meaningful significance from it. In his work on 4 Ezra, Eckhard J. Schnabel identified numerous "points of contact" with the wisdom tradition, and Joan E. Cook looked to the questions of 4 Ezra and their connection with wisdom traditions. In expanding horizons to 2 Baruch, Shannon Burkes has written an article called "'Life' Redefined"—for this and reference to Schnabel's work, see ibid., 41 n.1.

[38] Richard L. Schultz, *The Search for Quotation: Verbal Parallels in the Prophets*, ed. David J. A. Clines, Philip R. Davies, and John Jarick, JSOTSup 180 (Sheffield: Sheffield Academic Press, 1999), 21–22.

The inherent idea of authoritative transfer lay within Küper's work, particularly as it concerned Hosea and Micah's use of Isaiah.[39] Carl Caspari's (1843) writings also hinted at the underpinnings of authoritative transfer in Jeremiah's use of Isaiah.[40] Over the following 173 years, authoritative topoi remained in the implicit background of Tanakh scholarship.[41] For instance, in a 1980 article on the relationship between Gen 32:29 and Hos 12:5a, L. M. Eslinger argued Hosea used the narrative in Gen 32 as an authority to identify himself as a messenger to Israel.[42] Thus, according to Eslinger, Hosea identified himself as a messenger to Israel, and his claim depended on the Genesis narrative for authority, attributing canonized status to the text before 722 BCE.[43] This trend of seeking authority continued in canonical studies and subsequently, into apocalyptic scholarship. As such, some work has been done in the area of authority in apocalyptic writing. However, most of this work also assumed literary sources existed for Second Temple apocalyptic literature.

2.2.6. Ideas of Authority

Scholarship on authority in apocalyptic literature fell into four broad categories: Canonical authority by expansion, authority by the divine, prophetic authority, and authority by Torah. These categories are presented in order, identifying the scholar using authority in conjunction with Second Temple apocalyptic material.

---

[39] Augustus Küper, *Das Prophetenthum des Alten Bundes* (Leipzig Dörffling und Franke, 1870), 243–44. Although he may have rejected notions that later could be identified as authoritative transfer, his argument revealed that although implicit, the ideas were present in scholarly discussion at the time. See "definitions" for "authoritative transfer" as defined here.

[40] Carl P. Caspari, "Jesajanische Studien," *Zeitschrift für die gesammte lutherische Theologie und Kirche* 4.2 (1843): 10.

[41] For a summary of the methodology and search for parallels and quotations among the prophetic books, see Schultz, *Search for Quotation*, 18–61.

[42] Lyle M. Eslinger, "Hosea 12:5a and Genesis 32:29: A Study in Inner Biblical Exegesis," *JSOT* 18 (1980): 94.

[43] Ibid., 94–95. William Whitt and others challenged the concept of a canonized Gen 32:29 in Hosea's time. Whitt noted several scholars refused to confront the problem of "explaining the fact that Hosea seemed to know a Jacob tradition different from the traditions in Genesis" (William D. Whitt, "The Jacob Traditions in Hosea and Their Relation to Genesis," *ZAW* 103.1 [2009]: 18). However, Eslinger's work is included here for his concepts of authority transfer.

2.2.6.1. Canonical Authority: Scriptural Expansion

Todd Hanneken explored authority through scriptural expansion (and interpretation) but stopped short of venturing into the inner workings of authority. He claimed disinterest in seeking what he called "foreign influence" because it lay outside his work, but still admitted its importance. Subsequently, Hanneken, B. Z. Wacholder, and Martha Himmelfarb have continued to focus on authority and Jubilees.[44] Other studies in this area included a 2010 supplement to *The Journal for the Study of Judaism.* In this supplement, the authors focused on canon authority: Eibert Tigchelaar wrote an article titled "Authoritativeness of the Hebrew Scriptures…."[45] and John Collins focused on prophecy in "Prophecy and History in the Pesharim."[46] Other scholars have touched on this issue as well. Molly Zahn's 2013 work, for example, concerned the use and transfer of authority. She compared how Jubilean and Temple Scroll authors interact with Deuteronomy and the Sinai tradition:

> Trajectories that begin within the Torah itself—here, the idea of divinely revealed law and the creation of innovative ways to extend and transform that revelation—continue not only in rewritten scripture but also in D[euteronomy] and S[croll],

[44] Todd Hanneken, *The Subversion of the Apocalypses in the Book of Jubilees* (Atlanta: Society of Biblical Literature, 2012), 200; B. Z. Wacholder, "Jubilees as Super Canon: Torah-Admonition Versus Torah-Commandment," in *Legal Texts and Legal Issues: Proceedings of the Second Meeting of the International Organization for Qumran Studies, Cambridge, 1995, Published in Honour of Joseph M. Baumgarten*, ed. M. J. Bernstein, Florentino García Martínez, and J. Kampen, STDJ 23 (Leiden: Brill, 1997), 195–211; Martha Himmelfarb, "Torah, Testimony, and *Tablets of Heaven*: The Claim of Authority of the Book of Jubilees," in *A Multiform Heritage: Studies on Early Judaism and Christianity in Honor of Robert A. Kraft*, ed. Robert A. Kraft and Benjamin G. Wright (Atlanta: Scholars Press, 1999), 19–29.

[45] Eibert Tigchelaar, "Aramaic Texts from Qumran and the Authoritativeness of Hebrew Scriptures: Preliminary Observations," in *Authoritative Scriptures in Ancient Judaism*, ed. Mladen Popović, SJSJ 141 (Leiden: Brill, 2010), 157–172.

[46] John J. Collins, "Prophecy and History in the Pesharim," in *Authoritative Scriptures in Ancient Judaism*, ed. Mladen Popović, SJSJ 141 (Leiden: Brill, 2010), 209–26.

> traditions that have usually been analyzed in the context of other conversations entirely.[47]

Although authority was part of the discussion for these scholars, their focus was limited, and except for Hanneken, subjected to an a priori concern for sources. Moreover, as noted throughout this recital of history, assessments of sources developed from a general comparative literary approach rather than from focused assessments on how Second Temple authors used authority in specific passages. Nevertheless, this general approach identified three other types of authoritative topoi.

The first type was Pseudonymity, in which an author claimed authority through canonical expansion. Pseudonymity included most apocalyptic works because it allowed Second Temple apocalyptic authors to "appeal to the authority of a revered forefather."[48] However, research into pseudonymity extended far outside Second Temple scholarship. For instance, Thomas P. Waldemer examined the novel *Viva o povo brasiliero*, questioning if pseudepigraphy equaled forgery.[49] Loren Stuckenbruck, writing on Second Temple pseudepigraphy, concluded the authors were not guilty of forgery, but of humility arguing authors often used pseudepigraphy in humbleness, identifying their master or school of thought by name.[50] Questions concerning these approaches and others are explored in chapter 3. What should be noted here, however, is a second authoritative topos type behind Pseudonymity, which is Divine Authority.

---

[47] Molly M. Zahn, "Torah for 'the Age of Wickedness': The Authority of the Damascus and Serekh Texts in Light of Biblical and Rewritten Traditions," *DSD* 20.3 (2013): 208.

[48] Robby Waddell, "A Green Apocalypse: Coming Secular and Religious Eschatological Visions of Earth," in *Blood Cries Out: Pentecostals, Ecology, and the Groans of Creation*, Pentecostals, Peacemaking, and Social Justice 8 (Eugene: Wipf & Stock, 2014), 141. Waddell, John Collins, and others have argued, "All Jewish apocalyptic literature is pseudonymous" (John J. Collins, "Apocalypse Then," *AJS Perspectives: The Magazine of the Association of Jewish Studies*, Fall 2012, 6, http://www.bjpa.org/Publications/details.cfm?PublicationID=20997). The distinction between "most" and "all" apocalyptic works involved the canonical material, which was outside the purview of this study; consequently, all Jewish apocalyptic material in this study was pseudepigraphic.

[49] Thomas P. Waldemer, "Hijacking Authority: Writing and Forgery in *Viva O Povo Brasileiro*," *Hispanofila*.146 (2006): 49.

[50] Loren T. Stuckenbruck, "Apocrypha and Pseudepigrapha," *EDEJ* 154. An in-depth examination of scholarship on pseudepigraphy appears in chapter 3.

This topos type occurred when community members believed the works within the canon were a record of divine communication.

2.2.6.2. Authority by the Divine

John Bickley researched Daniel's dreams and visions as a mode of divine communication: "The ultimate authority, Yahweh, allows the dreamer [and] visionary to serve as the authorized mediator to reveal (in part) transcendent knowledge to the reader."[51] He concluded Second Temple authors based their "authorizing strategies" on a hierarchy of authority. Daniel's work was therefore authoritative because Yahweh chose Daniel. Bickley again touched upon this authority when he wrote, "The reader's (by way of the visionary's) portal to universal insight is closed—and the vision's or Visionary's final assertion of authority [the last five verses of Daniel] is made emphatically. He alone has access to these mysteries, and God alone is the one who determines when and to whom they are imparted."[52] For Bickley, then, Daniel was authoritative because of YHWH's call and because of the two authoritative topos types, Revelation of Secrets and Divine Authority. Another scholar, William Adler, wrote on the idea of divine authority but countered divine authority as an authority for authorship. Adler argued the early church rejected Jewish apocalyptic writings precisely because authors claimed "direct divine authority."[53]

2.2.6.3. Prophetic Authority

Scholars have researched several modes of divine authority, one of which was authority from elements of the prophetic movement or the

[51] John T. Bickley, "Dreams, Visions, and the Rhetoric of Authority" (PhD diss., Florida State University, 2013), 64, http://diginole.lib.fsu.edu/islandora/object/fsu:183664/datastream/PDF/view.

[52] Ibid., 62.

[53] William Adler, "Introduction," in *The Jewish Apocalyptic Heritage in Early Christianity*, ed. James C. VanderKam and William Adler, Jewish Traditions in Early Christian Literature: Section 3 of Compendia Rerum Iudaicarum ad Novum Testamentum, vol. 4 (Minneapolis: Fortress, 1996), 19–20. Adler argued the church rejected Jewish writings due to direct divine authority. In other words, his work agrees with the work here that Jewish authors were depending on Divine Authority in their writings. The focus is not whether the church community accepted pseuduepigraphy, but whether the Jewish authors did or did not use this topos type, and Adler goes so far as to say the early church recognized Jewish writers were using it.

interpretation of texts deriving from it (such as Pesher interpretation).[54] For instance, in Luca Arcari's 2012 article on otherworldly journeys, he argued apocalyptic material containing such journeys gained authority from both EAW cosmic journeys and the Hebraic prophetic movement. He did so by identifying how authors had based narratives on EAW cosmic journeys while incorporating "ecstatic modes of ancient Israel's prophecy."[55]

Marius Nel focused on Qumran modes of interpretation as an authority (although he did not use that term). He wrote, "The purpose of the pesher [was] to bridge the gap between the original prophetic word of encouragement and the present reality, to actualize and contextualize the message for different circumstances."[56]

2.2.6.4. Authority by Torah

A different mode of divine authority researched by scholars stemmed from the Torah. Moshe Weinfeld (1992) argued the Temple Scroll authors claimed authority by writing as though God revealed the scroll alongside the Torah.[57] Seven years later, Hindy Najman produced two papers; the first involved four authority-conferring strategies in Jubilees. Her second and subsequent material focused on natural and Mosaic Law. Najman argued for "Mosaic discourse" as an authority concerning the Temple Scroll and Jubilees. Through this discourse, "Revelation [was] renewed by re-presenting it in a new work that claim[ed] the same origins as the original revelation."[58] As such, Najman and the other scholars identified in this subsection came closest to the

---

[54] However, this authority was not based in the prophetic movement as the movement itself, but on specific elements that indicated divine authority.

[55] Luca Arcari, "The Otherworldly Journey of the Book of Watchers as the Source of a Competitive Authority," *Asdiwal* 7 (2012): 49.

[56] Marius Nel, "Daniel 9 as Part of an Apocalyptic Book?" *Verbum et Ecclesia* 34.1 (2013): 1–3. This study produced different conclusions for authority and Pesharim—see §6.3. "Qumran" (below).

[57] Moshe Weinfeld, "God Versus Moses in the Temple Scroll: 'I Do Not Speak on My Own Authority, but on God's Authority,'" *RevQ* 15 (1992): 175–80.

[58] Hindy Najman, "Interpretation as Primordial Writing: Jubilees and Its Authority Conferring Strategies," *JSJ* 30.4 (1999): 379–410; Najman, "The Law of Nature and the Authority of Mosaic Law," *SPhilo* 11 (1999): 55–73; Najman, "Torah of Moses: Pseudonymous Attribution in Second Temple Writings," in *Past Renewals: Interpretive Authority, Renewed Revelation, and the Quest for Perfection in Jewish Antiquity* (Leiden: Brill, 2010), 73–86.

work presented in this study. However, they still assumed sources existed as well as engaging in broader literary comparisons rather than limiting the focus to specific occurrences of a topos type.

2.2.7. A Summary of Preceding Scholarship and Reasons for the Present Study

Two trends in Jewish apocalyptic scholarship have therefore developed over the last century and a half. The first trend began in the late 1800s and consisted of an a priori drive to identify apocalyptic roots. This drive began soon after apocalyptic material rose to prominence and was heavily influenced by the concurrent philosophical, theological, and archaeological climate. The trend is still in evidence today. The second trend is a generalized comparative literary study that lacks a focus on *how* the elements being compared have been used. Scholars combined these studies to the a priori search for sources and then posited apocalyptic writing as the child of whatever culture or movement from which the supposed source or sources derived.

A few scholars have argued for multiple sources for Jewish apocalyptic literature, even focusing on authority to a certain degree. For example, in a 2008 article in the *Oxford Handbook of Eschatology*, Collins wrote, "Ultimately, Apocalypticism emerges in Judaism in the Hellenistic period as a new phenomenon, which draws on many sources, but combines them in novel ways."[59] Scholars have yet to research this statement on Apocalypticism exhaustively despite its rather obvious nature. Moreover, as shown above, no study has focused on Second Temple use of authority across the larger body of apocalyptic literature while eschewing an a priori belief in sources for apocalyptic material. The research herein was a first step in filling that niche. The basic method for doing so began with understanding the historical and cultural milieu in which the authors wrote.

2.3. A Brief History of the Second Temple Period

The Babylonian captivity began a turbulent period in Hebraic history. Jewish captives returned to Jerusalem with hope (Isa 40–44) and promises of blessings (Hag 2:5). However, they soon experienced a broken economy, unfilled expectations, conflict, and questions about what

[59] Collins, "Apocalyptic Eschatology," 44.

it meant to be Jewish.[60] These questions intensified after Alexander's conquest of the Persian empire (334–330 BCE). Although Judea was largely ignored in his campaigns,[61] the following Diadochi wars stemming from Alexander's death (323–281 BCE) eventually allowed for the Seleucid king, Antiochus IV Epiphanes, who forced Judea's Hellenization in 167 BCE.[62] Antiochus IV Ephiphanes rededicated the Jewish temple to Zeus and mandated Jewish participation in the Hellenistic cult, but he was not the originator of Jewish Hellenism. That designation falls to Jason, who bribed Antiochus IV in 175 BCE to gain the office of High Priest held by Onias III. Menelaus, who supplanted him with another bribe to Antiochus IV, continued these efforts until the Antiochian invasion in 168–167 BCE.[63] After the invasion, the Hasmonean dynasty rose amid Seleucid abuses (1 and 2 Maccabees) and provided Judea a degree of self-rule until Herod's reign under Roman authority in the first century BCE.[64]

Unfortunately, internal conflicts were commonplace among the Hasmonean heirs, and civil war erupted. Moreover, when not fighting for the throne, Hasmoneans fought outlying kingdoms to expand Judean boundaries. Eventually, the Judean kingdom incorporated both Samaria and ancient Edom. These historical and cultic issues drove responses from the various factions of early Judaism, including an emphasis on moral law over the official cult; concern for orthopraxis

---

[60] Joseph Blenkinsopp, *Judaism: The First Phase—the Place of Ezra and Nehemiah in the Origins of Judaism* (Grand Rapids: Eerdmans, 2009), 79, 123.

[61] Lester L. Grabbe, *An Introduction to Second Temple Judaism: History and Religion of the Jews in the Time of Nehemiah, the Maccabees, Hillel and Jesus* (London: T&T Clark, 2010), 5.

[62] Choosing "BCE" and "CE" over "BC" and "AD" expressed no theological statement; rather, it kept with postmodern convention against a Western metanarrative.

[63] A question existed whether Menelaus operated by nefariousness rather than by the Hellenistic ideal. Nevertheless, Antiochus IV twice installed Menelaus as the high priest, making Menelaus beholden to him and Hellenism. To the average Judean, the resulting circumstances would have been similar regardless of Menelaus's reasons behind his decisions. Chris Seeman, "From Alexander to Pompey," *EDEJ* 32–33.

[64] James C. VanderKam, *An Introduction to Early Judaism* (Grand Rapids: Eerdmans, 2001), 21. Questions exist about the extent to which the Hasmoneans rejected Hellenism. See, for instance: Erich S. Gruen, *Heritage and Hellenism: The Reinvention of Jewish Tradition*, HCS 30 (Berkeley: University of California Press, 1998), 1–40; for a treatise on the subject, see Lee I. Levine, *Judaism and Hellenism in Antiquity: Conflict or Confluence?* The Samuel and Althea Stroum Lectures in Jewish Studies (Seattle: University of Washington, 1998).

over orthodoxy; heightened particularism, exclusivism, and ideas of superiority; and a renewed interest in interpreting sacred writing for then-current issues.[65] From this milieu of conflict and religious concern arose the Jewish apocalyptic material. Therefore, this study on apocalyptic literature needed a methodology that incorporated both literary and historical concerns.

2.4. Definitions and Methodology

The first step to building such a methodology, however, was to define terms, starting with "apocalyptic" and "apocalyptic literature." Defining terms formed the foundation for understanding the term, "authoritative topoi," and following that, the methodology for studying them. The following section provides these definitions.

2.4.1. Defining Terms

The term "apocalyptic" follows Collins's suggestion in Semeia 14: Apocalyptic refers to "a genre of revelatory literature with a narrative framework, in which a revelation is mediated by an otherworldly being to a human recipient, disclosing a transcendent reality which is both temporal, insofar as it envisages eschatological salvation, and spatial insofar as it involves another, supernatural world."[66] Jewish writings that originated between the return from Babylonian captivity (538 BCE) and the destruction of Herod's temple (70 CE) and belonged to the apocalyptic genre were referred to herein as "apocalyptic literature" or "apocalyptic material." Further, "Jewish" or "Second Temple" often modified "Apocalyptic literature" or "apocalyptic material."[67] Finally, all Tanakh material was delimited

---

[65] This list was adapted from subtitles covering similar material in J. Julius Scott, *Jewish Backgrounds of the New Testament* (Grand Rapids: Baker Books, 2000), 122–26. Other scholars, however, have argued the influential theologies of Second Temple literature descended from the earlier Hebraic movements (prophetic, priestly, and wisdom), although these ideas were not mutually exclusive—see e.g., Richard S. Hess, *Israelite Religions: An Archaeological and Biblical Survey* (Grand Rapids: Baker Academic, 2007), 342.

[66] John J. Collins, "Introduction: Towards the Morphology of a Genre," *Semeia* 14 (1979): 9.

[67] Jewish apocalyptic authors continued writing after the first century CE; but three historic developments delimited their material from this study: Rome razing Herod's temple in 70 CE; the Bar-Kokhba revolt beginning in 132 CE; and the rising Christian influence beginning in the mid-first century. The first two were linchpins

from the term "apocalyptic literature" in this research as the focus here was noncanonical apocalyptic writing.

Other terms defined in this study included "Hebraic," which referred to the culture of a people group known diachronically as the Hebrews, the Israelites, and then, the Jews. "Canon" (or "canonical writing"), "OT," and "Jewish scriptures" were synonymous terms for the material collected in the Tanakh. The term "pseudepigraphy" related to the method of pseudonymous writing. Finally, all non-Hebraic material considered possible source material for Second Temple apocalyptic literature was labeled "external ancient world (EAW) literature" or "EAW material."

References to authors who wrote in the apocalyptic genre also needed to be defined. Concerning the Enoch literature, several questions of authorship and redaction existed. To avoid the attribution quagmire, "the Enochian author" or "the author of (1 or 2) Enoch" identified the writer(s) or redactor(s) of 1 and 2 Enoch in chapters 2–4 of this study. For other Second Temple apocalyptic literature included in this study, the following terms referred both to the author and redactor: "T. Levi author," as it pertained to the Testament of Levi; "T. Moses author" in connection with the Testament of Moses; "A. Levi author" designated the author[s] or subsequent redactor[s] of the Apocalypse of Levi; and the "Jubilean author" for Jubilees. The detail required in chapter 5, however, meant the terms, "redactor" and "author" were differentiated. Finally, references to authors in the context of pseudonymity followed the following pattern: P.author, P.Enoch, P.Moses, and so on.

---

on which Temple-oriented Judaism spun into Rabbinical Judaism introducing changes outside the scope of this study. The third affected the focus of apocalyptic authors, especially those Jewish authors who believed Jesus was the Messiah (for example, the Apostle John).

Note, extended textual corruption or doubtful origins postdating the fall of the temple negated texts from being included here. As such, only 1 and 2 Enoch, Jubilees, the Testaments of Moses and Levi, and the Apocalypse of Zephaniah were a part of this study. Also note, to avoid repetitiveness, the phrase was often shortened to Second Temple authors or Second Temple literature (or material). These phrases were intended to be synonymous with the apocalyptic authors and material studied here, unless context explicitly determines otherwise.

2.4.2. Defining an Authoritative Topos

As stated in the glossary, the term "authoritative topos" ("topoi") referred to a text-specific place where an author manipulated the reader's response by using available literary techniques, concepts, or references dependent on earlier writing or external knowledge.[68] Chaucer employed this technique by using an exemplar-clergy topos against the background of the anticlerical movement of the late fourteenth century. His character, Parson "established his own authority" against church corruption.[69]

This borrowing of authority is called an "authoritative transfer." In it, person B borrows authority from an older narrative to develop a new (but seemingly old) narrative for norming beliefs or behavior in a current situation. At the core of authoritative transfer is trust:

> Trust involves epistemic dependence: if H[earer] trusts S[peaker] on O[ccasion—meaning the occasion of the speaker speaking], then H epistemically relies on S on O, wherein the virtue of this reliance, at least some of the epistemic properties of S's trust-involving belief on O counterfactually depend on the quality of S's say-so on O.... [Moreover,] trust involves Hearer's Awareness: if H trusts S on O, then in some sense H is aware of this reliance.[70]

---

[68] Rebecca Belcher-Rankin, "Narrative Authority in Hawthorne's 'The Ambitious Guest,'" *Tennessee Philological Bulletin* (2008): 19. Belcher-Rankin focused on literary techniques by which American author Nathaniel Hawthorne moved his audience to "participate in interpretation" (21). Another way of stating this concept derived from Wallace Martin's presentation of flat and round characters. Reapplying his idea here and changing "character" to "authoritative topos," a flat topos was a literary technique or concept exhibiting little or no change—a static use of the topoi between the source and apocalyptic literature. A round topos evidenced a dynamic, the extent of which may prohibit authoritative transfer. Wallace Martin, *Recent Theories of Narrative* (Ithaca: Cornell University Press, 1986), 118.

[69] Larry Scanlon, *Narrative, Authority and Power: The Medieval Exemplum and the Chaucerian Tradition*, Cambridge Studies in Medieval Literature 20 (New York: Cambridge University Press, 2007), 7–9. Scanlon pointed out a contemporary of Chaucer, John Gower, "appeal[ed] to the same notion of exemplarity as Chaucer, connecting it even more explicitly to Christ" (9) to authorize his attack on church corruption.

[70] Sanford Goldberg, "Norms of Trust, *De Re* Trust, and the Epistemology of Testimony," in *Epistemology: Contexts, Values, Disagreement Proceedings of the*

Applied to the Second Temple apocalyptic authors, borrowed authority through authoritative transfer established the quality of the author's say-so because the hearers or readers already considered trustworthy the names under which they wrote.[71] This trust brought about preemption of prior beliefs (an idea known as preemption theory). Readers and listeners who accepted an author's narrative, their point of view, or belief replaced their constructs with the writer's in any related area. This act created normed responses:

> Through the acceptance of rules which set up authorities, people can entrust judgment to another person or institution which will then be bound, in accordance with the dependence thesis, to exercise its best judgment primarily based on the dependent reasons appropriate to the case. Thus, the mediation of authorities may, where justified, improve people's compliance with practical and moral principles.[72]

By self-aligning with a community or type of Judaism in the Second Temple period, hearers or readers of Jewish apocalyptic material inherently accepted that community's authority by accepting its norms and moral principles. Doing so precipitated a trust in the speaker or writer based on that person's use of authoritative transfer. In achieving such trust, the speaker or writer then obtained an epistemic advantage:

> Trusting a speaker, and thus responding to preemptive reasons for belief, makes one's belief less sensitive to [available evidence]. However, it also makes one's belief more sensitive to evidence available to the speaker. As a result, when speakers

34th International Ludwig Wittgenstein Symposium in Kirchberg, 2011, Publications of the Austrian Ludwig Wittgenstein Society 19 (Berlin: de Gruyter, 2013), 231–32.

[71] Since the hearers or readers considered the name trustworthy, they were also aware of borrowed authority. Therefore, no authority existed if an author broke trust by straying too far from the borrowed authority.

[72] Joseph Raz, "Introduction," in *Authority*, ed. Joseph Raz, Readings in Social and Political Theory (New York: NYU Press, 1990), 134. Christoph Jäger and Paul Faulkner have challenged preemption theory of late, but their questions concerned trust development, rather than whether hearer-speaker trust existed—see Christoph Jäger, "Epistemic Authority, Preemptive Reasons, and Understanding," *Episteme* (2016): 167–85; Paul Faulkner, "On Telling and Trusting," *Mind* 116.464 (2007): 875–902.

> have an epistemic advantage over audiences, audiences' epistemic position will often be no worse, and sometimes better, if they trust speakers instead of weighing their testimony against all evidence available to them. The clearest case is the one in which the speaker is not only honest and competent but also a known expert on the issue.[73]

This last sentence bears reiterating in the context of Second Temple literature. The best scenario for readers to trust the writer was for the speaker to be both honest and a known expert (as seen with P.Moses).

Applied to the texts in this study, all of which were pseudonymous, writing under a false name and using other sources garnered authority and trust.[74] Consequently, finding authoritative topoi in apocalyptic literature laid bare the sources by which authors made their claim and identified the true influences over Second Temple material.[75] To seek these sources, if they existed, the following methodology was employed.

2.4.3. Defining a Modified Postmodern Methodology

The methodology used here was derived from postmodern historiography based on its literary and historical origins. This approach was novel as Collins wrote in 2008, "For better or worse, the field has scarcely been touched by postmodernism."[76] The same is true nine years later; but what is a postmodern method, and why was it appropriate for this study of Second Temple history?

2.4.3.1. Ruptured History and Local Narratives

Several facets of postmodernism exist, but the key to this research was the French derivation (1960s), which contains links to Apocalypticism:

---

[73] Arnon Keren, "Trust and Belief: A Preemptive Reasons Account," *Synthese* 191.12 (2014): 2661–62.

[74] The question of deception by pseudepigraphical authors assuming such authority was outside the purview of this research, as was the legitimacy of revelatory claims. For discussion on the subject, including a summary of current arguments, see Armin D. Baum, "Revelatory Experience and Pseudepigraphical Attribution in Early Jewish Apocalypses," *BBRSup* 21.1 (2011): 65–92.

[75] Therefore, apocalyptic influences must have influenced both author and community.

[76] Collins, "Apocalyptic Eschatology," 55.

> French theories of a postmodern break in history were influenced by the rapid modernization process in France that followed World War II, exciting developments in philosophy and social theory during the 1950s and 1960s, and the dramatic sense of rupture produced by the turbulent events of 1968.... The apocalyptic impulses of the time were translated into the postmodern theories of a fundamental rupture in history and inauguration of a new era.[77]

The apocalyptic impulses of the French derivation became the postmodern understanding of ruptured history. It focused on how the Western metanarrative followed colonialization and ruptured local narratives. The postmodern response was to rupture the rupturing metanarrative, thereby breathing renewed life into the local narratives. A community reviving the local authoritative and norming narratives could, therefore, redefine itself as it sought to connect with history before the rupture.[78] This response spurred postcolonial scholars who similarly posited the Western metanarrative was responsible for subverting indigenous stories focused on local problems, issues, and national pride. By extension, this subversion also silenced the voices of indigenous authors and their communities.

The history of shattered, indigenous local narratives and subjugation to world powers paralleled Jewish history. According to Ezra-Nehemiah, the Babylonian returnees, or Golah, sought to reconnect with earlier Israelite history. In Ezra 1, the author narrated the return from Babylon as though it were a second exodus. The Golah became the covenant people

---

[77] Steven Best and Douglas Kellner, *Postmodern Theory: Critical Interrogations* (New York: Guilford Press, 1991), 17. Best-Kellner also suggested the French derivation was the most influential—an argument bolstered by the foremost scholar in postmodern philosophy, Jacque Derrida.

[78] John McLeod, *Beginning Postcolonialism*, Beginnings (Manchester: Manchester University Press, 2012), 13. Critics have often accused postmodernism of breaking all metanarratives; but traditionally, the only negated metanarrative is Western World History—a specific history driven by Western ideals and through a Western point of view. This negation allowed others to narrate their own histories. Please note, in this study, "local narrative" was used in lieu of "meta-" or "mininarrative," because a metanarrative may be understood as the Western construct of history pushed onto indigenous people contra their own construct of history (a community's mini-narrative), or a set of authoritative and norming narratives held by a small group of people contra an individual's story (which is an individual's mininarrative).

within a Persian hegemony that largely permitted local cultural autonomy. A focus on the lineages in Ezra 2 that connect to a precaptivity Judah confirmed this observation, as did the rebuilding of the temple and later covenant renewals. Two centuries later, Alexander the Great's conquest and the subsequent influence of Hellenism intensified the struggle for Jewish self-definition, similar to how modern indigenous people struggled against the Western metanarrative in colonialism. These similarities between Second Temple Judah, postmodernity, and post-colonialism made postmodern methodology a natural fit for this study.

2.4.3.2. Important Points for the Current Research

What, then, is a postmodern methodology? For this study, it was defined as a method of research guided by postmodern historiography but excluding the excesses often seen in certain elements of postmodernism.[79] Perhaps the most popular subset of postmodern historiography is New Historicism with its Foucauldian focus on power structures and societal norming. This focus is coupled with an economic lens through which postmodern researchers view history.[80] Essential to this study, however, was the way in which New Historicism incorporated the earlier History of Ideas movement of the mid-twentieth century. At the heart of the History of Ideas movement lay the question posed by Quentin Skinner: "What are the appropriate procedures to adopt in the attempt to arrive at an understanding of the work?"[81] Skinner suggested two textual approaches. The first was finding meaning from within the text. The second was finding meaning according to the surrounding culture, which provided the "ultimate framework for any attempt to understand" the text.[82] The present research incorporated both approaches—a common method shared by modernist and postmodernist scholars alike. However, a distinction occurred in the

---

[79] See the following paragraph for an example of these excesses or extremes. See also n.84 (below) for an example of the reading strategy used here.

[80] Michel Foucault's best work in this area was perhaps in his three-volume work, *The History of Sexuality* (New York: Vintage Books, 1988). In it, he began with the Victorian west, and then moved to ancient Greece to identify how power structures and norming occur concerning sexuality. Although his historiography in books 2–3 was questionable at times, the three-volume set serves well in defining his overall method.

[81] Quentin Skinner, "Meaning and Understanding in the History of Ideas," *HistTh* 8.1 (1969): 3.

[82] Ibid.

next touch point of New Historicism: the dual breach between author and historical event and between the author's historiography and the reader.

This breach prompted engaging a text by fostering its independent existence in a simulacrum. Postmodernists often have treated simulacra as hyperrealities with no outside referent, but not all scholars have reached this extreme. Linda Hutcheon wrote, "the postmodern [may] operate…in the realm of the representation [referentialism], not of simulation, even if it constantly questions the rules of that realm."[83] Postmodern historians such as F. R. Ankersmit and Hutcheon, therefore, have included referentialism and scientific method in historical research, but denied them the arbitrator's role; instead, they placed referentialism and various sciences such as archeology alongside other available tools. Based on these concepts, the reading strategy in this study began with a focus on the text, then moved to context. Finally, it incorporated a cross-text analysis. This method permitted referentialism but depended on authorial direction from within the text.[84]

2.4.3.2.1. Guarding against Inverted Causality

Using this text, context, cross-text method helped to avoid a fallacy called "inverted causality." Inverted causality occurs when scholars seek causes of historical events. The very act of seeking inverts the relationship: the historical event is now the cause, and any associated relationship is the result or the effect of the search. As defined within this study, inverted causality occurred because of a priori acceptance of the necessity of source material based on the History of Religions School and source theory influences. Thus, observations were prebiased

---

[83] Linda Hutcheon, *A Poetics of Postmodernism: History, Theory, Fiction* (New York: Routledge, 2010), 45.

[84] For example, in the text, "Joy at the Accession of Merneptah," the author referenced *ma'at* in the theophoric name preceding the authoritative topos. Through parallelism, the author was suggesting *ma'at* undergirded the events presented in the passage. However, no other information for *ma'at* was provided. Thus, the author signaled the need for modern readers to learn of *ma'at*. This approach balanced postmodern relativism and scientific-historicism, a balance Ankersmit and Hutcheon believed was necessary in such studies—see esp. F. R. Ankersmit, "Historiography and Postmodernism," *HistTh* 28.2 (1989): 53. Ian C. Werrett used a similar method researching the purity texts of the Dead Sea Scrolls. However, he refrained from the cross-text strategy, choosing to keep the texts independent and "free from the witness of so-called parallel texts" (Werrett, *Ritual Purity and the Dead Sea Scrolls*, STDJ 72, ed. Florentino García Martínez [Leiden: Brill, 2007], 288).

by the interpretative schema. To guard against creating inverted causalities in this research, Pierre Briant's method of searching for themes among historical documents was employed here.[85]

2.4.3.2.2. Postmodernism and Objectivity

In many postmodern schemas, objective observation has been considered impossible. Such observations have often been grounded in a belief that "the language of objective value presupposes a flawed, dualistic distinction between subjects and objects," or that all objective observations are based on subjective cultural values.[86] Other scholars, such as Robin Attfield, have engaged these arguments to support objectivity. However, even Attfield admitted underlying interpretations of objective observations exist.[87] Underlying interpretations are based on presuppositions either shared (as Attfield acknowledged) or unshared, which may promote bias. If understood, however, biases stemming from a worldview or belief system become a window into the framework of understanding, thereby allowing researchers to build correctives into their method. One of those correctives is writing in the first-person point of view.[88] Unfortunately, current norms mandated presenting research in the third person. Therefore, to use this corrective, but stay within current norms, only the following subsections of this chapter and one subsection in the conclusion of this work are presented in the first person.

2.4.3.2.3. Meta-research and Bias Correction

Before this study began, I believed Apocalypticism was a minor subcategory of the prophetic movement. To control that bias, I incorporated a general reading strategy in which I sought works from scholars who founded apocalyptic roots in various cultures or Hebraic movements; then, to strengthen that strategy, I refrained from formulating my arguments until I understood their positions on their

---

[85] For an example of this method, see Pierre Briant, *Historie de l'empire Perse: de Cyrus à Alexandre* (Paris: Fayard, 1996), 17–18.

[86] Robin Attfield, "Postmodernism, Value and Objectivity," abstract, *Environmental Values* 10.2 (2001): 145.

[87] Ibid. Attfield (perhaps unwittingly) identified these interpretations of observation by stating, "This essay appeals to the shared presuppositions of groups of human beings." In short, this argument depended on presuppositions to interpret objectivity.

[88] Doing so stood as a reminder to the author and reader that all observations are interpreted and thus, no research is free of bias.

terms. Engaging this control resulted in a shift to understanding Second Temple apocalyptic literature as writings of an independent movement necessitating study in its context. This shift led to yet another corrective—a comprehensive reading program of texts from each culture that modern scholars have proposed for source material. Therefore, the only texts delimited from this study were those texts that originated simultaneously or later than the passages in the Jewish texts to which they are being compared.[89] Another necessary step to limit the effects of bias in this work concerned personal conviction. I identify as an evangelical Christian and hold particular beliefs on biblical inerrancy; thus, delimiting canonical apocalyptic texts permitted assessing apocalyptic material without concern for faith-bias. Adding these correctives and controls allowed me to begin investigating authoritative topoi in both Jewish and EAW literature, beginning with step 1, as noted in the introduction to this research.

2.5. Excursus: Qumran

As an apocalyptic community represented in the literature, Qumran presented a unique challenge to this study. For instance, according to the *Habakkuk pesher,* the Teacher of Righteousness was responsible for "revealing…the divinely-inspired *nistar*, the hidden or secret interpretation."[90] Conversely, according to 1QS v:10–11, 1QS ix:17, 1QS x, and 1QH[a] xiii:25–26, the "counsel of the law" was hidden and the community was responsible not to reveal it to "men of injustice" (1QS ix:2).[91] The community also held an eschatological worldview "anticipat[ing] the old order would soon die and the messianic era would be established in their lifetimes."[92] This belief was part of a larger concept of dualism at Qumran.[93] How, then, should the

[89] "Simultaneous" is defined as originating within one hundred years to the origin of the Second Temple text. See Appendix B (below) for the texts included in this study.

[90] Lawrence H. Schiffman, *Qumran and Jerusalem: Studies in the Dead Sea Scrolls and the History of Judaism* (Grand Rapids: Eerdmans, 2010), 106.

[91] David Flusser, *Qumran and Apocalypticism,* vol. 1 of *Judaism of the Second Temple Period,* trans. Azzan Yadin (Grand Rapids: Eerdmans, 2007), 3. All Qumran documents in this study followed the newer numbering method for cave and document. Further location was written as f2.ii:5 (fragment, 2, column 2, line 5).

[92] Schiffman, *Qumran and Jerusalem*, 108.

[93] For an example of these tendencies, see Géza G. Xeravits, ed. *Dualism in Qumran*, LSTS, ed. Lester L. Grabbe (New York: T&T Clark, 2010).

presentation of this study commence? To be used in this study, Qumran material was required to meet at least one of two criteria: (1) the material directly related to other texts, or (2) subsequent research in this study located an authoritative topos in an apocalyptic text at Qumran. As such, beginning in chapter 3, a subsection on Qumran concerning the topos type appears in the "Text and Context, Use in Apocalyptic Literature" subsection, and then again in the evaluation (step 4f) portion of each topos type. Other mentions may occur in the cross-text section, but with a focus on individual texts, rather than on the authoritative topos at Qumran.

Chapter 3
PRELIMINARY RESEARCH

> *I am buried alive. And forgot. Now, I am remembering. I was in a library when it collapsed. And there I still lie. I am under the pressure of a thousand books all of various genres.*
>
> —JED, *Headswillroll*

3.1. Introduction

Preliminary research (steps 1–3) began the process stage of this study. The first step focused on identifying texts and authoritative topoi within Second Temple apocalyptic, Tanakh, and EAW literature. The act of culling topoi began in step 1d but was the focus of step 2 along with delineating the remaining authoritative topoi. In step 3, the final list of topoi from step 2 was quantified, and a final culling occurred before moving to step 4, presented in chapters 3 through 5.

3.2. Step 1: Text—Identifying Authoritative Topoi

The first step consisted of four substeps and a loop (steps 1a–d) incorporating a reading strategy focused on the text (rather than context or cross-text analysis). Step 1a focused on topoi in Second Temple apocalyptic literature. Likewise, steps 1b and 1c focused on topoi in Tanakh and EAW material, respectively. After completing step 1c, a loop to step 1a was introduced in order to identify several other possible topoi. Step 1d consisted of listing the discovered topoi types and striking three topos types that would have introduced circular argumentation (as explained in that subsection).

3.2.1. Step 1a

In step 1a, identifying topos types began by setting criteria for the inclusion of texts. First, the text had to be Jewish in origin. Second, the material had to incorporate apocalyptic elements. Third, it had to have a probable origin date before the destruction of the temple in 70 CE. Finally, no text considered canonical by Protestant Christianity would be included.

Concerns surfaced about origination dates of certain books or texts. For 1 Enoch, W. O. E. Oesterley identified all of 1 Enoch as written in the Second Temple period in 1917. Later, several scholars argued a third century CE date for the Parables of Enoch (1 En. 37–71). Of late, however, most arguments have moved to place the origins of the Parables in Second Temple Judaism.[1] Therefore, the Parables of Enoch were included in this study.

Another concern was 2 Enoch. In the late 1800s, Charles dated 2 Enoch to the early first century CE. He did so for three reasons: the book lacked references to the destruction of the temple, animal sacrifices were presented in the text as though the temple remained, and he noted an assertion of one place for worship reminiscent of temple-oriented Judaism. Others have argued for a Christian author, but their arguments have not "withstood scholarly scrutiny."[2] As such, 2 Enoch was included in this study based on the weight of evidence that tipped slightly toward a mid-first century CE date of origin. However, several questions remained concerning this date including origin dates of individual sections. As a result, in this study, no arguments concerning parent-child relationships hinged on findings from 2 Enoch. Instead, material from 2 Enoch was used to supplement findings from other texts.

The book of Jubilees also presented problems, but for other reasons. Many scholars considered only chapter 23 apocalyptic. However, James Kugel wrote that the overarching story of Jubilees concerned a god in a relationship with Israel long before the Sinaitic covenant. This relationship continued despite breaking the covenant and the subsequent Babylonian captivity (586–538 BCE). According to Kugel, the Jubilean author's belief in the continued covenant enabled

[1] Several modern scholars, such as Nickelsburg, have agreed with Oesterley's assessment. Oesterley, introduction to *The Book of Enoch*, by Robert H. Charles (London: SPCK, 1917), xiv–xv; George W. E. Nickelsburg, *1 Enoch*, vol. 1, *A Commentary on the Book of 1 Enoch, Chapters 1–36, 81–108*, Hermeneia: A Critical and Historical Commentary on the Bible, ed. Klaus Baltzer (Minneapolis: Fortress, 2001), 1. For scholars placing the parables of Enoch in Second Temple Judaism, see James H. Charlesworth and D. L. Bock, eds. *Parables of Enoch: A Paradigm Shift* (London: Bloomsbury, 2013).

[2] Andrei A. Orlov, "Enoch, Slavonic Apocalypse of (2 Enoch)," *EDEJ* 589. Nickelsburg provided the same reasoning in his discussion of 2 Enoch. Nickelsburg, *Jewish Literature between the Bible and the Mishnah*, 2nd ed. (Minneapolis, Fortress, 2005), 225.

consideration of historical events through the divine relationship presented in chapter 23.[3] By weaving the apocalyptic passage into the overarching narrative, the author provided a key to be used throughout the book of Jubilees for understanding the relation-ship between God and Israel.

Also included in Jubilees were apocalyptic traits in other passages such as angelic revelation, pseudonymous authorship, a connection to Enoch's dream vision (1 En. 85–90) and the apocalypse of weeks (1 En. 93:1–10; cf. 91:11–17), and finally, a recording of future events and a new creation of the world that included a lasting peace (Jub. 1:29).[4] For these reasons, Jubilees was included in this study as an apocalyptic work, along with 1 Enoch, 2 Enoch, the Apocalypse of Zephaniah, and the Testaments of Moses and Levi.[5] These texts were then examined and possible topoi marked in preparation for steps 1b–c.

3.2.2. Steps 1b–c

Step 1b consisted of a search in the Tanakh for topoi. Likewise, step 1c consisted of a search for topoi in one thousand EAW texts. Step 1c resulted in sixty-six possible topos types and 520 individual occurrences of possible authoritative topoi.[6] However, several of these topos types were similar and were therefore consolidated. Once this work was completed, the first loop was employed. The loop consisted of a return to step 1a (a search of the Second Temple apocalyptic literature). This loop was used to identify a larger sample of passages and possible topoi based on the findings in steps 1b–c, which resulted in locating several additional occurrences of topoi in Jewish apocalyptic literature. These topos types were listed in preparation for step 1d.

3.2.3. Step 1d

Step 1d began with comparing the lists and striking topoi absent from Second Temple apocalyptic material. The following topoi types remained: Anciency, Name, Common Knowledge, Covenant, Divinely

---

[3] James Kugel, *A Walk through Jubilees: Studies in the Book of Jubilees and the World of Its Creation* (Leiden: Brill, 2012), xxxvi, 48, 290.

[4] Michael Segal also noted several similarities between Jub. 5 and 1 En. 10–11—see Segal, *The Book of Jubilees: Rewritten Bible, Redaction, Ideology and Theology*, SJSJ 117 (Leiden: Brill, 2007), 115–17.

[5] See Appendix A (below) for delimited texts and the reasons for doing so.

[6] Genre was considered as it affected the context of the topos type.

Inspired Journeys, Prophetic Authority, Scribal Authority, Short Canonical Quotation (called "Short Quotation" in this research), Tablet(s), Wisdom Authority, and Righteousness. From this list, three topos types derived from ancient Hebraic movements (prophetic, wisdom, and scribal authority). Including these three topoi would have created a priori parent-child relationships; therefore, they were struck from the study.[7] The passages containing these topos types were reexamined at a more fundamental level and then reassigned according to constituent characteristics.[8] A fourth topos type, Short Quotation, was delimited from the preliminary work.[9] The remaining topoi were delineated and organized by category and subcategory (fig. 1),[10] which prepared the topoi for step 2.

3.3. Step 2: Context—Striking Passages and Delineating Authoritative Topoi

The second step consisted of a reading strategy focused on context as it pertained to the discovered authoritative topoi. In this step, the context of each topos-type occurrence from step 1 was examined to assess the way in which the author used authority. This process facilitated further defining, delineating, combining, and striking topos types from the study. The goal of this step was to produce a series of authority-focused literary comparisons ready to be quantified.

---

[7] Labeling topoi in apocalyptic literature by the names of the Hebraic movements presupposes a parent-child relationship because they have already been named as such. Instead, the analysis focused on what the author of each text was doing functionally and then the text was reassigned. Thus, each topos type occurrence could then be assessed on whether it was from the wisdom or prophetic movements without dealing with the problem of fighting a title that already assigned the text to a movement.

[8] Reassigning the passages meant subsequent analysis in step 4 could indicate Hebraic movements in parent-child relationships with Second Temple material.

[9] Because the Short Quotation topos type consisted of quotations from the Tanakh, they were examined separately in chapter 6, which is dedicated to material rooted in the Tanakh.

[10] Literary authority in figure 1 (below) contains references based in linguistics, storytelling, or concepts in stories. These referents may be physical in nature, but the focus is on the literary use of the referent, rather than the physical object.

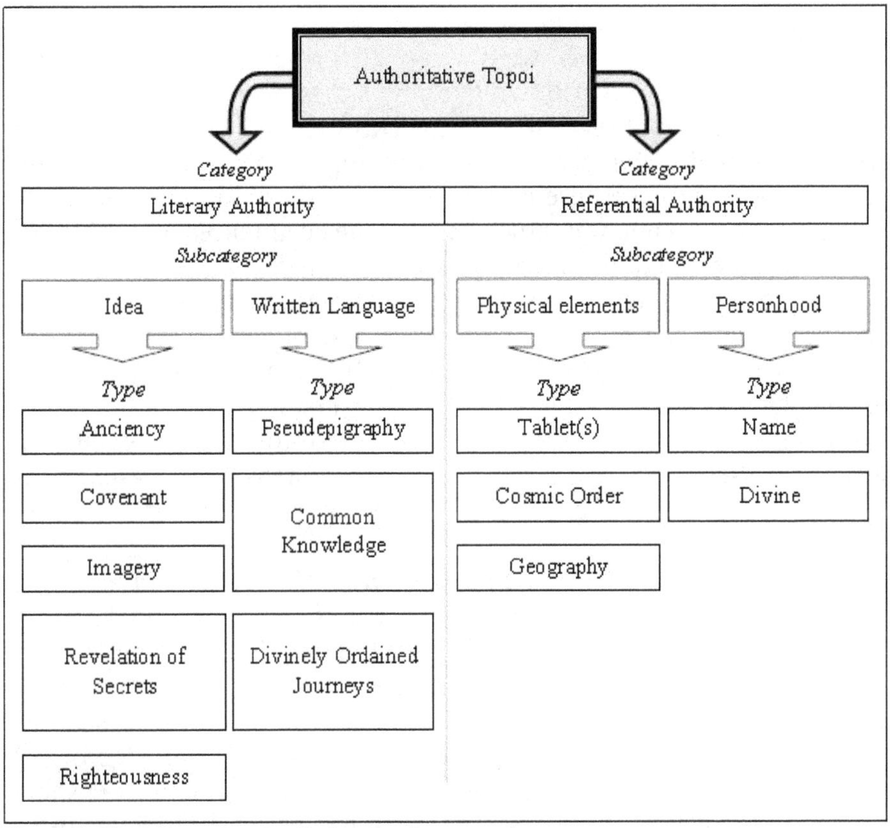

Figure 1. Flowchart of authoritative topoi.

3.3.1. Step 2a

Step 2a was an investigation of the topos types, which focused on context and presentation. For each text, the context of the topos type occurrence was noted with special attention devoted to the speaker, point of view, genre, setting, and the way in which the author used the authority. Then, the presentation of word pictures, concepts, and cognates was also noted. This focus on context and presentation helped further define each authoritative topos type, which enabled better identification of topoi. The work in Step 2a facilitated striking several passages from the Tanakh, EAW, and Second Temple material holding no authoritative appeal before continuing to step 2b.

3.3.2. Steps 2b–c

In step 2b, topos types were assessed for subtypes based on the work in step 2a. The following topos types were then struck or combined based on observations of the subtypes in step 2c. First, both topos types under the personhood subcategory were struck. Divine Authority was struck because it was definitional for cultic communities,[11] and Authority by Name was struck because the occurrences most likely to produce a parent-child relationship occurred in direct connection with pseudepigraphy. Therefore, all passages containing Authority by Name topos types were transferred to the Pseudepigraphy topos type.[12] Second, under the physical elements subcategory, Geography and Cosmic Order were demoted to subtypes under a new topos type, Cosmology.[13] Cosmology therefore referenced all naturally occurring celestial or terrestrial entia.[14] This work in steps 2a–c resulted in eleven topoi types (see fig. 2, below) ready for quantification in step 3.

3.4. Step 3: Cross-Text—Quantification of Authoritative Topoi

Step 3 incorporated a cross-text reading strategy. The goal of this step was to quantify the relationship between individual occurrences of topoi in Jewish apocalyptic literature and EAW or Tanakh material. Quantifying the relationship was the best way to determine a scoring method for later objective comparisons of text scores. This step began with a loop to step 1c. Once completed, the highest scoring relationships from each topos type were assessed for a parent-child relationship in step 4. Before beginning this quantification, however, another loop was needed.

---

[11] In Northwestern Semitic culture, identity was based on a tri-part relationship between a people, their god, and their land. Divine Authority was inevitable in each culture and thus, not helpful for this study. Daniel I. Block, *The Gods of the Nations: Studies in Ancient Near Eastern National Theology*, 2nd ed., Evangelical Theological Society Studies (Grand Rapids: Baker Academic, 2000), 18–20. Note, however, this topos type undergirded several other topos types and is referenced throughout chapters 3–5.

[12] However, it was referenced several times in connection with other topos types.

[13] A cosmological authority is a reference to a physical element that is authoritative because of what that element represents, such as a reference to Mount Sinai as the place upon which Moses received the law and thus, an authoritative reference to the law.

[14] Research into mountains as the navel of the earth (the *omphalos* myth) and by extension, the universe, supported combining Cosmic Order and Mountains under a single subtype as presented in the "Cosmology" subsection below.

3.4.1. Step 3 Loop

In the step 3 loop, another search through EAW material was performed (which was a return to step 1c). This step utilized a focused keyword search across the original one thousand EAW texts plus an additional one thousand EAW texts.[15] The keywords for this search were developed from the work in steps 1 and 2. New occurrences of

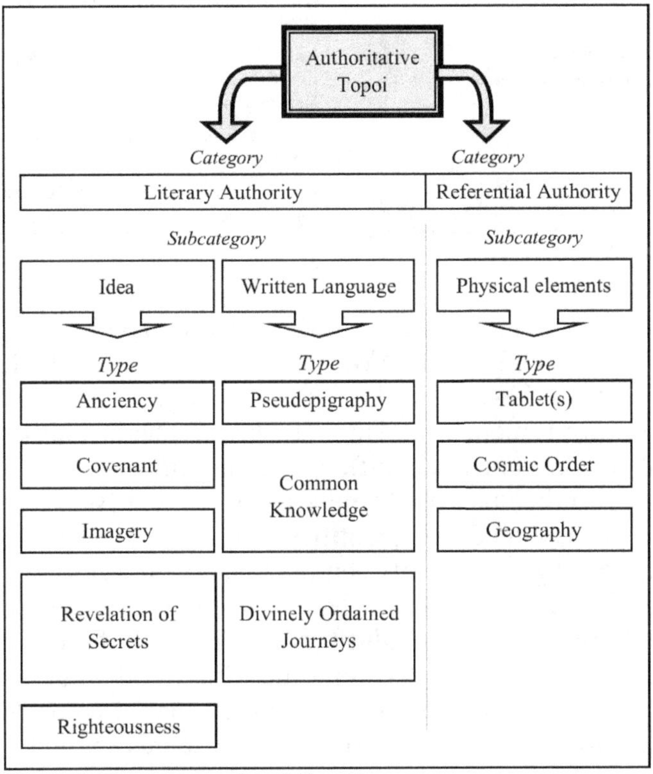

Figure 2. Topos types after delineation.

[15] The keywords for this search were developed from the work in steps 1 and 2. For instance, a search of the Cosmology topos type would include keywords such as sun, moon, stars, cosmos, celestial bodies, heaven, mountains, and the names of important mountains in the EAW and Hebraic cultures. A search for the A search for the Covenant topos type included key words such as "Covenant," "Treaty," "Agreement," and so on. See Appendix B (below) for the complete list of texts used in this loop, which exceeded twenty-two hundred texts, overall.

authoritative topoi were then resubmitted to step 2 where the context was examined and notated.[16] This loop resulted in a larger sample size for examination and quantification, beginning in steps 3a–b.

Table 1. Quantification of authorities

Similarity of Context	*Points*	*Similarity of Word Picture*
a dissimilarity detracts from any possible relationship	0	a dissimilarity detracts from any possible relationship
no similarities exist and dissimilarities do not detract from a relationship	null	no similarities exist and dissimilarities do not detract from a relationship
general similarities exist; nondetracting dissimilarities may also exist (genre, astral travel with story *A* to moon, *B* to stars)	1	general similarities exist (heavenly tablets in story *A* and *B*, no other similarities in word picture or linguistic units)
strong similarities exist with fewer dissimilarities (astral travel, *A* and *B* to moon, *B* also to stars)	2	multiple similarities exist (*A* and *B* have same tablets and heavenly figures, but different instructions)
distinct similarities exist (*A* and *B* to moon, then to stars)	3	distinct similarities exist (tablets, heavenly figures, and instructions all similar)

3.4.2. Steps 3a–b

Steps 3a–b were a comparison of similar topoi types among Jewish apocalyptic texts and the EAW material or the Tanakh. These comparisons were based on the work of steps 2b–c (concerning context and word pictures). The results of these authority-based literary analyses were then quantified, resulting in two scores. The first score represented the quantified similarity of context (step 3a), and the second score represented the quantified similarity of word picture(s), concepts, or verbiage found between the texts (step 3b). Each increase in the point scale represents less dissimilarities, and/or more similarities. In the final point values (points 2 and 3 of table 1 below), point value 2 includes some dissimilarities, but point value 3 includes no dissimilarities. As such, the similarities are classified as "distinct." At the conclusion of this step, two similarity scores existed. The first score (0–3) indicated the similarity of context. The second score (0–4)

---

[16] For instance, the keyword "Tablets" returned hits from texts such as the Song of Ullikummis, "Let us go before Ea to Apsu, let us ask for the old tablets with the words [of fate]!" and from the reverse side of the Nergal and Ereshkigal fragment A, "You be my husband and I will be your wife. I will let you hold dominion over the wide nether world. I will place the tablet of wisdom in your hand that [you] shall be master and I will be [the] mistress!"

indicated the similarity of the word picture. The criteria for each assigning a score are provided in table 1 (above).[17]

To illustrate, in step 1, the Revelation of Secrets topos type was located in 1 En. 89:2 (step 1a) and in the "Ascent of Enmeduranki" (step 1c). These passages were investigated in step 2 and notated for context and word picture. In step 2c, the Revelation of Secrets topos type was determined to have the subtype, positive revelation of secrets. Moreover, it was noted that the topos occurrences in 1 En. 89:2 and the "Ascent of Enmeduranki" both belonged to this subtype. In step 3a, the relationship between 1 En. 89:2 and the passage in "Ascent of Enmeduranki was quantified based on similarities of context, as noted in table 1. Then, in step 3b, the similarities of the word picture between the two texts were quantified (again, see table 1). Before these scores could be totaled, however, the strength of appeal also had to be quantified (step 3c).

3.4.3. Step 3c

In step 3c, a third score was calculated. This score quantified the strength of the author's authoritative appeal in Jewish apocalyptic work according to the criteria in table 2. This score for the strength of appeal elevated Jewish apocalyptic texts (and any EAW relationship to that text) according to the evaluation of the author's appeal to authority. Strength of appeal scoring assured texts with greater appeals to authority would be included in the overall assessment. Once completed, the study progressed to step 3d where the similarity scores and strength of appeal score for each occurrence was totaled in order to determine which occurrences and which topos types to include in Step 4 (chapters 3–5).

Table 2. Quantification of authoritative appeal

Strength of Appeal	*Points*
no authoritative appeal	0
appeal to authority possible: word or phrase carrying appeal to authority, more research needed before determining appeal, or appeal is implicit	1
appeal to authority evident in text, not paramount to story or is secondary to another appeal to authority	2
appeal to authority explicit and one of the following: weaved into narrative to strengthen narrative, explicitly mentioned as reason for legitimating a teaching or enabling an action, or paramount to story	3

[17] The following works informed but did not control this study: John S. Bergsma, "The Biblical Manumission Laws: Has the Literary Dependence of *H* on *D* Been Demonstrated?" in *A Teacher for All Generations: Essays in Honor of James C. Vanderkam*, ed. Eric Farrel Mason, SJSJ 153 (Leiden: Brill, 2012) 1:66–68; Richard B. Hays, *Echoes of Scripture in the Letters of Paul* (New Haven: Yale University Press, 1989).

3.4.4. Step 3d

In Step 3d, the two similarity scores and the strength of appeal score for each topos type occurrence were added together for a total (designated "Total One"). Then, these same three scores were multiplied for a second total (designated "Total Two"). Totals One and Two were then averaged (designated Overall Average).[18] For example, when comparing texts in which heavenly secrets are positively revealed to humanity, the story of Enmeduranki included the Revealed Secrets topos type where the gods revealed the secrets of extispicy to Enmeduranki. Comparing this occurrence to 1 En. 9:6 produced scores of 1 for similarity of context, 3 for similarity of word picture, and 2 for appeal to authority in the Jewish text, resulting in a score of 6 for Total One and 6 for Total Two with an Overall Average score of 6. This method, therefore, awarded better scores to texts with similarities across categories, but still awarded decent scores to topos occurrences with decent scores in one or two categories.[19] This method also compensated for possible inconsistencies within data collection and evaluation. Once the Overall Average was determined for each topos type occurrence, the top occurrences with the highest Overall Averages were included in chapters 3–4 if the topos type itself was included.

To determine which topos types to include in chapters 3–4, the Overall Average of the occurrences for each topos type were added together, then divided by the number of occurrences to produce a raw average score (*ras*). Then, one point was added to the *ras* for every five occurrences for a final *ras* score (designated, "Score").[20] As such, a topos type with a *ras* of 3.4 and 15 occurrences would receive a Score of 6.4.[21] The resulting Score for each topos type is noted in the following table.[22]

---

[18] To represent this step mathematically, let *sc* equal the score for similarity of context. Let *sw* equal the similarity score for word pictures. Let *aa* equal the score for appeal to authority. Let *oa* equal Overall Average. $oa = (sc+sw+aa) \times (sc \times sw \times aa)/2$.

[19] Conversely, comparisons of topoi type occurrences with any category scoring a 0 were heavily penalized in this method as Total Two then equaled zero.

[20] Adding one point to the *ras* per each five occurrences weighted the Score slightly toward topos types with several occurrences as more occurrences also indicated a slightly stronger possibility for locating a source of the authoritative topos type.

[21] Represented mathematically as Score = *ras* + (occurrences/5).

[22] If topos types had subtypes, the method for determining inclusion of topos types was also used to determine which subtypes to include in the following chapters.

Table 3. Quantification of topoi

Category	*Subcategory*	*Type*	*Score*
Literary	Written Language	Pseudepigraphy	Definitional[a]
Literary	Written Language	Common Knowledge	11.17
Literary	Idea	Covenant	9.63
Referential	Physical Elements	Tablet	7.83
Referential	Physical Elements	Cosmology	7.50
Literary	Idea	Righteousness	7.34
Literary	Written Language	Divinely Ordained Events	7.15
Literary	Idea	Revelation of Secrets	6.36
Literary	Idea	Anciency	6.25
Literary	Idea	Imagery (animal-manlike)	5.64

[a]*Definitional indicates the topos type is considered an essential element of the Apocalyptic genre*

As a result of the work in step 3d, the Imagery topos type was struck from the study for two reasons. First, it scored a full deviation lower than the mean (two full points below the mean of 7.65). Second, the imagery topos type scored 0.72 points below the next lowest topos type, Revelation of Secrets. Anciency was also struck, and its texts were reassigned to other topos types because too many similarities existed between it and the other topoi.[23] The Pseudepigraphy topos type was not included in this method of scoring because all Second Temple literature studied was pseudepigraphical and considered by many to be an essential part of the genre; therefore, inclusion of the Pseudepigraphy topos type was required.[24]

The quantification presented in steps 3a–d provided a consistent method for applying numerical values to subjective observations by examining them in a holistic manner.[25] After implementing step 3d, the

---

[23] Within the Anciency topos type, the two strongest subtypes were *ex-eventu* prophecy and chaos. *Ex-eventu* prophecy was heavily associated with pseudepigraphy in Second Temple literature and the scholarship thereof; the ancient chaos stories subtype was more accurately associated with the Common Knowledge topos type.

[24] But see chapter 2 n.48 (above) for limitations on this statement concerning canonical material.

[25] Quantification by this method also allowed for a postmodern focus on linguistics and discourse analysis. Kaya Yilmaz argues that postmodern methods have reduced the "emphasis on the role of language and discourse in shaping meaning and forming individual subjectivity" (Kaya Yilmaz, "Postmodernism and Its Challenge to the Discipline of History: Implications for History Education,"

Imagery topos type was struck from the study for two reasons. First, it scored a full deviation lower than the mean (two full points below the mean of 7.65). Second, the imagery topos type scored 0.72 points below the next lowest topos type, Revelation of Secrets. Anciency was also struck, and its texts were reassigned to other topos types because too many similarities existed between it and the other topoi.[26]

Nine topos types remained after step 3d, which were then investigated in step 4 (chapters 3–5). Of these remaining nine, the preliminary research identified the Revelation of Secrets, Righteousness, Divinely Ordained Journeys, and Tablets topos types as having the strongest possibility of deriving from EAW material; thus, these types were grouped for further study in chapter 3. The Pseudepigraphy, References to Common Knowledge, Covenant, and Cosmology topos types held an equal possibility of deriving from either EAW or Hebraic material and therefore were grouped for further study in chapter 4. Finally, the Short Quotation topos type was assigned its own chapter because it consisted of direct quotes from the Tanakh.

As noted in the introduction, the work in chapters 3 through 5 (representing the nine repetitions of step 4) was to discern whether the sources explored in each chapter were in a parent-child relationship with Second Temple apocalyptic literature. The goal of this exploration was to determine if the preliminary research and prima facia observations of possible parent-child relationships held up under greater scrutiny.

Educational Philosophy and Theory 42.7 [2010]: 779). Perhaps the most famous postmodern author concerning linguistics was Derrida, who introduced concepts on decentered language and wordplay. Taken to an extreme (and Derrida often did), decentering language and deconstruction resulted in an amorphous jumble of available signifiers lacking significance outside any inputted meaning by a reader. Authorial intent was therefore lost; signs become symbols and the textual world was available for any redesignation of its symbols. The above methodology attenuated these extremes.

[26] Within the Anciency topos type, the two strongest subtypes were *ex-eventu* prophecy and chaos. *Ex-eventu* prophecy was heavily associated with pseudepigraphy in Second Temple literature and the scholarship thereof; the ancient chaos stories subtype was more accurately associated with the Common Knowledge topos type.

Chapter 4
POSSIBLE PRIMA FACIE DERIVATION OF AUTHORITATIVE TOPOI ACCORDING TO PRELIMINARY RESULTS: EAW LITERATURE

Ten thousand things there are which we believe merely upon the authority or credit of those who have spoken or written them. It is by this evidence that we know...things that are at a vast distance from us in foreign nations or in ancient ages.

—*The Works of the Late Reverend and Learned Isaac Watts*

4.1. Introduction

The evidence about which Isaac Watts wrote was the authority of authors in distant lands or from antiquity. By this authority, a person believed what was not otherwise knowable. Pseudonymous authorship provided apocalyptic material a similar authority (explored in chapter 4). However, Second Temple authors also invoked other authorities, four of which were examined in this chapter (step 4): Revelation of Secrets, Righteousness, Divinely Ordained Journeys, and Tablets. These four types scored strongest for possible parent-child relationships with EAW literature.

In the following material, each subheading corresponded to the parts of each step (steps 4a–d). Step 4a was an overview of the authoritative topos in EAW material. This step focused on uses of the topos type and an introduction to its authority. Step 4b was a presentation of the topos type occurrences in Second Temple apocalyptic literature most likely to evidence a parent-child relationship with EAW or Tanakh material. In step 4c, germane scholarship informed the study on textual questions, significant contributions to the scholarly debate concerning the topos type, and other relevant issues. Steps 4d–e were the cross-text sections for each step in which the EAW and Tanakh material was examined. The final subsection (step 4f) was an evaluation of the topos type at the conclusion of these steps.

4.2. Literary Authority by Idea: Revelation of Secrets

The Revelation of Secrets topos type derived from mystery cults and religions incorporating elements of mystery. These cults and religions spanned the EAW world throughout classical antiquity. Examples included the Eleusinian and Dionysus cults in the West, the Isis cult in post-Ptolemy Egypt, and Mithraism in Persia. These religions focused on "salvation through closeness to the divine."[1] Yet, normal cultic activities were often separated from the secret elements, and only adherents who chose full initiation learned the mysteries;[2] consequently, initiation and revealed secrets became avenues to cultic salvation.[3] As such, a revealed secret within this context became authoritative because it brought about deliverance and often, salvation. How, then, was this topos type defined?

4.2.1. Step 4a: Text—Definition and Use of Authority

The Revelation of Secrets topos type was a place in a text in which an entity (usually an angel or a god) revealed a previously held secret to humanity that often resulted in deliverance or salvation. For Second Temple authors, secrecy was central to the apocalyptic genre. Their work consisted of narratives in which God (or another heavenly being) uncovered or revealed secrets to ancient figures who, in turn, preserved them for later audiences. In this way, a pseudonymous author (P.author) borrowed authority to promote or negate beliefs, teachings, or actions current to the Second Temple period.

---

[1] Walter Burkert, *Ancient Mystery Cults*, Carl Newell Jackson Lectures (Cambridge: Harvard University Press, 1987), 12.

[2] "In most cases, there existed forms of a 'normal' cult alongside the mysteries, that is, worship for the noninitiated independent of possible candidacy" (ibid., 10); cf. David Ulansey, *The Origins of the Mithraic Mysteries: Cosmology and Salvation in the Ancient World* (New York: Oxford University Press, 1991), 3.

[3] Arguments existed concerning the development of the nonmystery Persian Mithra cult into the Roman mystery religion. Manfred Clauss and Richard Gordon, however, argued no evidence showed such a link, at least between the Hellenistic and Roman versions of Mithras. On another note, many scholars believed the mystery cults postdated the period studied here, but Walter Burkert reminded his readers both Eleusis and Dionysus-Bacchus cults predated Hellenism in the Levant. Manfred Clauss, *The Roman Cult of Mithras: The God and His Mysteries*, trans., Richard Gordon (New York: Routledge, 2000), 7; Walter Burkert, *Ancient Mystery Cults*, 2–10.

The P.authors used this authority in several ways. One such way was the creation of eschatological scenarios in which "the secrets of the righteous" were "revealed and the sinners judged" (1 En. 38:3). This vision of judgment used secrets much like EAW mystery cults—those who were righteous could rely on the secrets to them for deliverance or salvation.[4] This salvation depended upon their knowledge, which was a revealed knowledge that condemned sinners at the judgment. As such, the topos type was used authoritatively to encourage the adherents in their struggles by assuring that salvation was coming through the judgment of the sinners.

Other ways P.authors used this authority were narrator provided secrets (1 En. 41:1) and secrets of specific knowledge; for instance, secrets of the heavenly city (Apoc. Zeph. 5:1). However, based on the preliminary work, two subtypes showed the strongest possibilities for a parent-child relationship. The first subtype was a positive revelation of secrets; the second subtype was a negative revelation of secrets.

4.2.2. Step 4b: Text and Context—Use in Apocalyptic Literature

Positive revelation of secrets was a sanctioned revelation with positive results. In contrast, a negative revelation of secrets was an unsanctioned revelation with negative results. P.Enoch used these topos subtypes to generate authority for or against a topic.

4.2.2.1. Positive Revelation of Secrets

In 1 En. 89:2, the author reminded the reader of divine protection through a positive revelation of secrets:

> Then one of those four went to those snow-white bovids and taught (one of them) a secret: he was born a bovid but became a person; and he built for himself a big boat and dwelt upon it. Three cows dwelt together with him in that boat, and that boat was covered (over) them.[5]

---

[4] The idea of salvation in this passage was found in verse 5; the kings and mighty were associated with the sinners (as seen in their being delivered to the righteous and holy and then perishing).

[5] All quoted apocalyptic texts in this work were from James H. Charlesworth, ed. *OTP*, 2 vols., Anchor Yale Bible Reference Library (London: Yale University

In this passage, the author withheld the origin of the secret revealed by the angel in 1 Enoch, but context led the reader to the flood narrative (6:9-9:17) in Genesis. There, God both originated the secret and approved its revelation to Noah. The result of this revealed secret was Noah's deliverance from the flood (1 En. 89:9). The opposite occurred in 1 En. 9:6, where the author wrote of a negative revelation of secrets.

4.2.2.2. Negative Revelation of Secrets

The occurrence of this subtype in 1 En. 9:6 was one example of a negative revelation of secrets. Here, it concerned the Watchers' interaction with humanity: "You see what Azazel has done; how he has taught all (forms of) oppression upon the earth. And they revealed eternal secrets which are performed in heaven (and which) man learned" (1 En. 9:6).[6] The concept of eternity as it applies to truth and the place of performance heightened the tension in this narrative. The secrets were heavenly, eternal, and belonged in the realm of the divine; yet, the Watchers released them upon temporal earth—the realm of man. Through this narrative, the author legitimized God's punishment of the Watchers while exonerating humanity (contrary to the Gen 6–8 flood account).[7]

4.2.2.3. Qumran

Positive and negative revelations of secrets were part of a binary system of belief at Qumran, based on הנגלות and הנסתרות (the revealed and the hidden law).[8] According to 1QS v:10–12, all Israel received הנגלות, but only the Qumran community or יחד received הנסתרות

Press, 1983–85). Translations from the Tanakh, Dead Sea Scrolls, Greek sources, and modern languages were mine, unless otherwise noted.

[6] Note, however, negative revelation topoi occurred in 1 En. 10:7, 65:6, and 69:1.

[7] Nickelsburg, *1 Enoch 1*, 203, 22. Himmelfarb argued a similar point, concluding the strength and thrust of the narrative "absolves humanity of the blame, or…some of the blame, for the evils around us" (Martha Himmelfarb, *The Apocalypse: A Brief History*, Blackwell Brief Histories of Religion Series [Chichester: Wiley-Blackwell, 2010], 18). Molenberg noted, however, that concepts of sin origins varied among Second Temple authors, paralleling the changing ideas among differing waves of Judaism—see C. Molenberg, "A Study of the Roles of Shemihaza and Asael in 1 Enoch 6–11," *JJS* 35.2 (1984): 136–46.

[8] Although usually translated "revealed" or "hidden things," the context in Qumran indicated that hidden thing was the law—see Schiffman, *Qumran and Jerusalem*, 202–03.

through "divinely-inspired study sessions." In these sessions, God revealed his will to the participants, which continued his relationship with the Qumran community—a community that believed its members alone were covenant-Israel.[9] Following this pattern, two texts from Qumran held a Revelation of Secrets topos type. The first text was a positive revelation, found in 4Q259 iii:16b–18:

> [He] leads them with knowledge [and thus to instruct them of the] mysteries of wonder and of truth and give them the secret pa[th of the men of] the Community, so that they wa[lk perfectly, one] with another, in all that has been revealed to them.

In the following lines, the Instructor taught the secret paths to proper cultic activity, and by obeying, the community separated from injustice according to the behavioral expectations of the sect. The Instructor's revelation, therefore, offered salvation to the adherents at Qumran.

A warning against a negative revelation of secrets occurred in 4Q270 f2.ii:12b–14:

> Whoever divulges the secrets of his people to the nations, or curses his people, or speaks rebellion upon those anointed with the spirit of holiness [...]. Against them, God has decreed to allow [...].

The gist of this warning was clear: A conflictual relationship between God and the revealer would exist if the congregant revealed secrets intended only for the Qumran community. Throughout Second Temple apocalyptic literature, these two subtypes of the Revelation of Secrets topos type indicated salvation (positive revelation) or contained warnings concerning cultic or ethical action (negative revelation).[10]

---

[9] Note the similarities to the mystery religions, for which salvation was available through membership into personal cultic mystery.

[10] See the following subsection for a presentation on the 1 Enoch 9 Watcher narrative as a warning to readers.

4.2.3. Step 4c: Text and Context—Germane Scholarship

According to Jacque Derrida, the act or wish to expose secrets within apocalyptic literature caused self-decentering, and eventually, self-deconstruction.[11] Elliot Wolfson summarized Derrida's thoughts on the apocalyptic genre: "With more than a touch of irony, Derrida viewed apocalyptic—a literary genre usually thought to be entirely mystifying—as that which imparts the desire for clarity and elucidation, a desire expressed…even to the point of demystifying or deconstructing the genre of apocalyptic itself."[12] Accordingly, revealing secrets in apocalyptic writing deconstructed the genre for that work. Yet, in that deconstruction came authority—a heavenly figure chose to violate secrecy because the message was too important to withhold from the receiver of the secret. Following the figure's leadership, the recipient then communicated the deconstructed secret to the community. Conversely, in Qumran, the decentered center (those to whom God reveals his secret), created a new center by commanding a new secrecy. This command set apart the Qumran community by creating a new recentered secrecy.[13]

Shifting to textual issues, Himmelfarb argued the context of 1 En. 9:6 was two separate origin-of-evil myths twined into a single story. One Enochian author placed responsibility on the Watchers for their sexual endeavors among women, the other wrote of revealed heavenly secrets associated with civilization. In this latter myth, the Revelation of Secrets topos type showed the dangerous misuse and abuse of divine knowledge.[14] Annette Reed agreed with Himmelfarb concerning the abuse of divine knowledge in the Book of the Watchers; however, she argued instances of revealed secrets and divinely ordained journeys posed serious epistemological concerns because they mixed what belonged in heaven with what belonged to earth, yielding horrible consequences. According to Reed, the author was driven by

---

[11] Jacque Derrida, "Of an Apocalyptic Tone Recently Adopted in Philosophy," *The Oxford Literary Review* 6.2 (1984): 22–23, 34–35.

[12] Elliot Wolfson, "Unveiling the Veil: Apocalyptic, Secrecy, and the Jewish Mystical Imaginaire," *AJS Perspectives: The Magazine of the Association of Jewish Studies*, Fall 2012, 18–20, http://www.bjpa.org/Publications/details.cfm?PublicationID=20997.

[13] Which, perhaps, explained (at least partially) why Qumran was such a unique challenge in this study, as noted in the introductory chapter.

[14] Himmelfarb, *Apocalypse*, 17.

this truth to limit authority of the Revealed Secrets and Divinely Ordained Journeys topos types by "attenuating the potentially radical epistemological ramifications of [Enoch's] access to knowledge through heavenly ascent."[15] Attenuation occurred by redacting chapters 12–19 into their current form, which "functions to link the revelations to Enoch to his predestined commission from God," and "presents a negative antediluvian paradigm for speculation into heavenly secrets."[16] Margaret Barker corroborated these assessments, noting such knowledge resulted in "the whole earth bec[oming] corrupted by this invasion of divine secrets."[17] These writings then served as a warning against those who "altered the calendar, which [was] a sign of their abuse of divine knowledge."[18]

The result of this scholarship was an understanding that properly revealed secrets produced divinely ordered events (as in 1 En. 89:2); but altered or improperly revealed secrets produced chaos and destruction.[19] Furthermore, the power of this once-secret knowledge added another layer of inherent authority to this topos type. Eternal, divine secrets were powerful enough to create order from chaos, but the inverse was also true: secrets incorrectly revealed were also powerful enough to introduce chaos into order.

Concerning Qumran, Samuel Thomas wrote, "Hidden matters were themselves guarded by the sect from the rest of Judean society."[20] Paul Heger also argued for a second instance of revealed secrets that were then secreted once more, this time by the Instructor from the community. Although several scholars have disagreed with Heger, they did agree on revealed secrets as a central teaching at Qumran.[21]

---

[15] Annette Reed, "Heavenly Ascent, Angelic Descent, and the Transmission of Knowledge in 1 Enoch 6–16," in *Heavenly Realms and Earthly Realities in Late Antique Religions*, ed. Ra'anan S. Boustan (Cambridge: Cambridge University Press, 2004), 66.

[16] Ibid.

[17] Margaret Barker, "Some Reflections Upon the Enoch Myth," *JSOT* 15 (1980): 9. "Divine secrets," as used here, was self-definitional: secrets held by the divine.

[18] Barker, "Reflections," 12.

[19] Ibid.

[20] Samuel Thomas, *The "Mysteries" of Qumran: Mystery, Secrecy, and Esotericism in the Dead Sea Scrolls*, EJL 25, ed. Judith H. Newman (Atlanta: Society of Biblical Literature, 2009), 134–35. The following paragraph was derived from his work.

[21] Thomas, *"Mysteries of Qumran,"* 134–35.

To summarize, Derrida's argument concerning deconstruction of the genre added a new layer of authority to Revelation of Secrets. That authority derived from the idea that the heavenly knowledge was so important, a heavenly being determined it should no longer be a secret. Himmelfarb, Reed, and Barker identified the P.author's concerns for using and misusing that heavenly knowledge and noted how it affected the negative revelation of secrets subtype. In Qumran, the heavenly secrets were heavily guarded—and perhaps resecreted (if Heger was right). The clarifications and points made by these scholars should help identify if the Revealed Secrets topos type in EAW material were in a parent-child relationship with the topos type in Second Temple apocalyptic literature.

4.2.4. Step 4d: Cross-Text—Possible EAW Sources

The Revealed Secrets topos type occurred in EAW sources ranging from Sumer, Babylon, and Persia to Egypt and Greece. The possible EAW sources with the highest scores from the third step were presented below in two subsections. The first subsection held three instances of a positive revelation of secrets. The second subsection held two instances of a negative revelation of secrets.

4.2.4.1. Positive Revelation of Secrets

Based on the scoring in steps 3a–c, the EAW sources most likely in parent-child relationships with Jewish apocalyptic literature within this typos type were (1) the "Ascent of Enmeduranki," (2) the Assyrian version of the *Epic of Gilgamesh*, and (3) "The Tradition of Seven Lean Years in Egypt." The first two narratives originated in Sumer. The latter, however, was Egyptian and possibly dated to Djoser's reign in the twenty-seventh century BCE.

4.2.4.1.1. "Ascent of Enmeduranki"

In the "Ascent of Enmeduranki," the gods Shamash and Adad gave a gift to Enmeduranki, king of Sippar in the antediluvian world:

> Enmeduranki [king of Sippar], the beloved of Anu, Enlil [and Ea], Šamaš and Adad [brought him in] to their assembly. Šamaš and Adad [honored him]. Šamaš and Adad [set him] on a large throne of gold. They showed him how to observe oil on

> water, a mystery of Anu, [Enlil and Ea] they gave him the tablet of the gods, the liver, a secret of heaven and [underworld].[22]

In the Sumerian text, two gods brought Enmeduranki into their presence in the heavens and then bestowed upon him a positively revealed secret: the gift of divination by extispicy. He then returned home, sharing the gift by divining and by teaching others to divine. Comparing this text with 1 Enoch revealed similarities. Enmeduranki and Noah both received positive revelations, both characters embarked on an astral journey, and both characters received knowledge. These similarities caused Collins to write, "To a great extent, [Enoch] *is modeled* on the mythological figure of Enmeduranki."[23] Thus, the condition of three verbal contacts between texts looked to be satisfied; however, the problem lay in the specifics.

The first problem was the positive revelation of secrets to Enoch not originating from a deity. Instead, it came from angelical beings (and the same held true for the positive revelations to Noah in 1 Enoch).[24] The second problem was the lack of divine gifts to Enoch (and Noah). Whereas Enmeduranki received the gift of divination,

---

[22] Wilfred G. Lambert, "Enmeduranki and Related Matters," *JCS* 21 (1967): 132; Lambert redacted line three of the translation, which was followed here. Andrei Orlov and Krzysztof Ulanowski are but two of the latest scholars to defer to Lambert's translation: Orlov, "The Learned Savant Who Guards the Secrets of the Great Gods: Evolution of Roles and Titles of the Seventh Antediluvian Hero in Mesopotamian and Enochic Traditions (Part 1: Mesopotamian Traditions)," *Scrinium: Journal of Patrology and Critical Hagiography* 1.1 (2005): 252; Ulanowski, "Mesopotamian Divination: Some Historical, Religious, and Anthropological Remarks," *Miscellanea Anthropological et Sociologica* 15.4 (2014): 17–19. Contemporary English replaces Old English inflections throughout this study.

[23] Collins, *Seers, Sibyls, and Sages*, 342—emphasis added. For Collins, Enoch and Enmeduranki were equivalent characters, acting as intermediaries between the divine and humanity. Collins based his exploration of likenesses on that equivalence (he also considered Utnapishtim a model). Others made this connection as well. Orlov, for instance, claimed the first to do so was Zimmern, who wrote of the "accidental coincidence in which of Enmeduranki, that seventh Babylonian king, and of Enoch, that seventh biblical forefather, is reported" (as noted in ibid., 341–42—citing Heinrich Zimmern, "Überblick über die babylonische Religion in bezug auf ihre Berührung mit biblischen Vorstellungen," in *Die keilinschriften und das Alte Testament*, 3rd edition, ed. Heinrich Zimmern and Hugo Winckler [Berlin: Verlag von Reuther and Reichard, 1903], 540).

[24] Likewise, 1 En. 108 closed with an angelic revelation.

Enoch received only instruction to relay to others. Finally, the third problem was the Enochian authors using Revelation of Secrets either as a rehearsal of history to explain those historical events and their repercussions or to reveal what was to come in the eschaton.[25] By comparison, Enmeduranki's revelation legitimized divination, which had no parallel in the Enochic accounts. These problems created two meaningful differences.

First, the receiver of secrets in 1 Enoch was not a true mediator. God tasked him to deliver a distinct message with no interpretive role. By comparison, although Enmeduranki repeated the divine teachings on divination, he also mediated in the role of haruspex by provoking the gods to answer human inquiry and then interpreting the response through extispicy.[26] Therefore, although Collins argued Noah was modeled on Enmeduranki, who was "a primeval archetypal mediator of revelation,"[27] their roles were only remotely similar.[28]

Second, the Enochian author did not create a new societal role or position for Enoch. Enoch functioned only as a go-between. The teleological purpose of Enoch's received secrets (and for that matter, Noah's) was an assurance and hope for future deliverance and punishment of the wicked.[29] By comparison, the teleological purpose in Enmeduranki's ascent was a divine ordination of divination and the establishment of a new societal role of haruspex within Nippur, Sippar, and Babylon. This role caused the diviner to be active in seeking

[25] Hence, the other topos subtypes mentioned in step 4a of this topos type. The crux of the argument was the vast differences in content, which denied similarities in the word-picture, and to a lesser degree, context. Consequently, if an author used this material as a source, then that author strayed too far from the original text, and borrowed authority was impossible, which negated a parent-child relationship.

[26] Known to the modern world as a practice in ancient Rome, "haruspex" was used here based on its Babylonian heritage. George Sarton, *Ancient Science through the Golden Age of Greece*, Dover ed. (New York: Dover Publications, 1993), 93.

[27] Collins, *Seers, Sibyls, and Sages*, 342.

[28] However, Orlov highlighted several roles in his dissertation dealing with 2 Enoch. See Appendix C (below) for Orlov's arguments on Sumerian influence in Genesis 5 and responses to his arguments. Orlov, "From Patriarch to the Youth: The Metatron Tradition in '2 Enoch'" (PhD diss., Marquette University, 2004), 77–93.

[29] George W. E. Nickelsburg and James C. VanderKam, *A Commentary on the Book of 1 Enoch, Chapters 37–82*, vol. 2 of *1 Enoch*, Hermeneia: A Critical and Historical Commentary on the Bible, ed. Klaus Baltzer (Minneapolis: Fortress, 2012), 133; Nickelsburg, *1 Enoch* 1, 37–39, 41. "Jewish Community" is a general term; scholars have continued to debate the question of the author's intended audience.

answers from the gods; something not found in the Enochian accounts. These meaningful differences persisted in the Enochian manuscripts at Qumran.

There, the manuscript evidencing the closest relationship to the Ascent text was 4Q201 i:4. In it, Noah declared he would speak for a future generation, but this manuscript only replicated the opening passage of 1 Enoch 1 in which Enoch declared he would write a parable or oracle, "a holy vision from the heavens which the angels showed me" (1 En. 1:2).[30] Therefore, meaningful differences denied a parent-child relationship between the Enochic topos (even at Qumran) and topos in the "Ascent of Enmeduranki."

4.2.4.1.2. Epic of Gilgamesh

The Revelation of Secrets topos type occurred twice in the Assyrian *Epic of Gilgamesh.* The first instance was found on Tablet xi, line 10:

> I will reveal to you, Gilgamesh, a hidden matter, and a secret of the gods will I tell you: Shurippak—a city which you know, (And) which on Euphrates' [banks] is situated—That city was ancient, (as were) the gods within it, When their heart led the great gods to produce the flood.[31]

The first revelation, Utnapishtim's story of protection to Gilgamesh, carried a second intrinsic revelation of a secret within Ea's instructions to Utnapishtim. These revelations produced deliverance from a flood, a similar result to that seen in 1 Enoch, but a closer reading showed Ea did not verbalize his secret. Instead, secrecy remained in the background, pushing along the plot. There was no revelation of secrets whereby the author tried to persuade the reader to a particular viewpoint.

---

[30] Florentino García Martínez and Eibert Tigchelaar inserted "oracle" in their text restoration, rather than "parable," as found in 1 En. 1:3—see Florentino García Martínez and Eibert J. C. Tigchelaar, ed. *The Dead Sea Scrolls Study Edition,* vol. 1 [hereafter DSSSE 1] (Leiden: Brill, 1997), 399. Two other Qumran manuscripts included this topos subtype. The first manuscript, 4Q206 f5.i:13–14, repeated the story of 1 En. 89:2 with no changes in Enoch's role. In the second manuscript, 1 QapGen ar vi:15–26, Noah received secrets, but no instructions concerning what he should do with them.

[31] "Akkadian Myths and Epics," trans. E. A. Speiser (*ANET*, 93).

Utnapishtim's secret to Gilgamesh read the same way. At the beginning of the tale, secrecy created an expectation; it was a storytelling device rather than an authoritative topos.[32] The result, then, was a story in which no authoritative Revelation of Secrets topos type held a parent-child relationship with Jewish apocalyptic material (including Qumran) as three points of verbal contact did not exist between the texts.

4.2.4.1.3. "The Tradition of Seven Lean Years"

The Egyptian text "The Tradition of Seven Lean Years" was inscribed on a rock found at Sehel. In it, the Egyptian king, Djoser, sought knowledge concerning the end of a drought:

> So he went, and he returned to me immediately, that he might *instruct* me on the inundation of the Nile,...and everything about which they had written. He uncovered for me the hidden spells thereof, to which the ancestors had taken (their) way, without their equal among kings since the limits *of time*.[33]

In this text, "he" was the Chief Lector Priest, Ii-em-Hotep, whom Djoser sought. No presentation of the hidden spells existed in the text, although context indicated Djoser received his request. Following this text, Ii-em-Hotep provided a bulls-impregnating-kine metaphor before the tale shifted (line 18) to Djoser dreaming of Khnum's teaching on the drought and subsequent cessation. Three verbal contacts existed with 1 En. 89:2 at first glance: (1) the bulls metaphor, (2) threat by water, and (3) necessary deliverance. However, as was true with the previous EAW texts, further review revealed several differences.

Both authors produced a striking picture of increase by relying on readers to understand and appropriately interpret the bull-virility metaphor; but, those interpretations differed based on context. The

---

[32] Beginning with line 185 of Assyrian tablet xi, Utnapishtim received "the secret of the great gods." The above text did not include this passage because the Revelation of Secrets topos type did not occur in it. Instead, Utnapishtim perceived the secret from a dream Ea gave to him, which resulted in the deification of Utnapishtim (line 194). Therefore, the text was too different to compare with 1 Enoch.

[33] "The Tradition of Seven Lean Years in Egypt," trans. James B. Pritchard (*ANET*, 31–32). The questions concerning the pseudepigraphical nature of this text were addressed in the first subsection of chapter 3 titled, "Pseudepigraphy," wherein this text was compared with other pseudepigraphical texts.

Enochic metaphor concerned antediluvian events up to the flood and included Noah, who received the whole secret and deliverance in 1 Enoch. Moreover, the bull in 1 Enoch changed into Noah—a created being. In comparison, the Egyptian bull was not Djoser, but a partial creator responsible for replenishing the land. Further, the focus in the Egyptian text was the cyclic nature of the Nile that irrigated Egypt. In it, Djoser received only partial knowledge from the chief lector, having to learn the rest from Khnum thereafter. Finally, no indication existed that deliverance came through Djoser learning the secret. Khnum told him only when the drought would end.

Thus, several meaningful differences and a dissimilarity of context indicated no parent-child relationship existed concerning authority between these two passages, despite three points of verbal contact. As a result, the positive revelation of secrets subtype in Second Temple apocalyptic literature showed no place in which it appeared as a child in a parent-child relationship to EAW material.

4.2.4.2. Negative Revelation of Secrets

The two stories most likely containing an authoritative negative revelation of secrets subtype in a parent-child relationship with Jewish apocalyptic literature originated from Greece and Babylon. The first was the well-known story of the Greek god, Prometheus. The second was a land grant from Babylon.

4.2.4.2.1. Prometheus Bound

Aeschylus's *Prometheus Bound* registered as the most striking EAW source for this study.[34] In it, a Titan named Prometheus sided with the Olympians in the Titanomachy, but his later protection of

[34] Aeschylus may or may not have been the original author, but the play came to modern awareness associated with his works. While the question of true authorship was beyond the purview of this research, it was worth noting scholars such as Ian Ruffell placed its writing at least in the fourth century BCE—see Ian Ruffell, *Aeschylus: Prometheus Bound*, Companions to Greek and Roman Tragedy (London: Bristol Classics Press, 2012), 10; By comparison, Paolo Sacchi placed the completed Book of the Watchers before 200 BCE—see Paolo Sacchi, *Jewish Apocalyptic and Its History*, trans., William J. Short, JSPSup 20 (Sheffield: Sheffield Academic Press, 1996), 47. And Nickelsburg dated it to before 150 BCE—see Nickelsburg, *Jewish Literature*, 46. For more on the issues surrounding authorship of Aeschylus, see Mark Griffith, *The Authenticity of Prometheus Bound*, Cambridge Classical Studies (Cambridge: Cambridge University Press, 2007), 1–17.

humanity put Prometheus in opposition to Zeus. After a series of machinations, Zeus hid fire from the humans, but Prometheus restored it, along with a second gift, hope:

> Burning fire, assistant of all arts, he stole and granted to mortals, as is his sin, he is bound to make requital to the gods, so to learn to be steadfast in the sovereignty of [Zeus] and stop dealing kindly [with man].[35]

The story continued thereafter with Prometheus admitting to giving humanity hope (line 252). Zeus then handed him to Hephaestus, who fettered him for punishment. At first, this story held several points of verbal contact with the Watchers including revealed secrets, a gift to humanity, and a deity's punishment for the gift.

These similarities have occasioned scholarly debate. Anathea Portier-Young stated "the Book of the Watchers adapt[ed] elements of the Greek Prometheus myth, assimilating the role of…Prometheus to two of its characters."[36] Furthermore, she argued the Enochic author was critiquing the Hellenistic pantheon through narrative inversion. Another scholar to find similarities was Kyle Roark, who examined the Watchers' punishment in the Enochic writings. He found the punishment and its location similar to that of Prometheus. Beyond these points, Reed noted the stories shared similarities concerning mining and metallurgy.[37]

---

[35] Translation mine, completed in correspondence with Herber W. Smyth, trans. *Aeschylus, with an English Translation by Herber W. Smyth*, vol. 1 of *Prometheus Bound* (Cambridge: Harvard University Press, 1926). Apollodorus's History 1.7.1 contained a similar account, but there, the focus of the narrative was Prometheus giving fire to humanity (ironically, by hiding it), and Zeus's punishment thereafter of Prometheus. Apollodorus's version of the narrative was not applicable here, however, because the story concerned fire not as a secret but as the element stolen for humanity.

[36] Anathea Portier-Young, *Apocalypse against Empire: Theologies of Resistance in Early Judaism* (Grand Rapids: Eerdmans, 2011), 15–16. David Suter also argued in this manner after stating, "Attempts to relate the myth of the fallen angels to Near Eastern and Hellenistic parallels have met with some success; however, the study of the myth cannot end at that point" (David Suter, "Fallen Angel, Fallen Priest: The Problem of Family Purity in 1 Enoch 6–16," *HUCA* 50 [1979]: 115).

[37] Kyle Roark, "Iron Age Heroes and Enochic Giants," in *New Vistas on Early Judaism and Christianity: From Enoch to Montreal and Back*, ed. Lorenzo DiTommaso and Gerbern S. Oegema (London: Bloombury T&T Clark, 2016), 45–

Portier-Young's and David Suter's works pointed to the reason for these similarities. The threat of Hellenism felt by the Jewish community drove this critique,[38] resulting in a narrative that "deconstruct[ed] the very epistemological claims of the Hellenistic empires and assert[ed] in their place a knowledge that reveal[ed] the universal sovereignty of the one God."[39] These narrative inversions identified Jewish cultic superiority over Hellenistic cultism, therefore denying a parent-child relationship between these texts.

Beyond this inversion, the Revealed Secrets point of verbal contact failed upon further examination. Secrecy was a plot-point in the Prometheus story as Zeus withheld fire as a punishment against Prometheus for tricking him. By comparison, the Enochic narrative held improperly revealed secrets and the Watchers' actions as dual origins of evil that brought about later chaos and destruction.[40] The topos type occurrence was an authoritative reminder of the otherness of God and the heavenly things, and subsequently, the responsibility for properly exercising revealed knowledge.

4.2.4.2.2. "Land Grant at Alalakh"

Another example of the negative revelation of secrets subtype was found in the Babylonian "Land Grant at Alalakh." There, Abbael (son of Hammurabi) and Yarimlim exchanged cities: "If ever in the future

---

46; Reed, *Fallen Angels and the History of Judaism and Christianity: The Reception of Enochic Literature* (Cambridge: Cambridge University Press, 2005), 39.

[38] Using Nickelsburg's dates for Enochic writings.

[39] Portier-Young, *Apocalypse against Empire*, 17. A work against Hellenism was believable at any point between Alexander's Conquest and Pompeii's occupation. That said, the threat presented by the High Priest Jason (175–172 BCE) followed by Menelaus's continued—and possibly more extreme—push in the following years to Hellenize Judaism, and by Antiochus IV Epiphanes's desecration of the temple and following dictates against Judaism, would be part of the historical milieu for the Book of the Watchers. Such a background provides a strong impetus for a polemical work.

[40] The Enochic story may be said to be in a general relationship with the Prometheus narrative. However, the focus of this research is parent-child relationships whereby an author directly borrowed authority from a previous text. As such, general relationships did not equate to borrowed authority as any borrowed authority had to be specific and identifiable from the earlier text rather than generalized. Moreover, by creating an inversion, the Enochic author also negated borrowed authority by directly challenging the very text from which authority would have been drawn.

Yarimlim sins against Abbael, or [if] he gives away Abbael's secrets to another king…his towns and lands he shall [forfeit].'"[41] However, no divinely held secrets appeared in this text, only hypothetical secrets between grantor and grantee. This occurrence was a loyalty oath rather than a Revelation of Secrets topos type, denying three points of verbal contact as well as holding several meaningful differences. As a result, no parent-child relationship exists between this text and Jewish apocalyptic literature concerning the Revelation of Secrets. This text also completed step 4d. In it, no EAW text was determined to be in a parent-child relationship with Second Temple apocalyptic literature concerning this topos type.[42]

4.2.5. Step 4e: Cross-Text—Possible Tanakh Sources

Turning to the Tanakh, only four passages were located in connection to this topos type. Two were in the Pentateuch (Gen 18:17; Deut 29:29), one in Psalm (25:14), and one in the prophets (Isa 48:6).[43] The first of these passages studied was Gen 18:17.

4.2.5.1. Genesis 18:17

The Revealed Secrets topos type occurred in relation to Abraham: "And then YHWH said, 'Should I hide from Abraham that which I am doing?'" Context placed this quote in the divine visit before God destroyed Sodom. God revealing his secrets created a scenario wherein Abraham responded as an intercessor. However, as noted earlier, Enoch was not an intercessor, nor did he plead for the lives of the Watchers. This meaningful difference in roles also denied a complementary context or word picture. Therefore, the meaningful difference and lack of three points of verbal contact denied a parent-

---

[41] "Land Grant *AT* 456," trans. Richard S. Hess (*COS* 2.137:369).

[42] A spell in *The Book of the Dead* titled "Rebellion, Death, and Apocalypse" also carried within it the idea of negatively revealed secrets. However, the text concerning secrets was short: "Since they have betrayed secrets in all you [Atum] have done," lives will be cut off. Little context existed for the betrayed secrets, except for who betrayed the secrets (the children of Nut—usually understood as Osiris, Set , Isis, and Nephthys), negating its usefulness in this study.

[43] Several other passages touched on revealed secrets but were not authoritative. For instance, in 1 Kgs 18:4, God revealed the hidden prophets to Elijah, but this revelation concerned secrecy as protection, and the revelation of the secret encouraged Elijah, but it carried no authority.

child relationship between these passages concerning the Revelation of Secrets topos type.

4.2.5.2. Deuteronomy 29:29

In Deut 29:29, the author wrote, "The hidden things are the Lord our God's, but the revealed things are for us, and for our sons forever to do all the words of this law." Little else within the text proved useful to interpret this phrase, and Jewish and Christian scholars alike have debated "the hidden things." For instance, Jeffrey Tigay wrote, "Moses's meaning is most likely that expressed in the Targum Jonathan: concealed acts are known to God, and he will punish them, but overt ones are our responsibility to punish."[44] Tigay followed that statement with other interpretations, including Maimonides's argument that the hidden things lay behind the commandments. However, the revealed things were the acts of Israel in submission to the law. Tigay then addressed several modern scholars who have often defaulted to interpreting the hidden things as real events in later history. As such, Israel was to live in the day based on the Torah, rather than focus on the future.[45] Another way to interpret this passage centered on God revealing Israel's future if (when) she descended into rebellion.[46]

These interpretive variations made any definite statement difficult except to say God revealed something that described an earlier hidden knowledge. From context, the revealed knowledge connected with covenant either to forestall Israel's apostasy or to provide postapostasy Israel with hope and a promised deliverance (30:2–5). Yet, the unclear revelation was troublesome. If the author provided no clear message, then there were no grounds to assume an authoritative topos.

At Qumran, however, the community made the passage itself authoritative. In 4Q259, new adherents received secrets in their induction into the community. These received secrets were considered revealed knowledge from God, making נגלות (revealed) the נסתרות (hidden laws).[47] Reading this text in connection to Gen 18:17,[48] God willed his

---

[44] Jeffrey H. Tigay, דברים; *Deuteronomy: The Traditional Hebrew Text with the New JPS Translation and Commentary*, The JPS Torah Commentary (Philadelphia: Jewish Publication Society, 1996), 283.

[45] Ibid,, 283.

[46] Peter C. Craigie, *The Book of Deuteronomy* (Grand Rapids: Eerdmans, 1976), 361.

[47] See n.8 (above) in this chapter.

secrets to be revealed by the Instructor, and in doing so, brought the community into proper cultic obedience. As such, a parent-child relationship may have existed between Deut 29:29 and the Qumran use of the Revealed Secrets topos type.[49] However, a similar relationship did not exist between Deut 29:29 and the authoritative topos type in other Second Temple material.

4.2.5.3. Psalm 25:14

Another possible Revealed Secrets topos type occurred in Psa 25:14: "The secret council of YHWHis for those who fear him; his covenant, for those who know him" (סוֹד יְהוָה לִירֵאָיו וּבְרִיתוֹ לְהוֹדִיעָם).[50] In this verse, the secret council belonged to God as סוֹד was in a construct chain forming a genitive of possession. By synonymous parallel, the secrets and the covenant also belonged to God and were for whoever feared and knew him. As such, the secrets were probably connected to the covenant. However, the lack of explicitness and differing contexts with Enochian material denied any points of verbal contact beyond the use of similar words. Therefore, no parent-child relationship existed.

4.2.5.4. Isaiah 48:6

Another positively revealed secret occurred in Isa 48:6: "I will cause you to hear new things from now on, even hidden things you have not known." This revelation reflected the covenant (48:12) and a prophesied future. Yet, compared to the Second Temple material, the narrative point of view was opposite that of Enoch. Further, no

---

[48] Note, however, no direct quote of this verse from Genesis was found in the Qumran scrolls, but 4Q180 f2–4.ii:5 included text from18:20–21 following the narration of Lot. The subject of this text, however, was the ages of creation; thus, care was necessary not to read too much into the missing authority of Gen 18:17.

[49] Based on the following verbal contacts: same words, context of the law, and the overall picture of revealed and hidden laws. However, the interpretation was solely dependent on Qumran understanding of an unclear verse, which resulted in the reluctance to state firmly the Qumran document sat in parent-child relationship with this text.

[50] Various translators rendered סוֹד as "intimacy," "friend," or "confide" in English bibles. Hebrew lexicons were similarly spread; however, "intimacy," according to the *DCH* authors, also connoted confidence. While not directly equal to "secret" as found in the *HALOT*, intimate conversation was one often not shared with the outside world, hence, the reason for the translated "secret" here. See David Clines, ed. "סוֹד," *DCH* 6:125–27; Ludwig Koehler, Walter Baumgartner, and M. E. J. Anderson, ed. "סוֹד," *HALOT* 1:745.

specifics were provided except for the fact that hidden things would be known "from now on." Therefore, the passage lacked two of the three points of verbal contact needed to establish a parent-child relationship with Jewish apocalyptic material concerning this topos type.[51]

4.2.6. Step 4f: Evaluation

The Mesopotamian texts lacked the specifics to be in a parent-child relationship with Jewish apocalyptic material, and the Egyptian and Hellenistic sources showed inversions. To this last point, Portier-Young and Roark argued the Watchers narrative was situated against Prometheus, pitting the Israelite god against a capricious Zeus. Likewise, a flood from which God delivered Noah inverts the story of Djoser enduring a drought in the "Seven Lean Years." Within this story, the bull in 1 Enoch changed into a man—a created being; the Egyptian bull was part creator.

Why would Second Temple apocalyptic authors have presented these inversions? The Watcher narratives containing 1 En. 9:6 "was completed by the middle of the third century BCE," according to Nickelsburg, in late pre-Maccabean times, according to E. Issac, or in the early second century BCE according to Crawford.[52] All three of these dates, and specifically, the latter two, placed the composition of this passage long after Hellenistic wars began raging across the region. These dates were conspicuous when placed alongside Portier-Young's argument concerning the Watcher narratives: "1 Enoch 6–11 implicitly assigns the negative value of each pair [of polarities such as civilized and uncivilized or moderate and excessive] to the 'Greeks' or, more accurately, the warring rulers, generals, and the armies of the Hellenistic empires."[53] Thus, the wars and the "unceasing violence and devastating appetite of the Hellenistic rulers and their armies suggest that…they are the mythic 'giants'" of the Watcher texts.[54]

This inversion between Jewish and Hellenistic culture extended to the Hellenistic gods and YHWH in the Dream Visions. These visions holding the Revelation of Secrets topos type in 89:2 were thought to have been

---

[51] This passage also related to hidden knowledge in Qumran, but the generalities in the passage allowed the community to change it as they saw fit.

[52] Nickelsburg, *1 Enoch* 1, 8; cf. Isaac, "1 (Ethiopic Apocalypse of) Enoch: A New Translation and Introduction," in Charlesworth, *OTP* 1:7; Sidnie W. Crawford, *Rewriting Scripture in Second Temple Times* (Grand Rapids: Eerdmans, 2008), 66.

[53] Portier-Young, *Apocalypse against Empire*, 20.

[54] Ibid.

written during the Maccabean revolt or soon thereafter.[55] In this period of Second Temple Judaism, both Ptolemaic and Seleucid Hellenism challenged Jewish identity, and in some cases, life. As referenced in the first chapter, Second Temple Jews endured war, had their customs and beliefs outlawed, and suffered abomination in their temple by Hellenistic hands, including the threat to make it a temple to Dionysus (2 Macc. 14:33). These threats and hardships gave birth to the polemic discourse presented by inversion in 1 En. 89:2, which served as narrative proof for the superiority of YHWH against Hellenistic gods.[56]

In terms of the Hebraic sources of the Revelation of Secrets topos type, P.Enoch wrote of deliverance for human recipients of revealed secrets who used them wisely and destruction for humans who employed them unwisely. The author also warned destruction comes for the wrong recipients of revealed secrets. The Tanakh material held no topos type occurrences similar enough to be in a parent-child relationship. However, a closer association between the Tanakh and Second Temple material may have occurred at Qumran.

The text of Deut 29:29 underwent authoritative transfer in Q259 wherein the Instructor borrowed authority to instruct the community on the hidden law. The question, then, was whether this authority connected to one of the movements of Ancient Israel. Deuteronomy 29:29 was part of Torah, which has often been tied to the priestly movement through source theory; however, using source theory failed

[55] Nickelsburg, *1 Enoch* 1, 8; see also Daniel Assefa, "Dreams, Book of," *EDEJ* 552; Isaac, "1 Enoch" in Charlesworth, *OTP* 1:7. Several scholars placed the first two visions earlier than the vision containing the authoritative topos in 89:2.

[56] Polemical discourse and inversion have also been seen in the contemporary writing of the book of Judith, which associated Holofernes with the Greek general Nicanor through a narrated beheading. In this text, several inversions existed. Perhaps, the strongest inversion concerned Judith penetrating the camp to kill Holofernes, which was written against the background of Judith inciting Holofernes's desire to penetrate her (and thus, by extension of Judith's name being a representation of the land, the kingdom of Judea). These acts occurred in sight of Scythopolis (Decapolis). Scythopolis was a city reportedly founded by Dionysus who was the Hellenistic god associated with YHWH. Scythopolis was also the home of Nysa, Dionysus's nurse who was both born and buried in the city. The city also housed temples to Dionysus and Zeus. Judith, then, was a story of inversion in which the death of Judah's Greek enemy, Nicanor, took place in view of a city that represented Dionysus. Thus, the inversion taught the superiority of YHWH over Dionysus. See Harold W. Attridge, "Greek Religions" *EDEJ* 700; Walter A. Elwell and Philip W. Comfort, "Scythopolis," *Tyndale Bible Dictionary* 167.

on two levels. First, the attribution of *D* was unclear: Was *D* a monarchic movement text intended to drive Josiah's reforms, a priestly source designed to establish laws for priests and people, or a prophetic source written by Jeremiah? Maybe the covenant-code editors influenced this verse? Second, using modern source theory steered the scholar into ignoring Second Temple understandings of the text, or worse, into reading modern scholarship into the thoughts of Second Temple authors. These issues rendered source theory unusable in this study.

From the perspective of the Second Temple author, Deut. 29:29 completed a passage of covenant relationship, promises, and warning concerning Israel's acts. Specifically, for Qumran, the community was formed after the chronological close of the passage—God's anger had already burned against Israel, uprooting them from their land and sending them into captivity (Deut 29:27–28; assuming the Babylonian captivity was the focus of this text). The adherents at Qumran subsequently thought of themselves as part of the Yaḥad, a renewed covenant community who received the hidden law from God.[57] The community may have consisted of marginalized Sadducean priests, but the authority on which they drew was not priestly.[58] Instead, the community held revealed secrets of God through righteousness based on a covenant relationship.

4.3. Literary Authority by Idea: Righteousness

The Righteousness topos type was found throughout the EAW. Some of the earliest references came from the Akkadian culture where it was often paired with "justice" (*kittum u mīšarum*) as an "ethical ideal." However, the same idea existed in Hebraic thought as the base

[57] Questions concerning Yaḥad as a technical name versus a broader designation existed in scholarship, as did questions about the origin of the name. However, "the community," whether it was Qumran only, Qumran as some part of the Essenes, or Qumran as one of several groups making up "the community" still connoted purity, and they remained separated from the Jerusalem priesthood to stay pure. For an in-depth discussion of the Yaḥad, see Alison Schofield, *From Qumran to the Yaḥad: A New Paradigm of Textual Development for "the Community Rule,"* STDJ 77 (Leiden: Brill 2009) 21–50.

[58] For more on the Sadduceen priests at Qumran, see Jodi Magness, "Qumran," *EDEJ*, 1126–31.

on which Torah worked.[59] For Hebraic authors, God was righteous, and he expected the same of Israel within the covenant relationship (Hos 10:12).[60] Therefore, righteousness was an authority through which God's covenant relationship with Israel continued.

4.3.1. Step 4a: Text—Definition and Use of Authority

The Righteousness topos type was defined as an authoritative topos by which a person was authorized to act or speak because of their ethical or cultic righteousness. Second Temple authors employed the Righteousness topos type through two subtypes: righteousness as authority to establish or nuance cultic reality, and righteousness as authority to bless God. In both subtypes, the P.author used this authority by affirming (or reaffirming) the righteousness of an ancient figure. The P.author then borrowed authority from that figure by making the figure a mouthpiece for the P.author. In this way, the P.author legitimized the message being delivered to the audience—it now came from a character in covenant with God.

4.3.2. Step 4b: Text and Context—Use in Apocalyptic Literature

Righteousness as authority to establish or nuance cultic reality presented the strongest possibility of a parent-child relationship with texts outside Hebraic culture. Therefore, it was examined first in the following subsection. The second subtype, righteousness as authority to bless God, showed stronger possible parent-child relationships with the Tanakh (and a possible connection to the *Yasnas*).[61]

---

[59] Richard G. Smith, *The Fate of Justice and Righteousness During David's Reign: Rereading the Court History and Its Ethics According to 2 Samuel 8:15–20:26*, LHBOTS 508 (New York: T&T Clark, 2009), 44.

[60] Willem VanGemeren, "Covenant," *BEB* 2:1860–61.

[61] An oblique reference to righteousness occurred in Apoc. Zeph. 4:8: "The angel said, 'Do not fear, I will not permit them to come to you because you are pure before the Lord. I will not permit them to come to you because the Lord Almighty sent me to you because you are pure before Him." The problem, however, was that Zephaniah's purity was not authoritative, but causative as the angel declared: "The Lord Almighty sent me." Thus, the P.author presented the angel's arrival through the Divine Authority topos type rather than the Righteousness topos type.

4.3.2.1. Righteousness as Authority to Establish or Nuance Cultic Reality

Two passages held the highest scores in steps 3a–c for this subtype. In Jub. 5:19, the Jubilean author began nuancing cultic reality by expanding Gen 6 concerning Noah's righteousness:

> But to any who corrupted their way and their counsel before the Flood, he did not show partiality, except Noah alone, for he showed partiality to him for the sake of his sons whom he saved from the waters of the Flood (and) for his sake because his heart was righteous in all of his ways just as it was commanded concerning him. And he did not transgress anything which was ordained for him.

Three verses later, the Jubilean author recapped the Gen 6:22 gloss: "And Noah made an ark in all respects just as he commanded him" (Jub. 5:22). With Noah's righteousness established, the author then introduced cultic nuances.

The first nuance concerned sacrifice. In Jub. 6:2, Noah "made atonement for the land" by sacrificing a goat before proceeding to several other named sacrifices.[62] These sacrifices in Jubilees specified a general list in Gen 8:20. Following these specifications, God covenanted with Noah. Thus, for the later readers of the text, the Jubilean flood story became authoritative through Noah's righteousness (Jub. 6:10).[63]

The author again borrowed authority to nuance cultic reality in the following verse:

---

[62] In Gen 8:20, Noah sacrificed from "all the clean birds." The Jubilean author, however, specified in Jub. 6:3 a turtledove and young dove, which, as part of the Columbidae family and therefore akin to pigeons, were the only family of birds considered clean, and thus, available for sacrifices in Levitical law (Lev 1:14). In Genesis, Noah also made offerings of "every kind of clean animal" as a burnt offering, but the Jubilean author again extended specificity to "the fat of the goat, a calf, a whole goat, a lamb, kids, and salt," all but the last found again in the Levitical laws. J. Fossum "Dove," in van der Toorn, *DDD* 263; D. Jeffrey Mooney, "Leviticus, Book Of," *The Lexham Bible Dictionary*, n.p.

[63] According to the Jubilean author, the Mosaic covenantwas a covenant renewal of the Noahic covenant, making Noah's cultic acts an example for all of Israel. This concept was explored in the subsection on the Covenant topos type in chapter 3.

> This testimony is written concerning you so that you might keep it always lest you ever eat any blood of the beasts or birds or cattle throughout all of the days of the earth. And the man who eats the blood of the beasts or cattle or birds throughout all of the days of the earth shall be uprooted, he and his seed from the earth. (Jub. 6:11)

Following the mandate for blood abstention, the Jubilean author again nuanced cultic reality for feasts based on Noah ordaining the times of the year (recorded in the Tablets of Heaven, Jub. 6:17–24), then moved to calendaring (6:30–38) and ethical living through abstaining from fornication, blood pollution, and injustice (7:20–39). Then, the Jubilean author narrated Noah's death in Jub. 10:15–17, but only after recounting his perfection. Thus, the author created an inclusio that began in Jub. 5:19 through the Righteousness topos type:

> On account of his righteousness in which he was perfected, his life on earth was more excellent than (any of) the sons of men except Enoch, for the work of Enoch had been created as a witness to the generations of the world so that he might report every deed of each generation in the day of judgment.

This inclusio highlighted Noah as an exemplar for faithful Second Temple Jews. To be righteous and covenant-worthy, one must live as Noah. This text also served two warnings. First, Enoch, who was more righteous than even Noah, would witness the activities of the generations and then recount them during the day of judgment. This warning informed the readers their acts would not go unnoticed.

The second warning informed the readers of humanity's openness to demonic control (Jub. 10:1–14). Accordingly, Noah's righteous lineage was dependent on apotropaic prayers and God's subsequent reprieve. This tension between Noahic righteousness and obligatory prayer produced an authorial assertion backed by the Righteousness topos type: do not rely on personal righteousness alone but seek God in prayer for deliverance from demonic control.

Another use of the Righteousness topos type in Jubilees focused on the cultic reality of God being just and righteous in his decisions:[64]

> And he is holy and faithful, and he is more righteous than all others, and there is no accepting of persons with him or accepting of gifts because he is a righteous God and he is the one who executes judgment with all who transgress his commandments and despise his covenant (Jub. 21:4)

The thrust of this speech occurred in the following verse: "And you, my son, keep his commandments and ordinances and judgments, and do not follow pollutions or graven images or molten images." These commands continued throughout the chapter and read as priestly instructions on proper sacrifices,[65] the impetus of which lay in recognizing God as the unswayable and righteous judge. He is involved in this world and executes his covenant responsibility. Moreover, according to the author, his righteousness demanded proper cultic and devotional responses. Together, the Righteousness topos type in these two passages presented God as a righteous, unswayable judge who responded not only to prayers but also to covenant violations.

The Testament of Levi also held a Righteousness topos type concerning worldwide judgment:

> Listen, therefore, concerning the heavens which have been shown to you. The lowest is dark for this reason: It sees all the injustices of humankind and contains fire, snow, and ice, ready for the day determined by God's righteous judgment. In it are all the spirits of those dispatched to achieve the punishment of mankind. In the second are the armies arrayed for the day of judgment to work vengeance on the spirits of error and of Beliar. Above them are the Holy Ones. In the uppermost

[64] Miryam T. Brand, *Evil Within and Without: The Source of Sin and Its Nature as Portrayed in Second Temple Literature*, JAJSup 9 (Göttingen: Vandenhoeck und Ruprecht, 2013), 179.

[65] James C. VanderKam, *The Book of Jubilees* (Sheffield: Sheffield Academic, 2001), 56.

> heaven of all dwells the Great Glory in the Holy of Holies superior to all holiness. (3:1–4)[66]

This passage concerned separation between God and punishment. The lowest heavens saw the injustices and carried the punishing fire, snow, and ice. The subsequent line of text expressed the place of the Holy Ones above the clouds. In the uppermost heaven, the Great Glory resided in the Holy of Holies.

The middle layers of heaven formed an "in-between world organized in a hierarchical fashion between [God and]...this world full of injustices."[67] God, therefore, performed righteous judgment from the Holy of Holies;[68] a reader was to trust God's righteous judgments because they came from God who was "superior to all holiness" (3:4). This passage also added a universal dynamic; God was the judge of the entire world.

4.3.2.2. Righteousness as Authority to Bless God

The righteousness as authority to bless God subtype occurred once, attributed to Enoch: "Then I raised up my hands in righteousness and blessed the Holy and Great One" (1 En. 84:1). Similarities between this passage, the Zoroastrian canon, and other outside sources made

---

[66] The quoted passage read differently in various manuscripts. Robert Charles noted Armenian Manuscripts A, B, H, and K lacked the latter half of the second verse, and two manuscripts from Mt. Sinai, along with a Vatican library codex (731) indicated corruption. Although Charles translated the end of the verse as "retributions for the vengeance on men"; three other divisions of manuscripts, including the Slavonic recension and Vatican library manuscript 1238, all read "retributions for vengeance on the lawless" (Charles, *Pseudepigrapha*, 306). See the introduction to the Twelve Patriarchs in *OTP* 1 for H. C. Kee's reasoning in following Charles (with variations) as quoted in the above text. Note also that Kee's interpretation benefits from additional scholarship and strong manuscript evidence—Kee, "Testaments of the Twelve Patriarchs: A New Translation and Introduction," in Charlesworth, *OTP* 1:775–77.

[67] Sacchi, *History of the Second Temple Period*, 319. Sacchi continued the idea concerning this world: It "does not let its secrets be understood except when God unveils their authentic reality to his chosen ones." If Sacchi was correct in attributing these thoughts to this verse, then a Revelation of Secrets topos type undergirded the Righteousness topos type.

[68] The attribution of holiness to God as associated with the Holy of Holies separated these texts from any Qumran understanding of God. There, God was called "divine" (4Q400–7). "Holy" described his angels (but see 1QM 12:7, 19:1). Ibid., 319 n.1.

examining it necessary. Zoroastrianism enamored early scholars, and similar Zoroastrian texts showed a proclivity toward authority. An inquiry, therefore, was needed for possible clarification of the Second Temple Author's use of EAW authoritative topos.

4.3.2.3. Righteousness at Qumran

Righteousness was essential for the Qumran community's understanding of itself and therefore, was available as an authoritative topos in many contexts.[69] One such context, according to the early Zadokite work *Admonition* was the Teacher of Righteousness, which designated the person whom God had raised and into whom he had instilled his interpretation (as seen in the *Pesharim*). This teacher instructed "from the mouth of God" those initiates who sought God "with a perfect heart" (CD–A i:12).[70] Through him came the future hope. To believe the teacher of righteousness and to follow his teachings assured righteousness and thus preparation for the eschaton; to reject the teacher was to dismiss hope of eschatological salvation.

Righteousness also occurred as a concept in 4Q181 f1.ii:3–4.[71] The author used antithetical parallelism to draw comparisons between the righteous (sons of heaven) and the wicked.[72] In 4Q521 f2.ii:5, an author wrote, "For the Lord will consider the godly ones and the righteous, by name he calls them." Righteousness, paired with "godly

[69] Any work on purity laws would have replicated the work of Hannah Harrington. Thus, her work stood in for the comparisons presented here—see Harrington, *The Purity Texts: Companion to the Dead Sea Scrolls* (New York: T&T Clark, 2004), 7–42, 112–127. See also, Werrett, *Ritual Purity*, 288–305.

[70] F. F. Bruce, *The Teacher of Righteousness in the Qumran Texts*, The Tyndale Lecture in Biblical Archaeology (London: Tyndale Press, 1957), 8–11.

[71] Its use here occurred in what Dimant called "a manner typical of the sectarian style." Devorah Dimant, *History, Ideology and Bible Interpretation in the Dead Sea Scrolls: Collected Studies*, FAT 90 (Tübingen: Mohr Siebeck, 2014), 418.

[72] Ibid., 421. Dimant also investigated the relationship between 4Q181 and 4Q180, permitting that a common source: 4Q181 represented a "slightly abbreviated and reworked citation." The relationship was important to this study because fragment 2, lines 7–10 contain references to the Watchers and their evil, including a "love for injustice" and inheritance of evil (yet the end of line 8 and the start of 9 were destroyed. The love for injustice and inheritance of evil could be attributed to another noun, but context indicated otherwise). This reference was the beginning of an interpretation of the Watchers that, while lost to present readers, can be surmised to depend upon the righteous/wicked binary. Also, note the "mysteries" in line 5 depended on the recipient's righteousness.

ones," became the authority by which the writer credited God's concern for the reader who sought him. Viewed across the texts in Qumran, the Righteousness topos type existed as part of a binary system authorizing or anathematizing beliefs and acts within the community. Whoever wore the label "righteous" was ready for the eschaton and an encounter with God.

The Righteousness topos type was used in several distinct ways. For non-Qumran authors, the topos type enabled them to cast their teachings on the lips of others or use the figures as exemplars. Doing so assured weight of the teaching by the character's covenant status with God or by their privileged position of blessing God. In Qumran, the author of the text used this topos type to set a particular path of belief leveraging hope for the eschaton. This study, however, was not the first to focus on the exemplar role of these figures.

4.3.3. Step 4c: Text and Context—Germane Scholarship

Scholars have identified several Antediluvian exemplars based on righteousness, as examined in the previous section, but little discussion has emerged on how it worked as an authoritative topos. For instance, Alex Jassen wrote in *The Oxford Handbook of Apocalyptic Literature*, the characters labeled "righteous" in Second Temple apocalypses "become exemplary models for the elect to ensure their own status as righteous and to secure their own salvation."[73] Following that same thought, Dimant stated the Jubilean author set Noah as lawgiver based on his righteousness. However, he also served as an exemplar for walking the righteous path in contrast with the Watchers who walked the wicked path.[74] Steven Fraade argued Enoch and others were not only exemplars but also anticipatory to modern righteous heroes for the Second Temple authors.[75] Finally, Hindy Najman wrote these "well-known biblical figures function as exemplars" based on their renown; they served as "part of a distinguished, holy, and inspired line

---

[73] Alex Jassen, "Scriptural Interpretation in Early Jewish Apocalypses," in Collins, *OHAL*, 81.

[74] Devorah Dimant, "Noah in Early Jewish Literature," in *BFOB*, ed. Michael E. Stone and Theodore A. Bergren (Harrisburg: Trinity Press, 1998), 130–31.

[75] Steven Fraade, "Enosh and His Generation Revisited," in Stone, *BFOB*, 61. His work focused on Ben Sira's writing. Dimant made a similar argument in her article—see n.74 (above).

receiving and transmitting the traditions."[76] These scholars' works underscored the importance of the label "righteous" in Second Temple apocalyptic literature. Each character labeled so was an example for emulation, and their lives, a guide for Second Temple readers.

4.3.4. Step 4d: Cross-Text—Possible EAW Sources

From the preliminary study, two EAW sources with the establishing or nuancing cultic reality subtype showed the strongest possibility for a parent-child relationship. The first source was from Sumer-Babylonian, and the second, Egypt. Likewise, two *yasnas* holding the subtype, righteousness as an authority to bless God, had a possibility of being in a parent-child relationship with Jewish apocalyptic material.[77]

4.3.4.1. Establishing or Nuancing Cultic Reality

Steps 3a–c identified the Babylonian hymn "Prayer of Lamentation to Ishtar" as a strong possible source for establishing or nuancing cultic reality. A second possibility was the Egyptian text "Joy at the Accession of Merneptah." This subtype also appeared in several other texts but scored too low for inclusion in this study.

4.3.4.1.1. "Prayer of Lamentation to Ishtar"

The "Prayer of Lamentation to Ishtar traced back to the Esagila temple in Babylon. The temple was dedicated to Ishtar, who was a conjoint goddess of the Semitic Eshtar and Sumerian Inanna:

> For you are great and you are exalted. All the black-headed (people) and the masses of mankind pay homage to your might. The judgment of the people in truth and righteousness you

---

[76] Hindy Najman, "Reconsidering Jubilees: Prophecy and Exemplarity," in *Enoch and the Mosaic Torah: The Evidence of Jubilees*, ed. Gabriele Boccaccini and Giovanni Ibba (Grand Rapids: Eerdmans, 2009), 241–42.

[77] The yasnas are liturgical texts in the Avesta, which is the collection of sacred Zoroastrian writings.

indeed do decide. You regard the oppressed and mistreated; daily you cause them to prosper. (24–26)[78]

Various cultures have associated Ishtar with sexual love, military conflict, life, death, randomness, and capriciousness. Authors have even assigned her simultaneous but conflicting traits.[79] These last two traits, randomness and capriciousness, also resonated with Second Temple authors as questions had emerged in their communities asking if the Hebraic god was capricious or malevolent.[80]

A second point of verbal contact existed in the divine reaction against injustices. Ishtar caused the "oppressed and mistreated" to prosper, and the Hebraic god punished the evils of his creation (T. Levi 3:1–4, Jub. 5–11; 21:4). Finally, authors from these cultures focused on both judgment and the underlying recognition of a deity's personality (including how that personality drove divine judgment). As such, three points of verbal contact were identified for further study. The problem, however, was the differences.

First, the judgment in the "Prayer of Lamentation" was akin to a Hebraic psalm of praise and adoration or a psalm of deliverance. The author focused only on the concept of judgment. Conversely, the Jubilean author referred to judgment as a warning for covenant violation, and the T. Levi author narrated a vision justifying the coming fire, snow, and ice as judgment for the injustices of humanity within a divinely ordained journey.

Second, the righteousness of Ishtar's judgments read as blandishments in prayer set within an encomium intended to sway divine response.[81] In contrast, the Jubilean and T. Levi authors were

[78] Muhammad Dandamaev, "Xerxes and the Esagila Temple in Babylon," *Bulletin of the Asia Institute* 7 (1993): 41; "Sumero-Akkadian Hymns and Prayers," trans. Ferris Stephens (*ANET*, 384).

[79] Tzvi Abusch, "Ishtar," *DDD* 452–54.

[80] Carol A. Newsom, "Theodicy," *EDEJ* 1304. According Charlesworth, the theodicy question for Second Temple Jews may "be synthesized as follows: 'Where is the God who elected us as a covenant people, and why does this God seemingly not care about what has been happening to us?'" (see James H. Charlesworth, "Theodicy in Early Jewish Writings," in *Theodicy in the World of the Bible*, ed. Antti Laato and Johannes C. de Moor [Leiden: Brill, 2003], 470–73). Answers to this question were at the heart of many apocalyptic writings in Second Temple Judaism.

[81] Such texts often were written to invoke action from a god, either by petition or, sometimes, through magic. An example of the latter was the "Prayer of the

narrating coming judgment. These dissimilarities created a meaningful difference in the teleological purposes of the texts. The "Prayer of Lamentation to Ishtar" was an attempt to curry the favor of a deity; the Jewish apocalyptic texts were recitals or warnings of coming judgment.

A third difference derived from these teleological purposes. Ishtar was thought to be swayable by such prayers, but the Hebraic god was presented as an unswayable and righteous judge, negating a point of verbal contact concerning personality. As such, the lack of three points of verbal contact and the meaningful difference denied a parent-child relationship.

4.3.4.1.2. "Joy at the Accession of Merneptah"

This passage concerned Merneptah's enthronement. It originated as a bureaucratic letter and only later was bundled with other writings for didactic reasons:

> Merneptah Hotep-hir-Ma'at—life, prosperity, health! All you righteous, come that you may see! Right has banished wrong. Evildoers have fallen (upon) their faces. All the rapacious are ignored.[82]

In context, the theophoric name, Merneptah Hotep-hir-Ma'at (Beloved by Ptah, Peace through Ma'at) ended a list of names ascribed to the king. In the following line, the author called the righteous to see "right has banished wrong." Two parallel results then referred to the banishment: "Evildoers have fallen on their face," and "the rapacious are ignored."[83] These parallels completed the opening phrase and served as a thematic inclusio highlighting the theophoric name. By this name, the author

---

Raising of the Hand to Ishtar," which morphed from prayer to magical incantation. In no way should the "Prayer of Lamentation" be considered a magical incantation, but the impetus of moving a god to action through prayer and use of language was strong in many cultic settings, Babylonian religions included (as opposed to earnestly beseeching a deity). See Robert W. Rogers, *The Religion of Babylonia and Assyria, Especially in Its Relations to Israel: Five Lectures Delivered at Harvard University* (New York: Eaton and Mains, 1908), 167–69.

[82] "Egyptian Hymns and Prayers," trans. John A. Wilson (*ANET*, 378).

[83] Ibid., 378. Hebraic reading strategies held heavy emphasis on parallelism, making it difficult to accept a Second Temple writer familiar with this text would miss the parallels.

suggested to the readers they needed a generalized understanding of *ma'at* to understand his presentation of peace.

Ma'at originated as the foundational order of creation. Kept by Pharaoh, *ma'at* held "ethical as well as metaphysical implications …rendered as truth, righteousness, or justice," from which scholars have argued a link with צדק.[84] *Ma'at* also tied into personal eschatological judgment, based on a person's "*ma'at*ian or *isfetic* life."[85] Contextualized to the Accession text, Pharoah taking the throne reinstated order against chaos (the opposite of *ma'at*), reestablished justice, and produced a rightness marginalizing the evildoer and the rapacious.

By comparison, the Jubilean and Testament of Levi texts concerned neither enthronement nor creating order from chaos through divine presence. Instead, the authors focused on correcting errant beliefs affecting theodicy and theology. Furthermore, the Accession text was a call to the righteous reader to affirm the king's peace and so affirm his occupancy of the throne (and thereby nuancing reality by accepting Merneptah as king), but the Second Temple apocalyptic material, however, contained no direct call to action. Instead, the P.authors nuanced cultic reality by picturing a righteous god and future judgment. Therefore, the synonyms for "righteousness" were the only point of verbal contact between these texts. Moreover, there were several meaningful differences. Thus, no parent-child relationship existed between the "Joy at the Accession of Merneptah" and this topos type in the Second Temple material.

4.3.4.2. Righteousness as Authority to Bless God

Five possible sources were located for righteousness as an authority to bless God, all in the Avesta. Four were hymns (*yasnas*), and one was a prayer of blessing. The two strongest candidates identified in steps 3a–b for parent-child relationships were *Yas.* 13:6 and *Yas.* 52:4.

---

[84] Klass A. D. Smelik, "*Ma'at*," *DDD* 534.

[85] Maulana Karenga, *Maat, the Moral Ideal in Ancient Egypt: A Study in Classical African Ethics*, African Studies (New York: Routledge, 2003), 85. For a description of scholarly development concerning this understanding, see Anna Mancini, *Maat, La Philosophie de la Justice de l'Ancienne Egypte*, 2nd ed. (Paris: Buenos Books International, 2007), 9–32.

4.3.4.2.1. Yasna 13:6

This *yasna* began with an invocation of Ahura Mazda to hear, followed by calls to the guardian beings, earth (earthen elements), and humans to worship, pray, and confess. These calls led to the following passage:

> By the kinship of the good kindred, by that of Righteousness the Good (Your righteous servant's nature) would we approach You, and by that of the good thrift-law, and of Piety the good.

In this text, the double use of "righteousness" (or "righteous") signified the importance and authority from which the performers of this hymn gained Ahura Mazda's audience. By comparison, Enoch's righteousness granted the prerogative to bless God (1 En. 84:1):

> I spoke with breath of my mouth and tongue of flesh which God has made for the children of the flesh, the people, so that they should speak with it; he gave them the breath and the mouth so that they should speak with it.

The authority to bless God (1 En. 84:1) or to intercede on humanity's behalf (1 En. 84:4–6) derived from existing as his creation. Therefore, the translated word, "praise" was the only verbal contact. Thus, no parent-child relationship existed between this text and the topos type in the Second Temple apocalyptic material. Moreover, any topos based on Righteousness was secondary to, and dependent upon, a greater authority—creation itself, which was similar to the topos type used in *Yas*. 52:4.

4.3.4.2.2. Yasna 52:4

In *Yas. 52:4* the Righteousness topos type came after a long prayer for sanctity and in relation to praise:

> For the sacrifice, homage, propitiation, and the praise of the Bountiful Immortals, for the bringing prosperity to this abode.... (And I pray for this) as I praise through Righteousness....

To understand the relationship between righteousness and praise, however, several passages had to be explored. In *Yas*. 11:18, righteousness received praise as an entity rather than as an attribute of mortals (or immortals):

> Here I give to you, O ye Bountiful Immortals! Sacrifice and homage with the mind, with words, deeds, and my entire person; yea, (I offer) to you the flesh of my very body (as your own). And I praise Righteousness. A blessing is Righteousness (called) the Best.

However, in *Yas*. 19:19, praise was integral to a deed well done:

> Question: What is the deed well done?
> Answer: It is that done with praises, and by the creatures who regard Righteousness as before all other things.

Completing a deed with praise alone did not qualify as deed well done, but only when righteousness was regarded before all else. Righteousness, then, had to accompany praise, opposite to *Yas*. 11:18. This relationship continued in *Afrinagan-i Gahambar* 1:

> I confess myself…for the worship, homage, propitiation, and praise of that lofty lord who is the 'Ritual Righteousness' [itself] (*A-i Gah*. 1).

Here, praise was for the lofty lord and connected with 'ritual righteousness,'[86] which the author defined in a following appositional clause:

> Yea, for the worship, propitiation, and the praise of the lords of days, months years, and seasons—for those lords of the ritual order who are of all the greatest, who are the regulators of the ritual at the time of Havani.

The *Yasna* writers, therefore, connected 'ritual righteousness' with ritualized order (the lords of the days and years, who were praiseworthy). Understanding 'ritual righteousness' in this way provided a trajectory for understanding righteousness in *Yas*. 52:4.

---

[86] Single quotes were used around 'Ritual Righteousness' as a disambiguation from the topos type, Righteousness.

'Ritual righteousness' received praise (*A-i Gah.* 1), and with praise, created the foundation for good works (*Yas.* 19:19), but righteousness was also a blessing deserving praise (*Yas.* 11:18). This dynamic resulted in a symbiotic relationship sharing righteousness in *Yas.* 52:4. In 1 En. 84:4, God's creative act and righteousness also coexisted as authorities, which created three points of verbal contact between these texts: (1) the creative act, (2) righteousness, and (3) their relationship.

The problem, however, was the role of these verbal contacts. In the *yasna*, the relationship was symbiotic and did not equal authority. In 1 Enoch, both the creative act and righteousness were used as authoritative topos types. Moreover, the Righteousness topos type and themes of interdependence were not unique to Zoroastrian literature. Therefore, the lack of authority caused meaningful differences in the text and denied a parent-child relationship with the texts in Second Temple apocalyptic literature concerning this topos type.

4.3.5. Step 4e: Cross-Text—Possible Tanakh Sources

A keyword search for the concept of righteousness (using the root צדק) produced 318 hits in the Tanakh; by sheer numbers, this authority had probable roots in the Hebraic canon, but what of the specifics? Four characters appeared prominently in the Second Temple apocalyptic narratives: Enoch, Noah, Levi, and Moses. The first two, however, "walked with God," and only Noah has been called righteous. The Righteousness topos type was not associated with Levi or Moses. The first two characters were examined next, followed by a general discussion of God and righteousness in the Pentateuch.

4.3.5.1. Enoch

The Tanakh held little information about Enoch—primarily, his lineage, lifespan, and a short account of his relationship with God. Nowhere in the Tanakh was he said to have been righteous. So, how did the concept develop in the Second Temple period? The textual construct of 5:22 appeared again concerning Noah in Gen. 6:9 (table 4, below). There, Noah also walked with God. These two passages contained the only occurrence of this phrase in the Tanakh, indicating what applied to Noah also applied to Enoch.

Table 4. Enoch-Noah clause comparison

Verse	*Translation*	*Hebrew*
Gen. 5:22	and walked Enoch with God	וַיִּתְהַלֵּךְ חֲנוֹךְ אֶת־הָאֱלֹהִים
Gen. 6:9	with God walked Noah	אֶת־הָאֱלֹהִים הִתְהַלֶּךְ־נֹחַ

4.3.5.2. Noah

The passage concerning Noah began with a parenthetic *waw* contrasting him and his generation, "But Noah found favor in the eyes of YHWH" (Gen 6:8). A few verses later, the author introduced the Noahic narrative and formulaic *toledot* in 9:1a with two occurrences of the Righteousness topos type. The first was "Noah was a man of righteousness," and the second, "He was blameless among his generation"; however, were these topoi authoritative? In 7:1, his deliverance was contingent on, not demanded from, his righteousness: "Go! You and your house, into the ark because you are righteous before me among this generation." Here, "because" (כִּי) introduced the clausal cause by which Noah's salvation became a reality: he acted righteously among his generation.[87] Righteousness caused deliverance, but his righteousness did not authoritatively require deliverance.

---

[87] Some controversy existed among scholars concerning the specific manner of this conjunction. Paul Kissling agreed with the causal "because" associated with righteousness, writing, "Because of that righteousness, he is chosen to be the new Adam" (Paul J. Kissling, *Genesis*, College Press NIV Commentary [Joplin: College Press, 2004], 292). William Reyburn and Euan Fry also agreed, but in the *UBS Handbook: Genesis*, they left out causality in their suggested translation: "You only are a straight man among all the people of the world" (see William David Reyburn and Euan McG. Fry, *A Handbook on Genesis* [New York: United Bible Societies, 1998], 166–67).

Victor Hamilton, however, followed W. M. Clark in reading this passage prospectively: "The explanation for Noah's righteousness is not merit, but rather the purpose of YHWH. God has chosen Noah…through whom humanity might be preserved" (Victor P. Hamilton, *The Book of Genesis, Chapters 1–17*, NICOT, ed. R. K. Harrison and Robert L. Hubbard, Jr. [Grand Rapids: Eerdmans, 1990], 286–87). Gordan Wenham's response to W. M. Clark was just as applicable to Hamilton, the gist of which was the strong repetitions with 6:9, 11, and 12—see Gordon J. Wenham, *Genesis 1–15*, WBC 1 (Dallas: Word, 1998), 176. Nevertheless, Hamilton's understanding, if correct, further reduced the importance of Noah's righteousness in the ongoing work of God in Genesis. The result of the reduction was

4.3.5.3. Righteousness in the Pentateuch

Righteousness was a standard apart from God in the Pentateuch. The author of Gen. 18:25 wrote, "Shall not the judge of all the earth do right?" thereby repudiating might-makes-right authority and rejecting actuated righteousness.[88] By using יַעֲשֶׂה מִשְׁפָּט (do [Qal perfect third masculine singular] right), the author suggested righteousness was a standard outside God's personhood (and his law). Michael Walzer wrote on this concept that "Moses's boast in Deuteronomy about the value of Israelite law carries the same implication as Abraham's rebuke: though the law is divinely delivered…it does not determine, but only realizes what is right." As such, the law of God does not determine right and wrong. Instead, it only identifies what is already right and wrong based on the external standard of righteousness.[89]

Therefore Enoch, Noah, and the general understanding of righteousness in the Pentateuch formed a background for righteousness in Second Temple apocalyptic literature. The two characters and their assessments in Genesis enabled P.authors to use the figures in Second Temple material, but righteousness as the authority to establish or nuance cultic reality was absent from these texts, as was righteousness as an authority to bless God. Moreover, the relationship between Enoch and righteousness was tentative through a link to Noah, and little was made of righteousness in the Genesis texts except to differentiate Noah from his peers. These observations show a meaningful difference between the passages in Genesis and the Jewish apocalyptic material, negating a parent-child relationship even though three points of verbal contact existed (Enoch, Noah, and Righteousness).

---

a greater distance between the text and the Second Temple use of the Righteousness topos type.

[88] Defined here as acts or events considered righteous because of the person or deity performing them; the opposite of someone actuated by righteousness. This concept paralleled a similar idea in a Zoroastrian Pahlavi text, *The Ḍinkarḍ*, 3:34. In it, five ranks of physicians existed. The highest-ranking physicians worked out of righteous motives, and the lowest acted from a love of money. The author therefore rejected actuated righteousness, opting instead to measure actualization *by* righteousness.

[89] Michael Walzer, *In God's Shadow: Politics in the Hebrew Bible* (New Haven: Yale University Press, 2012), 29. According to this argument, God does not define righteousness as there is an ultimate, independent guideline for righteousness in the universe.

4.3.6. Step 4f: Evaluation

For the establishing or nuancing a cultic reality subtype, the author of the "Prayer of Lamentation to Ishtar" used righteousness not as an authority, but as blandishment in a devoted follower's prayer. In the "Joy at the Accession of Merneptah," *ma'at* subjugated righteousness by the theophoric name and became the authority by which "right" drove away the Evildoer. Beyond *ma'at* righteousness, the topos also authorized a select group to watch the events. Therefore, both EAW texts held several meaningful differences while failing to hold three points of verbal contacts.

Concerning the righteousness as authority to bless God topos subtype, the Zoroastrian texts read in close parallel to the Second Temple texts, but the authority in *Yas.* 13:6 and 52:4 failed to match the authority of the only Second Temple apocalyptic passage concerning this righteousness subtype (1 En. 84:1). In it, the topos was secondary to creation as authority to bless God, which created meaningful differences with both *Yasnas* and lacked three points of verbal contact with *Yas.* 13:6. Therefore, no parent-child relationship existed between these texts and 1 En. 84:1.

The study then turned to the Tanakh. In Genesis, the author understood righteousness was external to the Hebrew deity—a law unto itself to which God conformed, but Second Temple authors muddied these distinctions. For the P.authors, God's righteous character legitimized judgment rather than leaving it to an external code of righteousness. He was now the "unswayable judge." A second difference in Genesis concerned Enoch's righteousness as the term applied to him only through a comparison to Noah. Moreover, the other Tanakh authors (except the author of 1 Chronicles) ignored Enoch completely. By comparison, Second Temple authors proclaimed the righteousness of Noah and Enoch, creating an authoritative topos type for nuancing cultic realities or legitimizing a right to bless God not found in the Tanakh. Therefore, three points of verbal contact did not exist with the texts of the Tanakh which denied a parent-child relationship.

In terms of the Hebraic movements, a scholar attributing prophetic authority to Enoch and Noah would have to contend with the absence of the Righteousness topos type in the prophetic material.[90] Likewise,

[90] While the Apocalypse of Zephaniah relied at least tangentially on the prophetic movement through Zephaniah, it contained no Righteousness topos type.

scholars tempted to link Moses or Levi to the priestly movement would have to contend with the absence of the topos type linked to Moses or Levi. The wisdom or scribal movement found stronger links. The Enochian author called Enoch "the scribe of righteousness" (12:4); however, if the label was an appositional description legitimizing Enoch through the Righteousness topos type, then righteousness became the authority by which a scribe acted prophetically, rather than by holding authority through the position of scribe in and of itself.

Overall, the differences between EAW, Hebraic, and the Second Temple literature indicated the Righteousness topos type developed from Second Temple traditions. Although based on Hebraic culture, the apocalyptic authors freely used characters considered righteous to fulfill their needs. As such, Second Temple theological concerns and traditions informed the narratives, and they alone imbued authority to the characters.

4.4. Literary Authority through Written Language: Divinely Ordained Journey

Divinely ordained journeys are journeys to destinations Second Temple authors believed existed in the physical world. However, these journeys fell under the category of literary authority through written language because the locus of authority for the journey was in the narrative, rather than the physical world.[91] In this work, the term, "divinely ordained journeys," replaced the more common "astral journey" to signify all Second Temple literary journeys, including celestial anabases and netherworld katabases. These journeys were authoritative based on their divine origination, connections with heavenly ascents into the divine council, and magical and ecstatic cultic events.[92]

---

[91] As an example, although a large body of knowledge developed in the Second Temple period on astronomy, the authority by which authors presented celestial bodies in 1 Enoch was not explicit to astronomy itself; rather, authority developed from the larger narrative. The astral journey in 1 Enoch contained both the journey and explicit observations of heavenly bodies. These observations created an authority for a solar calendar, rather than the celestial bodies themselves creating the authority. By comparison, Jubilean references to Mt. Sinai carried covenant overtones, regardless of whether such concepts were explicit in the current narrative—see Mladen Popović, "Astronomy and Astrology," *EDEJ*, 400.

[92] Paul A. de Souza Nogueira, "Celestial Worship and Ecstatic-Visionary Experience," *JSNT* 25.2 (2002): 180–83. For the heavenly council in Second Temple work, see Michael

4.4.1. Step 4a: Text—Definition and Use of Authority

The Divinely Ordained Journey topos type was a place in a text in which, by divine ordination, a person undertook a heavenly ascent, descent into Hades, a journey across lands, or an astral journey. Often, a heavenly being accompanied the person. P.authors used these journeys to legitimize their messages through an appeal to the divine. For example, in Enoch, a divinely ordained journey provided a firsthand account of how the universe worked. Because this journey occurred by divine will, the resulting observations (as the teleological purpose of the journey) were considered authoritative. In the case of Enoch, this topos type had parallels with the Righteousness topos type. As such, Enoch's report of heavenly movement became authoritative for a calendar.

4.4.2. Step 4b: Text and Context—Use in Apocalyptic Literature

These journeys occurred in several Second Temple apocalyptic texts. Qumran material also included two journeys of importance. The more interesting of the two occurs in the Book of Giants and builds on the Watcher story.

4.4.2.1. Apocalyptic Literature outside Qumran

In 1 Enoch, chapters 14–36, 37–71, and 72–82 all held divinely ordained journeys. The journey in 1 En. 14:17–36 was also incorporated into a larger journey through seven layers of heaven in 2 Enoch. Observations from the 2 Enoch journey focused on "cosmological elements [that] dominate the description of the first, fourth, and sixth heavens, whereas eschatological rewards and punishments receive attention in the second, third, and fifth."[93] Second Enoch, the Testament of Levi, and the Apocalypse of Zephaniah also recorded heavenly ascents. The Apocalypse of Zephaniah also contained a katabasis in the Akhmimic chapter 6.

S. Heiser, "The Divine Council in Late Canonical and Non-Canonical Second Temple Jewish Literature" (PhD diss., University of Wisconsin-Madison, 2004). For magic and Second Temple Judaism, see Ruth Langer, "Spiritual Practices: Mystical, Magical, and Apotropaic Prayer," in *Jewish Liturgy: A Guide to Research*, Illuminations: Guides to Research in Religion (Lanham: Rowman and Littlefield Publishers, 2015), 212. The work here was original but used Nicholas Wyatt's framework from *Space and Time in the Religious Life of the Near East*, vol. 85 (Sheffield: Sheffield Academic Press, 2001), 192–208.

[93] Daniel C. Harlow, "Ascent to Heaven," *EDEJ*, 388.

4.4.2.2. Journeys in Qumran Literature

In the Book of Giants (4Q530), a divine katabasis occurred in a giant's dream. God, with his heavenly court, descended to sentence the Watcher's offspring. Unfortunately, the broken text in the third column of the manuscript denied further reading, but a few observations were still possible. The text related to, and somewhat depended on, Dan 7:9–10—a throne-room scene wherein "one like the Son of Man" stood before "the Ancient of Days."[94] In this scene, the latter authorized the former's rule (Dan 7:14). Against this background, the dream katabasis of the heavenly courtroom and God condescending to earth in order to condemn was the authority confirming the judgment against the giants.

In 4Q213 f1.ii:15 through b:2, a probable ascent occurred, although the extant portions of text lacked any anabasis. In it, God moved Levi to his mountain and then instructed him on proper cultic activity. By extension, the instructions concerned proper temple sacrifices to be employed by the readers. Yet, the text most likely originated outside Qumran since the community did not engage in sacrificial rites.[95]

4.4.3. Step 4c: Text and Context—Germane Scholarship

Scholars have thoroughly documented divinely ordained journeys in the Jewish Second Temple material.[96] The focus, however, was

---

[94] Ryan E. Stokes, "The Throne Visions of Daniel 7, 1 Enoch 14 and the Qumran Book of Giants (530): An Analysis of Their Literary Relationship," *DSD* 15.3 (2008), 357. Stokes argued both this verse and 1 Enoch 14 depended on the Daniel passage.

[95] Carol A. Newsom, "Mysticism," *EDSS* 1:592. These scrolls were part of the Aramaic Levi texts, which included 1Q21 and 540–1.

[96] See, for instance, Martha Himmelfarb, *Ascent to Heaven in Jewish and Christian Apocalypses* (New York: Oxford University Press, 1993); *Tours of Hell: An Apocalyptic Form in Jewish and Christian Literature* (Philadelphia: University of Pennsylvania, 1983); John J. Collins and Michael A. Fishbane, *Death, Ecstasy, and Other Worldly Journeys* (Albany: State University of New York Press, 1995), 1–179; Fritz Graff, "The Bridge and the Ladder: Narrow Passages in Late Antique Visions," in *Heavenly Realms and Earthly Realities in Late Antique Religions*, ed. Ra'anan S. Boustan (Cambridge: Cambridge University Press, 2004), 19–33; Reed, "Heavenly Ascent, Angelic Descent," 47–66; for a succinct presentation of journeys in Second Temple literature, both apocalyptic and nonapocalyptic, see Harlow, "Ascent to Heaven," 387–90.

usually on origination and intent, making their work tangential to the current search for parent-child relationships through authoritative topoi.[97] Yet, a general background of scholarly work concerning origination was still useful to this study.

In discussions on EAW influence, scholars have usually taken one of three dominant positions concerning the journey in 1 En. 17, which for purposes of this research could be applied to all journey texts: (1) these journeys related to EAW ideas of "travel material" and "mythic geography," primarily from Babylonian sources; (2) journeys (and especially those of 1 En. 17–19) followed a pattern established in diplomatic relations whereby a person would escort foreign officials on a journey through his (or, perhaps, her) kingdom, highlighting its financial and militarity might; and (3) these texts followed Greek accounts of journeys, particularly, those of Nekyia.[98]

Illustrating the proclivity toward Babylonian sources by some scholars, Ursula Schattner-Rieser argued Hebraic interest in heavenly anabases grew after the Babylonian captivity because of the temple destruction and the need for continued experiences with the divine. This need coincided with the growth of Persian astronomy superseding an older understanding of layered heavens. Schattner-Rieser referenced John Collins's statement on the widespread belief of Babylonian influence on Jewish Apocalypticism, letting it stand as the assumption from which she sought her connections.[99] These three positions—especially the position of Babylonian backgrounds—loosely paralleled the prima facie findings in this research.

Concerning Hebraic influence, Paul Hanson understood the background of apocalyptic work to be a priestly work that encompassed Zadokite estrangement and their reactions to Hasmonean temple control. Thus, Jewish apocalyptic writing carried a charge

---

[97] However, see §4.2. (above) for Reed's argument concerning journeys and revealed secrets.

[98] Nickelsburg, *1 Enoch* 1, 279–80.

[99] Ursula Schattner-Rieser, "Levi in the Third Sky: On the 'Ascent to Heaven' Legends within Their Near Eastern Context and J. T. Milik's Unpublished Version of the Aramaic Levi Document," in *Dead Sea Scrolls in Context: Integrating the Dead Sea Scrolls in the Study of Ancient Texts, Languages and Cultures*, eds. Armin Lange, Emanuel Tov, and Matthias Weigold, VTSup 140 (Leiden: Brill, 2011), 808–10.

against the then-current temple administration.[100] Daniel Harlow, Himmelfarb, and others also held similar views. For instance, Harlow has argued "heaven [wa]s a temple, angels [wer]e priests, and the visionary assume[d] angelic status by taking on the role of a priest" in 1 Enoch.[101] Ascent texts, therefore, produced access to the heavenly temple. Perhaps, even more important, they provided information on proper cultic activity.

Other scholars accepted a prophetic background for the ascent texts. For instance, Nickelsburg and James VanderKam pointed to the Watchers directing Enoch to proclaim a sentence against the disobedient Watchers who defiled themselves with earthly endeavors. They further wrote that descriptions in this text resonated with Isaiah and Ezekiel in their commissioning texts as well as other heavenly scenes.[102]

The reasons for creating these journeys, as well as their similarities to the priestly or prophetic movements, was probably lost to antiquity. Nevertheless, Fredrick Murphy's conclusion on the subject is still applicable: journey texts and associated movements in Jewish history have led to a conclusion that "knowledge [bestowed by the characters] is complete and reliable."[103] This statement also validated divinely ordained journeys as an authoritative topos type.[104]

---

[100] Paul Hanson, "The Matrix of Apocalypse," in *CHJ*, vol. 2, *The Hellenistic Age*, ed. W. D. Davies and L. Finkelstein (Cambridge: Cambridge University Press, 1989), 530–33.

[101] Harlow, "Ascent to Heaven," 388.

[102] Nickelsburg and VanderKam, *1 Enoch* 2, 127–28.

[103] Fredrick Murphy, *Apocalypticism in the Bible and Its World: A Comprehensive Introduction* (Grand Rapids: Baker Academic, 2012), 132.

[104] Mark Elliott argued the purpose of these journeys was to support the dual destinies of Israel (heaven and hell) by revelational authority, an authority inherent in the divinely ordained journey topos type: "It is the dual feature of judgment and reward that suggests that the *primary concern* of these revelations of the cosmos is *to reveal the respective ultimate destinies of the elect and the damned* and thus to define the elect and the apostate by outlining their respective fates, the lengthy and detailed descriptions of the places of reward and torment adding revelational authority to the message that Israel is divided according to eternal destinies" (*The Survivors of Israel: A Reconsideration of the Theology of Pre-Christian Judaism* [Grand Rapids: Eerdmans, 2000], 300—emphasis added).

4.4.4. Step 4d: Cross-Text—Possible EAW Sources

After steps 3a–c above were completed, three texts were deemed most likely to hold an authoritative topos type in a possible parent-child relationship with Jewish apocalyptic work.[105] Those texts were the "Ascent of Enmeduranki," the "Divine Nomination of Thutmose III," and Plato's *Republic* (614b).

4.4.4.1. "Ascent of Enmeduranki"

As already noted in reference to another topos type, scholars have often posited the "Ascent of Enmeduranki" as source material for 1 Enoch:

> Enmeduranki [king of Sippar], the beloved of Anu, Enlil [and Ea]. Šamaš and Adad [brought him in] to their assembly. Šamaš and Adad [honored him]. Šamaš and Adad [set him] on a large throne of gold. They showed him how to observe oil on water, a mystery of Anu, [Enlil and Ea]. They gave him the tablet of the gods, the liver, a secret of heaven and [underworld].[106]

---

[105] Scholars have often posited as sources many of the texts that failed to qualify for authoritative topoi in this study. For instance, the Journey to Etana showed no authoritative topos; rather, the journey operated as an artifice. In the *Odyssey* (10:490–11:639), Circe told Odysseus he must sail into Hades and converse with Teiresias concerning his fate. Although Circe was a goddess, and Odysseus experienced a katabasis, Circe merely "advised [Odysseus] to make a journey to the lower world," according to Alexander Murray (*Manual of Mythology: Greek and Roman, Norse, and Old German, Hindoo and Egyptian Mythology* [New York: Charles Scribner's Sons, 1881], 305–06). Thus, little correlation existed between the Odyssey and the Divinely Ordained Journeys topos type as presented in this study.

The same held true for the story of Persephone and Demeter —both experienced katabasis based on the acts of a god, but neither correlated with divinely ordained journeys as presented here for authoritative topoi. Similarities between Enoch and Utnapishtim, when viewed through the lens of authoritative topoi, did not score heavily for inclusion, nor did the story, "Nergal and Ereshkigal," "The Journey of Etana" (which held no authoritative topos), Sophocles's "Ajax" (605), "Ishtar (and Inanna's) Descent to the Netherworld," the Egyptian story "Repulsing the Dragon," the Ugaritic account of "King Keret and the Language of Ritual," or the "Summons of Adapa."

[106] See n.22 (above) in this chapter for notes on translation.

This text began with Enmeduranki's ascension into an assembly of gods whereby he gained secret knowledge. His anabasis occurred to legitimize divination through his new role as a teacher. This journey, paired with secrecy, became the authority by which he could teach divination and by which later practitioners could claim legitimacy. In this text, the Secrecy topos type occurred based on its teleological purpose; however, for the Divinely Ordained Journeys topos type, teleological concerns had negligible effect as the focus shifted to the points of verbal contact concerning the divine journey itself.

Before further examination, three points of verbal contact existed between this text and Jewish apocalyptic literature. First, the identities of the characters making the journey were similar as both Enoch and Enmeduranki were seventh in the line of descendants. Second, they held similar character traits.[107] Third, both characters entered the heavenly assembly, and often into a deity's presence where they conversed.[108] Alongside these similarities, however, were several meaningful differences relating specifically to this topos type.[109] Concerning the first verbal contact, any possible relationship between Enoch and Enmeduranki based on the king lists was negated in 1 Enoch as Enoch's position in the Genesis *toledot* was ignored by the P.author(s). A second meaningful difference was Enmeduranki's journey-authority, which derived from his presence among deities. By comparison, Enoch's author

[107] James C. VanderKam, *Enoch and the Growth of an Apocalyptic Tradition*, CBQMS 16 (Washington: Catholic Biblical Association of America, 1984), 48–49. Orlov made this same connection (see n.28 [above] in this chapter, also Appendix C [below]). Helge Kvanvig went as far as writing, "Enoch was a Jewish literary crystallization of Sumero-Akkadian lore about the seventh antediluvian king, Enmeduranki" (*Roots of Apocalyptic: The Mesopotamian Background of the Enoch Figure and of the Son of Man*, WMANT 61 [Neukirchen-Vluyn: Neukirchener Verlag, 1988], 8). However, she approached the material differently compared to the above scholars. Kvanvig's work also highlighted the problems of a history of religions method. In the words of E. Earle Ellis, Kvanvig's "work shows both the help and the rather narrow limits of a 'history of religions' approach to understanding the Bible" (review of *Roots of Apocalyptic: The Mesopotamian Background of the Enoch Figure and of the Son of Man*, by Helge S. Kvanvig, *SwJT* 34.1 [1991]: 74).

[108] These ascensions occurred in several texts—see e.g., 1 En.14:20, 39:7–8; 2 En. 24:1–38:3, and 67 as the final ascension seen in Gen 5:24. Levi also ascended into God's presence in T. Levi 5:1–6.

[109] Not all scholars agreed with these similarities, either. For instance, Nicolas Wyatt questioned Enmeduranki's list position and the length he reigned, either six thousand or twenty-one thousand years—see *Space and Time*, 195.

wove together multiple authorities: divine presence began a journey, but the author relied upon additional authority from the Cosmology and Righteousness topos types. Finally, using 1 En. 14:8 as an example, the Second Temple author provided both setting and method by which Enoch ascended; yet, a close reading provided no setting or description for the Enmeduranki's anabasis. These meaningful differences and lack of a setting for Enmeduranki's ascent deny a parent-child relationship between this text and Second Temple material for this topos type.

4.4.4.2. "The Divine Nomination of Thutmose III"

"The Divine Nomination of Thutmose III" identified Thutmose's legitimacy as a ruler through a picture of Egyptian enthronement rites:[110]

> [He opened for] me the doors of heaven; he spread open for me the portals of its horizon. I flew up to the sky as a divine falcon, that I might see his mysterious form which is in heaven, that I might adore his majesty. (10)...I saw the forms of being of the Horizon God on his mysterious ways in heaven.
>
> Re himself established me, and I was endowed with [his] crowns [which] were upon his head, his uraeus-serpent was fixed upon [my brow]...I [*was equipped*] with all his states of glory; I was made satisfied with the understanding of the gods, like Horus when he took account of himself at the house of his father Amon-Re. I was [*perfected*] with the dignities of a god...[He established] my crowns, and drew up for me my titulary himself.[111]

In the second paragraph, the anabasis to Re's presence became Thutmose's divine approval. This work included three points of verbal contact to be examined: an anabasis, a revelation of secrets, and a worship scene.

In terms of journeys, Thutmose's journey differed from the Sumero-Babylonian account that lacked a discussion of the anabasis. Here, Re approached Thutmose, who, in his vision, ascended as a falcon:

[110] Ibid., 193.
[111] "The Divine Nomination of Thutmose III," trans. J. H. Breasted (*ANET*, 446).

> And behold I saw the clouds: And they were calling me in a vision; and the fogs were calling me; and the course of the stars and the lightning were rushing me and causing me to desire; and in the vision, the winds were causing me to fly and rushing me high up into heaven.

This divinely ordained journey was similar to 1 En. 14–20, but unlike 1 En. 14–20, the Thutmose text was an enthronement text making the teleological purpose meaningfully different.[112]

Zephaniah's anabasis in Apoc. Zeph. 2:1–5 also related to the Thutmose text. Zephaniah soared above his city, and with the Angel of the Lord, saw its activities. He eventually rose to find the world "hanging like a drop of water, which was suspended from a bucket when it comes up from a well." Implicit in Thutmose's trip as a falcon was a view of all his land over which he would soon reign, but this implicitness highlighted a significant difference. The author of the Apocalypse of Zephaniah produced a well-crafted setting absent in the Thutmose narrative. This absence signified detracting dissimilarities that negated the journey as a point of verbal contact. Consequently, while the journey was authoritative, meaningful differences denied a parent-child relationship with the Enochian journey, and the lack of three verbal contacts negated a parent-child relationship with the journey in the Apocalypse of Zephaniah.

4.4.4.3. Plato's Republic

In Plato's *Republic*, Socrates recounted a story to Glaucon. In this story, a warrior died only to awake on his pyre. Later, this warrior

---

[112] Hugo Odeberg, and later, Orlov argued Enoch's anabasis in 2 Enoch included a transformation into the "Prince of Presence," or Metatron—see Hugo Odeberg, *3 Enoch or the Hebrew Book of Enoch* (New York: Ktav, 1973); Andrei A. Orlov, *The Enoch-Metatron Tradition*, TSAJ 107 (Tübingen: Mohr Siebeck, 2005). These arguments focused on parallels to 3 Enoch and the larger Merkabah tradition and may hold more points of contact with the Thutmose text. One of the earliest texts in the Merkabah tradition was the "Four Who Entered Pardes," an ascension text found in the Tosephta and the Jerusalem and Babylonian Talmud (although not all scholars have made this connection). However, the dating of 3 Enoch and the Merkabah tradition developed mostly in the Common Era, putting such developments beyond the range of this study. See also Marvin A. Sweeney, "Pardes Revisited Once Again: A Reassessment of the Rabbinic Legend Concerning the Four Who Entered Pardes," *Shofar* 22.4 (2004): 43–44.

recounted a journey to a place of judgment where two apertures stood before him: one leading heavenward, the other, into a chasm. There, he received a charge to become a messenger to the living. After he agreed to it, souls visited him and provided their afterlife experiences so that he might fulfill his charge. Socrates used this story to identify an afterlife wherein a ten-fold repayment of deeds occurred. So, was the warrior's journey an authoritative topos? Emile Bréhier commented on this passage: "The place of judgment becomes the center of the earth; Platonic heaven becomes the fixed sphere."[113] Socrates's katabasis story was a descent to the place of judgment; the journey itself begot authority—the messenger awakened to recount his tales of heaven, the chasm, and the judgment that sent men to dwell in each. Plato used the story, placed on Socrates's lips, as authority for his arguments on the proper way to live (619ab). Likewise, Enoch reached a place where

> the actions of the sinners are weighed in the balance. And there [he] saw the dwelling place of the sinners and the company of the holy ones' and [he] saw the sinners—those who deny the name of the Lord of the Spirits—being expelled from there and being dragged off (1 En. 41:2–3).

A quick comparison showed three points of verbal contact: (1) both narratives expressed a place of judgment, (2) both visitors had to share their newfound knowledge, and (3) the authors of Enoch and Plato presented these journeys absent a divine being, but further study invalidated these points of contact.

In 1 Enoch, the author inserted the judgment in Enoch's journey after Enoch had visited God. Thus, although God was not mentioned at the place of judgment, the previous presence of God in the journey text signified divine appointment. The warrior's journey, however, ended at the place of judgment without visiting a deity. Further, his death occasioned the journey, which cast doubt on whether it was divinely appointed.

The focus of these journeys was different as well. In Plato's *Republic,* the location served as a place to learn enough of the afterlife so the warrior could fulfill his charge. In contrast, Enoch's journey contained several destinations and focused on learning cosmic secrets

---

[113] Emile Bréhier, *La Philosophie de Plotin* (Paris: Boivin, 1928), 29.

that the author could then use to direct cultic life. These differing contexts and purposes created meaningful differences between the two texts, denying a parent-child relationship based on the Divinely Ordained Journey topos type.[114] Thus, each of the three strongest possible EAW passages failed to show a parent-child relationship.

4.4.5. Step 4e: Cross-Text—Possible Tanakh Sources

For the Divinely Ordained Journeys topos type in the Tanakh, five passages were examined. Three were from the Pentateuch (Gen 5:24, 28:12–13; Exod. 24:10). Two were from the prophets (Isa 6:1–3; Ezek 8, 40).[115]

4.4.5.1. Genesis 5:24

The first text was the short account of Enoch from the antediluvian *toledot:* וְאֵינֶנּוּ כִּי־לָקַח אֹתוֹ אֱלֹהִים, ("And he was no more because God took him"—my translation). The problem lay in the word "took." Could it be read as an anabasis?

The Masoretes pointed the Hebrew root לקח as a Qal perfect. This root had a semantic range that included "take, grasp, or seize"; "take and go away with"; or "bring, acquire, purchase, and obtain."[116] Although movement was not a necessary part of this domain, as "purchase" or "acquire" indicated, context negated these terms as an option because no economic transaction occurred in the text.[117] Thus, the concept of "grasping" or "obtaining" remained as a nonmovement interpretation. Nevertheless, the phrase "And he was no more" (אֵינֶנּוּ)

---

114 A passage in Apoc. Zeph. 4:1–8 also indicated judgment, but in this text, Zephaniah saw strange angels carrying "the souls of ungodly men" to their place of eternal punishment. In 2 Enoch, an anabasis brought Enoch to the second heaven wherein he witnessed prisoners waiting for judgment, and in chapter 10, Enoch saw another place of torture and torment, but this place was in "the northern region" of what seemed in context to be the third heaven. As such, these narratives had little in common with texts presented above, except that one was a place for judgment to happen, and the other was a place for those who were judged unrighteous.

115 The ascent of Elijah in 2 Kgs 2:11 was not included here because it lacked several necessary elements found in the Divinely Ordained Journey topos type. The only points of commonality were a righteous man (although not called so in the pericope), and the ascent; however, this ascent was connected by לקח as seen in the following paragraphs.

116 Koehler, ed. "לקח," *HALOT* 1:534–35; Clines "לקח," *DCH* 4:564–76.

117 "Purchase" and "acquire" carry the concept of an economic transaction (or, perhaps, a transaction by force).

implied ceasing from existence. These two terms, לָקַח and אֵינֶנּוּ, occurred once each in a similar usage elsewhere in the Tanakh. For לָקַח, the context was 1 Kgs 19:4. There, Elijah asked YHWH to קַח נַפְשִׁי. The addition of נַפְשִׁי negated a direct correlation to Enoch, but the ultimate fulfillment of his wish—the ascension in the chariot—created a cessation of existence without death. Concerning, אֵינֶנּוּ, the Psalmist used it in Ps 37:10: "Still a little while, and the wicked will no longer be, and though you direct your attention upon his place, he will not be there."[118] The previous verse indicated the wicked were destroyed, and those people whose hope was in YHWH would inherit the land, which in turn indicated the wicked ceased to exist in the land. Therefore, it was difficult to determine the exact meaning of "and he was no more." Nevertheless, the word picture indicated Enoch was, and then he was not, as though he disappeared either in death or from existence. The latter may have hinted at a divine anabasis, but there was not enough evidence to declare it firmly from Gen 5:24.

Unfortunately, nothing more was said of Enoch in the Tanakh outside of a single reference in 1 Chronicles concerning lineage. Christian canonical writers, however, mentioned him twice. Enoch first appeared in the genealogy of Jesus (Luke 3:37). He also appeared in the list of faithful saints in Hebrews. There, the author wrote Enoch was "taken away so that he did not experience death, and he was not found because God took him" (11:5). Although a parameter of this study ruled out (as much as possible) Christian influence on Jewish Apocalyptic tradition, the passage from Hebrews illuminated how a community that included Jews understood Enoch; he was a man whose one-way divine journey to God defied death.[119] Therefore, Gen 5:24 may have been the beginning of a larger idea of divine journeys

[118] "וְעוֹד מְעַט וְאֵין רָשָׁע וְהִתְבּוֹנַנְתָּ עַל־מְקוֹמוֹ וְאֵינֶנּוּ׃"

[119] Other Second Temple traditions have portrayed him in a different manner. Josephus provided Enoch agency, exchanging the Hebrew לקח for the Greek ἀνεχώρησε (retire, withdraw). Thus, Enoch did not ascend from the earth, but withdrew or retired from it (*Ant.* 1:85). The (probable) Sicarii authors of the Masada Ben Sira manuscript likely removed Enoch from an exemplar list (he was first in the Greek and Cairo Geniza manuscripts), leaving instead a blank line for his entry. Later, early Rabbinic writers made him "a model of failure and betrayal," while others "removed [him] from the roster of the righteous and is added instead to the roster of the wicked," as found in Bereshith Rabba 25:1. See Stephan Pfann, "Abducted by God? The Process of Heavenly Ascent in Jewish Tradition, from Enoch to Paul, from Paul to Akiva," *Hen* 33.1 (2011), 122–24.

developed in the Second Temple period, but three points of verbal contact did not exist between it and Second Temple apocalyptic material.

4.4.5.2. Genesis 28:12

The first mention of ascending or descending occurred with Jacob in Gen 28:12: "And then he dreamed, and behold, a ladder was placed on the earth, and its top reached heaven. Behold, angels of God ascended and descended by it."[120] The author wrote in the following verse that YHWH stood עָלָיו; but how should עָלָיו be translated?

Two options were available: "beside him" and "above it" ("it" being the ladder). In the text, vertical movement and the ladder terminating in heaven made "above it" the correct translation, as evidenced in the ESV, NAS, NIV, NLT, and NKJV, among others.[121] Translated in this way, Gen. 18:12–13 included three points of verbal contact: (1) the ana- and katabases; (2) communication with the divine; and (3) divine, human, and angelic presence. Yet, a closer inquiry noted the ana- and katabases were angelic instead of human. As such, no Divinely Ordained Journey topos type existed in this text. However, in light of the Enochian narrative in Genesis, the passage may have contributed to an overall understanding of divinely ordained journeys.

4.4.5.3. Exodus 24:9–10

In Exod 24:9–10, Moses, Aaron, and seventy-two elders ascended the mountain to God's presence. There, Moses noted a change under

[120] The issue of translating סלם as "ladder" or "staircase" had little relevance to this study except for suggested connections a staircase would have had with Egyptian or Akkadian parallels. Certain scholars have made connections between this verse and ancient Ziggurats upon which priests ascended and descended. To read the connection into the passage, however, was to assume Second Temple apocalyptic authors recognized this connection in the second or first century BCE, four hundred years after Ziggurats fell out of favor for religious activity. Nevertheless, the Ziggurats informed the study concerning background information for heavenly journeys in Mesopotamia. See Kenneth A. Mathews, *Genesis 11:27–50:26*, NAC 1B (Nashville: Broadman & Holman, 2005), 449–50; Victor P. Hamilton, *The Book of Genesis, Chapters 18–50*, NICOT (Grand Rapids: Eerdmans, 1995), 240; Cornelis Houtman, "What Did Jacob See in His Dream at Bethel: Some Remarks on Genesis 28:10–22," *VT* 27.3 (1977): 43–45, 338.

[121] These versions all included the alternate translation, "beside him," in a note.

God's feet: "And then, they saw the God of Israel, and under his [God's] feet was something like sapphire flagstone, essentially as the skies in its purity."[122] Four key elements informed this study from this text. First, unlike Gen 28:12, human anabasis occurred. Second, this anabasis came about by divine command (24:1). Third, a change in substance highlighted entry into God's presence; they no longer resided on the natural mountainside. Whether the heavenly temple had descended to Mt. Sinai or the mountain itself had transformed, the word picture denoted standing in the skies.[123] Last, and perhaps most important, Moses received a divine command to go higher into the mountain where he received instruction on building the tabernacle and corresponding items of worship.

Missing from the narrative, however, was a supernatural anabasis. Supernatural anabasis occurred most often through a vision or assisted by an angel, but it was absent in Moses's movement from the mountain to the temple. Further, although the flagstone was representative of the boundary between the mountain and the temple, there was no evidence Moses stood upon the flagstone. Conversely, although the journey was an ascension to the temple of God and was divinely ordained, the ascension was unnecessary to provide authority for the story since the Covenant topos type was the authority through which cultic and political Israel understood herself. Yet, once again, this passage provided a sharper picture of anabasis compared to the previous passages studied in this subsection, which indicated a trajectory for this topos type in the Tanakh.

4.4.5.4. Isaiah 6:1–3

The text of Isa 6:1–3 was chronologically out of sequence in Isaiah. However, it contained a complete commissioning of the prophet, which began with a description of the setting in verses 1–3:

---

[122] "וַיִּרְאוּ אֵת אֱלֹהֵי יִשְׂרָאֵל וְתַחַת רַגְלָיו כְּמַעֲשֵׂה לִבְנַת הַסַּפִּיר וּכְעֶצֶם הַשָּׁמַיִם לָטֹהַר׃"

[123] השמים was translated "skies" rather than "heavens" to avoid an association with ascensions (ascending into heaven), as the comparison itself was meant only to describe the flagstone. Note, however, it may not only remind the reader of "the deep dark blue of an endless sky [but also] the building materials of legendary divine dwelling-places." John I. Durham, *Exodus*, WBC 3 (Dallas: Word, 1998), 344. For the symbolism of the sapphire flagstone, also see Walter C. Kaiser, Jr. "Exodus," in *Genesis, Exodus, Leviticus, Numbers*, vol. 2 of *The Expositor's Bible Commentary*, ed. Frank E. Gaebelein (Grand Rapids: Zondervan, 1990), 449.

> In the year of the death of king Uzziah, I saw the lord sitting upon a highly raised throne, and the seams of his robe filled the temple. Seraphim stood above him—six wings to each one; with two he covered his face, and with two he covered his legs, and with two he flew. And they called out to one another saying, Holy, Holy, Holy is the Lord of Hosts, and the whole earth was filled with his glory.

The basic elements for divinely ordained journeys occurred in this text, but the journey itself was implicit.[124] The text began with Isaiah's commissioning among the divine council, which occurred only because he had ascended to the council. Yet, the acts of the seraphim made this journey distinct from those found in Jewish apocalyptic literature. Here, the seraphim did not lead, guide, or transmit knowledge or secrets to Isaiah. Their participation was solely among the council acting out God's implicit commands.

This text may have begun the tradition of angels interacting with humanity in the Divinely Ordained Journey topos type, but the apex of Isaiah's ascent was a commissioning providing him with authority to prophesy. Thus, Isaiah ascended into the heavenly council through an implied anabasis, then returned to deliver a message authorized by his commissioning journey. The anabasis in this text, if considered with the other texts studied so far, provided a better picture of divinely ordained journeys, and extended the trajectory for the topos type in the Tanakh.

4.4.5.5. Ezekiel 8:3, 40:2

The author of Ezekiel expanded on the Divinely Ordained Journey topos type by changing the encroached space in 8:3:

> And then he stretched out an image of a hand and seized me by a lock of hair from my head, and then he carried me in the spirit between the earth and skies and brought me to Jerusalem in the vision(s) of God to the entrance of the inner gate facing

[124] The size of the throne indicated a heavenly vision, rather than an earthly one. John Watts favored this interpretation, as did George Nicol, who depended on the setting of the divine council in his article. See John D. W. Watts, *Isaiah 1–33*, rev. ed., WBC 24 (Nashville: Thomas Nelson, 2005), 106; Nicol, "Isaiah's Vision and the Visions of Daniel," *VT* 29 (1979): 504.

> north, where the dwelling of the idol that gives rise to indignation is (8:3).[125]

Ezekiel again travels laterally in 40:2:

> In the visions of God, he brought me to the land of Israel and set me down on a very high mountain. And upon its southern slope was something like a city structure.

The destination of these journeys provided another layer of authority whereby Ezekiel, led by an angel, spoke against current acts in the temple and addressed future restoration.

When this text was placed alongside other journey texts in the Tanakh, a clear picture of the Divinely Ordained Journey topos type emerged. However, the completed picture cannot be drawn from any one Hebraic movement, but from texts associated with the priestly movement, prophetic movement, and other texts not necessarily associated with any movement. As such, while occurrences of this topos type indicated a trajectory upon which apocalyptic authors built, no parent-child relationship existed with any specific Hebraic movement.

4.4.6. Step 4f: Evaluation

The EAW sources showed connections to the Divinely Ordained Journey topos type in Second Temple apocalyptic material, but the strength of the connections varied between texts. More importantly,

[125] A similar journey was Habakkuk's journey in *Bel and the Dragon* (33–39), which exhibited a horizontal journey between Jerusalem and Babylon and an angel taking Habakkuk by the hair. Yet, the purpose of his journey was only to feed Daniel, who was in the lions' den. William Daubney noted both prophets were moved against their will, although it was difficult to see that point in the text beyond questioning Habakkuk's announcement that he had never seen Babylon and knew nothing of the den (cf. *Bel and the Dragon* 35—see William H. Daubney, *The Three Additions to Daniel: A Study* [Cambridge, Deighton Bell, 1906], 221). This journey was included here to note a similar story to Ezekiel's as Bel and the Dragon was neither part of the Tanakh, nor identified in chapter 2 as part of the apocalyptic works studied here (the journey being the only possible identification of the apocalyptic genre, and as such, a prototype like Ezekiel).

every EAW text held meaningful differences that negated a parent-child relationship with Jewish apocalyptic literature.[126]

In the Tanakh, it was unclear whether the Genesis account of Enoch referenced an anabasis. Moreover, the later debates in Judaism showed a lack of consensus concerning Second Temple understanding of Enoch. The Jacob story held both ana- and katabases of angels but lacked the anabasis of the main character. These two stories, however, began a trajectory that was completed in Isaiah and expanded horizontally in Ezekiel. This trajectory resulted in a parent-child relationship between the topos type in the Tanakh and Second Temple material.

At Qumran, the texts had too little in common with EAW texts for a parent-child relationship. The Hebraic texts held more similarities. However, the katabasis in 4Q530 concerned judgment as opposed to the anabases of Isaiah and Ezekiel for commissioning as a prophet, and Levi's katabasis in 4Q213 focused on specific instructions for temple purity, contrary to Ezekiel's measuring angels that symbolized future hope. Therefore, Qumran authors may have followed the Second Temple apocalyptic authors in identifying and further building on the topos type from the trajectory found in the Tanakh material. However, any similarities were with the overall topos type, negating a parent-child relationship with any of the Hebraic movements.

In general, the Second Temple apocalyptic authors had at their discretion several divine journey traditions from which they drew, but their work remained unique to Second Temple Apocalypticism. While a trajectory showed a parent-child relationship between the whole of the Tanakh material and Second Temple apocalyptic literature, it was possible the relationship was also influenced by the Divinely Ordained Journey topos type in the EAW literary culture based on the similarities.

4.5. Referential Authority through Physical Elements: Tablets

In EAW literature, the Tablets topos type gained authority through the message written on the tablet or its author. Examples of authority through a message are adoption tablets, sale tablets, and Suzerainty treaties. On

---

[126] Another significant difference between EAW and Second Temple texts is that no single EAW source produced an intricate, woven set of authorities (Plato's *Republic* came closest, with prophetic authority, secret knowledge, and a possible divine journey) as found in Second Temple material.

these tablets, the message dictated the relationship (or conclusion thereof) between parties.[127] Tablets gaining authority through the author are exemplified by prayers (on tablets) laid beside idols, and the pseudonymous Orpheus tablets. Naturally, this authorial authority for tablets also depended on Authority by Name and often, Pseudonymity.

4.5.1. Step 4a: Text—Definition and Use of Authority

The Tablets topos type was defined as a place within written literature whereby an author referred to tablets for the sake of using the authority represented by them. Two tablets were referenced most often in apocalyptic works. The first tablets were the Tablets of the Law. These tablets referred to that on which God had written the law for Moses. The second tablets were the Tablets of Heaven and referred to that from which the law was copied and upon which both history and the actions of humankind were written. These tablets were thought to contain the literal truths of heaven and the history of the world. Knowledge obtained from these tablets was incontestable by those adherents who accepted the larger narrative from which the Tablets topos type derived. P.authors called on the authority of these tablets to confirm the incontestability of their teaching.

4.5.2. Step 4b: Text and Context—Use in Apocalyptic Literature

The Tablets topos type occurred thirty-six times in Jubilees, five times in 1 Enoch, and once in the Testament of Levi. In Jubilees, the author referenced four sets of tablets: Tablets of the Division of Years, Tablets of Heaven, Tablets of the Law, and Jacob's Tablets. The Jubilean author also referred to Tablets of the Law, but devoid of authority. Contrary to the Jubilees P.author, the Enochian P.author was consistent, referring only to Tablets of Heaven. Likewise, the T. Levi P.author used this authority once with the title "Tablets of the Fathers," which prompted a question: Was the Jubilean variation important?

---

[127] "Mesopotamian Legal Documents: Nuzi Akkadian," trans. Theophile J. Meek (*ANET*, 217–22). Concerning Suzerainty treaties, see Kenneth Kitchen and Paul J. N. Lawrence, *TLC* 1, 3. Joseph A. Fitzmyer, "The Aramaic Suzerainty Treaty from Sefire in the Museum of Beirut," *CBQ* 20.4 (1958): 444–76, esp. 45; Martin L. West, *The Orphic Poems*, Oxford University Press Academic Monograph Reprints Series (Oxford: Clarendon Press, 1983), 3. On cultic prayers, see Murray, *Manual of Mythology*, 14.

4.5.2.1. Jubilees

The Jubilean P.author referenced tablets in the introductory paragraph, which read as a descriptor: "When [Moses] went up to receive the Tablets of the Law and commandment by the word of the Lord." These tablets played a major role in the overall understanding of the Tablet topos type.

4.5.2.1.1. Tablets of the Law

The term "Tablets of the Law" first appeared in Jub. 1:1:

> In the first year of the Exodus of the children of Israel from Egypt, in the third month on the sixteenth day of that month, the LORD spoke to Moses, saying, "Come up to me on the mountain, and I shall give you two stone Tablets of the Law and the commandment, which I have written, so that you may teach them."

This passage was the foundation for later authoritative topoi in Jubilees through a textual link with Exod 24:12:

> YHWH said to Moses, "Come up to me *on* the mountain and wait there. And I shall give you tablets of stone—the law and the commandment—which I have written to instruct them."

Through this link, the author wove together two elements to support this topos type. The first element was history: Mount Sinai and the Torah highlighted the corporate memory of Israel's national birth when Moses received the covenant.[128] Second, the author referenced Exod 24:12 to remind the reader that God himself delivered the law written on tablets. Then, the author inverted cause-and-effect by postulating the Tablets of Heaven as the source.[129] The narrative logic

[128] See chapter 5 for the Covenant and Cosmology topos types.

[129] VanderKam, *Book of Jubilees*, 12, 24. VanderKam wrote the Angel of Presence "dictate[d] the remainder of the book to Moses from inscribed celestial tablets" (24). The current text was therefore "revelation in the form of direct speech…and the several stages in the process of revelation guaranteed the accuracy and authenticity of the message: God commanded that the message be communicated, that message was already fixed on Tablets of Heaven…and no less an authority than Moses himself made the earthly copy of the heavenly message. Jubilees thus presented itself…as an absolutely authoritative work whose divine message compelled acceptance and

was reduced to an if-then statement: If the Torah, written on the Tablets of the Law, was authoritative, then the Tablets of Heaven from whence it came also held equivalent authority. Consequently, the author established both history and authoritative correction through this occurrence.

4.5.2.1.2. Tablets of Heaven

In Jub. 3:10, purity laws gained authority based on the Tablets of Heaven topos type:

> And therefore, the command was written in the heavenly tablets for one who bears, "If she bears a male, she shall remain seven days in her impurity like the first seven days. And thirty-three days she shall remain in the blood of her purity. And she shall not touch anything holy. And she shall not enter the sanctuary until she has completed these days which are in accord with (the rule for) a male (child). And that which is in accord with (the rule for) a female is two weeks—like the two first weeks—in her impurity. And sixty-six days she shall remain in the blood of her purity. And their total will be eighty days."

These remarks carried the weight of law because they had been inscribed on the Tablets of Heaven.

Another reference occurred in Jub. 24:33: "It is written and engraved concerning him in the Tablets of Heaven to be done to him in the day of judgment." This reference concerned Isaac's curse on the Philistines. In it, the author created a picture like that seen on curse tablets, which extended the various uses for Tablets of Heaven in this period.[130]

A third use was in Jub. 23:32 occurring at the end of the only specific apocalyptic section of Jubilees: "And you, Moses, write these words because thus it is written and set upon the Tablets of Heaven as a

---

obedience" (ibid., 12). Tablets of Heaven both gained authority and became an authoritative topos for the message delivered to the author's audience.

[130] Charles recognized these distinctions in 1913: "[Tablets of Heaven] are at times a record [of] contemporary events (14:9; 30:20; 31:23), or a heavenly copy of Levitical Laws (3:8, 31; 4:32; 5:13; 6:17; 15:25; 16:29; 24:33; 28:6; 32:15, and so on)" (Charles, *Pseudepigrapha* 2:17).

testimony for eternal generations." This prophecy, inscribed on the Tablets of Heaven (and thus, eternal and trustworthy), carried the weight of Torah. Eschatological hope drove this use. The hope was for an increase in lifespan and a future lacking only the presence of a satan or evil one (23:26–29).[131] A second prophetic use of the topos type occurred four times in Jubilees 6 concerning the feasts and the solar calendar:

> For I know and henceforth I shall make you know—but not from my own heart, because the book is written before me and is ordained in the Tablets of Heaven of the division of days—lest they forget the feasts of the covenant and walk in the feasts of the gentiles, after their errors and after their ignorance. (6:35)

The author based his command to obey the feasts on the solar calendar, itself based on authority "ordained in the Tablets of Heaven" rather than on authority founded in pseudepigraphical Moses. However, these tablets were paralleled with the Tablets of the Division of Years.

4.5.2.1.3. Tablets of the Division of Years

A reference to these tablets occurred once in all Second Temple literature used in this study:

> And the angel of the presence, who went before the camp of Israel, took the Tablets of the Division of Years from the time of the creation of the law and testimony according to their weeks (of years), according to the jubilees, year by year throughout the full number of jubilees, from [the day of creation until] the day of the new creation when the heaven and earth and all of their creatures shall be renewed according to the powers of heaven and according to the whole nature of earth, until the sanctuary of the LORD is created in Jerusalem upon Mount Zion. And all of the lights will be renewed for healing and peace and blessing for all of the elect of Israel and

[131] VanderKam correctly stated eschatology rested not at the Jubilean forefront, but on Tablet authority at the end of this passage, which shifted the narrative from a potential future to a foregone fact and a foundation of hope—see VanderKam, *Book of Jubilees*, 132–33.

> in order that it might be thus from that day and unto all the days of the earth. (Jub. 1:29)

By introducing the tablets at the close of the first chapter, the author stamped the Jubilean divisions of history with the Tablets topos type, rather than the authority of Moses. Doing so relied on authoritative transfer from the Tablets of the Law, as well as on the same angel who orated the Tablets of the Law to Moses. Paired with the Tablet of the Law, these tablets produced the authoritative book of Jubilees.[132] Finally, the author referenced a fourth set of tablets: Jacob's tablets.

4.5.2.1.4. Jacob's Tablets

Jacob received these tablets at Bethel with a warning to refrain from building a sanctuary:

> And he saw in a vision of the night, and behold an angel was descending from heaven, and there were seven tablets in his hands. And he gave (them) to Jacob, and he read them, and he knew everything which was written in them, which would happen to him and to his sons during all the ages. 22 And he showed him everything which was written on the tablets. 23 And he said to him, "Do not build this place, and do not make an eternal sanctuary, and do not dwell here because this is not the place." (Jub. 32:21–23)[133]

Jacob's Tablets held history similar to the Tablets of the Division of Years, but these tablets specifically contained the authoritative history for understanding God's injunction against a sanctuary at Bethel. This

---

[132] Najman wrote the author of this type of transfer "rewrit[es], or more generally, imitate[es] textual traditions to which authority was already attached" by using already accepted authoritative texts to justify religious interpretations—see Hindy Najman, "The Inheritance of Prophecy in Apocalypse," in Collins, *OHAL*, 39. In the technical sense, this authoritative transfer was part of the complex authority structure referenced in the opening paragraph of this work, but here, the transfer was from an already understood literary authority to the book of Jubilees as a second authority from which the readers could operate in light of current temple practice and personal piety.

[133] The tablets were labeled "Jacob's Tablets" in this work for clarification.

history also undergirded Jubilean reliability.[134] As a whole, the four types of tablets listed here represented a single concept: writing that was explicitly (or even implicitly) ordained by God and inscribed on tablets was an authoritative recording of the unchanging, eternal truth.[135]

4.5.2.2. 1 Enoch 81.2

By comparison, the Enochian authors only referenced the Tablets of Heaven. P.Enoch presented the contents of these tablets in 1 En. 81:2:

---

[134] The Bethel-cultic tradition in Second Temple Judaism, including a possible post-captivity active temple, provided context to the necessity of Tablet authority against Bethel cultic activity. Esther Eshel, "Jubilees 32 and the Bethel Cult Traditions in Second Temple Literature," in *Things Revealed: Studies in Early Jewish and Christian Literature in Honor of Michael E. Stone*, SJSJ 89 (Leiden: Brill, 2004), 22.

[135] García Martínez argued the Tablets of Heaven were "the divine, pre-existing archetype of the Torah [Tablets of the Law]" (see Florentino García Martínez, *Between Philology and Theology: Contributions to the Study of Ancient Jewish Interpretation*, ed. Hindy Najman and E. J. C. Tigchelaar, SJSJ 162 [Leiden: Brill, 2012], 51–52). He referenced a variant of the Testament of Asher (variants *c, h, I,* and *j*) where a redactor interchanged the term "Tablets of Heaven" with "Tablets of the Law" to conclude these two sets of tablets were the same.

The problem, however, was this argument negated the differences between Torah and what was written in the text. In Jub. 4:32, Exod 21:12–35 seemed to be referenced; yet, as "ordained in the Tablets of Heaven," not only was punishment an eye for an eye, as the Torah stated, but a midrash was incorporated. "Eye for an Eye" was interpreted as "With the weapons with which a man kills his fellow, he shall be killed, just as he wounded him, thus shall they do to him." In 5:12, the punishment of the Watchers was written on the Tablets of Heaven as well. In 16:3, the Tablets of Heaven were a record of "ordained names, a list of sorts of those in history God had chosen"; and similarly, in 19:9, Abraham was "recorded as a friend of the Lord in the Tablets of Heaven." From these examples alone, it was difficult to conclude the Tablets of Heaven and Tablets of the Law were equivalent.

A preferred understanding was to see the text of the Tablets of the Law as part of the larger corpus, known as the Tablets of Heaven. Nevertheless, if García Martínez was correct, no inversion existed as argued above; rather, the source of authority was God writing the text with his finger, as Susan Niditch identified (discussed in the following subsection), which signified God's approval of both tablets through Divine Authority.

> Then he said unto me, "Enoch, look at the tablet(s) of heaven; read what is written upon them and understand (each element on them) one by one. So, I looked at the tablet(s) of heaven, read all the writing (on them), and came to understand everything. I read that book and all the deeds of humanity and all the children of the flesh upon the earth for all the generations of the world."

A variant reading of verse 2 provided clarification: "I read the book *of* all the deeds of humanity."[136] God's command to read, found in the first verse, dictated this book was equivalent to the Tablets of Heaven: "Enoch, look at the Tablets of Heaven; read what is written upon them and understand each element on them one by one." These Tablets of Heaven, therefore, equaled the Jubilean tablets of the same name containing the history of human activity up to the coming judgment (Jub. 24:33). The other three references to Tablets of Heaven in 1 Enoch followed this same pattern: "I...understood from the Tablets of Heaven" (93:2); "For I know this mystery, I have read the Tablets of Heaven" (103:1–2); and "The Lord has revealed (them) to me and made me know—and I have read (them) in the Tablets of Heaven" (106:19).

4.5.2.3. Testament of Levi

Like the Enochian P.author, the T. Levi author used only one name for tablets, although he called them the Tablets of the Fathers:

> At that time, I [The Angel Who Makes Intercession] put an end to the sons of Hamor, as is written in the Tablets of the Fathers. And I said to him, "I beg you, Lord, teach me your name, so that I may call on you in the day of tribulation." (5:4)

What were the Tablets of the Fathers? In context, they were historical documents—although not the Tablets of Heaven, they carried similar weight because the official version of the story occurred in them.

---

[136] Although late, two manuscripts, EMML 2080 from the fourteenth or fifteenth century and the Princeton Ethiopic 3 text from the eighteenth century (designated here as $\mathfrak{E}^{2080}$ and $\mathfrak{E}^{3}$, respectively), provided a clear reading that complemented the tristich found in these first two verses—cf. Isaac, "1 Enoch," in *OTP* 1:6; Nickelsburg, *1 Enoch* 1, 338–39.

Considering Second Temple Judaism, this statement most likely referenced some form of the Pentateuch.

Taken as a whole, tablets in Jewish apocalyptic literature represented a deposit of trustworthy writing. Authors who referenced them referenced unchanging truth, by which they gained authority. Authorial need dictated the type of tablet and reason for inclusion, but the tablets all symbolized delivery of eternal truth, except in Qumran. There, the tablets dictated preordination.

4.5.2.4. Qumran

Tablets of Heaven at Qumran focused on the ages of creation, which reflected an Enochian understanding:

> An interpretation concerning the ages which God made, an age to conclude [all that is] and will be. Before creating them, he established [their] work [according to every arrangement of the ages.] Age to age is engraved upon the tablets [of the heavens] for the [sons of man][for] all the ages of their dominion this is the arrangement of the son[s of Noah from Shem to Abraham]. (4Q180 f1:1–3)

In this text, authority fell not on the passage itself, but on the interpretation (as noted in chapter 5, "Qumran and Pesharim"). The focus of Qumran's authoritative topos, therefore, was strengthening the interpretation of God's ages and the following preordained earthly events.[137]

4.5.3. Step 4c: Text and Context—Germane Scholarship

This topos type related to an understanding of the power of inscribed words. The origin of *defixiones*, for instance, traced to a fourth century BCE Cretan tablet, and execration texts to at least 2000 BCE. The discussion of Orphic writings and tablets ventured into similar territory, although it focused more on Orphism as a craft of magic rather than religion and the nature of Orphic writing therein.[138] The power of

[137] Devorah Dimant, "Ages of Creation," *EDSS* 1:11.

[138] Rebecca Lesses, "Amulets and Angels: Visionary Experience in the Testament of Job and the Hekhalot Literature," in *Tablets of Heaven: Interpretation, Identity and Tradition in Ancient Judaism*, ed. Lynn R. Lidonnici and Andrea Lieber, SJSJ 119 (Leiden: Brill, 2007), 56; John G. Gager, "Introduction," in *Curse Tablets and Binding*

inscribed words also worked in tablet authority as seen in the curses set against anyone who changed or defaced the inscribed words on a tablet. Glenn Corbett identified similar ideas behind Num 5:11–28: "A woman accused of adultery is made to consume 'the water of bitterness,' a cloudy concoction infused with the washed-off ink from the words of a written curse."[139] This verse, along with Ezek 2:9–3:11, provided "clear indications that writing was often thought to have tangible, even magical properties."[140] These passages set the stage for early Judaic thought in which, by using different names of God in ritual, a person could "control angelic forces and powers."[141] Another concept of tablet authority was focused on the tablet itself. For instance, Susan Niditch argued that in Exod 31:18, God created the tablets by his finger and thus imparted his power into them, which resulted in "God [being] invested in the tablets."[142]

In the Jewish apocalyptic literature these concepts seemed to combine. For instance, Charlesworth, writing on the Testament of Levi, concluded the Tablets of the Fathers were a "record of divine historical decrees" and therefore unchangeable, equal to the law in divine origin.[143] Other scholars have noted tablets represented a well-used medium bearing inherent authority based on the inscribed words. Mark Elliott wrote that (heavenly) tablets described by Jewish apocalyptic authors "composed a storehouse of knowledge and contained the contents of the

---

Spells from the Ancient World, ed. John G. Gager (New York: Oxford University Press, 1999), 6, 28; Radcliffe G. Edmonds, "Sacred Scripture or Oracles for the Dead? The Semiotic Situation of the 'Orphic' Gold Tablets," in *The 'Orphic' Gold Tablets and Greek Religion: Further Along the Path*, ed. Radcliffe G. Edmonds (Cambridge: Cambridge University Press, 2011), 258.

[139] Glenn Corbett, "Word Play: The Power of the Written Word in Ancient Israel," *Bible History Daily: Biblical Archaelogy Society*, May 15, 2015, http://www.biblicalarchaeology.org/daily/biblical-artifacts/artifacts-and-the-bible/word-play/.

[140] Ibid.; also see Gabriel Barkay, "The Divine Name Found in Jerusalem," *BAR* 9.2 (1983): 14–19.

[141] S. Daniel Breslauer, "Secrecy and Magic, Publicity and Torah: Unpacking a Talmudic Tale," in *Magic and Ritual in the Ancient World*, ed. Paul Allan Mirecki and Marvin W. Meyer, RGRW 141 (Leiden: Brill, 2002), 265.

[142] Susan Niditch, *Oral World and Written Word: Ancient Israelite Literature*, ed. Douglas A. Knight, LAI (Louisville: Westminster John Knox Press, 1996), 79–80.

[143] H. C. Kee, "Testaments of the Twelve Patriarchs," in Charlesworth, *OTP* 1:790 n.4c.

perfect law, various secrets regarding God's plan for the righteous,... names of good and evil persons, and a list of their respective deeds."[144] Further, he noted the tablets were a connection to the covenant in Enoch.[145] From these examples, it seems that together, author, written word, and message all worked to create the Tablets topos type.

4.5.4. Step 4d: Cross-Text—Possible EAW Sources

Tablet inscriptions date back to at least the fourth millennium BCE, and perhaps, to the sixth.[146] References to an authoritative Tablets topos, however, were seldom found, and references to named tablets were rare.[147] Researchers have uncovered only five such tablets: the Covenant Tablet, the Tablet of Destinies, the Tablets with the Words of Fate, the Holy Tablet of the Heavenly Stars, and the Tablet of Wisdom.[148] In steps 3a–c, the first two tablet concepts scored highest for a possible parent-child relationship with Jewish apocalyptic writing.

---

[144] Elliott, *Survivors of Israel*, 287.

[145] Ibid., 288.

[146] The Dispilio tablet, found in Greece, was dated to the late sixth millennium BCE, as was the Tărtăria tablet, which was found in a dig in Transylvania. Both tablets were said to contain a form of writing; however, for the Tărtăria tablet, controversy surrounded both the dating, and the find itself.

In Mesopotamia, as far back as the third millennium, "the idea of books and tablets in heaven, in which the destinies and the behavior of men are written down in advance, or in the beginning, is widespread" (Yorgos Facorellis, Marina Sofronidou, and Giorgos Hourmouziadis, "Radiocarbon Dating of the Neolithic Lakeside Settlement of Dispilio, Kastoria, Northern Greece," *Radiocarbon* 56.2 (2014): 526; cf. Marco Merlini, "Settling Discovery Circumstances, Dating, and Utilization of the Tărtăria Tablets," in *Proceedings of the International Colloquium: The Carpathian Basin and Its Role in the Neolithisation of the Balkan Peninsula*, ed. Sabin A. Luca, ATS 7 [Lucian: Blaga University, 2008], 112, 117; Hans Bietenhard, *Die Himmlische Welt im Urchristentum und Spätjudentum* [Tübingen: Mohr, 1951], 231).

[147] See, for instance, the story of "Ba'al and Yam," lines 25–26; "Edict of Ammisaduga"; "The Egyptian Famine Stela"; the Unchangeable Tablet found in the *Tukulti-Ninurta* epic where the Babylonian king complained about an "unopposable treaty of my fathers"; and as mentioned above, the scribal notes or curses concluding a tablet.

[148] "Words of Fate" may have been a description and not a title. The term "Tablets of Law" occurred twice in Cicero (*Divination* 1.19; 2.47) but the reference was to general tablets containing laws, and more importantly, it was not used authoritatively.

4.5.4.1. Covenant Tablet: "Second Oracle of Salvation (to Esarhaddon)"

As a phrase, "covenant tablet" occurred in the cuneiform tablets among the oracles uncovered in Nineveh; one oracle, however, doubled as Ashur's covenant, occasioning Esarhaddon's enthronement:

> I slaughtered your enemies and filled the River with their blood. Let them see it and praise me, for I am Ashur, lord of the gods! This is the oracle of peace placed before the statue. This covenant tablet of Ashur enters the king's presence on a cushion. Fragrant oil is sprinkled, sacrifices are made, incense is burnt and (the tablet) is read out before the king.[149]

Although debatable whether the term was an actual title, its use here represented a single tablet. The context for this topos type occurrence was significant: a king sought deliverance from his enemies, and in response, the head deity delivered him by destroying the enemy through fire and brimstone. In this case, the tablet became the covenant medium carried on a cushion and read before the king. In comparing this covenant to the Tablets of the Law in Hebraic literature, one difference came immediately to light: in the Tanakh material, a prophet delivered the God-initiated covenant to Israel.[150] In an ironic twist to other authoritative topoi, however, these differences in context highlighted similarities.

First, God covenanted with Israel through the Tablets of the Law after delivering them from Egypt. Likewise, Esarhaddon received the covenant tablet as a promise of deliverance. Second, God commanded all Israelites to hear the reading of the covenant, but for the Ninevite Covenant Tablet, the audience was only the king—however, the Assyrian king and Israelite nation were the intended recipients of their respective covenants. Third, the Tablets of the Law remained in the ark, which served as YHWH's seat in the temple, whereas the Covenant Tablet rested on a cushion delivered to the king. However, the Israelite temple also represented a

---

[149] "Oracle to Esarhaddon," trans. Choon L. Seow (*Prophets and Prophecy in the Ancient Near East*, SAA 9 3.2:119); Eckart Otto, *Das Deuteronomium: Politische Theologie und Rechtsreform in Juda und Assyrien*, reprint ed., BZAW 128 (Berlin: de Gruyter, 1999), 80. See step 4d under the Covenant topos type for a further discussion of the context concerning this tablet.

[150] The author of Deut 18:15, 18, and 34:10 called Moses a prophet.

throne room,[151] and the king, in his throne room, received the Covenant Tablet amid cultic activity (sprinkled oil, sacrifices, and incense).[152] Unfortunately, these commonplace likenesses extended to covenants and treaty tablets across several EAW cultures, which negated the influence of any single covenant document over Jewish apocalyptic literature. Therefore, while a parent-child relationship may exist with a general idea of Covenant in the EAW world, no apparent relationship exists between Jewish apocalyptic and EAW texts or Hebraic movements.[153]

4.5.4.2. Tablet of Destinies

The Tablet of Destinies appeared in several EAW writings. The three strongest possibilities were the Babylonian version of the Akkadian Anzu story, the "Enūma Elish," and "Erra and Ishum." These stories all originated as Mesopotamian narratives.[154]

4.5.4.2.1. Babylonian Version of the Akkadian Anzu Story

"Tablet of Destinies" occurred once in what remained of the Old Babylonian version of the Akkadian Anzu story and eleven times in the standard Babylonian version. The tale concerned Anzu's theft of Enlil's Tablet of Destinies, which disrupted authority and sent the universe spinning toward chaos:

---

[151] Marc Z. Brettler, *God Is King: Understanding an Israelite Metaphor*, JSOTSup 76 (Sheffield: JSOT Press, 1989), 92.

[152] The "Assyrian scholars...generated[ed] an Assyrian ideological program centered on the figure as the human agent of the supreme god, Aššur." Moreover, the "king's primary task [was] securing cosmic order." Beate Pongratz-Leisten, *Religion and Ideology in Assyria*, Studies in Ancient Near Eastern Records 6 (Boston: de Gruyter, 2015), 390.

[153] See, for instance, Kitchen and Lawrence, *TLC* 1. Another tablet attributed to Esarhaddon was found at Tel Tayinat. This tablet, however, was meant to bind loyalty to Esarhaddon's son, Ashurbanipal through an oath. The oath was hung in the temple at Tel Tayinat, but several reasons may have existed for doing so. It was thought this oath might have been read publicly. Note the difference between this oath and the covenant referenced above. See also Gary M. Beckman, *Hittite Diplomatic Texts*, ed. Harry A. Hoffner, WAW 7, 2nd ed. (Atlanta: Scholars Press, 1999), 11–124; Jacob Lauinger, "Some Preliminary Thoughts on the Tablet Collection in Building XVI from Tell Tayinat," *Canadian Society for Mesopotamiam Studies* 6 (2001): 12; "Esarhaddon's Succession Treaty at Tell Tayinat," *JCS* 64 (2012): 89–90.

[154] Note, the Nimrud tablets, once sealed, became the Tablet of Destinies. These tablets, however, originated as covenant tablets (or, more precisely oath tablets). See A. R. George, "Sennacherib and the Tablet of Destinies," *Iraq* 48 (1986): 133–46.

> Anzu often watched the father of the gods, the god (of) Duranki, and in his heart imagined removing the supremacy: "I myself will take the gods' Tablet of Destinies and gather the assignments of all the gods. I will win the throne, be the master of the offices! I will give command to all the Igigi!" (tablet 1: 69–76).[155]

The referential authority of the Tablet of Destinies did not move readers to action but reminded them of the gods' assigned roles. By removing the Tablet of Destinies, Anzu erased the authority by which the gods worked: "To the Tablet of Destinies his hands reached out. The supremacy he took—suspended are the offices!" (lines 81–82). The power of this tablet came in 2:66–67: "As [Anzu] raised the Tablet of Destinies of the gods with his hands, the darts, carried by bowstring, could not approach his body." Thus, the tablet held authority for deity assignments and warded against enemies. These roles were absent in Second Temple apocalyptic literature, which created a meaningful difference among a lack of three verbal contacts and denied a parent-child relationship.

4.5.4.2.2. "Enūma Elish"

The Tablet of Destinies also appeared in the "Enūma Elish." On tablet 1:148, Tiamat raised Qingu (or "Kingu" in some translations) as her consort and placed him in charge of all the Annuna gods. The author symbolized this role by having Tiamat hand Qingu the Tablet of Destinies and remarking, "As for you, your command will not be changed, your utterance will be eternal" (1:57–58). Later, Marduk took the Tablet of Destinies from Qingu and "sealed it with a seal and affixed it to his chest" (tablet 4:121); thus, the Tablet topos type announced his victory and supremacy.

Although associations might be made with the Israelites receiving the tablets at Mount Sinai after their god's victory against Egypt, no such argument occurred in Jubilees (or the other apocalyptic writings studied here). Instead, the P.author chose to associate the tablets with an ongoing covenant between God and Israel (as explored in chapter 4 under the Covenant topos type). As a result, three points of verbal contact did not exist between these texts, but meaningful differences did, which negated a parent-child relationship.

---

155 "The Akkadian Anzu Story," trans. Marianna Vogelzang (*COS* 3.147:327–34).

4.5.4.2.3. "Erra and Ishum"

A third narrative in which this tablet appeared was in "Erra and Ishum," a wandering story of a war narrowly avoided. Ishum recounted his accomplishments to Erra before moving to a series of woes from Marduk. The final woe was to Babylon: "Woe to Babylon, which I have taken in my hands like the Tablet of Destinies and will not deliver to anyone else."

Without other contextual clues, the reader had to refer to other EAW sources to understand the tablet name. The Tablet of Destinies, therefore, referenced a divinely held tablet whose bearer became heaven's sovereign. Thus, the sovereign was authorized to assign offices to deities, one of which could be a keeper of the tablet (such as Marduk's son, Nabû, who kept the tablets for Marduk).[156]

As noted for the previous two occurrences, these uses and roles for the tablets were absent from Second Temple apocalyptic material, creating meaningful differences and a lack of three verbal contacts. Therefore, a parent-child relationship did not exist between the "Erra and Ishum" text and Second Temple apocalyptic material.

4.5.5. Step 4e: Cross-Text—Possible Tanakh Sources

A search for "tablet" in the Tanakh produced forty-three hits for variants of לוח and two for גלה. Of the latter, neither employed authority nor referred to the concepts explored here. For the former, the author(s) of Exodus and Deuteronomy used לוח for concepts significant to this study thirty-two times (sixteen times per book). Other biblical authors used this term twice in Proverbs (where it was a metaphor), and once each in 1 Kings, Isaiah, Jeremiah, Habakkuk, and 2 Chronicles. So, how did these uses align with the Second Temple apocalyptic authors' uses of "tablet"?

References to the Tablets of Heaven, the Tablets of the Division of Years, and Jacob's Tablets were absent from the Tanakh, leaving only the Tablets of the Law. Starting in Exod 24:12, the author wrote, "And then YHWH said to Moses, 'Come up to me on the mountain

[156] According to Jean-Jacques Glassner, in the New Year festival of Babylon, "the gods set down in writing on the 'Tablet of Destinies' the destiny of the king and the country for the following year" (*Mesopotamian Chronicles*, ed. Benjamin R. Foster, WAW 19 [Atlanta: Society of Biblical Literature, 2004], 81). This concept followed the general idea above—the holder of the tablet assigned the roles (and in this case, the destiny).

[and] remain there! And I will give to you the tablets of stone.'" Was the reference to the Tablets of Stone synonymous with Tablets of the Law? In Deut 9:9, the following clause modified or further identified the Tablets of Stone: "When I ascended the mountain to take the tablets of stone; tablets of the covenant that YHWH wrote for you." This pattern repeated in 9:10, "And then YHWH gave me two tablets of stone written by the finger of God"; and again in 9:11, "YHWH gave to me two tablets of stone, tablets of the covenant." The same held true for this term in 1 Kgs 8:9, creating a pattern also found in the conclusion of Exod 24:12: "And I will give you the tablets of stone and the law and the commandments that I wrote for their instruction." These modifications and clarifications indicated "Tablets of Stone" was not a stand-alone title synonymous with Tablets of the Law, but an adjectival phrase needing further delimitation.

If Jewish apocalyptic authors drew Tablets of the Law from this phrase, they did so by creating a title where one did not originally exist in the Tanakh or in relation to a Hebraic movement. As a result, three points of verbal contact did not exist for Tablets of the Law. Furthermore, shifting "tablets of the law" from an adjectival phrase to a title in Second Temple apocalyptic material created a meaningful difference. Therefore, no parent-child relationship existed for this topos type between the Tanakh and Second Temple apocalyptic literature.[157]

4.5.6. Step 4f: Evaluation

Similarities existed between Esarhaddon's Covenant Tablet and Tablets of the Law as Jewish apocalyptic writers understood it. However, evidence showed these similarities existed across the EAW. Therefore, no parent-child relationship existed between a specific EAW text or culture and Second Temple apocalyptic literature.

References to the Tablet of Destinies in EAW texts had only one verbal point of contact with the Tablets of Heaven in Jewish texts: they both recorded events. However, the Tablets of Heaven also incorporated the Jewish Torah. Further, missing from the Jewish Tablets of Heaven was the concept of possession equaling divine supremacy and authority to

[157] This argument did not negate tablets of stone deriving from the Tanakh and being based in the Sinaitic event, rather, it negated tablets of stone existing as its own topos type in the Tanakh.

assign offices. These significant differences and lack of three verbal contacts negate a parent-child relationship between EAW literature and Jewish apocalyptic material.

The Tanakh also failed to hold three points of verbal contact while evidencing meaningful differences. However, the Jubilean author grounded authority for the Tablets of Heaven in the Tablet of the Law in the historical (from the Second Temple author's point of view) Sinai event. Therefore, a general idea of tablet authority most likely derived from Mosaic law, but Second Temple Judaism shaped the meaning for the apocalyptic P.author.

Likewise, Second Temple Judaism shaped the understanding of this topos type in Qumran. There, the Tablets of Heaven were part of the community's understanding of God's historical program, predestination, and the coming eschaton. Although a superficial similarity existed in the use of Tablets of Heaven, too many meaningful differences negated any relationship. As such, there was no parent-child relationship between EAW literature and Qumran material for this topos type.

4.6. Chapter Evaluation

Observations of the four topoi types in this chapter led to the conclusion that general similarities existed with EAW sources, but the points of verbal contact often disappeared amid closer research, distracting dissimilarities, and meaningful differences. In three texts, however, the verbal contacts withstood scrutiny. Two of these texts were related to the Revelation of Secrets topos type (the "Tradition of Seven Lean Years" and *Prometheus Bound*). These texts held strong, multiple similarities, but they were inversions—proofs against other gods. The third text was the "Second Oracle of Salvation," but the points of verbal contact with this text were not unique. Instead, they were based on covenant formulas found throughout the EAW and therefore indicate a parent-child relationship to the overall concept in the EAW (although most-likely filtered through the Tanakh).[158] As a result, the four topos types studied in this chapter were not in a parent-child relationship with EAW material.

---

[158] The focus of the apocalyptic texts concerning covenants on tablets was the Sinaitic covenant, which was specific to the Tanakh. Therefore, the parent-child relationship extended to both EAW and Tanakh texts.

Concerning the Hebraic movements, although several similarities existed, no authoritative topos type could be linked to a Hebraic movement. The topos type coming closest was Divinely Ordained Journeys. However, this topos type showed a trajectory in the Hebraic material that was completed in the Second Temple period. The trajectory indicated a parent-child relationship with the Tanakh, but the texts were too dissimilar to associate them with a Hebraic movement. Likewise, the concept of tablets also existed in the Tanakh, but the occurrences lacked specificity for assigning a parent-child relationship between topos type occurrences.

How, then, did Second Temple authors establish authority concerning the topoi presented in this chapter? They borrowed from widely available concepts across the EAW and from the Tanakh, but they were filtered through the milieu of Jewish Second Temple culture and history. The authority for these topos types lay in Second Temple Judaism, and through these authorities, the authors commended their readers to certain beliefs or practices. In a few instances, however, an author used an authoritative topos to signify an inversion arguing for Jewish cultic or cultural superiority. In these texts, the authoritative topos was used to make the connection between the texts.

In the next chapter, the four topos that, prima facie, stemmed equally from the EAW and Hebraic roots were examined. Were these topos types used in similar patterns? To answer that question, Step 4 was repeated four more times.[159]

---

[159] Again, the observations made in chapters 3–5 concerned literary comparisons only as they pertained to authoritative topos types.

Chapter 5
POSSIBLE PRIMA FACIE DERIVATION OF AUTHORITATIVE TOPOI ACCORDING TO PRELIMINARY RESULTS: EAW OR TANAKH LITERATURE

So-and-So never slays dragons. Only famous persons do famous things.

—Christopher Collins, *Authoritative Metaphors*

5.1. Introduction

In his work on orality and stories, Christopher Collins proposed names attached to tales became references that recalled entire narratives. In such narratives, the character associated with the name survived trials and ordeals. These stories, and later, the characters who invoked memories of the stories, were authoritative and available as referents for subsequent authors.[1] One such authoritative topos drawn from these stories was Pseudepigraphy.[2] EAW and Jewish P.authors alike appropriated ancient names from these stories to legitimize or strengthen their didactic tales. Such stories also took on a second authority as it morphed into common knowledge.

Pseudepigraphy and Common Knowledge were investigated in this chapter, along with Covenant and Cosmology. Of the nine topos types, these four evidenced a prima facie possibility of deriving from EAW or Tanakh literature equally. As previously described, the study of these topos types was divided into six substeps (4a–f). Step 4a provided an overview of the authoritative topos type in EAW material concerning its use in Second Temple apocalyptic literature. Thus, it served to introduce each topos type. Step 4b was a presentation of the topos type occurrences in Second Temple apocalyptic literature most likely to evidence a parent-child relationship with EAW or Tanakh

[1] Christopher Collins, *Authority Figures: Metaphors of Mastery from the Iliad to the Apocalypse* (Lanham: Rowman and Littlefield Publishers, 1996), 51, 57.

[2] Pseudepigraphy and pseudonymity were synonymous in this study, differing only in the sense that the former term focused on the written material, and the latter, on the author.

material. In step 4c, germane scholarship informed the study on textual questions, significant contributions to the scholarly debate concerning the topos type, and other relevant issues. Steps 4d–e were the cross-text sections for each step in which the EAW and Tanakh material was examined. Finally, step 4f was an evaluation of the topos type after observation. These substeps were applied to the Pseudepigraphy topos type first.

5.2. Literary Authority through Written Language: Pseudepigraphy

Pseudepigraphy as a method of writing had been well documented from several cultures in the EAW, as well as in Second Temple Judaism. It should be noted, however, that the method has not been limited to the apocalyptic material. For instance, in the Letter of Aristeas, the P.author portrayed himself as a Ptolemy II court member writing etiologic Septuagint tales. The purpose was to propose the Septuagint as "an independent scriptural authority for Alexandrian Jews."[3] Consequently, by writing as a Ptolemaic Gentile, the Jewish author also pushed other Alexandrians to understand "the centrality of Moses as a legislator and the Septuagint for Jewish identity."[4] This example exemplified the central tenant of pseudepigraphy: writing under another's name provided an authority not originally available to the P.author.

5.2.1. Step 4a: Text—Definition and Use of Authority

Within this study, the Pseudepigraphy topos type was defined as writing under a false name that carried authority as it pertained to apocalyptic literature. Authors chose to write under these false names because the names transferred authority. Therefore, if an author borrowed the name of Moses, for instance, this process would allow "a 'new' law ...[to be] characterized as the Law of Moses."[5] For that characterization to occur, however, the borrowed name had to be recognized within the intended audience's community as an authoritative figure. As a result, the

[3] Benjamin G. Wright, "Pseudonymous Authorship and Structures of Authority in the *Letter of Aristeas*," in *Scriptural Authority in Early Judaism and Ancient Christianity*, ed. Isaac Kalimi, Tobias Nicklas, and Géza G. Xeravits, DCLS, ed. Friedrich V. Reiterer, Beate Ego, and Tobias Nicklas, vol. 15 (Berlin: de Gruyter, 2013), 45–46.

[4] Ibid., 58.

[5] Hindy Najman, *Seconding Sinai: The Development of Mosaic Discourse in Second Temple Judaism* (Leiden: Brill, 2003), 13.

Pseudonymity topos type inherently relied on the Authority by Name topos type for legitimization.

5.2.2. Step 4b: Text and Context—Use in Apocalyptic Literature

Reading each apocalyptic writing synchronically,[6] the authoritative topos began in the superscriptions. The superscriptions help establish authority for the author's message.

5.2.2.1. Literature Outside of Qumran

In 1 Enoch, a P.author produced the following superscription before its final Ethiopian form:

> The blessing of Enoch: with which he blessed the elect and the righteous who would be present on the day of tribulation at (the time of) the removal of all the ungodly ones.[7]

When the P.author substituted Enoch for Moses in Deut 33:1 ("And this is the blessing with which Moses, the man of God, blessed the Israelites before his death"), a paired topos was created consisting of Authority by Name and Authority through Pseudepigraphy, which drew again from a third topos type—Short Quotation.[8]

Choosing Enoch as the P.author for 2 Enoch built on the earlier 1 Enoch traditions; however, his character was distinct in 2 Enoch, wherein he transmuted into a heavenly being "exalted above the angelic world."[9] The superscription to 2 Enoch was peculiar as well, in the sense that certain discrepancies existed among manuscripts. Although the A recension lacked any introduction, J began, "The story of Enoch: how the Lord took him to heaven," which built on Gen 5:24: "Enoch walked with God, and he was no more because God took him." Thus, the P.author

---

[6] The synchronic approach was not intended to ignore temporal issues. Instead, it was a recognition that authors much closer to the date of origin for these texts identified the authority (Authority by Name) by which the messages were delivered.

[7] Pre-Qumran, the introduction was thought to be the final written section, according to "the consensus of critical scholars" (see E. Isaac, "1 Enoch," in Charlesworth, *OTP* 1:7). Nickelsburg presented the superscription as being "for the successive stages of 1 Enoch for which chapters 1–5 served as the introduction" and therefore, possibly an earlier origination—see Nickelsburg, *1 Enoch* 1, 135.

[8] Isaac, "1 Enoch," 7. Short quotation was explored in chapter 4 (above).

[9] Orlov, "Enoch, Slavonic Apocalypse of," 589.

identified authority for the narrative in the Genesis account and then borrowed it for his 2 Enoch work.

In terms of the book of Jubilees, the Jubilean P.author opened with an expanded version of Moses's stay on Sinai:

> In the first year of the Exodus of the children of Israel from Egypt, in the third month on the sixteenth day of that month, the LORD spoke to Moses, saying, "Come up to me on the mountain, and I shall give you two stone Tablets of the Law and the commandment, which I have written, so that you may teach them."

By doing so, the Jubilean P.author paired P.Mosaic authorship with Torah authority, drawing from Exod 31:38: "And he gave to Moses—when he had finished speaking to him on Mount Sinai—two tablets of the testimony, tablets of stone inscribed by the finger of God." The P.authors of the Testament of Moses and Testament of Levi followed likewise, although not as explicitly. Overall, these superscriptions in apocalyptic texts invoked shades of the prophetic movement, in the sense that, like "Isaiah, Jeremiah, Ezekiel, and Zechariah,...[they] speak with supernatural authority."[10] Thus, these superscriptions show the P.authors' authority was borrowed from ancient names and possibly from the prophetic movement; yet these pseudonymous writers also intertwined several additional authoritative topoi to advance their messages.

5.2.2.2. Literature from Qumran

Jubilees and 1 Enoch constituted the largest body of pseudepigraphical writing at Qumran. Additionally, archeologists found fragments of the Testaments of Levi, Judah, and Naphtali in the caves.[11] Beyond these texts, however, the community also kept material concerning the Giants, Noah, and over thirty other pseudepigraphical writings, most or all of which were "not obviously

---

[10] Baum, "Revelatory Experience," 75.

[11] John Collins argued these scrolls and fragments were not renderings, but copies of source material for the Testaments of the Twelve Patriarchs—see Collins, "Apocrypha and Pseudepigrapha," *EDSS*, 37. Note, the paragraph containing this citation followed the basic outline of Collins's subsection on Pseudepigrapha.

or necessarily of sectarian origin."[12] Stuckenbruck also noted the non-Qumran origins of the Aramaic material found among the scrolls.[13] However, Moshe Bernstein went further, stating no pseudepigraphical apocalyptic material was native to Qumran and that "pseudepigraphy was superfluous for the writing of legal codes."[14] Consequently, all that remained to study at Qumran stemmed from pre-Qumran origins.[15] As such, Qumran was not a factor for studying this topos type among the Jewish apocalyptic literature.

5.2.3. Step 4c: Text and Context—Germane Scholarship

Was it possible for a falsely authored document to be authoritative for Second Temple religious communities?[16] Waldemer labeled these

---

[12] Ibid., 38.

[13] Loren Stuckenbruck, "Pseudepigraphy and First Person Discourse in the Dead Sea Documents: From the Aramaic Texts to Writings of the Yaḥad," in *Dead Sea Scrolls and Contemporary Culture: Proceedings of the International Conference Held at the Israel Museum, Jerusalem (July 6–8, 2008)*, ed. Adolfo Roitman, Lawrence H. Schiffman, and Shani Tzoref, STDJ 93 (Leiden: Brill, 2011), 296–97.

[14] Moshe Bernstein, "Pseudepigraphy in the Qumran Scrolls: Categories and Functions," in *Pseudepigraphic Perspectives: The Apocrypha and Pseudepigrapha in Light of the Dead Sea Scrolls; Proceedings of the International Symposium of the Orion Center for the Study of the Dead Sea Scrolls and Associated Literature, 12–14 January, 1997*, ed. Esther G. Chazon, Michael E. Stone and Avital Pinnick, 1–26, STDJ 31 (Leiden: Brill, 1999), 24, 26, 9. He also argued a complete absence of attributions to sapiential fathers, such as Solomon—cutting across scholars attributing apocalyptic work to the wisdom movement.

[15] Any work in this study on Qumran would have largely replicated Bernstein. Therefore, his conclusions concerning Qumran apocalyptic material were accepted here.

[16] A follow-up question was *why* use forgery, or pseudonymity, in the ancient world? Charles argued three issues stood in the way of Jews keeping "fresh faith and truth," and it was because of these three issues that pseudepigraphy came about: (1) the end of prophetic spirit; (2) the rise of the Torah as supreme authority; and (3) textual stagnation and eventual canonicity—see Robert H. Charles, *A Critical History of the Doctrine of a Future Life in Israel, in Judaism, and in Christianity, or, Hebrew, Jewish, and Christian Eschatology from Pre-Prophetic Times Till the Close of the New Testament Canon*, 2nd rev. ed. (London: A. and C. Black, 1989), 202–04. Metzger identified at least seven reasons (the following list is a combination of direct copy and consolidated ideas): (1) desire for financial gain; (2) malice; (3) love and respect for the supposed author; (4) modesty; (5) accidents, such as erroneous attribution of authorship to treaties; (6) identification with ancient figures; and (7) unknown reasons—see Bruce M. Metzger, "Literary Forgeries and Canonical Pseudepigrapha," *JBL* 91.1 (1972): 5–10. For a history of scholarship on this issue, see David G. Meade, *Pseudonymity and*

documents "forgeries," arguing that forgery "competes with or subverts the authorized production and circulation of meaning."[17] He further stated that forgeries "counterfeit authority" because identity relied solely on "the nature and authority of the original it has stolen or mimicked."[18] The problem in the apocalyptic literature, however, was that with the exception of Moses, the names associated with the writings often carried no literary authority for the P.author to borrow (see, for instance, the figures of Enoch and Levi, both of whom supposedly authored apocalyptic works, but held no Tanakh material). Thus, by modern standards and a definition of forgery as the replication of writing and passing it off as the original, few pseudepigraphs deserved consideration as forgeries (sans the Testament of Moses).

Vicente Dobroruka agreed with this assessment: "To assume that pseudepigraphic apocalypses are an imitation of something else supposes, evidently, that there are originals to be imitated.... And, if a forgery is to be successful it depends upon the skillful imitation of the original."[19] The issue of forgery and modern standards raised another (and more important) question: How did cultures in classical antiquity view this material, and subsequently, how did they view authority borrowed by the P.author?

Stuckenbruck believed pseudepigraphical authorship was "not only widespread but also widely received" among Jews and Gentiles in the Second Temple period;[20] so well received, in fact, that communities would not reject known pseudepigraphical writings for that reason alone. He argued students following Pythagoras and Plato wrote not in their names but used the names of Pythagoras and Plato, which was how they "express[ed] their humility, indebtedness, and devotion in relation to the received tradition."[21]

Canon: An Investigation into the Relationship of Authorship and Authority in Jewish and Earliest Christian Tradition (Grand Rapids: Eerdmans, 1987), 4–12.

[17] Waldemer, "Hijacking Authority," 49.

[18] Ibid.

[19] Vicente Dobroruka, *Second Temple Pseudepigraphy: A Cross-Cultural Comparison of Apocalyptic Texts and Related Jewish Literature*, Ekstasis: Religious Experience from Antiquity to the Middle Ages, ed. John R. Levison, vol. 4 (Berlin: de Gruyter, 2014), 134.

[20] Stuckenbruck, "Apocrypha and Pseudepigrapha," 154.

[21] Ibid., 155.

In other circumstances, authors scribed texts against competing interpretations in intermural disputes. Stuckenbruck offered 1 En. 104:10–11 as an example:

> And now I know this mystery: For they (the sinners) shall alter the just verdict and many sinners will take it to heart; they will speak evil words and lie, and they will invent fictitious stories and write out my Scriptures on the basis of their own words. And would that they had written down all the words truthfully on the basis of their own speech, and neither alter nor take away from my words, all of which I testify to them from the beginning!

Indeed, the Enochian author accused others of "invent[ing] fictitious stories and writ[ing] out my scriptures based on their own words" when they published material in their own names,[22] thereby leading the community astray. The P.author, therefore, believed himself to be the "authentic interpreter and transmitter of Enochic revelation"; and others "[had] subverted or misrepresented the Enoch tradition they [had] all received."[23] Not all modern scholars, however, accepted this position. Dobroruka dismissed the respectful-pseudonymity argument. He wrote the idea was "something which cannot be proved to have ever existed."[24] Likewise, pointing to a Tertullian passage often quoted for praising pseudonymity, he argued it was impossible to infer any such understanding, leaving respectful-pseudonymity a construct of modern scholarship.[25]

Armin Baum, also looking at intent in authorship, concluded recipients of a "genuine visionary experience" who wrote under a pseudonym intended to deceive; however, if the author "published his book orthonymously under his own name," then he intended no deception.[26] Baum's underlying argument concerned legitimacy. He believed deceptive naming delegitimized a work and made it

---

[22] Ibid., 156.

[23] Ibid.

[24] Dobroruka, *Second Temple Pseudepigraphy*, 136.

[25] Ibid., 137.

[26] Baum, "Revelatory Experience," 92. Baum defined "genuine" in "genuine visionary experience" as any experience an author believed to have received.

unacceptable for a faith community.[27] Nevertheless, whether or not the communities accepted pseudepigraphical writing, the author still used pseudepigraphical writing with the intention of gaining acceptance for the text within the community. As such, the author was still using pseudepigraphy as an authority. The follow-up question is why would an author write under a false name if doing so failed to hold authority? Doing so would invalidate the author's purpose of writing. Therefore, it follows that the targeted community most-likely accepted the text as suggested by the translation of 1 Enoch, Jubilees, and other such books into a second language (and later, as they passed into the Christian church, into a third or fourth language) as well as their inclusion at Qumran. Although it would be remiss to argue positive reception occurred anywhere except in the circles responsible for duplication and transmission, it would also be remiss to negate positive reception probably occurred in these communities.[28] The question, then, is where did this topos type originate?

5.2.4. Step 4d: Cross-Text—Possible EAW Sources

From the observations in steps 3a–c, the three cultures showing the strongest potential sources for a parent-child relationship were the Akkadian, Egyptian, and Greek cultures. Note, however, the Akkadian stories often originated in Sumer and as often, descended through Babylonian culture.

---

[27] In a follow-up article, Baum interacted with Petr Pokorný's theological argument justifying NT pseudepigraphical writing based on Jacob's deceptions in Genesis 27. He concluded Petr Porkorný's arguments were "not conclusive" because they "are not in keeping with the inner logic of the analogy, which is based on a distinction between the actor and his deed." However, he left open the possibility of "more convincing arguments" in the future—see Armin D. Baum, "A Theological Justification for the Canonical Status of Literary Forgeries: Jacob's Deceit (Genesis 27) and Petr Pokorný's Sola Gratia Argument," *JETS* 55.2 (2012): 289–90; see also Petr Pokorný and Ulrich Heckel, *Einleitung in das Neue Testament: Seine Literatur und Theologie im Überblick*, Uni-Taschenbücher 2798 (Tübingen: Mohr Siebeck, 2007).

[28] Moreover, whether or not the communities accepted pseudepigraphical writing, the author still used pseudepigraphical writing with the intention of gaining acceptance for the text from the community. As such, the author was still using pseudepigraphy as an authority. Of course, the follow-up question is why would an author write under another name if that name failed to carry authority? Doing so would invalidate the author's entire purpose of writing and as such, it follows the targeted community most likely accepted the text.

5.2.4.1. Akkadian-Akkad-Babylonian

Of the Sumer-Akkad-Babylonian pseudepigraphic works, "The Adad-Guppi Autobiography," "The Autobiography of Idrimi," "The Marduk Prophecy," and "The Dynastic Prophecy" were perhaps the most famous. However, for this study, the "Autobiography of Idrimi" and "The Marduk Prophecy" failed to further the discussion on the Pseudepigraphy topos type and thus was not examined in this work.[29]

5.2.4.1.1. "The Adad-Guppi Autobiography"

In this tale, the P.author claimed to be Adad-Guppi, the "mother of Nabunaid, king of Babylon, a worshipper of Sin, Ningal, and Nusku, and Sadarnunna, my gods, for whose divinity I have cared since my youth."[30] Her story read like a hagiography, creating authority for the final exhortation:

> [Whoever] you are—whether king, prince [ ] in the land. [Continually stand watch] for Sin, the king [of the gods], the lord of the gods of heaven and earth, his great divinity and reverence [the divinities of heaven and] earth who [ ] dwell in Esagil and Eḫulḫul and pray (to the divinities) in heaven and earth and [ ] the command of Sin and Ishtar who saves [ ] keep your seed safe forever and ever.

Of greatest concern was the worship of Sin (and perhaps, Ishtar). The authority for this exhortation to worship derived from righteousness, but the author had to build the character in the eyes of the reader. The author, therefore, depended on recognized cultic acts and a storytelling ability to manufacture authority, rather than a Righteousness topos type. This dependence negated righteousness as a point of verbal contact with Jewish apocalyptic texts. Further, the teleological purpose of this

[29] The focus of Idrimi's autobiography was recounting Idrimi's life before announcing a curse on anyone who removed the statue. Although it may be argued the writer used an authoritative topos by using the Pseudepigraphy topos type—writing in Idrimi's name to protect the statue—it was a stretch to argue it was an attempt to norm beliefs or behavior. However, even if considered an authoritative topos (by norming behavior toward the statue), the scores for context and word picture would have delimited it in the preliminary study.

[30] "The Adad-Guppi Autobiography," trans. Tremper Longman III (*COS* 1.147:477–78).

narrative focused on proving Adad-Guppi's righteousness from which the P.author could then urge general cultic activities and perspectives. Conversely, the P.authors of 1 and 2 Enoch explicitly declared their character's righteousness, which was paired with the Authority by Name topos type. The teleological purpose of this narrative was not to be a proof for righteousness but to be a didactic tool legitimated by righteousness. This distinction created a meaningful difference and, coupled with no points of verbal contact, disallowed a parent-child relationship between this text and Second Temple material concerning the Righteousness topos type.

5.2.4.1.2. "The Dynastic Prophecy"

Two problems with "The Dynastic Prophecy" bore mentioning before examination: (1) time and elements severely damaged the original text, and (2) the author was not pseudepigraphic, but anonymous (unless otherwise named in missing parts of the text). The prophecy was included here because two themes were similar to Second Temple apocalyptic material and necessitated a closer study: prophetic utterances and an eschatological motif. These two themes created two points of verbal contact, and anonymous authorship originally created a third, albeit weak point of verbal contact before further investigation.

Beginning with prophecy, the author portrayed a war ending with a king taking control; later, a prophesied rebel prince would rise and establish the Harran dynasty, reigning for several years. The current text ended with Enlil, Shamash, and Marduk, who would engage in divine warfare at the side of another king and overthrow the Hanaean army. This text resembled Dan 11:2–45,[31] and held similarities to Second Temple material.

The eschatological theme began with the rebel prince and ended in the following passage:

> Afterward [his ar]my will regroup and raise their weapons. Enlil, Shamash, and [Marduk] will go at the side of his ar[my]. He will bring about the overthrow of the Hanaean army. He will [carry] off his extensive booty [and bring] it into his palace. The people

[31] "The Dynastic Prophecy," trans. Tremper Longman III (*COS* 1.149:480–81).

> who had ex[perienced] misfortune [will enjoy] well-being. The mood of the land [. . .] tax exemption [...].

Unfortunately, the line broke at this point, but the following was evident: (1) divine intervention existed for the people, (2) the gods would deliver victory over oppressing enemies, and (3) a promise of restorative acts existed. This text, therefore, compared favorably to Second Temple material on the surface, but closer scrutiny revealed detracting dissimilarities that negated these points of verbal contact. The first distracting dissimilarity was a lack of didactic interest in "The Dynastic Prophecy" text (other than recounting history). In comparison, the Second Temple P.authors referenced a later historical period through pictures of antediluvian actors that actualized authoritative transfer. This authoritative transfer laid the foundation to push for cultic and ethical responses in their community. Thus, history was recounted precisely for didactic interests. Another distracting dissimilarity was the anonymous author, which resulted in the text missing an Authority by Name topos type. These two distracting dissimilarities disallowed the prophetic and eschatological contexts from being points of verbal contact, negating a parent-child relationship with Second Temple material.

5.2.4.2. Egyptian

The study of Egyptian pseudepigraphy focused on two pieces of literature. The first story was "The Tradition of Seven Lean Years," which is also known as the Famine Stela. The second story was "The Legend of the Possessed Princess."

5.2.4.2.1. "The Tradition of Seven Lean Years"

The P.author scribed a stela concerning the famine in Egypt and Khnum's theophany to the king; the explanation for the tale began in the final lines:

> Freed of fatigue I [Djoser] made this decree on behalf of my father Khnum. A royal offering to Khnum, lord of the cataract region and chief of Nubia: in return for what you have done for me, I offer you Manu as western border, Bakhu as eastern border, from Yebu to Kemsat, being twelve *iter* on the east and the west, consisting of fields and pastures, of the river, and of

> every place in these miles. From this point, the instructions continued, granting taxes for foodstuffs from anyone in the named territory to support the temple.

In the Ptolemaic period, an issue arose concerning the temple. Scholars have suggested it concerned strengthening local tax authority, but others have argued larger political issues of the Ptolemaic rule were at the center.[32] Regardless of the specifics, the P.author worked to legitimize continued taxation in support of the Khnum temple priests.

On the surface, three points of verbal contact existed: the concern with anciency, divine authority, and legitimation. Upon a closer examination of these similarities, the Egyptian P.author portrayed the tax law as existing from ancient times by using P.Djoser to confirm the tax authority of the Khnum temple. This law, then, was to continue based on precedent. In contrast, the norms or laws set in Jewish pseudepigrapha stemmed from eternal covenants (the Tablets of Heaven) and by the hand of God (literally). The one from whom Jewish P.authors borrowed authority was thought to have still lived, and his laws, current. Authority stemmed not from an Anciency topos type, but from divinity and law written on the Tablets of Heaven. Therefore, similar to the case for Adad-Guppi, the reliance on differing underlying authorities disallowed these similarities to exist as verbal points of contact. Therefore, a parent-child relationship did not exist with this text.

5.2.4.2.2. "The Legend of the Possessed Princess"

"The Legend of the Possessed Princess" is also known as "the Bentresh Stela." Found at Karnak, the story was based on Ramses II and his marriage to a Hittite princess who bore the Egyptian name Maatnefrure. This legend originated after Egypt fell to Cambyses II (or possibly after the Ptolemaic period). In it, a Bakhtan prince asked Ramses to act as an intercessor for her deliverance.[33] Ramses agreed, sending the god Khons-the-Provider-in-Thebes to deliver her. After a series of events, Khons-the-Provider returned to Thebes with gifts

---

[32] "The Famine Stela (on Sehel Island)," trans. Miriam Lichtheim (*COS* 1.53:130).

[33] "Bakhtan" most likely related to the Bactrian kingdom while the name of the prince, Bentresh, was probably Canaanite—see ibid., 135 ns.4, 7.

given to "the house of Khons-in-Thebes-Neferhotep."[34] From this tale, three possible points of verbal contact were of interest for this study.

The first point involved spiritual possession and dependence on divine deliverance. In this narrative, Bactria asked Pharaoh to send a god (Khons-the-Provider) to deliver the princess; likewise, in Jubilees, the righteous depended on prayers for divine deliverance from evil spirits.[35] The second point concerned the Egyptian and later Jewish P.authors, who found themselves and their people subjected to foreign rule—and possibly the same foreign rule. The third point concerned the incorporation of the Anciency topos type, which referred to times extending into the past and thus, beyond their current political climate.[36]

However, a closer inspection of the text concerning spiritual possession showed the P.author of "The Legend of the Possessed Princess" focused singularly on possession. Conversely, the Jubilean P.author produced a multipurpose work legitimizing proper calendaring, directing a proper understanding of covenant, and expanding an already authoritative text. Spiritual possession was one of several themes in Jubilees (and, perhaps, a minor one in comparison). The historical background of the text differed as well. Although both authors were subject to foreign rule, the Jews experienced wide-ranging persecution by Seleucid leaders. The Egyptians, however, often lived in peace in Ptolemaic Egypt. Later Ptolemaic rulers even accepted counsel from Egyptian leaders.[37] Finally, a meaningful difference also existed in the teleological purpose of the texts. The Jubilean P.author was concerned with proper understanding and obedience to the law, and the author used authority from several topoi in the teaching. In contrast, the focus of the

---

[34] Miriam Lichtheim, *AEL*, vol. 3, *The Late Period* (Berkeley: University of California Press, 1973), 90; "The Legend of the Possessed Princess," trans. Miriam Lichtheim (1.54:134–36). The difference between the manifestations of Khons-the-Provider and Khons-in-Thebes-Neferhotep was one of position: The first referred to the trait of the healer, the other, the "leading position." Lichtheim declared this text "propaganda," but for what reason and against whom, it is difficult to know. Yet, by locating the princess in Bactria, the author provided a location ruled at various times by Assyrian, Babylonian, Persian, and Hellenistic empires, against the rulers of which the author may have targeted the work.

[35] See §4.3.2 (above).

[36] The Anciency topos type was delimited from the study (see §3.4.4 [above]).

[37] Günther Hölbl, *A History of the Ptolemaic Empire* (London: Routledge, 2001), 25–29.

Egyptian tale was singular—Egypt's superiority. No cultic or ethical instruction occurred in the text. As a result, three points of verbal contact could not be established, and furthermore, a meaningful difference in the teleological purpose of the text disallowed a parent-child relationship.

5.2.4.3. Greek

Pseudepigraphy was rampant among Greek writing compared to the writing of other cultures, which has prompted questions concerning the rise of Jewish pseudepigraphy concurrent with Hellenistic contact and the overall relationship between the two. However, because it was an active method of writing among the Greeks concurrent with the material studied here, several Greek narratives were delimited because of similar dates of origin.[38] Of the remaining texts, the Homeric Hymns and Orpheus garnered attention, beginning with the "Hymn to Demeter," which was said to have originated in the eighth century BCE.[39]

5.2.4.3.1. "Hymn to Demeter" (Homeric Hymns)

The "Hymn to Demeter" centered on Demeter's daughter Persephone, whom Hades (the god) inveigled from her friends before driving his chariot to the earth's surface, snatching her and then descending into Hades (the place). Demeter, unable to find her daughter, embarked on an astral journey to Helios with the Titaness Hecate (a moon-goddess) . After an intervening tale that established or authorized the Demeter cult and Eleusinian mysteries, Zeus sent Hermes to rescue Persephone. Hades, however, tricked Persephone into returning each winter. This hymn was an etiological myth for the four seasons, the Demeter cult, and the Eleusinian mysteries.[40] On the

---

[38] Unfortunately, Hermes Trismegistus fell into this category, dated to the second century CE. However, he was an interesting character—he was later associated with Thoth (the Egyptian God of scribes), Greek Hermes (as evident in the name), and the Hebraic Enoch figure. See Frances A. Yates, *Giordano Bruno and the Hermetic Tradition* (Chicago: University of Chicago Press, 1964), 2–5, 48.

[39] Karl Kerényi, *Eleusis: Archetypal Image of Mother and Daughter,* vol. 4, *Archetypal Images in Greek Religion*, trans., Ralph Manheim, Bollingen Series 64 (New York: Bollingen Foundation, 1967; repr.; Princeton: Princeton University Press, 1991), 13. Although debated, an eighth century or earlier date for the hymn was common in scholarship.

[40] Mark Cartwright, "Eleusis," Cambridge University Press, January 14, 2015, http://www.ancient.eu /Eleusis.

surface, this myth holds three points of verbal contact with Second Temple material: the Divinely Ordained Journeys and Revealed Secrets topos types, and a descent of a nonhuman figure.

The similar journeys in apocalyptic literature occurred in Apoc. Zeph. 6:16 and 2 En. 40:12.[41] The author of 1 Enoch also wrote of journeys to the netherworld for eternal punishment. However, Persephone's journey to the underworld was a kidnapping; a violation of self-agency ending in forced marriage, and Hermes's journey was a rescue mission. By comparison, the journeys in Jewish literature were guided by angelic beings to educate the person taking the journey in light of cultic realities. These distracting dissimilarities denied the journey as a verbal point of contact. Furthermore, the teleological differences for these journeys created a meaningful difference. The anabasis of Demeter to Helios, escorted by Hecate, also matched astral journeys in Second Temple literature. Both texts had characters ascending to gods. However, both characters on the journey were gods in the Demeter account, rather than a human and a divine being as found in Second Temple apocalyptic literature.[42] Second, Demeter's anabasis was to a defeated god no longer holding power. The Titans had lost to the Olympians in the distant past of this narrative. By comparison, anabases in Second Temple apocalyptic literature to a deity was a journey to an all-powerful deity. Third, Demeter's anabasis was an astral journey to the sun with a single purpose of finding her daughter. Second Temple astral journeys were scientific in nature in that they concerned the workings of the universe. For these reasons, the Divine Journey topos type was not a verbal point of contact between the "Hymn to Demeter" and Second Temple apocalyptic literature.

The preliminary study showed both texts also held a Revealed Secrets topos occurrence, but further study indicated the revealed secret in the "Hymn to Demeter" was not an authoritative topos. Demeter did learn the secret of Persephone's disappearance from Helios, but the reader already knew this secret. Consequently, the author of "The Hymn to Demeter" used secrecy and revelation not as an authority but as a plot device. The impetus behind the narrative conflict was Hades's decision to take

---

[41] Another journey perhaps similar to that found in "Hymn to Demeter" was in T. Levi 3:1–2; but, the context was judgment rather than a permanent destination or a place of suffering.

[42] But see n. 112 (above) in chapter 4 for a closer parallel with 3 Enoch.

Persephone as his wife (and Zeus's complicity in the act). The topos occurrence did not establish authority for a Demeter cult, nor did it legitimize the Eleusinian mysteries. Thus, the occurrence of revealed secrets was not a topos of authority, which denied it as a point of verbal contact. As a result, a single point of contact remained among several distracting dissimilarities and meaningful differences, disallowing a parent-child relationship.

However, the Pseudonymity topos type also focused on the author. As such, questions concerned similarities in the names P.authors chose to associate with their stories. Homer was the supposed author of the "Hymn to Demeter." He (and his poetry) garnered "immense cultural authority" in Hellenism—inciting Dio Chrysostom to write the merism that Homer was "'the beginning, middle, and end' of culture."[43] Among modern scholars, arguments have continued regarding Homer's position as a divine sage and prophet. Any literature associated with Homer garnered Homeric authority to shape both cultic and social realms; thus, similarities existed concerning authority by name for pseudepigraphical literature in both Greek and Second Temple apocalyptic literature. This similarity also occurred with the pseudepigraphical works written under the name of "Orpheus."

5.2.4.3. Orpheus

The general narrative of Orpheus centered on his wife, Eurydice, who died from a snakebite. Orpheus descended into Hades and convinced the god Hades and Persephone, to release Eurydice. They agreed but made him promise not to look back during his anabasis. However, as he reached the surface, he did so, only to see Eurydice fall back into Hades.[44] Unfortunately, the current Greek pseudepigraphic material postdated the Jewish Second Temple period leaving no viable comparisons for this

---

[43] Lawrence Y. Kim, *Homer between History and Fiction in Imperial Greek Literature*, Greek Culture in the Roman World (Cambridge: Cambridge University Press, 2010), 2, 5, accessed September 16, 2016, ACLS Humanities E-Book.

[44] What drew authors to write under his name was his adaptability—a trait that also ignited writers in the Renaissance to take on Orpheus's name associated with "a variety of narrative roles" including "creator, lover, philosopher, musician, magician, historian, civilizer, prophet, and priest" (A. Leigh Deneef, "The Poetics of Orpheus: The Text and a Study of Orpheus His Journey to Hell," *Studies in Philology* 89 [1992]: 20). This diversity presented various opportunities for authority, as seen in the later Jewish work "Poetae Epici Graeci" where the author "postulates the righteousness and originality of Jewish wisdom." René Bloch, "Pseudo-Orpheus," *EDEJ* 1009.

study.[45] How, then, did Homer and (to a lesser degree) Orpheus compare to Jewish apocalyptic P.authors? Little evidence existed concerning the authority of the name Enoch in Jewish literature, but the same was not true for other names attached to such material. Moses was authoritative as Israel received the Torah from God through him; Levi, through his descendants, received the role of priest and temple keeper; and Zephaniah gained authority through the prophetic movement. These figures carried similar authority to that of Homer, but the narratives themselves shared little except generalized themes,[46] and the same held true for Orpheus and the Egyptian figures of Djoser and Ramses II.[47]

Thus, there existed a tradition in both Hellenistic Greece and Egypt whereby authors appropriated names for reasons of authority—but the stories to which they attached those names varied tremendously. The Akkadian writings held a similar idea, but the Adad-Guppi P.author depended on proving righteousness as an authority more than the name itself, and "The Dynastic Prophecy," although holding several similarities, was anonymous. As a result, there was no parent-child relationship between a specific EAW text or texts and Second Temple apocalyptic literature. However, the use of the Pseudepigraphy topos type across the EAW created a parent-child relationship between the EAW in general and Second Temple apocalyptic literature.

5.2.5. Step 4e: Cross-Text—Possible Tanakh Sources

A postmodern approach to this research reminded both researcher and reader that written work often revealed more about the author than the author's subject. This idea found no greater evidence than in the vast swath of literature on Tanakh authorship. Who wrote the Pentateuch? How many Isaiahs existed and who was the author or authors? Was

---

[45] Elizabeth Sears, "Orpheus," in *The Classical Tradition*, ed. Anthony Grafton, Glenn W. Most, and Salvatore Settis, Harvard University Press Reference Library (Cambridge: Harvard University Press, 2010), 664.

[46] Levi carried such authority not because of his role as a historical person, but as the father of the Aaronic priesthood.

[47] Scholars have long considered the Greek-Zoroaster writings pseudepigraphy. In 1878, William Smith claimed, "There were…several works bearing the name Zoroaster, but these writings were forgeries" ("Zoraster," in *A Classical Dictionary of Greek and Roman Biography, Mythology and Geography*, rev. ed. [London: John Murray, 1904], 1018). The Hellenistic P.authors assumed Zoroaster's name because the Greeks considered him a sage. These writings held too few similarities otherwise with Second Temple apocalyptic literature to be investigated further in this study.

Daniel a book written by a prophet of the same name, or was it a set of court tales to which redactors added later apocalyptic work? Scholars too often have answered these questions based on already-set views. Therefore, a different strategy was employed concerning the Tanakh. Rather than identifying possible pseudonymous material in the Tanakh, the characters named as authors in Jewish apocalyptic works were revisited with an eye to authority accorded to them in the text, beginning with Enoch.

5.2.5.1. Enoch

The author of Genesis wrote Enoch "walked with God" (Gen. 5:22) and then stretched the uniqueness of the statement to Noah, who also "walked with God" (Gen 6:9). A closer reading of the text containing Enoch established a repetition not present for Noah. The repetition began with the following, "And, Enoch walked with God," after the *toledot* age statement. This phrase repeated at the close of the passage. Enoch thus began and ended in righteousness.[48] Likewise, the report on Noah started with "and Noah walked with God," but ended in sin and Noah cursing a son who saw him naked (table 5).

---

[48] Comparisons have been made between Enoch and Utuabzu, the seventh antediluvian king in the Babylonian king lists who entered heaven. Note, however, this name and heavenly ascent was also found in the list of primeval fish, part of the *Bīt Mēseri* (protected house) incantations in Uruk, which dated to 165/164 BCE, and a similar list concerning names in Greece according to Berosus's Babyloniaca, written around 290 BCE and was perhaps the result of a different transmission history. Of corollary interest and possible assistance was the tenth name on the Uruk Adad tablets—Ummanu, or, according to the tablet, the person the Aramains called "Aḫuqar." Work concerning him was found at Elephantine, and he also appeared twice in Tobit. What, then, might be made of the connection between Enoch and Utuabzu? Cultures across the EAW shared narratives. The connection of the tenth king between Jewish and other cultures made it possible, if not likely, that Utuabzu was known among Second Temple Judaism. The concurrent rise of Enochian myths among Jewish authors therefore may have been related, but Jewish authors also situated Enoch within the Tanakh narratives of their own culture and through the names of their own antediluvian heroes. Whether the author of Genesis was influenced by stories of Utuabzu was outside the purview of this research; however, for Jewish apocalyptic authors, it seemed their dependence on Hebraic culture was at least as strong as their dependence on any specific culture concerning Utuabzu. Thus, a parent-child relationship was denied, although left open was the real possibility that generalized Utuabzi myths became a significant part of Enochian lore. For more on this, see Helge S. Kvanvig, *Primeval History: Babylonian, Biblical, and Enochic: An Intertextual Reading*, SJSJ 149 (Leiden: Brill, 2011), 106–13.

Table 5. Enoch and Noah cycle comparison

Enoch	*Noah*
A. birth announcement	A. birth announcement
B. walked with God	B. walked with God
C. lived 300 more years	C. earth is corrupt
A. birth announcement	A. birth announcement
B. walked with God	B. Noah drunk/Canaan cursed
C. Enoch no longer lives	C. Noah dies

This connection to curses heightened with the verb, הלך—the author had already used it in Gen 3:7, referring to God seeking Adam in the garden.[49] Consequently, Enoch was the only man who began and ended his life walking with God.[50] He was the high point between the first and last men of the antediluvian period, both of whom began by walking with God, but ended in sin and curses (perhaps with Enoch picturing what Israel should be and Adam and Noah picturing what Israel is). Enoch was

[49] Paul Kissling made this connection between Gen 3:7 and 5:22, "by thus echoing the experience of Eden, Enoch's relationship with God is compared to that of Adam and Eve prior to the fall" (*Genesis*, 255; see also Kenneth A. Mathews, *Genesis 1–11:26*, NAC 1A (Nashville: Broadman & Holman, 1996], 258).

[50] Philip Alexander suggested another interpretation of "God" in this verse is angels, which then allowed Enoch to be "someone who had a special relationship with the angels. This interpretation opened the possibility that he ascended to heaven and learned secrets from the angels, or acted as an intermediary or intercessor between earth and heaven" (Philip S. Alexander, "From Son of Adam to Second God: Transformations of the Biblical Enoch," in Stone, *BFOB*, 92). The problem, however, as Alexander noted earlier on the same page, was the title "Sons of God." The Hebrew, הָאֱלֹהִים was the same as found in 5:22, 24, and 6:9, where Enoch and Noah walked *with God*. Was it too much to assume Second Temple apocalyptic authors would move from הָאֱלֹהִים as God to assigning the same articulated term—in the same pericope—a lesser, pluralized interpretation? Angels took on a semidivine nature in context of the divine assembly and perhaps were believed to be semidivine among certain Second Temple Jewish communities. However, if placed alongside the Adamic passage mentioned above, context indicated the interpretation of הָאֱלֹהִים should be "God." Moreover, the delineation between righteous Enoch and the wicked Watchers in the Book of the Watchers and its connection to the flood story weighed in favor of understanding הָאֱלֹהִים as God in 5:22, 24, and 6:9. This understanding is especially true in light of the Righteousness topos type the Enochian author often used with Enoch. See Hava Tirosh-Samuelson, "Jewish Mysticism," in *The Cambridge Guide to Jewish History, Religion, and Culture*, ed. Judith R. Baskin and Kenneth Seeskin (Cambridge, Cambridge University Press, 2010), 401.

the pinnacle of righteousness—an exemplar who walked with God without failure and bore God's truth without the taint of sin.[51]

5.2.5.2. Moses (Levi)

In Num 12:6–8, the author wrote of the importance of Moses:

> Listen to what I say: If there is a prophet among you from the LORD, I make Myself known to him in a vision; I speak with him in a dream. Not so with My servant Moses; he is faithful in all My household. I speak with him directly, openly, and not in riddles; he sees the form of the LORD.

The context of this passage was Miriam and Aaron's criticism of Moses for marrying an Ethiopian woman. The underlying distinction was clear: Moses was greater than the prophets, the wise men, or the priests represented by Aaron, against whom God sided.[52] At the close of the Pentateuch, two more statements set Moses apart from other Hebraic personalities—no greater prophet had come, and YHWH knew him face-to-face (Deut 34:10). Furthermore, the narrator informed the readers no Israelite had ever matched Moses in signs and wonders; he was the greatest Tanakh personality.[53] Therefore, the names with which Second Temple P.authors associated their writings were available to them much like the names of Djoser and Ramses II for the Egyptian authors, or Homer and Orpheus for Greek writers further signifying a parent-child relationship to the overall Pseudepigraphy topos type in EAW material (and perhaps, more specifically in western EAW material).

5.2.6. Step 4f: Evaluation

The Akkadian sources produced similarities in prophecy and exhortation; likewise, the Egyptian sources evidenced a thematic link.

---

[51] Yet, as referenced in chapter 3 n. 119 (above), Enoch took on the opposite role in later Second Temple and early Mishnaic material.

[52] This text was not to be read as a condemnation of the prophetic movement based on 11:29. There, Moses defended two men prophesying in camp, stating he wished all of Israel would do so.

[53] Zephaniah was not included in this list because there was nothing said about him except that he was a prophet of God in the days of Josiah (Zeph 1:1). Concerning Levi, he gained legitimacy by begetting the tribe who received the priesthood.

When coupled with the Revealed Secrets discussed in chapter 3 of this study, the similar authoritative topoi were not a surprise.

"The Legend of the Possessed Princess" displayed Jubilean similarities that reminded readers of the Enochic passages on demonic possession, but those similarities were not strong enough to present three points of verbal contact. Therefore, no parent-child relationship existed. The Greek "Hymn to Demeter" also showed similarities to Second Temple literature, but the points of verbal contact failed to hold up under further scrutiny. Furthermore, meaningful differences also existed concerning the teleological purposes of the narratives. The practice of associating names, however, held a stronger connection. Starting with Homer, the P.authors in Greek, Egyptian, and to a lesser degree, Akkadian pseudepigraphs carried authority beyond simple name recognition. These names held cultic, and often, royal authority within society.[54]

In comparison, the Hebraic P.authors held cultic, but not royal authority. Righteous Enoch was singular in Tanakh personalities. He was the only man to walk *with* God throughout his life. Noah and Adam, by comparison, began with God but ended in sin and curses. Moses was elevated above everyone else including priest and prophet. Together, Enoch and Moses became the exemplars of cultic obedience and the pseudepigraphic authors of perhaps the earliest two noncanonical apocalyptic books. Levi received legitimation as the originator of the priesthood, yet, it was notable how little material Second Temple authors attributed to him, and the same held true with Zephaniah, considering his prophetic authority. Consequently, a type of relationship existed between the Hellenistic and Jewish pseudepigraphy in the names they invoked, but a similar reliance occurred in Hellenistic Egypt when the Khnum temple priests relied on pseudepigraphic authority (and perhaps, to a lesser extent, on the author who wrote "The Legend of the Possessed Princess").

To summarize, although possibly originating in Akkad, pseudonymity and pseudepigraphic material changed in the authority claimed and the message delivered. These changes similarly occurred in the Greek, Egyptian, and Jewish material in the Second Temple era. No single relationship, therefore, existed between EAW cultures or ancient Hebraic texts and Second Temple apocalyptic authors. Instead, a multitude of

---

[54] An exception may have been Adad-Guppi; yet, she was playing off the name of her son, the king, who held cultic authority within the kingdom.

similarities evidenced a method of writing spread across the Persian and Hellenistic worlds. However, this method changed as it moved west and was subsequently employed by various authors. Focusing on the Tanakh, scholars have long attributed several books or parts of books in the Tanakh to P.authors, which may have led to a stronger influence on Second Temple literature. This influence, however, could not preclude the thematic likenesses with EAW sources, which left Jewish pseude-pigraphical material available to be influenced from the EAW in general and Hellenism in particular, but unique in its application among Second Temple Judaism.

5.3. Literary Authority through Written Language: Reference to Common Knowledge

Reference to Common Knowledge invoked two questions: What was common knowledge, and how could it be authoritative? Common knowledge referred not to shared knowledge in a community but to the knowledge that members of a community *knew* they shared among themselves.[55] Using a contemporary illustration, a letter sent to every community member does not constitute common knowledge of the enclosed content as each recipient knows only that he or she has received the letter. In order for the content to become common knowledge, the community members must also know the rest of the community received the same letter.

Jaakko Hintikka provided the following explanation for this idea: "If I know that you know that *p* is true, I virtually know myself that *p* is true. Hence, if you tell me that you know that *p* is true, I cannot (defensibly) deny that I know myself whether *p* is true without indicating that I do not wholly trust you."[56] Here, commonality of knowledge was based on both knowing that the other knows (the

---

[55] Michael Chwe, *Rational Ritual: Culture, Coordination, and Common Knowledge* (Princeton: Princeton University Press, 2001), 13–16.

[56] Jaakko Hintikka, *Knowledge and Belief: An Introduction to the Logic of the Two Notions*, ed. Vincent Hendricks and John Symons, Texts in Philosophy 1 (London: Kings College Publications, 2005), 48–49. This statement is focused on two people, both of whom believe *p* is true. In that case, the recipient of the knowledge cannon deny *p* without denying the trust in the provider of the knowledge of *p* concerning whether *p* is true. Therefore, in a community, a person cannot deny something the community knows without denying the community in that area. Common Knowledge, therefore, is something the community accepts as true and as such, becomes available for authority.

information on the billboard), but also knowing the other knows it is true (each party knows the other party has seen the information on the billboard), which reinforces self-belief. In this way, common knowledge reinforced corporate truths that subsequently would become authoritative.

The process of narratives becoming authoritative begins with a set of shared historical focal points—e.g., the events of December 7, 1941 and September 11, 2001; or Neil Armstrong's moon landing. These focal points were past narratives that highlighted decisions made within them. The decisions then became the precedent for similar future situations. Individual knowledge of community acceptance predetermined accepting this precedent-employment. Thus, common knowledge became authoritative for a person when it was accepted as community precedent.[57]

5.3.1. Step 4a: Text—Definition and Use of Authority

Applied to this current study, the Common Knowledge topos type was defined as a reference in a text to a commonly known narrative that carried authority, such as the Noahic flood and its purpose of judgment. Second Temple apocalyptic authors used this topos type by referencing focal points of shared history to influence an audience to accept their message. This topos type was used in the Qumran texts and by the P.authors of 1 and 2 Enoch, and Jubilees.

However, the Jubilean P.author's use of the Common Knowledge topos type required a short comment. Although the author widened the general narrative scope to most of Genesis and Exodus, specific focus was placed on particular events within the larger narrative. Thus, the P.author engaged the Common Knowledge topos type for the larger narrative and then sharpened individual elements of that narrative as

---

[57] Charles Sanft, *Communication and Cooperation in Early Imperial China: Publicizing the Qin Dynasty*, Suny Series in Chinese Philosophy and Culture (Albany: State University of New York Press, 2014), 22–24. Sanft interacted with Chwe in the introduction to his work, then moved in his discussion of power and political systems to discussing Foucault's analysis of power—that power was not static or singular, but relational and multifaceted; accepted and agreed upon with "some degree of choice on the part of the subject" of power (29). Applied here, the readers of the text were to accept authority of the early narratives from which common knowledge was developed. Note, however, Chwe and Sanft both argued for authority using common knowledge in political systems, whereas the arguments in this work presented common knowledge as the authority by which current interpretations were delivered to a community.

necessary for his message. After these and other observations were made and quantified in steps 3a–d, the two narrative focal points with the greatest possibility of holding three points of verbal contact with Hebraic or EAW narratives were the flood narratives and the Watchers.

5.3.2. Step 4b: Text and Context—Use in Apocalyptic Literature

In Jewish apocalyptic literature, authors often connected the flood and Watchers stories, creating etiological tales of evil, but they varied their presentations. The P.authors of 1 and 2 Enoch made quick references to the flood. However, The Jubilean P.author provided a full rehearsal of the flood story.

5.3.2.1. Enoch

The Enochian author of 1 Enoch connected the focal points of the flood and the Watchers for a Common Knowledge topos in 10:2b–4a:

> "The Deluge is about to come upon all the earth; and all that is in it will be destroyed. And now instruct [Noah] in order that he may flee, and his seed will be preserved for all generations." And secondly, the Lord said to Raphael, "Bind Azazel hand and foot (and) throw him into the darkness!"

In 54:7–10, a P.author introduced a flood story connected to Azazel. Whether Azazel related to the Watchers depended on how a person read the textual strains:

> And in those days, the punishment of the Lord of the Spirits shall be carried out, and they shall open all the storerooms of water in the heavens above, in addition to the fountains of water which are on earth. And all the waters shall be united with (all) other waters. That which is from the heavens above is masculine water, (whereas) that which is underneath the earth is feminine.[9] And they shall obliterate all those that dwell upon the earth as well as those that dwell underneath the ultimate ends of heaven, on account of the fact that they did not recognize their oppressive deeds which they carried out on the earth, they shall be destroyed by (the Flood).

A longer account incorporating dialogue between Noah and Enoch echoed the flood-Watchers connection in chapters 65–67. In chapters 83–90, the author made no clear causal link between the flood and Watchers; however, an implicit narrative cause-and-effect connected the flood and the Watchers in 1 En. 88–89. A subsequent explicit link occurred in 106:13b–15:

> And behold, [angels] commit sin and transgress the commandment; they have united themselves with women and commit sin together with them; and they have married (wives) from among them, and begotten children by them. There shall be a great destruction upon the earth; and there shall be a deluge and a great destruction for one year.

5.3.2.2. 2 Enoch

The author of 2 Enoch shifted responsibility for the flood to humanity in 34:1:

> For I know the wickedness of mankind, how they have rejected my commandments and they will not carry the yoke which I have placed on them…. And that is why I shall bring down the flood onto the earth, and I shall destroy everything, and the earth itself will collapse in great darkness.

This theme continued in 2 En. 68:5–6:

> For in his days there will be a very great breakdown on the earth, for each one has begun to envy his neighbor, and people against people have destroyed boundaries, and the nation wages war. And all the earth is filled with vileness and blood and every kind of evil. And even more than that, they have abandoned their LORD, and they will do obeisance to unreal gods, and to the vault above the sky, and to what moves above the earth, and to the waves of the sea. And the adversary will make himself great and will be delighted with his deeds, to my great provocation.

Thus, the 1 Enoch P.authors connected the flood and Watchers stories, identifying the Watchers as the origin of evil. In 2 Enoch, however, humanity shouldered the blame. In either case, the P.authors warned the readers through the Common Knowledge topos type that to act counter to God was to invite punishment.[58]

5.3.2.3. Jubilees

The Jubilean author expanded the Tanakh flood story in 5:24–29:

> And the LORD opened the seven floodgates of heaven, and the mouths of the springs of the great deep were seven mouths in number; and these floodgates sent down water from heaven forty days and forty nights, and the springs of the deep sent up water until the whole world was full of water. And the water increased upon the earth, fifteen cubits the water rose over every tall mountain; and the ark rose from upon the earth, and it moved upon the surface of the water. And all of the water stayed upon the surface of the earth five months, one hundred and fifty days. And the ark went and rested on the top of Lubar, one of the mountains of Ararat. And in the fourth month the springs of the great deep were closed and the floodgates of heaven were held shut. And on the new moon of the seventh month, all of the mouths of the deeps of the earth were opened. And the water began to go down into the depths below.

At the close of the Noahic Jubilee, the author again expanded upon the story:

> For on account of [Noah's sons] the Flood came upon the earth. For (it was) because of the fornication which the Watchers, apart from the mandate of their authority, fornicated with the daughters of men and took for themselves wives from all whom they chose and made a beginning of impurity. (7:21)

---

[58] In Jub. 5:19, for instance, the author warned Second Temple readers, "Any who corrupted their way and their counsel before the flood" did not receive the partiality of God. Noah received it, and his salvation, because "his heart was righteous in all of his ways as it was commanded concerning him. And he did not transgress anything which was ordained for him." This thinly veiled warning implied a threat to the reader: transgress righteousness and suffer as the unjust did in the great flood.

The Watchers were responsible for evil, but God's purpose for flooding the world shifted to protecting the righteous line from which Israel descended in contradistinction to the Enochian punishment-only theme. By using Common Knowledge authority, the author conveyed a message whereby God protected his righteous from evil.

5.3.2.4. Qumran

Of the eleven scrolls concerning the flood (not including copies of 1 Enoch), a Common Knowledge topos type occurred only in 4Q370 with a focus on exhorting readers to a righteous life. The exhortation began in column 1, line 4 with a description of the flood and continued for at least 14 lines to column 2, line 9. The Watchers' offspring appeared in line 6. Unfortunately, sections of the scroll were damaged, and some of the text (i:10 and the ends of ii:1–3, 6–8) were missing. From what remained, column 2 began with a discussion of iniquity and how YHWH would cleanse it, then ended in the extant text with the negative imperative, "Do not oppose the word[s of YHWH]." Thus, it was reasonable to infer the author focused on members of the community who opposed his teaching by drawing from an authoritative flood topos and the following judgment.[59]

The author of the Qumran Damascus Document (CD–A i) taught on God's strength. The author referenced the Babylonian Captivity (col. 1, lines 5–6), which then led to the Golah realizing their iniquity and guilt (line 8–9); however, they were like the blind, "groping for a path over twenty years" (line 10). Because they later sought him with a whole heart, God raised a Teacher of Righteousness to "direct them in the way of his heart" (lines 10–11). The captivity, repentance, and following need for a leader authorized the Teacher of Righteousness; the following lines informed the reader what judgments God passed on others, leading to column 2, lines 17–19:

> The Watchers of heaven were trapped because they kept not the commands of God and their sons who were as tall as cedars, and their bodies were like mountains.

Following this passage, the author reiterated the cause: They had failed to keep God's commandments, which brought about his wrath. Stephen Hultgren argued the form was a didactic psalm; the purpose was to

[59] John C. Reeves, "Noah," *EDSS*, 2:612–13.

instruct on God's works and deeds, focused on the law and Israel's disobedience. If Hultgren was correct, the teleological goal became an exhortation to proper ethical behavior as part of God's elected remnant (4Q266 f5.1b:12–19).[60] Moreover, the author applied the Common Knowledge topos type for both the Teacher of Righteousness and for accepting the community's place in God's eschaton.[61]

Each Second Temple narrative referenced a historic focal point, and most referenced the same pair—the flood and the Watchers. An issue, however, arose when locating the event within a community's historiography. The historical foundations of the flood, for instance, were easily located at the beginning of Hebraic founding narratives. Unfortunately, the historical foundations for the Watchers were harder to locate; yet, in an ironic twist, this difficulty strengthened the Common Knowledge authoritative topos type where it concerned the Watchers.

The preceding paragraphs highlighted the ways in which this topos type was used in Second Temple apocalyptic material. Many scholars have commented on these narratives as well. In the following step (4c), germane scholars were identified, and their observations were a help in this study.

5.3.3. Step 4c: Text and Context—Germane Scholarship

Himmelfarb, Barker, and others have focused on etiological meaning displayed through disparate narrative strains as presented in chapter 2 of this work. Nickelsburg and Collins, however, focused on sources. Nickelsburg worked through the account of Azazel and Šemiḥazah, drawing parallels from Jewish literature for these stories from the OT and Second Temple literature.[62] Collins, however, argued, "The story of the

---

[60] Stephen Hultgren, *From the Damascus Covenant to the Covenant of the Community: Literary, Historical, and Theological Studies in the Dead Sea Scrolls*, STDJ 66 (Leiden: Brill, 2007), 380–81. Also 4Q534 (Aramaic Noah) contained a possible authoritative topos in column 2, line 16, but the text was too fractured to legitimize an argument from the material.

[61] Albert I. Baumgarten, "Perception of the Past in the Damascus Document," in *The Damascus Document: A Centennial of Discovery: Proceedings of the Third International Symposium of the Orion Center for the Study of the Dead Sea Scrolls and Associated Literature*, ed. Joseph M. Baumgarten, Esther G. Chazon, and Avital Pinnick, STDJ 44 (Leiden: Brill, 1999), 12.

[62] George W. E. Nickelsburg, "Apocalyptic and Myth in 1 Enoch 6–11," *JBL* 96.3 (1977): 384–86.

Watchers does not have a clearly identifiable referent."[63] Yet, for Collins, the Watcher narrative became "a paradigmatic model which is not restricted to one historical situation, but can be applied whenever an analogous situation arises."[64] Although using different terms, Collins thus concluded the author introduced the narrative (to use the nomenclature of this work) as a reference to common knowledge, confirming the observation made in the third step of this study.

Shifting to Noah and Qumran, Geza Vermes argued the Qumran community saw themselves as equal with Noah as a "community of penitents who were separated residents from the region of iniquity."[65] Dorothy Peters identified over two dozen Qumran texts (both sectarian and nonsectarian) concerning the Noahic tradition in her 2008 book on Dead Sea Scroll traditions of Noah. Scholars such as Wayne Baxter have argued for a possible Book of Noah (although others, such as J. P. Lewis and C. Werman, have argued against a separate Noahic corpus).[66] Their work highlighted the flood as a Common Knowledge subtype (at Qumran, at least). Which narrative or narratives of the flood did Second Temple authors use, and what sources might there be for the Watchers? Answering that question began by applying step 4d.

5.3.4. Step 4d: Cross-Text—Possible EAW Sources

The EAW sources for this topos type were divided between flood accounts and stories concerning a type of Watcher. For the latter, however, similarities were necessary for one of three specific areas for the sources to be considered here.[67] The first was a text showing divine judgment narratives as authoritative for warning readers about future decisions. Second, a text contained an authoritative etiological account of evil that derived from deity-human conjugal relations. Finally, the

[63] John J. Collins, "The Apocalyptic Technique: Setting and Function in the Book of the Watchers," *CBQ* 44.4 (1982): 97.

[64] Collins, "Apocalyptic Technique," 98.

[65] Geza Vermes, "La communauté de la Nouvelle Alliances d'après ses écrits réemment découverts," *ETL* 27 (1951): 73.

[66] Dorothy Peters, *Noah Traditions in the Dead Sea Scrolls: Conversations and Controversies of Antiquity*, EJL 26 (Atlanta: Society of Biblical Literature, 2008). Although Peters dedicated her entire book to this discussion, a summary can be found in pages 1–3; cf. also Baxter, "Noachic Traditions and the Book of Noah," *JSP* 15.3 (2006): 186–87.

[67] Common knowledge did not equate to general knowledge, which was the reason for specificity, as noted here.

offspring from the conjugal relations sought to possess humans, which produced instructions on apotropaic protection. As such, this subsection contains an exploration of EAW narratives holding at least one of these three criteria.

5.3.4.1. Flood Accounts

The "Eridu Genesis" narrative scored highest for a possible parent-child relationship in step 3. Several related stories also scored well, but because of limited space, only the second highest scoring account was included here: the Akkadian "Atrahasis." The third highest scoring account occurred in Apollodorus's History.

5.3.4.1.1. "Eridu Genesis"

In the Sumerian "Eridu Genesis" account, the main character Ziusudra endured a flood:

> All the evil winds, all stormy winds gathered into one and with them, then, the flood was sweeping over (the cities of) the half-bushel baskets for seven days and seven nights. After the flood had swept over the country, after the evil wind had tossed the big boat about on the great waters, the sun came out spreading light over heaven and earth.[68]

A first read provided three points of verbal contact between this text and Second Temple apocalyptic literature. The first point of contact was a god that commanded a flood. The second was the specifics of the flood, including its height, a specific period that included a day-night merism, and the ceasing rains. The third point of verbal contact was the sacrifice by the main human character.

Several differences highlighted specific cultural references rather than negating the verbal contacts. In "Eridu Genesis," cities provided a better reference to height than did mountains in the Tanakh Genesis account, as the Zagros range was far to the north. Another cultural reference was numbers. Seven was a common number in myth and

---

[68] "The Eridu Genesis," trans. Thorkild Jacobsen (*COS* 1.158:513–16).

held several meanings other than a literal count of days in the same way that "seven" or "forty" has been used in Hebrew.[69]

However, noncultural differences also existed that negated these points of verbal contact. In "Eridu Genesis," the "evil wind" was a destructive force, driving the rain and tossing the ship. In the Tanakh, the wind played an opposite role helping the waters to recede.[70] More important, however, was the divine decree. In "Eridu Genesis," the decree for the flood was not punishment for angelic wrongs or humanity's unrighteous actions; rather, it existed at the whim of divine beings, born of a god's unrest, and thus played out in an intermural dispute between deities. In the account found in Second Temple apocalyptic literature, the decree came as a result of the action of the Watchers and was a condemnation of either the revelation of secrets or of inappropriate actions of divine beings (the Watchers).

As such, the driving purpose for the flood, the context in which it occurred, and the lessons derived from it changed the overall message of the text. The flood accounts in Second Temple apocalyptic literature were punishments for etiological evil, a teleological purpose missing from "Eridu Genesis." This meaningful difference negated a parent-child relationship. These same similarities and differences repeated in the Akkadian "Atrahasis" story.

5.3.4.1.2. Akkadian "Atrahasis"

In the Akkadian flood story, gods created humanity to bear the drudgery of physical labor and relieve the Igigi of the task. When humanity increased, their noise disturbed the gods. The latter then determined humanity's destruction under Enlil's leadership. Enki, however, opposed the decision. Standing outside Atrahasis's dwelling place, he spoke to the wall, rather than directly to Atrahasis to remain faithful to the heavenly council by technicality. After learning of the

---

[69] See, for instance Reinhold Gotthard, ed. *Die Zahl Sieben Im Alten Orient: Studien Zur Zahlensymbolik in Der Bibel und Ihrer Altorientalischen Umwelt* (Frankfurt: Peter Lang, 2008); Yosef Green, "Who Knows Seven?" *JBQ* 41.4 (2013): 259–60; Noel Weeks, "The Bible and the 'Universal' Ancient World: A Critique of John Walton," *WTJ* 78.1 (2016): 18–19. For the Hebrew *forty*, see James Swanson, "אַרְבָּעִים," *Dictionary of Biblical Languages*; Johannes P. Louw and Eugene A. Nida, eds. "ἔτη τεσσεράκοντα," *L&N* 1:640.

[70] Note, however, this difference alone did not negate a point of verbal contact as it did not meet the definition of "meaningful difference."

flood, Atrahasis approached the city elders and reported all he had heard. A feast began the next readable text, followed by Atrahasis and his family embarking on the ship amid the rain. The text describing the storm broke at this point, but was still available for comparison to Second Temple literature:

> [ ] The storm [ ] were yoked. [Anzu rent] the sky with his talons, [he] the land and broke its clamor [like a pot]. [ ] The flood [came forth], its power came upon the peoples [like a battle]. One person did [not] see another, they could [not]recognize each other in the catastrophe. [The deluge] bellowed like a bull, the wind [resound]ed like a screaming eagle. The darkness [was dense], the sun was gone, [ ]...like flies[the clamor (?)] of the deluge.[71]

The flood finished, the gods repented of their destruction and agreed to limit humanity by slowing birth rates and establishing death.

Compared to the Second Temple material, the conflict in this text was between two gods. Enki and Enlil were equals, but Enki protected and conversely, Enlil destroyed. Humanity, on the other hand, represented a mere annoyance. The tale was an etiological account of creation, death, and class-authorization. Based on the authority of the gods, only certain classes could reproduce. Although a flood occurred in "Atrahasis," a capricious god caused it, and although secrets were revealed, the method of revelation discounted both righteousness and relationship, which was essential to the Enochian and Jubilean author s. Moreover, the Akkadian flood tale lacked an etiological account of evil, instead authorizing offspring by class. Therefore, although it was possible this text contributed to the story represented in this Common Knowledge topos type, there were several meaningful differences negating a parent-child relationship between "Atrahasis" and Jewish apocalyptic literature.

5.3.4.1.3. Apollodorus

In the Apollodorus's account, Zeus destroyed humanity by flood, but a single human, Deucalion, constructed the ark on Prometheus's advice:

---

[71] "Atrahasis," trans. Benjamin R. Foster (*COS* 1.130:450–53).

> When Zeus willed to destroy the bronze-aged ancestors, Prometheus advised Deucalion to build an ark, and [after] he put in what was necessary, he embarked with Pyrrha. Zeus poured out a great rain from heaven and flooded the greater part of Greece so that all men were destroyed, few fled separately, and they took refuge in the neighboring mountain (range). And, at that time, the Thessalian mountain separated, and what was outside the isthmus and Peloponnese was all overwhelmed. But the ark carried Deucalion through seas for nine days and nights to Parnassus. (Hist. 1.7.2)

The text ended with Deucalion's sacrifice to Zeus and a list of his descendants. This account followed the familiar line of a god coaching a human to build an ark, who then rides the ark through a storm, comes to land, and sacrifices to a god; but a closer examination revealed several distinctions.

First, Apollodorus provided no reason for the flood.[72] Second, Prometheus chose Deucalion because of a familial connection rather than righteousness or devotion to Prometheus. Third, the author reminded the reader this flood devastated only Greece and left untouched the Grecian mountain tops to which a few men had fled. The lack of reasoning, the familial connection determining salvation, and the provincial boundaries of the flood created several distracting similarities that negated any points of verbal contact.

It also created a meaningful difference in the teleological purposes between the stories. Therefore, a parent-child relationship did not exist between the Greek flood story and Second Temple apocalyptic accounts of the flood.

5.3.4.2. Watchers

The minimal number of Greek texts holding a possible connection with the Watchers in Second Temple Jewish literature meant every text was investigated here, beginning with Hesiod's *Works and Days*. Next, Apollodorus's *History* 2.1.1 and a text from Philo of Byblos was

[72] A possible reason may have existed based on translating the Greek text in 1.7.2. The important clause was "ἐπεὶ δὲ ἀφανίσαι Ζεὺς τὸ χαλκοῦν ἠθέλησε γένος." The translation was either "And when Zeus would destroy the bronze-aged ancestors" or "And when Zeus wished [or wanted] to destroy the bronze-aged ancestors," depending on how ἀφανίσαι was translated. However, *wish* or *want* still left the reader with no reason except the desire of a god.

examined. Finally, both versions of "The Myth of Illuyankaš" concluded this subsection. The older version was Hittite, and the latter, Greek.

5.3.4.2.1. Hesiod

In *Works and Days*, Hesiod touched on the idea of immortals watching men:

> For thirty thousand are upon the bountiful earth, Zeus's immortal Watchers of mortal men. They watch the judgments and abominable actions, clothed in air [mist?] as they are moving everywhere upon the land (WD 252–55).

At first, this passage held three points of verbal contact: the term, "Watchers," an etiology of evil, and the Watchers' role in watching humanity. However, "Watchers" translated Hesiod's φύλακες: a person who is on guard or watches.[73] In the Jewish literature, the English term "Watchers" translated ἐγρήγοροι. These terms were not synonymous, denying "Watchers" as a point of contact.[74] Second, Hesiod wrote that humanity was responsible for evil (he termed it "abominable actions"), but the Enochic and Jubilean authors made the Watchers responsible, inverting the origin of evil. These differences denied three verbal contacts and thus, a parent-child relationship.[75]

5.3.4.2.2. Apollodorus

Greek mythology was replete with gods cohabitating with women and producing offspring. In most situations, these offspring were heroes, such as Perseus or Heracles; however, Apollodorus wrote Zeus's copulation with Niobe, a human female, resulted in the one hundred-eyed watchman named Argus. Three points of verbal contact existed before further examination: divine-human copulation, non-human offspring, and a

---

[73] Logos Bible Software, "φύλαξ," *The Lexham Analytical Lexicon to the Septuagint* n.p.; also, Rudolf Kassühlke and Barclay M. Newman, "Φύλαξ," *Kleines Wörterbuch zum Neuen Testament: Griechisch-Deutsch* 204.

[74] According to John Collins, who wrote, "The word for watchers here, φύλακες, [was] not the same as that used in Daniel or Enoch" (Collins, "Watchers," *DDD* 894).

[75] Contrary to T. Reub. 5:1–7, wherein women bore fault because they "allured the Watchers" (5:6).

connection to seeing, or watching (as noted in the one-hundred eyes). However, further study negated these contacts.

First, a deity-human union produced Argus who could be likened to the Watchers, but in Jewish literature, the Watchers were the heavenly beings committing the connubial act. Second, Argus was neither a giant nor a menace to humanity. Finally, Argus was not tasked with the role of "Watcher." These distracting dissimilarities negated the points of verbal contact; therefore, they disallowed a parent-child relationship between the topos type in Apollodorus's work and in the Jewish Watcher narratives.[76]

5.3.4.2.3. Herennius Philo of Byblos

Herennius Philo wrote of Watchers, or "Observers of Heaven," within Phoenician cosmology:

> Living things which had no sense of perception, from which living beings possessed of intellect were born. And they were called *Zophasēmin*, that is, "Observers of the Heavens, and they were formed like the shape of an egg."[77]

Many problems existed with this passage, including its date and origins. Scholars have argued this writing was a "derivative pastiche of Hesiod's *Theogony*" or a "Hellenized rendering of older Phoenician materials."[78] The heavenly Observers may have contributed to a Common Knowledge topos type, but they were neither divine nor angelic. Instead, they were beings "like the shape of an egg." Further, the author mentioned nothing of their role or of their interaction with humanity. Collins provided a succinct conclusion of the reference, "[The Observers were] assigned no function which might be compared to the Jewish Watchers...."[79] Collins's observations confirmed the observation that three points of

---

[76] Apollodorus also showed confusion concerning Argus as he writes in the following passage of a man named Agenor begetting Argus, "the all-seeing one" (2.1.2).

[77] Translation compared with: Albert I. Baumgarten, *The Phoenician History of Philo of Byblos: A Commentary*, Ëtudes préliminaires aux religions orientales dans l'Empire romain 89 (Leiden: E. J. Brill, 1981), 97; James Barr, "Philo of Byblos and His 'Phoenician History,'" *BJRL* 57.1 (1974): 23.

[78] J. R. C. Cousland, "Philo of Byblos," *The New Interpreter's Dictionary of the Bible*, 4:513.

[79] Collins, "Watchers," 894.

verbal contact did not exist. Therefore, no parent-child relationship existed between these texts for this topos type.

5.3.4.2.4. "The Myth of Illuyankaš"

"The Myth of Illuyankaš" was an etiological myth establishing the *Purulli* festival.[80] In the older Hittite version, the Dragon Illuyankaš defeated the Storm God. The Storm God then called the other gods to his side against Illuyankaš, including his daughter Inara. Inara later sought Hupašiyaš (a married human) to join her in defeating the dragon. Hupašiyaš agreed to help, but only if she consented to coitus. After fulfilling his terms, they go in search for Illuyankaš. Carole Fontaine narrated the capture of the dragon:

> [Inara] hides Hupašiyaš, adorns herself, and proceeds to lure the Illuyankaš-dragon and his cohorts…from his lair. The Illuyankaš-dragons become sated and overcome with drink, to the point that they are unable to regain their burrow, whereupon Hupašiyaš springs out and binds them with a rope. The advance work being accomplished, the Weather-god enters and slays the dragon(s), while the pantheon looks on.[81]

After Illuyankaš was captured, Inara built a cliff-top house and held Hupašiyaš captive as her mate. She commanded him not to peer through the window lest he looked upon his wife and then demand to leave. Later, Inara returned from a trip to find Hupašiyaš had disobeyed her and longed to return home. In the ensuing argument, she killed him.[82]

This story held three points of verbal contact before further study: heavenly conflict, sexual relations between a heavenly being and a human, and punishment. Closer scrutiny, however, negated these contacts. First, the conflict in this myth involved two gods, and the author

---

[80] Harry A. Hoffner, *Hittite Myths*, ed. Gary M. Beckman, 2nd ed., WAW 2 (Atlanta: Scholars Press, 1998), 11–12. Little was known about this festival, limiting further investigation.

[81] Carole Fontaine, "The Deceptive Goddess in Ancient Near Eastern Myth: Inanna and Inaraš," *Semeia* 42 (1988): 95.

[82] Contra Harry Hoffner, who argued Inara may have let him go home in *Hittite Myths*, 10. This summary and that of the later version was based on the translation in "Hittite Myths," trans. Albrecht Goetze (*ANET*, 125–26).

provided no reason for the conflict. In the Jewish apocalyptic literature, the conflict arose between a God and his created beings as punishment for the latter overstepping their boundaries through cohabitation with women. This variance created a distracting dissimilarity that denied this point of verbal contact. Second, although both stories pictured sexual interaction between deity and humanity, they differed greatly through inverted roles. The Jewish authors presented the heavenly beings (Watchers) as male sexual antagonists. In "The Myth of Illuyankaš," the heavenly being was female and the one from whom copulation was requested. However, once they completed the act, the male lost self-agency to the female partner. In the Watchers, neither participant lost self-agency. This variance created a distracting dissimilarity that denied the second point of verbal contact. Finally, punishment existed in the Watcher stories and the Illuyankaš myth, but it, too, held a distracted dissimilarity. The Watchers received just punishment for their intercourse with women and the subsequent destruction it caused. Hupašiyaš, however, died in an argument—a passion murder—when he wished to return to his wife and children. These distracting dissimilarities, coupled with the different etiological purposes of the stories, negated all three points of verbal contact. Therefore, no parent-child relationship existed between the older version of the myth and the Watchers story in Jewish apocalyptic literature.

In a later version of the Illuyankaš myth, the Storm-god lost his eyes and heart to Illuyankaš. To garner revenge, he fathered a son with "the daughter of a poor man."[83] Once the son came of age, he took Illuyankaš's daughter in marriage. Through him, the Storm-god requested the return of his eyes and heart, which he subsequently received. Sometime later, however, the Storm god again warred against Illuyankaš, only to have his son side against him.[84]

As with the earlier version, three points of verbal contact existed before further study. First, the stories held a deity-human relationship. Second, a woman or women bore children. Finally, no punishment was sent specifically to the women (the Watcher's flood was directed towards everyone on the earth). However, a closer examination failed to sustain these points of verbal contact. First, in the Illuyankaš myth, revenge drove the deity-human relationship, whereas lust drove the relationships in the

---

[83] Alberto Green, *The Storm-god in the Ancient Near east,* BJSUCSD 8 (Winona Lake: Eisenbrauns, 2003), 148.

[84] Ibid.

Watchers story. Second, the role of the offspring was meaningfully different. The Storm God's child married Illuyankaš's daughter with the purpose of retrieving the Storm God's eyes. In the Watcher's narrative, the offspring wrought destruction and evil. Finally, part of the teleological purpose for the story in Enoch and Jubilees was apotropaic information, which was a purpose missing from the Illuyankaš story. The distracting dissimilarities denied two of the three points of verbal contact, and the difference in teleological purposes created a meaningful difference. As a result, the newer Illuyankaš myth was not in a parent-child relationship with the Watchers narratives.[85] Therefore, no EAW tale held three points of verbal contact and several meaningful differences were present. As such, no EAW text was found to be in a parent-child relationship with Jewish apocalyptic material concerning this topos type.

5.3.5. Step 4e: Cross-Text—Possible Tanakh Sources

From the later Second Temple perspective, the flood and Watchers narratives originated in Genesis, but references to floods were found in other Tanakh texts. These references often symbolized God's judgment. Conversely, references to the Watchers were few and varied. These references were examined in step 4e, beginning with the story in Gen 6.

5.3.5.1. Genesis Flood

The author of Genesis provided an account of the flood in 6:9–9:17, but the decreed judgment began in 6:5:

> And YHWH saw the evil of man was great upon the earth—even every inclination from the thought of his heart was continually evil (evil the whole day). And then YHWH repented that he made man on the earth, and he was deeply hurt

[85] Scholars have also linked the Book of the Watchers with the story "Erra and Ishum," but the story was not presented here because it presented no possibility of a parent-child relationship. Parallels were still noted, however. According to Kvanvig, both stories (1) contained "information about mythical concepts from the first millennium"; (2) expressed the earthly results of factional war in the heavens; and (3) highlighted a reading whereby an earlier event became the "backdrop for a new catastrophe hitting humans later in history" (Kvanvig, *Primeval History*, 428). Kvanvig concluded on the next line that "Erra and Ishum" were not in the background of 1 En. 6–11 (or probably the larger Watcher myths), but rather, "traditions from the Mesopotamian flood story have influenced both Genesis and the Watcher story" (ibid.).

> in his heart. And then YHWH said, I will blot out man whom I created from upon the face of the land, from man to the beast, to the creeping things, even to the birds of the sky, because I regret that I made them. But Noahfound grace in the eyes of YHWH.

Humanity was evil, and God regretted his creation. Yet, the language of divine response was neither justice nor righteousness, but emotional pain (נחם—Niphal, "to repent, be sorry, rue, grief"; עצב—Hitpa'el, "to feel hurt, be grieved, filled with pain").[86] This judgment did not receive the label "righteous"; rather, it was a judgment born of sorrow and pain. Exegeting Isa 54:8–9 strengthened this observation.

5.3.5.1.1. Isa. 54:8–9

In this text, God was speaking to captive Judah:

> For a moment, I abandoned you, but with great compassion, I will gather you, in a flood of anger I hid my face for a moment from you, but I will have compassion on you with covenant love forever. This, to me, is just as Noah, when I swore the waters of Noah would not again pass over the earth.

Isaiah pictured God angry with Judah, yet he likened the picture to the Genesis flood story and identified a later Judean restoration. Note the

---

[86] Of this emotional pain, Glenn Kreider wrote, "God's grief and pain are channeled into judgment that will 'destroy all life under the heavens'" (Glenn R. Kreider, "The Flood Is as Bad as It Gets: Never Again Will God Destroy the Earth," *BSac* 171.684 [2014]: 424; cf. Klines, "נחם," *DCH* 5:663–65. "עצב."; Koehler, "נחם," *HALOT* 1:688–89; Koehler, "עצב," *HALOT* 1:864). Note, however, עצב might also result in positive actions such as consoling or gaining satisfaction but tied up in that concept was an occurrence for which one must be consoled or dissatisfaction that must be relieved. Also note, נחם was a debated term often concerning the question of God "relenting" (stopping a course of action because of a desired result, such as Moses interceding for Israel at Sinai in Exod 32:12–14) or "repenting" (changing of one's mind, such as in the context of Exod 13:17).

This debate, however, overlooked the issue of perspective of the writer, who was anthropomorphizing God. Thus, the question was not whether God relented or repented, but how the *author explained* the acts of God. However, regardless of the correct answer, what was not debated was the emotional element, which was the focus here.

words "abandoned," "anger," and "compassion."[87] These terms were not associated with righteousness, but with decision born of emotion. How, then, did Second Temple authors read judgment into this narrative?

5.3.5.1.2. Flood as Judgment

The following passages all referred to flood as judgment: 2 Sam 5:20 (repeated in 1 Chron 14:10); Ps 78:47 (referring to the Exodus flood); Isa 8:8; 28:2; Dan 9:25; and Nah 1:8. In them, God literally or metaphorically destroyed by flood based on either his judgment or deliverance (which entailed judgment). Second Temple authors paired these later judgments and delivery accounts with the earlier Noahic story to declare God's future deliverance of their community. Consequently, origins of this Common Knowledge topos type were found in the Tanakh. However, understanding the Genesis flood as a judgment against the origin of evil was a Second Temple occurrence. This occurrence created several meaningful differences between the texts. Therefore, while the Genesis account of the flood and other Tanakh passages heavily influenced this topos type, no one Tanakh passage or Hebraic movement was in a parent-child relationship with this topos type in Jewish apocalyptic material.

5.3.5.2. Watchers

The Second Temple authors associated Watchers with the "Sons of God" in the opening verses of Gen 6:1-4:

> And it came about when men began to be numerous upon the face of the land, and daughters were born to them. And the sons of God (בְנֵי־הָאֱלֹהִים) saw the daughters of man, that they were desirable, and they took for themselves wives from all, whomever they chose. And then YHWH said, my spirit will not dwell with man forever, for they are flesh; his days will be 120 years. The Nephilim were on the earth in those days with them, and thereafter, when the sons of God entered into the daughters of man and they bore them, they were heroes, who were from anciency, men of the name (men of renown).

[87] "Compassion," which translated רָחַם in this verse, took on the concept of deep-seated love, often that of a parent loving a child, and most often was associated with God in the Tanakh. See Koehler, "רחם," *HALOT* 2:1216–18; R. Laird Harris, Gleason L. Archer Jr., and Bruce K. Waltke, "רחם," *TWOT* 843.

The punishment fell not on the Sons of God, but on man: "His days will be 120 years"; yet the question lay in interpreting "man"—for whom was this limit intended? Scholars have divided into three camps. John Sailhamer argued this punishment was against all humanity. Gordon Wenham claimed the Nephilim, whose lifespan almost equaled immortality, was the intended target. Still others, such as Donald Gowan, concluded, "Any explanation is guesswork."[88] While scholars have significantly disagreed over the interpretation of this passage, Jewish apocalyptic authors unanimously connected them to the Watchers by expanding the biblical text:

> And it came to pass when the sons of men had multiplied, born to them were beautiful daughters. And the watchers lusted after them and were led astray following them, and they said to one another, "Let us choose for ourselves wives from the daughters of men upon the earth" (Syncelli Greek text of 1 En. 6:1–2).[89]

Here, the P.Enoch author substituted "Watchers" for "Sons of God," but from whence did this concept appear? The late texts of Job and Daniel, plus three other verses found in copies at Qumran helped in this research.

---

[88] Wenham, *Genesis 1–15*, 145–46; John H. Sailhamer, "*Genesis*," in *Genesis, Exodus, Leviticus, Numbers*, vol. 2 of *The Expositor's Bible Commentary*, ed. Frank E. Gaebelein (Grand Rapids: Zondervan, 1990), 76; Donald E. Gowan, *From Eden to Babel: A Commentary on the Book of Genesis 1–11* (Grand Rapids: Eerdmans, 1988), 85.

[89] Variations existed across different manuscripts and recensions. The Qumran community had this text as well, catalogued as 4Q202. There was little change between it and Ethiopian Enoch, except the dittographic "beautiful." In Codex Panopolitanus [CP] and Syncelli, the first mention of "men" in Gen 6:1 expanded "sons of men." CP agreed with the Aramaic 4Q202 dittography of beautiful but supplied a synonym rather than a true repetition. Syncelli, however, followed the MT and LXX with only one description of the daughters. The Ethiopian Enochic text followed the Greek tradition found in CP, but expansion of the text came in the second half of verse two. The MT and LXX produced the words of the angels, but the Greek Enoch texts showed significant expansion—the angels lusted after the daughters and then enticed each other to take wives who would bear them children. The Ethiopic text followed this pattern, evidencing a proclivity to the CP over Syncelli. Note Jubilees, at this point, followed the MT and LXX.

5.3.5.2.1. Job 7:20

Job asked in 7:20, "If I sin, what have I committed against you, Watcher of Man, why have you set me as a target for yourself? Now I am a burden to myself." The word, "Watcher," translated נֹצֵר, located as Qal participle (the watching one, or Watcher). So, to whom has Job directed his question? Context implied Eliphaz, but invoking intertextuality identified God as the recipient. Job's speech in 7:6 began with an imperative to remember, reflecting Ps 78:40 (table 6), which was written as a prayer to God. Job's speech then continued to "parody…Psalm 8 in verses 17–18,"[90] which established God as the audience in verse 1.

Table 6. Comparison of Job 7:6 and Psa. 78:40

	English Text	*Hebrew Text*
Job 7:6	Remember that my life is a breath, my eye will not turn to see good.	זְכֹר כִּי־רוּחַ חַיָּי לֹא־תָשׁוּב עֵינִי לִרְאוֹת טוֹב
Psa. 74:40	For he remembered that they were flesh, a passing breath that won't return.	וַיִּזְכֹּר כִּי־בָשָׂר הֵמָּה רוּחַ הוֹלֵךְ וְלֹא יָשׁוּב

In 7:12, Job questioned why God placed a מִשְׁמָר "guard" in his presence, but the semantic domain included "watch," as in one standing watch. John Hartley has argued this passage "dr[ew] on the rich, mythopoeic imagery of primordial conflict" in which Job showed his "fear that he [became God's] cosmic foe."[91] Job, therefore, occupied a similar position to the Watchers of Second Temple literature, who was God's foe through rebellion, secret-revealing, and (or) cohabiting with human women. There, the Job passage held a term that could later be understood as the Watchers, and also held the concept of a cosmic foe, although the Watchers were not the foe in this passage.

5.3.5.2.2. Isaiah 24:21

An indirect reference available for later adaptation to the Watchers occurred in Isa 24:21. The context of this passage was the day of judgment:

---

[90] Roland E. Murphy, *Wisdom Literature: Job, Proverbs, Ruth, Canticles, Ecclesiastes, and Esther*, FOTL 13 (Grand Rapids: Eerdmans, 1981), 26.

[91] John E. Hartley, *The Book of Job* (Grand Rapids: Eerdmans, 1988), 149.

> And it will come about in that day, YHWH will punish the hosts of the heaven of heavens and the kings of the earth upon the earth. The captive prisoners will be gathered upon the pit, and they will be shut up in prison, and in many days, be punished. And the moon will be ashamed, and the sun will be ashamed, because the Lord of Hosts reigns on the mountain of Zion and in Jerusalem, and before his elders in glory (24:21–23).

Several scholars have posited Isaiah originally referenced fallen angels based on the context of verse 22, but this position ignored the paralleled moon and sun in verse 23.[92] John Oswalt allowed for a reference to pagan gods whom the EAW religions associated with celestial bodies.[93] Yet, the textual evidence weighed against this connection. The Tanakh author avoided the expectant שֶׁמֶשׁ and יָרֵחַ (Semitic names of the sun and moon gods), choosing לְבָנָה and חַמָּה instead.[94] Oswalt, however, was correct when he wrote,

> The use of *height* for heavens suggests that this terminology is primarily used to convey God's implacable enmity against all which raises itself against him, whether a star in heaven or a

[92] *Hosts of the Heaven of Heavens* in verse 21 paralleled "gathered upon the pit" in 22, and the sun and moon suffering shame in verse 23. Likewise, the "kings of the earth" in verse 21 paralleled "shut up in prison" in verse 22, and "Because the Lord of Hosts reigns" in verse 23. The result was the heavenly hosts and kings of the earth were imprisoned because the Lord of Hosts reigned supreme upon the earth. These parallels forced the Hosts of the Heaven of Heavens in verse 21 to equate with the sun and moon in verse 23.

[93] John Oswalt, *The Book of Isaiah, Chapters 1–39*, NICOT (Grand Rapids: Eerdmans, 1986), 444. For scholars who argued a reference to the fallen angels, see Geoffrey W. Grogan, "Isaiah," in *Isaiah, Jeremiah, Lamentations, Ezekiel*, vol. 6 of *The Expositor's Bible Commentary*, ed. Frank E. Gaebelein (Grand Rapids: Zondervan, 1986), 155; Gary V. Smith, *Isaiah 1–39*, NAC 15A (Nashville: Broadman & Holman, 2007), 424. A third option by Edward Young claimed the phrasing incorporated both angels and heavenly bodies as a kind of literary merism. Edward Young, *The Book of Isaiah: Chapters 19–39*, vol. 2 of *The Book of Isaiah* (Grand Rapids: Eerdmans, 1969), 178–79.

[94] B. B. Schmidt, "Moon," *DDD* 586. The author also tapped into a couplet appearing only in poetic texts, which highlighted the fluidity among ancient Hebraic movements. This fluidity heightened the difficulty in positing a single Hebraic movement in a parent-child relationship with Second Temple literature.

> king on earth. While a more involved symbolic structure...is certainly possible, nothing in the context demands it, and much in the context suggests that the imagery was chosen primarily for its impact.[95]

Thus, any reference to fallen angels in this verse occurred through inverted causality; that is, reading Second Temple interpretation into First Temple texts. Perhaps a clearer reference to Watchers occurred in Dan 4:13–23.

5.3.5.2.3. Dan 4:13–23

The passage began, "I was looking in the visions of my head, upon my bed, and behold, a Watching and Holy One was coming down from the heavens." The title "Watching and Holy One," translated from עִיר וְקַדִּישׁ, was repeated in Second Temple literature (often pluralized) as "Watchers and Holy Ones."[96] In the Daniel passage, this Watcher acted in God's service similar to the Watchers in Second Temple Judaism. Yet, a Watcher serving God linked neither to the Sons of God in Genesis nor to Watchers faining connubial relationships with the daughters of men in Second Temple apocalyptic literature.

However, reading these passages together indicated a trajectory of the Watcher concept into the Second Temple period. This trajectory was admittedly weak, and most-likely also depended on concepts in the EAW. However, that dependence only strengthened the conclusion that no parent-child relationship existed between Second Temple apocalyptic literature and passages in the Tanakh, let alone with a specific Hebraic movement as it concerned the Watchers topos subtype.[97]

---

[95] Oswalt, *Book of Isaiah*, 455.

[96] Nickelsburg provided an excurses on this subject in his 1 Enoch commentary. There, he reflected on both וקדישין and עירין די שמיא, determining "Watcher" had "defined a particular class of heavenly beings" from the larger collection of angels designated as Sons of Heaven (God) or Holy Ones in various places—see Nickelsburg, *1 Enoch* 1, 140.

[97] In the Watchers texts of 1 Enoch and Jubilees, the Common Knowledge topos was specifically the Watchers who revealed secrets or took wives. The connection to a general idea of Watchers indicated not a parent-child relationship to Dan 4, but to a building concept of Watchers developed in the Second Temple period.

5.3.5. Step 4f: Evaluation

EAW literature held basic similarities to Second Temple flood and Watcher stories; furthermore, little reason existed to deny many of these stories inhabited the background from which Jewish apocalyptic authors drew. However, meaningful differences in the texts negated a parent-child relationship with "Eridu Genesis" and "Atrahasis," as well as Apollodorus's flood account. A close reading of the text also negated the three points of verbal contacts in Philo and the Illuyankaš myths. The same was true for Hesiod's Watcher narratives, which also included an inversion between it and Second Temple apocalyptic literature. Thus, no parent-child relationships existed between EAW material and Jewish apocalyptic literature for this topos type.

Individual texts in the Tanakh provided a few connections between the flood and the actions of the Sons of God in both Qumran and non-Qumran texts. However, those connections were not firm. Instead, they created a trajectory starting in the Genesis text; the Isaiah text provided latitude for later reading as well as a possible link for readers to connect Daniel with Genesis. This trajectory also hinted faintly at a prophetic influence, but the reference in Isaiah was not authoritative and thus was not factored into the discussion.

As for Daniel, the argument relied on an early date for authorship and recognizing Daniel as part of the prophetic movement, two very tenuous positions to hold in modern scholarship. In summary, a Common Knowledge topos type most likely drew on a general knowledge shared by many cultures; however, as the stories were generalized and then filled with additional details and meaning in succeeding cultures, the authority carried in these stories were localized to those cultures. Thus, in the Hebraic culture, elements of the flood and Watchers stemmed from the Tanakh, but the specifics and therefore the authority for these two uses of the Common Knowledge topos type was unique to the Second Temple world.

5.4. Literary Authority through Written Language: Covenant

The vast body of Hittite covenants provided a good picture of suzerainty in the EAW. Such documents included rights, responsibilities, and edicts to vassals. Several of these texts referred to Hittite-Egyptian treaties, including the treaty between Ramses II and Hattusilis after the

Battle of Kadesh.[98] These treaties inundated EAW cultures as well as forming the core of the Hebraic covenants. Perhaps, the two most-often cited scholars concerning EAW influence in Hebraic covenants have been Meredith Kline and Kenneth Kitchen. Kline compared Deuteronomy and EAW covenant structures, and Kitchen extended the work to Exodus, Leviticus, and Joshua 4.[99]

Scholars debate the first occurrences of covenant in the Tanakh, with some seeing a reference to a type of covenant in Gen 2:23.[100] Other scholars (especially dispensationalists) identify a pre- and postfall Adamic covenant. Nevertheless, the first clear reference to covenant occurs in the story of Noah, which is followed by references to the Abrahamic covenant in Gen 15 and 17. [101] These covenants and later covenant renewals occurred throughout the Pentateuch and later material.[102] Despite the EAW influence, the covenants in the Tanakh were unique in two ways. First was the three-part promise of land, seed, and nationhood in the Abrahamic covenant; the second was the demarcation of Israel's birth through the Mosaic covenant.[103]

The Second Temple authors specifically focused on the Abrahamic and Sinaitic covenants in their material and therefore, the Covenant topos type referenced only the Tanakh covenants. However, the relationship between Second Temple Jews and the Hebraic covenants was ripe for influence from outside sources. This situation was based on the intervening centuries of conflict, captivity, return, and restoration. The intervening history resulted in a forced historical catenation with the precaptive Hebraic culture driven by the problems

---

[98] Amnon Altman, "Rethinking the Hittite System of Subordinate Countries from the Legal Point of View," *JAOS* 123.4 (2003): 741; Wilson, "Egyptian Treaty," 199. This treaty may have occurred in preparation for a war against the Sea People.

[99] Meredith G. Kline, *Treaty of the Great King: The Covenant Structure of Deuteronomy: Studies and Commentary* (Grand Rapids: Eerdmans, 1963), 13–26; Kenneth Kitchen, *On the Reliability of the Old Testament*, revised ed. (Grand Rapids: Eerdmans, 2003), 284–85; also see Kitchen, *TLC* 1 ANE Covenants.

[100] Walter Brueggemann, "Of the Same Flesh and Bone, Gn 2:23a," *CBQ* 32.4 (1970): 539.

[101] Paul R. Williamson, *Abraham, Israel, and the Nations: The Patriarchal Promise and its Covenantal Development in Genesis*, vol. 315 (Sheffield: Sheffield Academic Press, 2000), 26–38.

[102] Rolf Rendtorff, *The Covenant Formula: An Exegetical and Theological Investigation* (Edinburgh: T&T Clark, 1998), 93.

[103] Peter C. Craigie, "Covenant," *BEB* 1:533.

of identity in postcaptivity Judaism. So, which element—EAW or Tanakh—had a larger influence on Second Temple authors' covenant understanding? If the latter held more influence than the former, did these references stem from the prophetic or priestly movements? Answering these questions depended on first identifying covenant references in apocalyptic literature.

5.4.1. Step 4a: Text—Definition and Use of Authority

A Covenant topos type was defined as a covenant or treaty, or a reference to a covenant or treaty, for the sake of the authority derived from it. Second Temple apocalyptic authors writing in a name other than Moses made little use of the Covenant topos type. For instance, the 1 Enoch P.authors made several references to righteousness and demanded the feasts be kept based on proper calendaring, but seldom directly through a Covenant topos.[104] In contrast, the Jubilean and Test. of Moses authors wrote in Moses's name and together, produced over fifty references to "covenant."

5.4.2. Step 4b: Text and Context—Use in Apocalyptic Literature

As already mentioned, the authors of 1 Enoch seldom referenced "covenant." In the few places where such references were made, however, the authors used two Ge'ez words: *maḥalā*, and *šerʿat*. These words were examined in the following subsections.

5.4.2.1. Maḥalā in 1 Enoch

Maḥalā translated into English as "oath," "treaty," "covenant," or "adjuration."[105] Ge'ez writers used *maḥalā* in place of διαθήκη for Coptic Exod 6:4, which Greek writers translated from the Hebrew ברית.[106] Thus, *maḥalā* had a direct connection to "covenant." In 60:6, the author used this term to describe Enoch's eschatological vision:

---

[104] Nickelsburg, *1 Enoch* 1, 50.

[105] Wolf Leslau, "Maḥalā," *Comparative Dictionary of Ge'ez: (Classical Ethiopic); Ge'ez-English, English Ge'ez with an Index of the Semitic Roots [CDG]* 335.

[106] Nickelsburg-VanderKam, *1 Enoch* 2, 238. Although based on Nickelsburg's work here and his article on Enochic Wisdom (see "Enochic Wisdom: An Alternative to the Mosaic Torah," in *Hesed Ve-Emet: Studies in Honor of Ernest S. Frerichs*, ed. Jodi Magness and Seymour Gitin, BJS 320 [Atlanta: Scholars Press, 1998], 124–26), the list of verses in this subsection depended on Kelley Cobelentz

> And when this day arrives—and the power, the punishment, and the judgment, which the Lord of the Spirits has prepared for those who do not worship the righteous judgment, for those who deny the righteous judgment, and for those who take his name in vain—it will become a day of covenant for the elect and inquisition for the sinners.

Nickelsburg identified the Noahic covenant as the referent, based on similar references in 55:1–2.[107] However, *Maḥalā* only occurred 60:6. Intertextuality indicated the referent was Exod 6:4, pointing to the Abrahamic covenant. Nevertheless, the question of a parent-child relationship was not dependent on differentiating between Tanakh covenants.

The Covenant topos type was used here as an eschatological hope by contrasting the judgment of sinners. As such, the P.author promised a covenant to those who continued in the ethical norms established in the community. However, this passage also held a warning. To forgo the norms was to forgo the covenant. Hence, the author used this topos type to manipulate beliefs and the worship of God. Another use of this topos type occurred with the word *šerʿat*, which focused more heavily on eschatological hope.

5.4.2.2. Šerʿat in 1 Enoch

In 93:4, an Enochian translator used *šerʿat* in reference to an increase of great, evil things and deceit: of great evil and deceit: "After it is ended, injustice shall become greater, and he shall make a law [covenant] for the sinners" (93:4). Nickelsburg argued this occurrence referred to the Noahic covenant, but he argued *šerʿat* as "law," rather than "covenant."[108] The word appeared again two verses later in what Bautch called "the only explicit mention of the Sinai covenant."[109] In 1 En. 93:6, the context was

---

Bautch's 1 Enoch work—see *A Study of the Geography of 1 Enoch 17–19: No One Has Seen What I Have Seen*, SJSJ 81 (Leiden: Brill, 2003), 290.

[107] Nickelsburg-VanderKam, *1 Enoch 2*, 238.

[108] Nickelsburg, *1 Enoch* 1, 50.

[109] Coblentz Bautch, *Study of the Geography*, 289. Coblentz Bautch took this statement from Nickelsburg, who wrote it "refer[s] to the eternal covenant…although the translation, 'law,' was not excluded" (*1 Enoch*, 446). Nickelsburg also argued, "The final redactor of the Book of the Watchers may allude to this covenant in 1:4…perhaps indicating that God is coming to condemn the transgression of the Sinaitic covenant" (ibid., 50).

the Apocalypse of Weeks, but note the Tablets of Heaven acted as a secondary authority:

> Then after that, at the completion of the third week a (certain) man shall be elected as the plant of the righteous judgment, and after him, one (other) shall emerge as the eternal plant of righteousness. After that at the completion of the fourth week visions of the old and righteous ones shall be seen; and a law [covenant] shall be made with a fence, for all the generations.

Depending on the translation, *šerʿat* appeared a third time in 99:2. The context was a series of woes that read like a polemic against religious rivals:

> Woe unto you who alter the words of truth and pervert the eternal law [covenant]! They reckon themselves not guilty of sin, they shall be trampled on upon the earth.

The final occurrence was in 106:13, where the recension 𝔊ᵖ used "covenant of heaven" in place of the "law of heaven":

> For in the generation of Jared, my father, they transgressed the word of the Lord, (that is) the law of heaven [covenant of heaven]. And behold, they commit sin and transgress the commandment.[110] If manuscripts A, B, and C represented the earlier reading, then a later author may have written covenant into the text. If 𝔊ᵖ and Ethiopian Enoch represented an older text, then later authors may have written covenant out of the text.[111] More likely, however, these distinctions identified

[110] The following material is a direct quote from Isaac's notes on this text: "Or 'the regulation or order (or rule, commandment, principle, custom) of heaven'; so A [Kebrān 9/II], B [𝔈³], and C [(𝔈²⁰⁸⁰] read *ʾemaʿelta samāy*, 'from the heights of heaven' or 'from heaven above,' instead of *ʿemserʿāta samāy*. 𝔊ᵖ [Chester Beatty papyrus] read 'from the covenant of heaven'" (Isaac, "1 Enoch," in Charlesworth, *OTP* 1:87 n.*x*2).

[111] Standard textual criticism was to accept the rougher or shorter read as closer to the original and assume any explanatory phrases, longer reads, or smoother texts as later additions; but not always. Emanuel Tov posited rougher reads may be the result of scribal mistakes (see *Textual Criticism of the Hebrew Bible*, 2nd rev. ed. [Minneapolis: Fortress, 1992], 303), and Philip Comfort wrote that after Wescott and Hort, text critics moved to accept the "most likely original is the one that best

differing interpretations—no reason existed to assume a normative text and its variations.[112]

For the Enochian authors, the Covenant topos type and the authority that came with it were used primarily for judgment or eschatological hope. In the later Ge'ez, Maḥalā references to covenant included both, whereas *šer'at*, often translated as "law," referenced what was established in the eschaton or what was violated (which then brought about judgment).

5.4.2.3. Jubilees and Testament of Moses

Jubilees, as an expansion of Genesis and Exodus, contained over forty references to the covenants. Moreover, the references were specific—for example, "My [God's] covenant" (1:10, referring to the Sinai covenant), "the covenant with Noah" (6:3), and "the covenant with Abram" (14:16). These covenant texts, however, did not simply reproduce the covenants in the Tanakh. Instead, they expanded the text.

Likewise, the Testament of Moses, which concerned the transfer of power from Moses to Joshua, held nine Covenant topoi. The author referenced the Sinaitic covenant in several ways, including a reminder of the land declared for Israel "through the leadership of Joshua" (1:10),[113] reminders that Israelites would break the covenant (2:7), and cries to God to remember "his" or "your" covenant (4:2, 5). In these references, the author repeatedly provided information, authority, or a warning that replicated what was found in the Tanakh. Other references to covenant existed in Second Temple apocalyptic literature, such as blessings, cursings, oaths, and so on. The volume of references in Jubilees and the

---

explains the variants" (*Encountering the Manuscripts: An Introduction to New Testament Paleography and Textual Criticism* [Nashville: Broadman & Holman, 2005], 292). Applied to this passage, it would seem likely that covenant was read back into the text as a clarification.

[112] The variant, "The sanctuary of the eternal covenant" in 12:4, based on 𝔊 and interpreted as such by Knibb, occurred in a single text; further, it was a translation not widely accepted. "Tabernacle" or "sanctuary," as suggested by Matthew Black, was the preferred reading. Matthew Black, *The Book of Enoch, or 1 Enoch: A New English Edition: With Commentary and Textual Notes*, SVTP 7, ed. A. M. Denis and M. De Jonge (Leiden: E. J. Brill, 1985), 143.

[113] "Leadership of Joshua" clarified the covenant reference to the Sinaitic covenant, rather than the Abrahamic covenant.

Testament of Moses prompted a focus on those two books. Although only a few covenant references existed in 1 Enoch, the issue of covenant in 1 Enoch has been widely discussed in modern scholarship. As such, covenant references in 1 Enoch were also explored.

5.4.2.4. Qumran

The Qumran Covenant topos type was distinct from other Second Temple topoi since the community believed they alone were the remnant-inheritors of the Tanakh covenants. This reality was found in the phrase ברית היחד (Covenant of the Community), "A term indicating that the sectarians saw themselves as banding together to observe the 'renewed covenant' of God with his chosen ones, the members of the sect."[114] The members of the covenant community considered themselves "the sons of light" who were headed by the Archangel Michael. The sons of light were engaged in a war against the "sons of darkness" (consisting of all who rejected their teachings) led by Belial.[115] The covenant community belief also set the foundation for ethical purity, occasioning thirty-one references to covenant in 1QS (Rule of the Community). As such, covenant was definitional to Qumran identity.

This focus on covenant at Qumran, and in other Second Temple texts as well, has inspired much scholarly debate, but only two discussions were germane to this study. The first was covenant and identity. The second helped inform this study on the Covenant topos type.

5.4.3. Step 4c: Text and Context—Germane Scholarship

Covenant as identity began with the Abrahamic and Mosaic covenants, which lay at the core of Tanakh Hebraism; but in the Second Temple period, "being Jewish" incorporated several concepts. E. P. Sanders proposed two strains of Judaism existed during the Second Temple period: a normative strain he called "common Judaism" and a second strain he called "covenantal nomism," which then anchored

[114] Schiffman, *Qumran and Jerusalem*, 102.

[115] Adapted from: Flusser, *Judaism* 1, 2. These beliefs occasioned hostile attitudes against outsiders (CD-A iii) . However, Hultgren argued elements in the CD were written against community members who failed to leave behind outside influences. His argument would indicate even greater separation and antagonistic beliefs. See Hultgren, "Damascus Covenant," 12–29.

common Judaism. He listed several defining elements: dependence, belief, obedience, and continuation of the Sinaitic covenant with a hope of purity and deliverance. Within these strains, a central tenant implied the covenant promises were still current, based on Israel's eternal election. Thus, no danger existed concerning God refusing to fulfill his promises.[116] Scholars and later archaeological discoveries have since challenged Sanders's proposal. Jacob Neusner, for instance, proposed multiple Judaisms, arguing they cohered to the same general Jewish canon, but each strain appealed to distinct parts.[117] James Davila argued for the single term "Judaism" but understood the term as members of a group who self-identified as Jews and had several common traits. Such traits included "worship of God of Israel alone,…following of the customs, laws, and rituals mandated in those scriptures; participation in or support of the temple cult in Judaism…[and accepting] Palestine as the Holy Land."[118] In these traits, Davila included several key covenant concepts: land, worship the God of Israel alone, Torah obedience, and active participation in the Hebraic cult.

All of these concepts carried implicit or explicit connections to covenant, such as worshipping only God and participation in the temple cult, both of which were Mosaic concepts. Therefore, the idea of covenant was still important to Second Temple Judaism. Moreover, they were especially important to Qumran as noted in the previous section. This brief review of scholarship served as a reminder that community members self-identifying as Jews shared ideas of covenant, but they also held several distinctions, and these distinctions appeared within the apocalyptic material. As such, uses of the Covenant topos type were more susceptible to context compared to other topoi types, and the meaning and

---

[116] E. P. Sanders, *Paul and Palestinian Judaism: A Comparison of Patterns of Religion* (Philadelphia: Fortress Press, 1977), 422; cf. 104–06; Portier-Young, *Apocalypse against Empire*, 283.

[117] Jacob Neusner, "Preface," in *Judaisms and Their Messiahs at the Turn of the Christian Era*, ed. Jacob Neusner, William Scott Green, and Ernest S. Frerichs (Cambridge: Cambridge University Press, 1987), xii, accessed 1987. Note, however, Neusner's *Judaisms* read more as Christian denominations (or Christianities) than independent religions, and he argued as much on page xi.

[118] James Davila, *The Provenance of the Pseudepigrapha: Jewish, Christian, or Other?* SJSJ 105 (Leiden: Brill, 2005), 19. According to Davila, there was no key trait or traits that all people *must* hold to be considered Jewish, rather, he claimed a group of traits, most of which have been accepted by most others who self-identified as Jews.

necessity of covenant may have varied across the broad spectrum of Judaism.[119]

5.4.4. Step 4d: Cross-Text—Possible EAW Sources

The three sources with the Covenant topos type examined in step 3 that scored well enough to include in step 4d were the "Second Oracle of Salvation," the Amulet from Arslan Tash, and "The Marduk Prophecy."[120] The Legend of King Keret, while including a repeating covenant refrain, was too different in both context and word picture (as defined in chapter 1). The same was true for Urakagina's Reforms (Ensi of Lagash).

5.4.4.1. "Second Oracle of Salvation" (to Esarhaddon)

As mentioned in the discussion of the Tablets topos type in chapter 3, the oracles in this tablet described Ashur's covenant that occasioned Esarhaddon's enthronement:

> I slaughtered your enemies and filled the River with their blood. Let them see it and praise me, for I am Ashur, lord of the gods! This is the oracle of peace placed before the statue. This covenant tablet of Ashur enters the king's presence on a cushion. Fragrant oil is sprinkled, sacrifices are made, incense is burnt and (the tablet) is read out before the king.

The deity promised peace through divine warfare, opposite many inscriptions in the EAW whereby the king went to war to reinstate

---

[119] Although considered an independent topos type, Covenant also may have been paired with the Authority by Name topos type. Najman and Portier-Young argued the term "Torah of Moses" in the early Second Temple period was not the name of a body of literature, but "serves as a category and a claim to authority"—see Najman, *Seconding Sinai*, 116; Portier-Young, *Apocalypse against Empire*, 283. If Najman and Portier-Young were correct, then any use of "Torah of Moses" was a use of both Covenant and Authority by Name.

[120] The plethora of covenants among EAW empires and people were not presented here because of the stipulation they were the predominant influence for covenants in the Tanakh, and because the question at hand for this research concerned how authors borrowed authority using a Covenant topos type, not how covenants themselves were authoritative.

the justice of his god.[121] This covenant contained promises that resembled certain Tanakh promises (such as Deut 9:1–3); however, was it similar to Second Temple apocalyptic texts? Ashur's covenant reviewed his deliverance of Esarhaddon; his oracle of salvation was a reminder of the victory.[122] Similarities occurred in 1 En. 60:6, wherein the assurance of a coming day of covenant meant deliverance for the elect; "And when this day arrives—and the power, the punishment, and the judgement…it will become a day of covenant for the elect and inquisition for the sinners" (1 En. 60:6). The future promise was one of victory. Both texts, therefore, assured peace through the enemy's destruction (past tense for Esarhaddon, future tense in 1 Enoch), which created a point of verbal contact.

The text of "The Second Oracle of Salvation" was part of a larger group of texts that most likely represented "a description of a procession leading to Esarhaddon's enthronement festival in Ešarra, the Aššur temple of Ashur."[123] It began with a call for the Assyrians to listen to what Ashur had done; that is, delivering the king from his enemies (10–22). Thus delivered, Esarhaddon then took the throne (implicit in the text). A narration followed concerning his covenants with Ashur, their placement before the statue of Ashur in the temple (line 26), and a public reading in the presence of the king (27–31).[124] Together, the three texts concerning

[121] The Sumerian king, Eanatum, was currently the earliest known king to claim divine instruction or order for war. He worked to regain his father's losses in the twenty-fifth century BCE, claiming the blessings of Inanna, Ninhursag, and Ningirsu (and later, Enlil) in his quest. Peeter Espak, "The Emergence of the Concept of Divine Warfare and Theology of War in the Ancient Near East," in *ENDC Proceedings* 14.2 (2011): 122–25.

[122] According to Simo Parpola, "The soteriological significance of the present passage was based on the fact that it referred to events that actually took place." Simo Parpola, trans. "Second Oracle of Salvation," in *Assyrian Prophecies,* State Archives of Assyria, ed. Simo Parpola and Robert M. Whiting, vol. 9 (Helsinki, Helsinki University Press, 1997), Collection 3.3 n21.

[123] Seow, trans. "85. SAA 9 3.2," in Machinist, *Prophets and Prophecy*, 118 n.*c*.

[124] Parpola, "Second Oracle," Collection 3.3 (see n.27 for a discussion of placement in the Holy of Holies and n.32 concerning the coronation ritual). Concerning the translation of "covenant" in Theodore Lewis's work on the identity and function of EAW gods, Lewis looked at "The Role of Deity as a Treaty Partner," (a subheading within his work). He wrote, "Special note should be made of the expression, tuppi adê…. It makes…sense not to lose the force of the word adê and thus to translate it as 'the tablet of the adê treaty/oath/agreement'" (Theodore J. Lewis, "The Identity and Function of

Esarhaddon represented a yearly rehearsal of his enthronement. The renewal carried similarities to the yearly celebrations of the Feast of Tabernacles (even though the Mosaic law was read aloud once every seven years; Deut 31:10–11) and to several covenant renewals throughout the Tanakh, but these elements were absent in 1 En. 60:6.

A second possible point of verbal contact was the promised punishment of the enemies. However, the Esarhaddon text concerned only the deliverance of the king, followed by his ascent to the throne. The festival was a reminder of what Ashur did and who he was: "I slaughtered your enemies and filled the river with their blood. Let them see (it) and praise me, (knowing) that I am Ashur, lord of the gods" (lines 22–26). By comparison, the text of Enoch concerned righteous punishment and deliverance of a suffering people. It was the fulfillment of a covenant promise, rather than a reminder of a covenant associated with a king's enthronement. These observations led to the conclusion that only one point of verbal contact existed and therefore, the topos type was not strong enough to warrant a parent-child relationship with occurrences in Second Temple material.

5.4.4.2. Amulet from Arslan Tash

The Covenant topos type also occurred in the amulet from Arslan Tash, found on the reverse side (specifically, lines 8–9). The script wrapped around (and through) a depiction of a warrior-god bearing a hatchet or small ax (fig. 3 [below]):

> The court I tread, you shall not tread! Ashur has made an eternal covenant with us. He has made (a covenant) with us, along with all the sons of El and the leaders of the council of all the Holy Ones, with a covenant of the Heavens and Eternal Earth, with an oath of Ba'al.[125]

El/Baal Berith," *JBL* 115.3 [1996]: 406–08). However, Lauinger has proposed adê, which was seen in other texts "as the direct object of tamû (to swear), and in apposition with māmītu, (oath)," as "oath" or "destiny," thus, tuppi adê is an oath tablet. Moreover, once it was sealed by Ashur, it became a Tablet of Destinies—see Jacob Lauinger, "The Neo-Assyrian adê: Treaty, Oath, or Something Else?," *Journal for Ancient Near East and Biblical Law* 19 (2003): 105–15.

[125] Several scholars considered this amulet a forgery. The amulet was included here not due to conviction of authenticity, but due to a desire for not delimiting

Figure 3. The Arslan Tash amulet. Drawing by C. G. Häberl, used with permission.

Several key points existed in this text: (1) the amulet-maker labeled the covenant "eternal"; (2) Ashur made the covenant with "us"; (3) the text included a covenant of the Heavens and Holy earth; and (4) the covenant formed the basis for protecting the owner of the amulet "against the Flyers, the goddesses, against Sasm son of Padrishisha' the god, and against the Strangler of the Lamb" (lines 1–6 obverse side). Thus, this topos functioned as an apotropaic incantation, depicting a warrior-god protecting the bearer from evil,[126] but did it exist in a parent-child relationship with Second Temple literature?

Frank Cross and Richard Saley believed the amulet was a forerunner of the mezuzah, calling it "a pagan prototype of the…the Israelite portal

---

material that later may be considered valid. For a discussion on this issue, see P. Amiet, "Observations sur les 'Tabletter Magiques' d'Arslan Tash," *Aula Orientalis* 1 (1983): 109. Also, see Noel Weeks, *Admonition and Curse: The Ancient Near Eastern Treaty/Covenant Form as a Problem in Inter-Cultural Relationships* LHBOTS 407 (London: T&T Clark, 2004), 132.

[126] "An Amulet from Arslan Tash," trans. P. Kyle McCarter (*COS* 2.86:223); cf. also Chuck G. Häberl, "Unpublished Paper on the Arslan Tash Amulet No. 1," https://www.academia.edu/5074216/Arslan_Tash_Amulet_No._1_AT1. Note, the evil has been interpreted as the evil eye, or that which kept away the spring water among other things. André Caquot, "La seconde tablette ou 'petite amulette' d'Arslan-Tash," *Syria* 48.3–4 (1971): 394–95.

inscription."[127] If they have correctly assessed the amulet, they have opened Hebrew culture (and later Judaism) to Northwestern Semitic influences beyond common linguistics and etiological narratives, but what was the strength of this influence? The concepts of an eternal covenant and polemic writing implied two points of verbal contact between the amulet and 1 En. 99:2. Although a third point of verbal contact did not exist, the amulet was still included in this research as Cross and Saley's argument concerning the connection of the amulet to the mezuzah may be correct. Therefore, it was accepted as a point of historical contact.

A closer reading of the text and a broader historical view, however, negated these points of verbal contact. First, although seldom phrased as an "eternal covenant" in EAW literature, the idea was tacit in many treaty texts. The parity treaty between Hattusilis III and Ramesses II, for instance, proclaimed a "relationship…determined from eternity by the gods."[128] In "The Marduk Prophecy," Marduk promised a covenant to the king who "will ever cause him to enter Der and the Ugal-kalama."[129] In the Legend of King Keret, after the king lost everything, Eldescended in a dream and offered "friendship by covenant and vassalage forever" (line 54). The phrase repeated in line 128 and 140, almost as a refrain.[130] Several scholars have also argued the Abrahamic and Davidic covenants in the Tanakh were eternal. Therefore, eternality was not unique to the Arslan Tash amulet.

Second, the polemic similarity also failed after examining the context. The amulet was an incantation-inscribed apotropaic trinket; by comparison, the Enochic text was a prophetic woe leveled against the wicked, the liars, and those who prevented the covenant. Therefore, only the historical point of contact remained, which disallowed a parent-child relationship with Jewish apocalyptic material based on the Covenant topos type.

---

[127] Frank M. Cross and Richard J. Saley, "Phoenician Incantations on a Plaque of the Seventh Century BC from Arslan Tash in Upper Syria," *BASOR* 197 (1970): 49.

[128] Weeks, *Admonition and Curse*, 73.

[129] "The Marduk Prophecy," trans. Tremper Longman III (*COS* 1.149, 481). See §5.4.4.3 (below) for a discussion on "The Marduk Prophecy."

[130] "Ugaritic Myths, Epics, and Legends," trans. H. L. Ginsberg (*ANET*, 143–45).

5.4.4.3. "The Marduk Prophecy"

According to Tremper Longman III, "The Marduk Prophecy" was a "fictional biography" with a prophetic conclusion:

> That prince will [rule all] the lands. And I, the god of all, will [covenant] with him. He will destroy Elam. He will destroy its cities. The city and its swamps he will turn away. He causes the great king of Der to arise in his doorframe. He will change its deathly silence. His evil [...]. His hand he will seize. He will ever cause him [the Prince] to enter Der and the Ugal-kalama.[131]

Marduk confirmed the king's reign through a covenant reference, which signaled this Covenant topos type.[132]

At first, this text looked to be archetypical to Jewish material because of the permeating apocalyptic overtones and an inverted natural order:

> The corpses of the people block the gates. Brother consumes brother. Friend strikes his friend with a weapon. Aristocrats stretch out their hands (to beg) from the commoner. The scepter grows short. Evil lies across the land.[133]

Further, in ii19, the author promised a future king who would set the inversion right, including a positive response from nature:

---

[131] Longman, "Marduk Prophecy," 480. Longman used "befriend" instead of "covenant," yet the contextual meaning of "befriend" held the idea of "covenant," which was why it was changed here.

[132] Scholars have debated translating *ki* (*itti*)-*šu salmāku* as "befriend" or "covenant"—see Weeks, *Admonition and Curse*, 32. Theodore Lewis argued earlier scholars "have documented the regular use of the verb, *salāmu*, for political alliances and covenants" (Lewis, "Identity and Function," 406). Lewis also referenced Simo Parpola's work ("Neo-Assyrian Treaties from the Royal Archives of Nineveh," *JCS* 39.2 [1987]: 161–89), allowing a possible rendering of "to make peace" or "to seek détente." The latter translation prevailed in this study in order to cast a wider net for possible sources.

[133] "Inverted nature" appeared often as a symbol of divine abandonment, wrath, or theodicy in EAW work, such as the Sumerian "Lamentation over the Destruction of Ur," the Akkadian Myth of "Erra and Ishum," and "Poems of the Righteous Sufferer"; the Hittite "Wrath of Telipinu"; the Egyptian Coffin Text Spell 1130, and the "Book of the Dead" 175; and the Neo-Assyrian "Atrahasis" (version 2).

> The rivers will carry fish. The fields and plains will be full of yield. The grass of winter (will last) to summer. The grass of summer will last to winter. The harvest of the land will thrive. The marketplace will prosper."

Together, Marduk and the king righted all wrongs, disposed of evil, and restored the natural order to its most bountiful and pristine state. The apocalyptic overtones, inverted nature, and later work of the king created three possible points of verbal contact to be examined. Two differences, however, denied setting this text as an archetype to apocalyptic literature, let alone holding a parent-child relationship with Second Temple authoritative topoi.

First, Marduk created a theopolemus in the king.[134] Doing so legitimized the king's wars and reign but worked against Marduk's immanence. He only worked at arm's length through the king who fought the battles. In Enoch, God prepared the Day of the Covenant in 60:6 without a theopolemus. Although the author of 1 En. 93:4 may have followed "The Marduk Prophecy" pattern, further scrutiny identified neither deliverance nor a theopolemus. Additionally, although Noah received a covenant after deliverance, his covenant was "for the sinners" and not himself (nor did Noah act as a theopolemus). Furthermore, the following texts (1 En. 99:2; 106:13) held no literary or word picture similarities with "The Marduk Prophecy" except for the covenant itself. As for the Jubilees and Testament of Levi topoi, the P.authors set both stories amid God delivering Israel from Egypt; the Divine Warrior delivering his people through direct acts.

A comparison to Moses also failed. According to the Jubilean author, God delivered Moses from Mastema (48:4), executed vengeance on Egypt because of his covenant with Abraham (48:8), smote the magicians of Egypt (48:11), stood between the Egyptians and Israelites and then brought them through the sea (48:13), and destroyed the Egyptians (48:14). Consequently, Moses was a herald rather than a theopolemus; he announced, but God brought about the

[134] "Theopolemus" is defined as "God's warrior," a god's hero for earthly battles. This definition should be understood separately from the person, Theopolĕmuś, "a man who, with his brother Hiero, plundered Apollo's temple at Delphi" (J. Lempriére, "Theopolĕmuś," *A Classical Dictionary,* n.p.).

action.[135] This shift from a theopolemus to a herald created a meaningful difference: in Jewish apocalyptic literature, God was intimately involved in delivering his people. Second, "The Marduk Prophecy" served as a future promise for the king's victories, but most of the Covenant topos type occurrences in Second Temple literature concerned instructions, judgments, or warnings against explicit, unrighteous acts. In 1 En. 93:4 and Jub. 6:4, the authors focused on historiographic Noah, and in Jub. 6:11, the Noahic story became a foundation for action with Moses in the Sinaitic covenant. Judgments and warnings came in the 1 En. 60:6 vision, in the 99:2 woe-text, and in the instructive and judgment texts of 1 En. 106:13 and Jub. 1:10. These meaningful differences negated setting "The Marduk Prophecy" in a parent-child relationship with Second Temple writing; yet, they indicated an overarching EAW covenant idea that may have filtered to Second Temple authors through the OT.

5.4.5. Step 4e: Cross-Text—Possible Tanakh Sources

A search for "covenant" produced between 260 and 340 hits in English versions of the Tanakh, 284 in the MT (using בְּרִית [lemma search]), and 344 in the LXX (διαθήκη [lemma search]); often, several references occurred within a single pericope. The high number of hits showed the concept of covenant was important across most of the Tanakh. Second Temple Jews looking to re-establish or strengthen connections to older narratives because of their ruptured history would have found a prominent theme in the Covenant topos type. However, the vast number of hits in the search through the Tanakh mandated a more effective method for engaging this topos. That method was reading the Tanakh through the perspective of the Second Temple authors with the help of modern scholars.

---

[135] However, Orville Wintermute's footnote (d) on this text in *OTP* 2:139 is worth replicating here in full: "In his translation, Charles suggested this emendation. The Eth. MSS have 'to do,' which makes a difficult reading. Perhaps one could retain the Eth[iopian] text by assuming a command to work sympathetic magic: 'Everything was sent in your hand so that you might act (it out) before it was done.'" This rendering seemed to lend more credence to Moses as a theopolemus, but in the two scenes where an enemy came to take life (Mastema against Moses; the Egyptian army against Israel), it was still God alone who acted according to Jubilees.

5.4.5.1. OT Covenant and Enoch

In the second line of 1 En. 99:2, the author wrote, "And pervert the eternal covenant." Charles connected this "eternal covenant" with the Mosaic covenant, as did Matthew Black.[136] Nickelsburg disagreed, "The only clear reference to [the Mosaic Torah] in the Epistle is in 93:6, although 99:14 may be another instance."[137] He referred to recited wisdom in 1 Enoch 82 and promoted as equal to Torah, although he provided a caveat for the "passage [being] clearly concerned about divine law" based on parallelisms in 99:2.[138]

5.4.5.2. OT Covenant and Jubilees

As mentioned in the section on tablets, the Tablets of the Law stemmed from the Tablets of Heaven in the book of Jubilees, which contained the Torah and written history according to the Jubilean P.author. By process of inversion, the Tablets of Heaven gained authority from the Tablets of the Law in Hebraic history. These tablets represented the covenant with Israel; a single eternal covenant God entered with Noah and then renewed with Abraham and Moses.

Beginning with the Jubilean version of the Noahic covenant, the author included days and seasons, which assured proper festival observance. Elements of the law on ingesting animal blood also appeared, as did the Festival of Weeks, which linked to creation in Jubilees. Thus, "The correct calendar becomes part of the eternal covenant between the Lord and the members of the chosen line,"[139] from whom Sinaitic Israel descended.[140] In the Jubilean version of the Abrahamic covenant, the practice of circumcision stemmed from the Tablets of Heaven and extended even to certain angels (Jub. 15:25, 32). The P.author opened the pericope in chapter 15 by identifying that Abram sacrificed and feasted on the first fruits, celebrating the Festival of Weeks in the third month of the year. According to VanderKam, the Jubilean author set aside the festival as a time of covenant renewal, making Abraham's covenant a renewal of Enoch's covenant with

---

[136] Charles, *Pseudepigrapha* 2:271; Black, *Book of Enoch*, 304, 23.

[137] Nickelsburg, *1 Enoch* 1, 489.

[138] Ibid.

[139] VanderKam, *Book of Jubilees*, 36.

[140] Outside the purview of this study were questions concerning a "great mixture" of people who had no Abrahamic ties. Did Israel at Sinai include this mixture in Jubilees?

additions.[141] Moreover, these covenant additions were permissible because they originated from the Tablets of Heaven. The Jubilees-Mosaic covenant also began in the third month, making it a Noahic renewal with additions as well.

This idea of renewal also provided a possible clarification for the "the eternal covenant" reference in 1 En. 99:2. The referent was the divine law of God, which derives from wisdom (Nickelsburg's claim). However, that wisdom was enshrined in a single covenant made with Noah and then renewed by Abraham and Moses. One way to test this idea was investigating if the P.author followed a similar pattern of connecting the covenants in the Testament of Moses.

5.4.5.3. Testament of Moses

The T. Moses P.author referenced land that God promised through both the Abrahamic and Mosaic covenants (1:9), the latter of which Moses mediated (1:14). Covenant references following chapter 1 prophetically referred to Israel's tribes falling away from God. The focus, however, was the covenant-forefathers: "Then all the tribes will lament, crying out to heaven and saying, God of Abraham, God of Isaac, and God of Jacob, remember your covenant" (3:9). In the fourth chapter, the reference was to the "covenant which [God] made with their fathers" (4:5); but the verse concluded with "[God] will openly show his compassion," a promise from the Mosaic covenant (Deut. 30:3). Each book thus connected the covenants; specifically, the author of Jubilees established one covenant and many renewals based on the Tablets topos type (Tablets of Heaven and Tablets of the Law).

Consequently, a strong connection existed between Tanakh covenants and the topos type in Second Temple apocalyptic literature. However, the Enochian absence of Tanakh covenants and other P.authors' proclivity to read a connection between them showed several meaningful differences and a trajectory of the topos type. The authority for these topoi derived from Second Temple beliefs on the Covenant topos. Therefore, no parent-child relationship existed between specific texts in the Tanakh and the Jewish apocalyptic literature for this topos type.

---

[141] VanderKam, *Book of Jubilees*, 37.

5.4.6. Step 4f: Evaluation

The EAW texts initially seemed promising, but the Esarhaddon text was a covenant following the EAW treaty form. Any likenesses between it and the Tanakh covenants, let alone with Second Temple Covenant topoi, were attributable to widespread familiarity. Therefore, only one point of verbal contact remained between it and Second Temple apocalyptic literature. This lack of verbal contacts and presence of similar contacts across the EAW negated a parent-child relationship. The Amulet from Arslan Tash held a Covenant topos and may even have influenced later Hebraic culture.

However, the topos itself occurred inside an apotropaic spell warding against evil whereas 1 En. 99:2 was a woe—a prophecy against unrighteous and covenant-breaking humans. These meaningful differences and distracting dissimilarities in the context negated the verbal points of contact. "The Marduk Prophecy" showed closer similarities. However, the meaningful difference of the king as theopolemus and the context of the ex-eventu prophecy mandating his reign denied a parent-child relationship.

The Tanakh provided a stronger connection—the Noahic, Abrahamic, and Mosaic covenants all influenced Jewish apocalyptic literature, but the understanding of these covenants developed in a trajectory that placed the authority of the topos in the Second Temple community. In Jubilees, the differing covenants were each established in the third month signifying these covenants were all renewals of the Noahic covenant. This addition created meaningful differences from the Tanakh covenant texts. Moreover, 1 Enoch and the Testament of Moses followed similar patterns, although not to the same extent. Therefore, no parent-child relationship existed between a specific text or Hebraic movement and Jewish apocalyptic literature.

The Covenant topos type most-likely stemmed from both the EAW and Tanakh material. However, the topos type was stripped of EAW peculiarities; and, to a lesser degree, Tanakh peculiarities. To this last point, the P.authors combined covenants in so-called priestly accounts and D-source material with Noahic and Abrahamic covenants. Further, the Noahic covenant contained an abundance of wisdom elements even as it provided the Sinai law-giving material. Therefore, an authoritative topos developed with roots in the EAW and Hebraic material alike, but was distinct in Second Temple apocalyptic work, most likely based on a

Second Temple tradition that interwove wisdom and priestly traditions with the larger EAW understanding.

5.5. Referential Authority through Physical Elements: Cosmology

In this study, "cosmology" referred to celestial bodies and terrestrial elements such as mountains, rivers, and seas, which included their order and patterns of movement. Celestial bodies held a deified position in most EAW cultures as they were "all-encompassing…permanent and immutable features of the cosmos."[142] They also played a part in an EAW Platoesque concept now labeled "archaic ontology," which scholars have defined as believing "the terrestrial realm [is] a copy of the celestial one."[143] Within archaic ontology, correspondence existed between celestial and human bodies that represented cosmic singularity.[144] This correlation between micro- and macrocosm occurred across the EAW and beyond. For instance, in Malaysia, beliefs concerning the nine emperor gods were matched to the nine planets and nine human orifices. For Zoroastrianism, the micro-macrocosm correlation appeared in ceremonies as practitioners worked through rituals based on "verbal events, mainly comprising recitation of texts…. Mistakes in the verbal (and non-verbal) performance [were] dramatic since they undermine[d] the cosmic order and strengthen the evil powers."[145] Finally, an inversion to the micro-macrocosm correlation occurred in Rome. There, sexually penetrating a Vestal Virgin negated protection, inviting enemy penetration. In reality, the macrocosm, represented by the threats against Rome, caused accusations in the

---

[142] Jacques M. Chevalier Chevalier, *A Postmodern Revelation: Signs of Astrology and the Apocalypse* (Toronto: University of Toronto Press, 1997), 52.

[143] Jonathan Z. Smith, introduction to the 2005 edition of *The Myth of the Eternal Return: Cosmos and History*, by Mircea Eliade, 2nd paperback ed., Bollingen Series 46 (Princeton: Princeton University Press, 2005), xiii.

[144] Philippe Gignoux, "Microcosm and Macrocosm in Pre-Islamic Iranian Thought: the Theory of the Correspondence between the Different Parts of the Human Being and Those of the Cosmos," in *Encyclopaedia Iranica*, ed. Ehsan Yarshater (New York: Encyclopaedia Iranica Foundation, 2004), http://www.iranicaonline.org/articles/microcosm-and-macrocosm; Albert Amao, *The Birth of a New Consciousness and the Cycles of Time* (Bloomington: AuthorHouse, 2016), II.3.

[145] Michael Stausberg, "Zoroastrian Rituals," in *Encyclopaedia Iranica* (New York: Encyclopaedia Iranica Foundation, 2014), http://www.iranicaonline.org/articles/zoroastrian-rituals.

microcosm—a Vestal Virgin accused of sexual activity.[146] The micro-macrocosm concept is so common in the ancient world that K. A. H. Hidding wrote of *Makroanthropos*—the phenomenon of humanity projecting the micro as macro-reality, making the gods and the cosmos in humanity's image as defined by the community.[147]

Another element of the Cosmology topos type were sacred mountains that often housed a deity. Moreover, sacred mountains were central to the *omphalos* myth, which considered them the navel of the earth.[148] References to sacred mountains, celestial bodies, or other cosmic elements were authoritative if those references were intended to change or encourage belief or behavior through the appeal. An example from Greek writing was oaths sworn by Mount Olympus. This oath was accepted because the referent had the authority to dictate allegiance to the oath since the sacred mountain housed Olympian gods.[149]

5.5.1. Step 4a: Text—Definition and Use of Authority

The Cosmology topos type was defined here as references to a celestial or terrestrial body or element in which the author declared a truth in relation to that body or element. The P.Enoch authors used this topos type as proof of God's authority to judge in chapter 41. In chapter 43, they identified that which was greatest—the cosmos and its order—before leveraging that information in a "the creator is greater than the creation" argument. Toward the close of 1 Enoch and also in 2 Enoch 19, ordered creation was used as an authority for praising God and placing hope in his justice. The Jubilean P.author made the authority subservient to God as well (Jub. 12:16b–18), but the P.author also used it to legitimize a solar calendar (Jub. 2:8–9). Finally, the

---

146 Cheu Hock Tong, "The Festival of the Nine Emperor Gods in Malaysia: Myth, Ritual, and Symbol," *Asian Folklore Studies* 55.1 (1996): 63, 68–69; Robin L. Wildfang, *Rome's Vestal Virgins: A Study of Rome's Vestal Priestesses in the Late Republic and Early Empire* (London: Routledge, 2006), 51–55, 76–108.

147 K. A. H. Hidding, "Der Hochgott und Der Mikrokosmische Mensch," *Numen* 18.2 (1971): 96–98.

148 David B. W. Phillips, "Center of the Land," *Lexham Bible Dictionary* n.p. Phillips produced a list of both Tanakh and intertestamental period literature identifying mountains as the navel of the world; the work here heavily depended on this list.

149 Other elements of the cosmos can be included here, but only those listed were authoritative. Moreover, cosmic forces were not limited to Jewish apocalyptic writing. See, for instance, the role of the cosmos during the Exodus according to Jewish wisdom literature, in Beauchamp, "Le salut corporel des justes," 498.

P.authors of the Qumran documents used this topos type in several ways, as displayed in step 4b.

5.5.2. Step 4b: Text and Context—Use in Apocalyptic Literature

In parts of Judaism, creation stemmed from the Torah. The Torah represented order through the law and was the microcosm from which the order of the universe emerged.[150] Therefore, the cosmos was an authoritative reflection of the Torah and able to correct understanding, move adherents to praise God, or lend authority for explaining divine judgment in Jewish literature. These authoritative topoi appeared in 1 and 2 Enoch and Jubilees.

5.5.2.1. 1 Enoch

The first topos began in 2:1 where the author urged Second Temple readers to gaze at the cosmos and use it as a plumb line for God's order (5:2). The author then accused them of violating it. In 1 Enoch 17–19, the author pictured divine journeys with a rich setting of peculiar geographical references. Coblentz Bautch noted these "chapters present themselves like an abbreviated travelogue and, with only a cursory reading, it is tough to reconstruct from obscure descriptions the course of Enoch's journey and the geography that stands behind the various sites appearing in 1 Enoch 17–19."[151] Yet, Coblentz Bautch identified certain geographic items, such as equating Mt. Zaphon with the mountain in 1 En. 17:2, which gained importance as Ba'al's dwelling place. More important for this study, however, was her conclusion the overall travelogue was "dominated by sacred sites."[152]

In 1 En. 26:1–2, the *omphalos* myth appeared: "And from there I went into the center of the earth and saw a blessed place, shaded with branches which live and bloom from a tree that was cut. And there I saw a holy mountain." The author wrote of the rivers flowing from this mountain, noting they caused him to marvel deeply (26:6). By providing this setting, the author claimed to have visited the center of the world where heaven and earth connected and communication

---

[150] Herbert W. Basser, "The Development of the Pharisaic Idea of Law as a Sacred Cosmos," *JSJ* 16.1 (1985): 115–16.

[151] Coblentz Bautch , *Study of the Geography*, 278.

[152] Ibid., 60–61, 278.

between God and man occurred (the same mountain upon which Jerusalem and thus the temple sat).

The Enochian author depended on the *omphalos* myth to claim approval of his message. Within this journey, the Watchers received the label "The Seven Stars of Heaven" (21:3), which Daniel Olson argued was a "condemn[ation of the] widespread ancient worship of the seven planets (Sun, Moon, Mercury, Venus, Mars, Jupiter, Saturn).[153]

Enoch's journey continued through chapter 36 where the author concluded:

> And when I saw (this) I blessed—and I shall always bless—the Lord of Glory, who performed great and blessed miracles in order that he may manifest his great deeds to his angels, the winds, and to the people so that they might praise the effect of all his creation—so that they might see the effect of his power and praise him in respect to the great work of his hands and bless him forever (36:4).

These cosmic references became grist for praise and authoritative for setting the standard of his mighty deeds. God created the cosmos and set the stars, wind, dew, and rain to come forward (36:1) so angels and man could worship him when viewing these works. Consequently, the cosmos was authoritative for praise, but the cosmic authority was testimony, not self-contained authority. Conversely, if Olson was correct in stating the author slighted EAW beliefs, the topos became authoritative concerning cosmogony. The Enochian author, therefore, would have rejected EAW cosmic origination narratives, instead

---

[153] Daniel C. Olson, "1 Enoch," in *Eerdman's Commentary on the Bible*, ed. James D. G. Dunn and John W. Rogerson (Grand Rapids: Eerdmans, 2003), 913. Olson's full argument is that "the author is probably condemning the widespread ancient worship of the seven planets (Sun, Moon, Mercury, Venus, Mars, Jupiter, Saturn). Their transgression, enigmatically dated 'to the moment of their first rising,' leaves 'an empty place outside of heaven' (18:15). This explains why the visible luminaries are still there and functioning properly: they are innocent and obedient, but in a parallel realm 'outside of heaven' the skies are blackened since the seven planetary angels, who have perhaps been accepting worship as gods are cast down and bound, awaiting final punishment" (ibid.).

positing the Jewish god created and controlled the celestial bodies, as found in 1 En. 41:3.

In 1 En. 41, the text began, "And after that, I saw all the secrets in heaven, and how a kingdom breaks up." The narrative meanders through punishing sinners before focusing on the cosmic secrets of storms, precipitation, and the mysteries of the wind. In the following verse, the author reflected on the sun and moon patterns becoming authoritative for praising God; they followed their paths by his command, allowing the proper celebration of festivals. In the closing verses of this chapter, cosmic movement (and signs) begot authoritative transfer through a reference to their creation. The author transferred this authority to God as the judge: he ordered his creation, and it worked as he intended. Since angels and humans did not work as intended, God must judge them.[154]

In 43:1–2, the author presented stars to show God's wisdom. He did so by showing God knowing the names of the stars and by their obedience as they followed set patterns. This theme emerged again in chapters 52–56, wherein Enoch saw "a part of the earth hidden from the inhabited [world]...where final and eternal punishment [was] being prepared for the kings and the mighty."[155] Here, God prepared future punishment for angels and kings contravening God's order by revealing secrets or oppressing the righteous; he would set in proper order all that was out of order.

The topos type also occurred in 1 En. 72–82. This section was most likely developed from the Aramaic Book of Heavenly Luminaries, which was a treatise on astronomy outlining both solar and lunar calendars; however, little information was available for determining its purpose. The same was true for determining the purpose of the Ethiopic text (also 2 En. 11–16). Ethiopian editor of 1 Enoch located 72–82 after the Book of Similitudes (chapters 37–71). Thus, the editor may have intended to support the Similitudes through a detailed order of the cosmos.

Several scholars posited (and was argued earlier in this work as well) the original intent of the Enochic Book of Heavenly Luminaries (72–82) was to act as an authority for solar or lunar calendaring for festivals and feasts. However, this idea was based on one passage

[154] Nickelsburg-VanderKam, *1 Enoch* 2, 39.
[155] Ibid., 40.

beginning in 1 En. 82:7: "[Uriel] has revealed to me and breathed over me concerning the luminaries, the months, the festivals, the years, and the days." This idea was repeated two verses later: "These are the orders of the stars which set in their (respective) places seasons, festivals, and months." Although calendaring probably was the purpose of the text, proof of the author's intent has been lost to antiquity. Nevertheless, that purpose, whatever it may have been, was based on the cosmos according to the content of these chapters.[156]

The arguments for judgment, punishment, and cosmic authority for praising God, and for the righteous ones' hope of justice appeared in 1 En. 100–102:2. Starting in 1 En. 100:10, that which followed the proper order and could view humanity from an elevated physical position could judge humanity. Thus, the astral bodies, angels, clouds, mist, and dew bore witness to human activity; however, this occurrence of the Cosmology topos type also incorporated the Righteousness topos type (100:10).

5.5.2.2. 2 Enoch

In 2 En. 19, the angels recorded and studied the movements of the heavenly bodies for "evil activity," and worked to "harmonize all existence, heavenly and earthly" (19:3). The author also expanded Gen 1:14, reminiscent of Jubilees, connecting newborns and horoscopes by the authority of the Cosmology topos type:

> And I appointed the sun over the illumination of the day, but the moon and stars over the illumination of the night. And the sun goes in accordance with each animal, and the twelve animals are the succession of the months. And I assigned their names and the animals of their seasons, and their connection with the newborn, and their horoscopes, and how they revolve. Then evening came and morning came—the fifth day.

Finally, in 2 En. 48:1–4, the path of the sun and movements of the cosmos were authoritative and eternal witness to God's wisdom: God fixed days and hours "by his own wisdom, that is everything visible and invisible." This authority authorized the instructions in 2 En. 48:6 for Enoch's children to "hand over the books [concerning the solar

[156] Ibid., 359–68.

movements] to your children, and throughout all your generations...and among all nations who are discerning so that they may fear God, and so that they may accept them."

5.5.2.3. Jubilees

In Jubilees, references to the Cosmology topos type developed from a reading of the first chapter of Genesis, as seen in the Jubilean author's focus on the sun:

> And on the fourth day he made the sun and the moon and the stars. And he set them in the firmament of heaven so that they might...rule over the day and the night....[9] And the LORD set the sun as a great sign upon the earth for days, sabbaths, months, feast (days), years, sabbaths of years, jubilees, and for all of the (appointed) times of the years (2:8–9).

The Genesis text (1:14) read "and let them be signs for appointed times and days and years."[157] By dropping the moon in the Jubilean text, the P.author designated the sun as authoritative for calendaring, and therefore, for assigning dates for feasts.[158] However, that authority was subservient to God:

> Abram sat up during the night on the first of the seventh month, so that he might observe the stars from evening until daybreak so that he might see what the nature of the year would be with respect to rain. And he was sitting alone and making observations; and a word came into his heart, saying, "All of the signs of the stars and the signs of the sun and the moon are all in the hand of the LORD. Why am I seeking? If he desires, he will make it rain...and if he desires he will not send (it) down; and everything is in his hand" (Jub. 12:16b–18).

---

[157] "וְהָיוּ לְאֹתֹת וּלְמוֹעֲדִים וּלְיָמִים וְשָׁנִים:." Note, לְאֹתֹת located as feminine plural absolute, referencing both the sun and the moon.

[158] Unfortunately, the Qumran Jubilees text (4Q216) was not in the best condition, but it seemed to follow Ethiopian Jubilees. This could not be verified as the extant text on line 7 began, "[Gr]eat [upon the earth] for day[s] and for [sa]bbaths and for [months]. Thus, although it was likely Qumran Jubilees dropped the moon from its role as a sign, the similarity of text made this statement unprovable.

The P.author condemned Babylonian stargazers, whose lunisolar calendars contained what James Cornell called "irregularities."[159] Such irregularities were dangerous for the Jubilean author; feasts had to occur on the proper days to keep Torah, lest they suffer a second Babylonian-type captivity. Condemning Babylonian stargazers was further supported by the narrative of Cainan in 8:3. There, Cainan read and transcribed "the teaching of the Watchers by which they used to observe the omens of the sun and moon and stars within all the signs of heaven." The P.author noted Cainan sinned because he learned knowledge specific to astronomy from the Watchers. The sun, moon, and stars, therefore, carried authority, but this knowledge was not for humanity.

A different authority occurred concerning references to Mount Sinai. For the P.author, the passage was historiographic and therefore authoritative through an appeal to history. However, the authority for the topos type lay in referencing a physical location that represented both Torah reception and God's home before he dwelt among the Israelites. In Jub. 8:19–20, the author also included the *omphalos* myth to mark Mount Zion as a holy place alongside Mount Zion and Eden:

> And he knew that the garden of Eden was the holy of holies and the dwelling of the LORD. And Mount Sinai (was) in the midst of the desert and Mount Zion (was) in the midst of the navel of the earth. The three of these were created as holy places, one facing the other. And he blessed the God of gods, who placed in his mouth the word of the LORD, and also the Eternal God.

Therefore, according to the P.author, Mount Zion was the permanent center of divine outworking in human history (how God *does* history).[160]

---

[159] James Cornell, *The First Stargazers: An Introduction to the Origins of Astronomy* (New York: Scribner, 1981), 111. But see the Aramaic Book of Luminaries at Qumran for possible acceptance of this calendar.

[160] Depending on the date of the original writing, this passage may have provided another authority for the Jerusalem temple, and thus, repudiated the idea the temple at Leontopolis was transformed into a Jewish temple by Onias IV sometime after 171 BCE (the death of High Priest Onias III). Another possible target for repudiation was the Samaritan temple on Mt. Gerizim. For those who dated

5.5.2.4. Qumran

A few texts contained the Cosmology topos type at Qumran. One such reference was 1 QapGen ar xii wherein the author detailed inverted nature. Unfortunately, the text was broken making it difficult to understand the context. However, an inversion began based on xii:17 wherein God saved Noah and his family from the flood (xi:15). Noah's salvation was followed with references to the sun, the moon, stars, and other elements of creation acting destructively. By referencing the cosmos negatively, the author indicated broken order, and by metaphor, pictured an encompassing antediluvian evil. Outside this passage and the flood story, however, negative cosmic references Carried no authority in the manuscripts researched.

The 1Q27 f1.i:5–6 (4Q299 f1 and 4Q300 f3) text held two references. However, the references were comparative, not authoritative. The first reference regarded the light-dark binary in line 5: "evil will disappear before justice as [da]rkness disappears before light." The second reference referenced the sun: just as sun regulated the world, so "justice will be revealed." As such, the author did not use these references to authorize his teaching, only to clarify it.

Cosmic references also occurred in five passages of 1QH[a]. There, the Cosmology topos type led to praise (ix:10–14):

> Everything [which it contains] you have [es]tablished according to your will, and powerful spirits, according to their laws, before they became h[oly] angels [...] eternal spirits in their realms: luminaries according to their mysteries, stars according to [their] circuits, [all the stormy winds] according to their roles, lightning and thunder according to their duties and well-designed storehouses according to th[eir] purposes [...] according to their secrets. *Blank.* You have created the earth with your strength, seas and deeps [...] you have founded their [...] with your wisdom, everything which is in them you have determined according to your will.[161]

Jubilees late, the text read as a justification for John Hyrcanus extirpating the temple and city.

[161] "*Blank*" equals a space in the text where no letters appear. The translations in this subsection were from García Martínez, *DSSSE* 1.

Reminiscent of 1 En. 36 and 41, this passage guided the reader to understand God's might and power encompassed the celestial bodies as God created the entire realm. The other 1QH[a] cosmic references were chronological or metaphors reminiscent of 1Q27. However, a noncanonical psalm in 4Q381 f1:5 also held a Cosmology topos type occurrence that led to praise based on God's creative act.

Calendaring is factored into cosmic authority in CD–A x:15. The author instructed the reader, "No one should do work on the sixth day, from the moment when the sun's disc is at the distance of its diameter from the gate." The author then quoted from Deut 5:12 concerning Sabbath observation. In this text, cosmic authority regulated when certain laws were active in the community. This authority extended to astrology in 4Q318 f2.ii:6–9:

> If it thunders in the sign of Taurus, revolutions against [...], and affliction for the province and a sword in the court of the King and in the province [...] there will be. And for the Arabs [...] famine. And they will plunder each other. If it thunders in the sign of Gemini, fear and distress from the foreigners and [...].

According to this text, the sun and stars were signs that foreshadowed terrestrial events, which was closer to an EAW understanding of the celestial bodies than concepts found in the Tanakh. However, not all Qumran texts agreed. For example, 11Q19 lv:18 held a clear warning against worshipping the sun, the moon, or the "legions of heaven." This issue of astrology at Qumran hinged on the personification or deification of celestial bodies. The 4Q318 reference seemed to have personified the Heavenly Host within God's order whereas 11Q19 held a negative reference against deification. This latter reference was against the worship of gods represented by the celestial bodies. The author of this reference, therefore, negated the authority and practices of worshiping celestial bodies often found in the EAW world.

The only authoritative reference to mountains occurred in 11Q19 li:6b–8a: "And they shall not defile themselves with those things which I tell you on this mountain, and they are not to become unclean." The reference to Sinai as the mountain on which Moses obtained the Torah signified an equivalency in authority to the rules in the text.

Overall, cosmic authority showed broad applicability for Second Temple authors. They used it to engender praise, demand proper obeisance, foster obedience to a specific calendar, and refer to larger EAW concepts. These references have also caused several debates among scholars. Two such discussions concerned dating and origination, occasioning further research into the beginnings of astronomy in the EAW.[162]

5.5.3. Step 4c: Text and Context–Germane Scholarship

The Aramaic Book of the Luminaries was the oldest extant, noncanonical Hebraic set of didactic narratives yet found. Paleographic studies dated it to the third century BCE (or earlier).[163] The subject matter in these writings focused on the cosmic movement and calendaring, which the Second Temple authors presented as "revealed information…in excruciatingly long-winded detail."[164] Concerning its origination, Michael Stone looked to the Babylonian and Persian empires, although he "depend[ed] on those who are more learned than [he] in the natural sciences in antiquity."[165]

Several scholars have agreed with him. For instance, Silverman wrote an article concerning such influences, titled "Iranian details in the Book of Heavenly Luminaries," in which he sought differing influences on Enochic literature.[166] Additionally, Seth Sanders argued the author of the Aramaic book of Luminaries "[wrote] in the cosmopolitan, high-cultural register of the lingua franca of the

---

[162] Most of the references in Qumran to the sun, moon, or stars were delimited because they concerned chronology, portions of the Tanakh and apocalyptic literature already examined in the above subsection, metaphors that were not applicable, or texts with no Cosmology topos type. One such series of references not included was the metaphorical references to the Teacher of Righteousness as a star (CD–A vii:18–19). These references paralleled other references to stars in Homer's *Iliad*, "The Coronation and Consecration of Šulgi in the Ekur", "The Gebel Barkal," and "The Stela of Thutmose III." Yet, the cosmic topoi (astral topoi) were not authoritative in these texts; rather, they were reflections of the physical world in metaphor. The cosmic reference in 4Q213 f3–4 was too difficult to discern because of poor preservation (although an inversion of nature was evident).

[163] This statement referenced full didactic narratives; there were several extant inscriptions, ostraca, letters, and so on that were dated earlier than the Aramaic Book of Luminaries.

[164] Michael Stone, "Enoch, Aramaic Levi and Sectarian Origins," *JSJ* 19.2 (1988): 160–61.

[165] Ibid., 161.

[166] Jason Silverman, "Iranian Details in the Book of Heavenly Luminaries (1 Enoch 72–82)," *JNES* 72.2 (2013).

Babylonian and Persian empires known as the Standard Literary Aramaic."[167] Other scholars, however, have disagreed.

Popović used network analysis to investigate the relationship between the Aramaic text found at Qumran and Babylonian calendars. He posited several scenarios in which the Babylonian calendars affected Judaism. In one scenario anchored in the Uruk traditions, he proposed families kept scribal learning among themselves and seldom taught others; but, economic considerations drove them from their lands, thus spreading the Babylonian calendar.[168] Based on his analysis, Popović argued the difference in scholarship between Babylon and Judea of the Second Temple period indicated strong generalization:

> [Researchers] should look for network connections at other places than the centers of Babylonian learning.... We [should not] perceive of the transmission of Babylonian astronomical and astrological material to the Second Temple period Palestine as having taken place in a direct manner but rather through various intermediaries, Aramaic and other channels, as well as via a—more vague—continuous tradition.[169]

Using terms from this current research, Popović concluded no parent-child connection existed between Babylonian astronomy and Second Temple Jewish literature; however, the stars still played a major role in apocalyptic material.

In her dissertation, Coblentz Bautch wrote stars "were depicted as sentient beings in the Second Temple period" holding self-determination and agency.[170] Consequently, her work supported this study by reinforcing Second Temple cosmology. Sentient celestial

---

[167] Seth Sanders, "'I Was Shown Another Calculation' (אחזית חשבון אחרן): The Language of Knowledge in Aramaic Enoch and Priestly Hebrew," in *Ancient Jewish Sciences and the History of Knowledge in Second Temple Literature*, ed. Jonathan Ben-Dov and Seth Sanders (New York: NYU Press, 2014), 69–70.

[168] Mladen Popović, "Networks of Scholars: The Transmission of Astronomical and Astrological Learning between Babylonians, Greeks, and Jews," in *Ancient Jewish Sciences and the History of Knowledge in Second Temple Literature*, ed. Jonathan Ben-Dov and Seth L. Sanders (New York: New York University Press, 2014), 172–73.

[169] Ibid., 192.

[170] Coblentz Bautch, *Study of the Geography*, 47.

bodies never misstepped in their nocturnal dance set by God, proving his order. These beings were judged when called by God, proving his justice. They were also majestic, providing the impetus for praising God.

Turning to the *omphalos* myth, Arent Wensinck identified five mythic themes within Semitic cultures: (1) reverence for the homeland, (2) the locale as the birthplace of the world, (3) the center of the world, (4) a place of interaction with heaven and the netherworld, and (5) a place for feeding the world.[171] However, not every reference to mountains concerned this myth. A close textual reading limited *omphalos* references to topoi containing a share of the above themes and using the *Omphalic* myth in an authoritative manner. These concepts and observations from scholars were helpful in the cross-text steps of 4d–e.

5.5.4. Step 4d: Cross-Text—Possible EAW Sources

Several EAW ontological beliefs existed concerning celestial bodies. Therefore, the following material was divided by culture, beginning with Mesopotamian texts. An Egyptian hymn and a coffin spell followed. The final two texts were a Greek play and a philosophical treatise. Unfortunately, terrestrial references generated few authoritative topoi; to illustrate this dearth, a quick tour of Ugaritic and Hittite material ends this section before the discussion moved to the Tanakh.

5.5.4.1. Celestial Bodies

References to celestial bodies and their order occurred throughout the EAW, but the problem lay in distinguishing between references to natural elements and references to gods by theophorism or representation. Striking passages that focused on a deified sun or stars, on astrology, or on those containing metaphors or references to heavenly bodies as chronometers helped delimit several texts. Of those texts that remained, the following scored the strongest in step 3 for a possible parent-child relationship concerning the Cosmology topos type.

---

[171] Adapted and partially reworded from Arent J. Wensinck, "The Ideas of the Western Semites Concerning the Navel of the Earth," *Verhandelingen der Koninklijke Akademie van Wetenschappen: Nieuwe Reeks* 17.1 (1916): xi.

5.5.4.1.1. Mesopotamian Texts

Two texts from Mesopotamia evidenced this topos type. The first was the Babylonian tale "Nabonidus's Rise to Power." This tale was a retelling of Nabonidus's story through a cultic perspective. The second text was *Yas.* 44:3–4. This unnamed *Yasna* was a song used in Zoroastrian worship.

5.5.4.1.1.1. "Nabonidus's Rise to Power."

This stela recounted the history between Assyria and Babylon, ascribing the deliverance of Babylon to Marduk. In the following passage, two messengers appeared to Nabonidus:

> I became apprehensive (but) (in a dream) a...man came to my assistance, saying to me: "There are no evil portents (involved) in the impending constellation!" In the same dream, when my royal predecessor Nebuchadnezzar and one attendant (appeared to me) standing on a chariot, the attendant said to Nebuchadnezzar: "Tell me what good (signs) you have seen!" And I [Nabonidus] answered him, saying: "In my dream, I beheld with joy the Great Star, the moon and Marduk (i.e., the planet Jupiter) high up on the sky and it (the Great Star) called me by my name!"[172]

Nabonidus's response to "What good signs you have seen" held a reference to celestial bodies as portents of the future and a determiner of events.[173] However, two meaningful differences denied a parent-child relationship with Jewish apocalyptic material.

First, Nabonidus's tale reflected common EAW astromythology in which the cosmos had both will and agency, but the cosmos in 1 and 2 Enoch was subservient to—and a symbol of—God's order. Second, in Nabonidus's tale, celestial bodies foretold events, but in Jewish apocalyptic literature, celestial bodies evidenced God's wisdom (1 En. 43:1–2; 2 En. 48:1–4). Furthermore, in the book of Jubilees (8:3; 12:16b–18), the author condemned astrology because "all the signs of the stars and the signs of the sun and moon are all in the hand of the Lord." According to the Jubilean author , YHWH was Lord over the

---

[172] "Babylonian and Assyrian Historical Texts," trans. A. Leo Oppenheim (*ANET*, 310).

[173] Many texts from the EAW included celestial bodies as portents of the future.

cosmos; he was the determiner of actions and the orchestrator of the celestial dance.

5.5.4.1.1.2. Yasna. 44:3–4.

In this Yasna, a few lines reflected YHWH's speech in the Tanakh version of Job, but here, a human asked these questions without sarcasm or irony:

> This I ask Thee, tell me truly, Ahura. Who is by generation the Father of Right, at the first? Who determined the path of sun and stars? Who is it by whom the moon waxes and wanes again? This, O Mazda, and yet more, I am fain to know. This I ask Thee, tell me truly, Ahura. Who upholds the earth beneath and the firmament from falling? Who the waters and the plants? Who yoked swiftness to winds and clouds? Who is, O Mazda, creator of Good Thought?

No call upon or command from authority existed; yet, the concept still appeared. By questioning who created the cosmos, the author sought to find the one labeled "The Father of Right." An underlying belief indicated the creator was greater than the cosmos, which became the hinge for a rhetorical statement judging the identity of the Father of Right. These texts reflected the Enochian use of this topos in 1 En. 41–43, and several points of verbal contact existed until closer inspection proved otherwise.

First, the cosmic order was the authority in the *yasna* by which the author sought the Father of Right who was sovereign over creation. However, the text was a hymn for service—a rhetorical set of praises for Ahura Mazda. This setting created a ritualistic context in which the topos was used. By comparison, the authors of the apocalyptic material exhorted the readers to proper beliefs concerning God and the coming world. Although these contexts were different, they were not dissimilar enough to distract a reader from the similarities. The problem, however, was the lack of two or more distinct similarities in the context to create a point of verbal contact.

Second, the authors of the *yasna* and the Jewish apocalyptic material began with a wish to praise a deity (1 En. 41:7–9). They did so by calling on the Cosmology topos type by which they then identified the sovereignty of their deity. Thus, a similar theme existed in the text. However, a meaningful difference discounted it as a point of verbal contact. The teleological purpose of *yasna* was a praise to Ahura for worship whereas the purpose of the Enochian passage was didactic.[174]

Third, there existed similarities on a broader scale when incorporating the Hebraic Wisdom movement. As such, the work of Job caused problems for this analysis in the sense that any argument for *Yasna* 44 was also an argument for Job in a similar relationship. In Job, the author began with a character seeking wisdom about his circumstances and God. God later intervened with a series of rhetorical questions elevating his sovereignty, which ended with Job's recognition (note the same in *Yas*. 44:4) and praise. However, both texts were different from Jewish literature as they derived from a wisdom-style of writing with terseness. Conversely, the Enochian text was not a wisdom-style of writing but a narrative concerning Enoch who was receiving heavenly wisdom—an element lacking in both Job and the *yasna*.

This heavenly wisdom encouraged understanding of God's wisdom to judge in 1 Enoch (41:3ff; 52–56; 101:1; and 102:1–2 and a judge for judgment in 100:10). Conversely, God's wisdom to judge was questioned in Job and missing in *Yasna* 44.[175] In 2 Enoch, a similar pattern occurred, focused on either judgment or on calendaring. For Jubilees, the concern was calendaring (2:8–9), sovereignty (Jub. 12:16b–18), and condemning astrology (8:3). As a result, *Yasna* 44 was not in a parent-child relationship with Second Temple apocalyptic texts because the *yasna* did not hold three points of verbal contact with 1 En. 41–43. Meaningful differences also existed between it and other Second Temple apocalyptic texts. At the most, it contributed to a

---

[174] Note, the distinction here were the teleological purposes of the texts that rendered a meaningful difference. In the previous paragraph, the concern was whether context alone was complimentary between the texts. Thus, teleological purposes were not weighed in that text.

[175] In Job 38–41, God responded, "Who are you to question me?" and proved this question by invoking the Cosmology topos type. The use of the topos type was different than in Enoch where the author employs the topos type to answer the question, "Why can God be trusted in his judgment?" The different purposes of the text negated a parent-child relationship between 1 Enoch and Job (and thus, the Wisdom movement) for this topos type.

larger reality of cosmic authority in the EAW from which Jewish apocalyptic authors drew.

5.5.4.1.2. Egyptian Texts

In the two following texts, authors used the cosmos to symbolize a deity's greatness, beginning with "The Great Hymn to Osiris." In the coffin text spell, the focal point was an annunciation acting as one of the two elements of magic that created the spell: "The creative expression of a thought through the medium of the spoken word."[176]

5.5.4.1.2.1. "The Great Hymn to Osiris."

In the following text, the author established the might of Osiris:

> Plants sprout by his wish, Earth grows its food for him, sky and its stars obey him, the great portals open for him. Lord of acclaim in the southern sky, sanctified in the northern sky, the imperishable stars are under his rule, the unwearying stars are his abode.[177]

The cosmic elements listed here served as a measuring stick by which the author claimed Osiris's might. A key reference was the first mention of the sky and stars, which obeyed Osiris much like the celestial bodies obeyed God within the Hebrew writings. Obedience, coupled with the Cosmology topos type, formed two points of verbal contact. However, a distracting dissimilarity negated obedience.

The Egyptian author specified cosmic obedience to show the greatness of Osiris. In 1 and 2 Enoch, however, cosmic obedience symbolized God's wisdom and the proper order of the universe, rather than his greatness. Moreover, this order was broken by humanity (Jubilees) or the Watchers (1 Enoch). As such, Jewish texts legitimate God's judgment, which was missing from the Osiris text. This distracting dissimilarity negated obedience as a point of verbal contact, leaving only one contact. Therefore, a parent-child relationship did not exist with Jewish apocalyptic literature concerning the Cosmology topos type.

---

176 "Coffin Texts Spell 261," trans. James P. Allen (*COS* 1.11:17–18).

177 "The Great Hymn to Osiris," trans. Miriam Lichtheim (*COS* 1.26:41–43).

5.5.4.1.2.2. Coffin Texts Spell 261.

The coffin text concerned creation and magic in Heliopolis mythology. In this mythology, "Magic [was] the divine force that translated the creator's will into reality."[178] A picture of personified magic occurred in the following text:

> I am the one whom the Sole Lord made before two things had evolved in this world, when he sent his sole eye, when he was one, when something came from his mouth, when his million of ka was in protection of his associates, when he spoke with the one who evolved with him, than whom he is mightier, when he took Annunciation in his mouth.[179]

According to James Allen's textual note, the "one who evolved with him, than whom he is mightier," had a parallel in the Bersheh version that read "when he spoke to Scarab."[180] Through intertextuality, this parallel identified magic as mightier than the sun. Like the Osiris myth, this text used a cosmic element as a measuring stick by which the author claimed the might of magic. However, this passage lacked references to obedience, let alone three points of verbal contact outside of an obscure reference to the Cosmology topos type built through intertextuality. Therefore, this passage did not sit in a parent-child relationship with Jewish apocalyptic material.

5.5.4.1.3. Greek Texts

The first Greek play studied was a play by Aristophanes. In it, the chorus spoke to the audience about different events. These events led to the audience's choice of a general who was "hateful to the gods." The reference to cosmology occurred in the aftermath of this choice. The second text was attributed to Plato, called *Epinomis*. The context of the passage was an attempt to identify science and instill wisdom. The speaker made this attempt by speaking of what or whom he believed to be God.

---

[178] "Coffin Texts Spell 261," trans. James P. Allen (*COS* 1.11:17–18).

[179] Ibid.

[180] The Bersheh version was part of a series of texts found at Deir el-Bersha. The place was "known primarily for a row of tomb chapels in the cliffs, most of which were constructed for the twelfth-dynasty provincial governors (c. 1991–1783 BCE)." Ian Shaw, "Deir el-Bersha," *A Dictionary of Archeology* 196–97.

5.5.4.1.3.1. Aristophanes Clouds 575

The following passage described the aftermath of picking the wrong general:

> And then, when you were for choosing as your general the Paphlagonian tanner, hateful to the gods, we contracted our brows and were enraged; and thunder burst through the lightning; and the Moon forsook her usual paths; and the Sun immediately drew in his wick to himself, and declared he would not give you light, if Cleon should be your general.[181]

Choosing Cleon disrupted the cosmos, but by whose hand? A close reading indicated it was the gods who disrupted the cosmos through their anger, but the elements of the cosmos also held self-agency. These elements acted on their own as seen in the sun declaring judgment. Two observations were made from this text.

First, choosing Cleon caused the microcosm to affect the macrocosm. The same was true for the author of Jubilees, where the microcosm (the law) created the macrocosm (the cosmos). However, the microcosms were meaningfully different. In *Clouds,* the microcosm was human beings, but in Jubilees, the microcosm was the law. Thus, the context of the topos type held distracting dissimilarities and could not be used as a verbal point of contact. Second, self-agency was attributed to the cosmos as it condemned human choice. In Jewish apocalyptic literature, the cosmos was not to condemn autonomously but to be a picture of God's wisdom. As such, the purpose of the cosmos included in the text was meaningfully different.[182] These observations negated a parent-child relationship between *Clouds* and Second Temple apocalyptic literature.

5.5.4.1.3.2. Epinomis, 977b

In this text, Plato used the cosmos much as the author of Yas. 44:3–4, wherein the cosmos became a tool to identify the creator:

---

[181] Plato, *Menexenus, Cleitophon, Timaeus, Critias, Minos, Epinomis*, trans. W. R. M. Lambert (Cambridge: Harvard Press, 1925), line 977b.

[182] Although more similarities existed with 1 QapGen ar xii, including self-agency, the focus of that passage was a cosmos acting selfishly rather than condemning human choice alongside the gods.

> For if one enters on the right theory about it, whether one be pleased to call it World-order or Olympus or Heaven—let one call it this or that, but follow where, in bespangling itself and turning the stars that it contains, it produces all their courses and the seasons and food for all.

This heaven provided wisdom for created order. Plato used what was seen (the stars and cosmos) to proclaim the greater power, and thus, he proclaimed the divine by cosmic order (also note the link to the *omphalic* myth through a reference to Olympus). However, In Enoch, the cosmos was not used to identify God himself, but to identify God as wise and thus, a wise judge, and praiseworthy. The difference in teleological purpose negated this passage being in a parent-child relationship with Jewish apocalyptic literature, as did the lack of three verbal contacts.

5.5.4.2. Sacred Mountains

In Ugaritic writings, Eldwelt on a sacred mountain and was head of the local pantheon like Marduk and Zeus. Outside of these two similarities, nothing else reflected the Second Temple material; no authoritative topos existed except perhaps a general reference to holy mountains for identifying deities. In the Hittite material, however, a ritual purification referenced the sacred mountains: "'Let it go into the sacred mountains. Let it go into the deep wells.' He breaks a thick loaf and libates wine."[183] "It" in context was the "bloodshed and impurity of this house." The question here was whether the sacred mountains referenced geography or authority. The context indicated geography as the author paired sacred mountains with deep wells and the seas (found in the previous line). This pattern followed in both Egyptian and Hellenistic work: similarities in references to mountains and the *omphalos* were negated by meaningful differences and a lack of verbal contacts. The EAW texts, therefore, showed similarities with Second Temple apocalyptic literature, but no parent-child relationships.

5.5.5. Step 4e: Cross-Text—Possible Tanakh Sources

In the Tanakh, a general search for elements of the cosmos (sun, moon, or stars) produced approximately 215 hits, depending on the English text. The BHS provided significantly more hits than the English

[183] "Purifying a House: A Ritual for the Infernal Deities," trans. Billie J. Collins, (*COS* 1.68:170).

texts because חֹדֶשׁ was often translated as "month" rather than as the celestial body, "moon." On account of the vast number of hits, the following section was organized by theme: order and praise, court cases and judgment, divine wisdom, and mountains.

5.5.5.1. Order and Praise: Gen 1:14

Jubilees 2:8–9 reflected Gen 1:14, which was a central text for various Hebraic cosmic beliefs. However, the Tanakh author chose not to discern between the heavenly bodies directing festivals and feasts: "And then God said, 'Let there be lamps in the firmament of the heavens to separate between the day and the night, and let them be signs for festivals, days, and years.'" The Tanakh author then described the sun and the moon as equal signs for calendaring in general and the proper time for festivals, specifically; וְהָיוּ לְאֹתֹת וּלְמוֹעֲדִים וּלְיָמִים וְשָׁנִים: "Let them be signs for festivals, days and years." The sun and the moon then assumed a larger role in Gen 1:16: "And then God made two great lamps; the greater lamp for domination of the day and the smaller lamp for domination of the night; and the stars." In this domination, they reigned in the heavens, but now held little authority on earth except marking time.[184] In Jub. 2:9, however, the Jubilean author specified the sun only as the authority for marking time on earth. This change caused a meaningful difference, especially as the Jubilean text read as an apology for the solar calendar. As such, a parent-child relationship did not exist between these texts.

Turning to Qumran, for all the speculation of calendaring and Babylonian influence, the Genesis texts of 4Q2 f1.i (4QGen^{b}) and 4Q10 f2 (4QGen^{k}) followed the MT (and LXX in translation) faithfully. The only questionable text is 4Q7 (4QGen^{G}), which drops part of the verse (indicated here with an ellipsis), "and then God said, 'Let there be a lamp in the expanse…and between the night and let it be a sign'" (table 7 [below]). This missing text makes the sentence difficult to understand in Hebrew (as well as English) and therefore evidences a scribal mistake

---

[184] Mathews, *Genesis 1–11:26*, 154. But see Reyburn and Fry, who proposed seasons referred "mainly not to the seasons of the year but rather to fixed times for carrying out a human activity." A similar conversation occurred concerning the translation and understanding of "signs" in the text. None of these discussions, however, negated the idea of the sun and moon appointed both to rule over the heavens and to track the passing of time. Wenham, *Genesis 1–15*, 22–23; Reyburn and Fry, *Handbook on Genesis*, 42.

rather than purposed editing.[185] Consequently, the scrolls at Qumran showed a proclivity for faithful interpretation, rather than following the Jubilee author's rewrite.

Table 7. MT-Qumran comparison of Gen. 1:14

MT	וַיֹּאמֶר אֱלֹהִים יְהִי מְאֹרֹת בִּרְקִיעַ הַשָּׁמַיִם לְהַבְדִּיל בֵּין הַיּוֹם וּבֵין הַלָּיְלָה וְהָיוּ לְאֹתֹת וּלְמוֹעֲדִים וּלְיָמִים וְשָׁנִים
4QGenB	ויאמר אלהים יהי מארת ברקיע השמים להבדיל בין היום ובין הלילה והיו לאתת ולמועדים ולימים ושנים
4Q7GenG	ויאמר אלהים יהי מארות ברקיע ובין הלילה ויהיו לאתות ולמעדים לימים ושנים
4QGenK (frag 2)	ויאמר אלהים יהי מארות ברקיע השמים להבדיל בין היום ובין הלילה והיו לאתות ולמעדים ולימים ולשנים

5.5.5.2. Order and Praise: Other Verses

Joshua 10:12–14 and Judg 5:20 stood out as the two strongest verses outside Psalms for order and praise. In Josh 10:12–13, the context was the Israelite conquest and a battle against the Amorites. The crux of the text was Joshua's command for the sun and the moon to stand still (verse 12b) and their obedience to his command (vs. 13). However, the following verse clarified YHWH stilled the sun and the moon (YHWH listened to man's voice because YHWH fought for Israel). Implicit in this narrative was God's cosmic authority. A similar topos type occurred in Judg 5:19–20. The context of this passage was Deborah's song about Israel's deliverance from Jabin and his commander Sisera: "The kings came, and they fought; then the kings of Canaan fought by Taanach upon the waters of Megiddo, profits of silver they did not take. From the heavens, the stars fought, from their paths they fought with Sisera." In this passage, the order of God goes to war alongside Israel.

The problem with both passages, however, was the Jewish authors did not include the context of war with this topos type. Furthermore, the teleological purpose of the topos type in the apocalyptic narratives concerned God's wisdom or praise based on God's order rather than his deliverance. As such, the Joshua and Judges texts lacked three points of verbal contact. They also displayed a meaningful difference in the teleological purposes of the texts.

In Ps 104:19, the author noted the moon regulated festival activity: "He made the moon for the festivals; the sun knows its setting." The setting of this passage was a psalm of praise. Furthermore, in verse 24,

[185] The missing text included (1) the noun doing the dividing or determining *between* two entities, and (2) the second entity from which the noun was determining or creating division.

the psalmist stated, "How many are your works, O YHWH! in your wisdom you have made them all." Two points of verbal contact existed between this passage and 1 En. 36:4. First, the context of both passages was praise due to God's creation. Second, both passages contained a word picture of God constructing his work. Unfortunately, a third point of verbal contact did not exist, and the reference to wisdom in the psalm was missing in the Enochian passage, which created a detracting similarity concerning the context. Therefore, only one point of verbal contact remained, denying a parent-child relationship between Ps 104:19 and 1 En. 36:4.[186]

5.5.5.3. Court Cases and Judgment

Two passages in Deuteronomy called on the cosmos to witness against Israel. In 4:26, the heavens were to hear Moses's words for future generations when they (the generations) failed to follow God. The heavens would then be a witness and testify that Moses had declared their destruction. In Deut 30:19, Moses again called on the heavens to witness he had provided Israel with the law and noted Israel's responsibility to follow it. This court case motif continued in Psa. 50:4. The psalmist wrote that God called the heavens not as a witness, but as a judge (with the earth). Isaiah opened with the court case motif in 1:2, calling on the heavens and the earth to adjudicate his complaint. Judgment also appeared in Isaiah through creation-inversion in Isa 13:10 as the stars, sun, and moon failed to shine their light.[187]

---

[186] Negating a parent-child relationship did not negate all influence of the psalm over the Enochian passage. The problem was that without three points of verbal contact, it was difficult to assess whether the topos type was used directly from this psalm or if the Enochian P.author and psalmist were both drawing from an earlier topos type. The same was true for this topos type in Pss 8:3; 19:1; 74:16; 136:8–9; and 147:4. Another passage was 2 Sam 22:1–51. There, the author had David providing a hymn of praise that included the shaking earth and trembling foundation of heaven among many other cosmological responses to God's power David was praising.

[187] See also Ezek 32:7–8 and Joel 2:1-31. The idea of inversion had little reference in Second Temple apocalyptic literature—specifically that of sun and moon failing to shine (day inverting to night or other such cosmic inversions); yet, the inversions listed above found kindred texts in twelve different EAW sources. Those inversions varied from the idea of natural order reversing itself (sheep neglecting the lambs, and a cow, its calf in the Hittite Telepinus myth) to a complete reversal of creation in the Book of the Dead (text 175).

These passages, however, all sat within the context of a court case whereby God or Moses brought charges against Israel. The stars, sun, and moon were witnesses or impartial judges. In the Second Temple material, the stars, sun, and moon were the entities that, when observed, testified to God's wisdom allowing him to judge, or proved God was worthy to be praised. As such, the meaningful difference in context disallowed a parent-child relationship.

5.5.5.4. Identifying Divine Wisdom

Divine wisdom was a third way Tanakh authors used cosmic authority and occurred in Jer 10:11–13. The context was Jeremiah condemning Judah for believing in other gods:[188]

> The gods that did not make the heavens or the earth, they will perish from the earth and from under these heavens. He made the land by his strength and established the world by his wisdom, and by his understanding he stretched out the heavens.

Creation through wisdom and strength repeated verbatim in Jer 51:15. The purpose of these passages was teaching God's superiority over false gods according to his wisdom. A point of verbal contact occurred based on the cosmos highlighting God's superiority, and a second point occurred based on the idea of wisdom at the heart of these passages. However, further scrutiny identified the context of the Enochian passages was an anabasis that provided proof for proper calendaring and trusting God's judgment. The purpose in Jeremiah was proof that YHWH was greater than "the gods that did not make the heavens and the earth." Therefore Jer 10:11–13 held a meaningful difference as well as lacked a third point of verbal contact, denying a parent-child relationship.

5.5.5.5. Mountains

The geographical references for mountains in Second Temple Judaism were mostly the same as references found in the Tanakh. Perhaps, the two most notable references in the Tanakh were Mount

---

188 Jeremiah 10:11 was a single Aramaic verse within this passage. The question of this verse being a gloss rather than original did not affect this study as the possible gloss was also found in 4Q71 f1 and the LXX. Therefore, if this verse was a gloss, it was made early in the Second Temple period.

Sinai and Mount Zion. The first played a large part in the Exodus. The second was the temple site and center of Israelite political life from David's reign until c. 925 BCE, and then that of Judah through 586 BCE. However, only two references to mountains were linked to the *omphalos* myth in the Tanakh. This link occurred in Judg 9:37 and Ezek 38:12 where the LXX translators used ὀμφαλός for טַבּוּר. The first reference examined was the story of Abimelech.

5.5.5.5.1. Judges 9:37

The author of Judges placed the reference *omphalos* myth on Gaal's lips. Gaal had earlier entered Shechem and tried to turn the city against Abimelech. Zebul, ruler of Shechem, sent messengers to Abimelech telling him to go at night and set up an ambush. The next morning, when Gaal saw them, he cried they were coming from the mountain tops. A second time, he cried they were coming from the navel of the earth (ὀμφαλοῦ τῆς γῆς). Finally, he warned of soldiers coming from the Diviner's Oak. These three references associated mystical or cultic centers with Abimelech's soldiers, which provided them a veneer of invincibility.[189]

This narrative held two points of verbal contact with Jewish apocalyptic literature before further scrutiny. The first point was the reference to a mountain, and the second, a reference to the *omphalos* myth. The problem, however, was the differing meanings found in 1 En. 26:1–2 and Jub. 8:19–20. The Enochian topos type occurred in Enoch's divine journey and vision of Mount Zion and worked to paint a verbal picture of an eschatological reality. The Jubilean topos type occurred in the context of the Garden of Eden. This context worked to establish the Garden as the center of the world. By comparison, the Tanakh author's use of this topos type identified Abimelech's warriors as invincible. The authors, therefore, painted vastly different word pictures creating meaningful differences while negating one of the points

---

[189] Trent C. Butler, *Judges*, WBC 8 (Nashville, Thomas Nelson, 2009), 247. Not all have accepted the *omphalos* connection. Daniel Block produced evidence for other "Aramaic, Biblical Hebrew refer[ences]" to "umbilical cord," and instead, argued a better rendering was "elevated ground," a rendering that "suits the only other occurrence of this phrase, Ezek. 38:12" (*Judges, Ruth*, NAC 6 [Nashville: Broadman & Holman, 1999], 329). Whether Block was correct or not concerning authorial intent, the LXX translator's choice in translation opened the connection to the myth for Second Temple apocalyptic authors.

of verbal contact. Therefore, a parent-child relationship did not exist between Judg 9:37 and the passages in 1 En. 26:1–2 and Jub. 8:19–20.

5.5.5.5.2. Ezekiel 38:12

In Ezek. 38:12, the author may have introduced the omphalic myth by referencing the people "who live at the center of the earth." Scholars such as Samuel Terrien have argued the omphalic myth entered the Hebraic cultic world through the Jebusites: "Solomon's temple [wa]s built on a rock which is the earth-center, the world mountain, the foundation stone of creation, the extremity of the umbilical cord which provide[d] a link between heaven, earth, and the underworld."[190] Moreover, Walther Zimmerli understood the phrasing orchestrated a mythical background by drawing from a parallel concept in Ezek 5:5.[191] Accordingly, if Terrien and Zimmerli are correct, this passage referenced a restored Jerusalem and through the *omphalos* myth, Mount Zion.

Ezekiel 38:12 showed three points of verbal contact with 1 En. 26:1–2 and two with Jub. 8:19–20 in the beginning: the *omphalos* myth, a reference to mountains, and, for 1 En. 26:1–2, an eschatological setting. However, further study noted the Ezek 38:12 passage made no direct reference to mountains. The connection occurred only through the *omphalos* myth, which negated "mountains" as a point of verbal contact. Yet, the remaining points of verbal contact reflected the *omphalos* myth as understood across the EAW. As a result, no parent-child relationship existed between Ezek 38:12 and the passages in 1 En. 26:1–2 and Jub. 8:19–20. Conversely, a parent-child relationship may have existed between the myth as used in Second Temple apocalyptic literature and the overall understanding of the myth in the EAW.[192] However, this understanding would have been drawn through Jewish Second Temple culture.[193]

---

[190] Samuel Terrien, "The *Omphalos* Myth and Hebrew Religion," *VT* 20 (1970): 317.

[191] Phillips, "Center of the Land" n.p.; Walther Zimmerli, *Ezekiel 2: A Commentary on the Book of the Prophet Ezekiel*, ed. Frank Moore Cross et al., trans., Ronald E. Clements, Hermeneia: A Critical and Historical Commentary on the Bible (Philadelphia: Fortress, 1979), 311.

[192] If Terrien and Zimmerli were right in their assessments.

[193] A trajectory may exist between these texts and Second Temple apocalyptic literature for the *omphalos* myth, but the lack of textual references and Block's argument (see n.189 [above]) concerning the reference in Ezek 38:12 considerably weakened this possibility.

5.5.6. Step 4f: Evaluation

The EAW and Hebraic sources varied in relationship to Second Temple apocalyptic literature. Jubilees and at least one Qumran manuscript read as a condemnation of the astrological elements, such as seen in "Nabonidus's Rise to Power." The *Yasna* text and the Epinomis text read as differing ways to understand the divine, ways that incorporated some similarities, but failed to hold three points of verbal contact with Second Temple apocalyptic literature. Moreover, meaningful differences appeared in both texts as well. The same held true for the Egyptian texts, which lacked three points of verbal contact and held meaningful differences. The Aristophanes text also lacked three points of verbal contact and evidenced meaningful differences as the cosmos held self-agency. Finally, the references to mountains from outside sources showed no authoritative topos, but rather, a reliance on the generalized myths of mountains and the *omphalos* myth. This reliance suggested a parent-child relationship existed with the general EAW culture concerning mountains as a topos type, but no relationship existed with a specific text or culture.

In the Tanakh, passages under the "Order and Praise" subheading failed to generate a parent-child relationship. Genesis 1:14 held similarities to Jub. 2:9, but the Jubilean author elevated the sun as the sole marker of days and festivals, contra Genesis. Joshua 10:12–14 and Judg 5:20 both lacked three points of verbal contact and also held meaningful differences. Psalm 104:19 also lacked three points of verbal contact. This same pattern occurred with Tanakh passages grouped under the subheadings: "Court Cases and Judgment," and "Identifying Divine Wisdom." Finally, vastly different word pictures and meaningful differences negated such a relationship between Jewish apocalyptic literature and Judg 9:37 or Ezek 38:12, but a parent-child relationship was possible between the Second Temple apocalyptic literature texts and a general concept of the *omphalos* myth in the EAW.

5.6. Chapter Evaluation

Observations of the four topoi types in this chapter led to the conclusion that general similarities existed with EAW sources, but closer scrutiny revealed a lack of verbal contacts, contextual dissimilarities, and meaningful differences. Three of the topos types, however, showed a broad use in the EAW that suggested a parent-child relationship. The first type was Pseudepigraphy. The practice of associating known names to writings occurred in the Adad-Guppi text from Mesopotamia as well as the Egyptian and Greek texts studied in this chapter. The second type was Covenant. Three texts were explored with one of them, "The Second Oracle of Salvation" suggesting a parent-child relationship between the texts. However, further research identified parts of a common treaty formula evident across the EAW, which broadened the parent-child relationship to the general culture of the EAW, a culture that presumably also shaped the Tanakh covenant texts. The third type was Cosmology. The general topos type was revised significantly in Jewish apocalyptic literature to negate any parent-child relationships with the EAW or Tanakh. However, the subtype, "mountains" showed a parent-child relationship through the *omphalos* myth to the larger EAW world, but to no particular texts including the Tanakh.

Concerning References to Common Knowledge, the study of this topos type focused on the Watcher and flood narratives. Meaningful differences and a lack of verbal contacts occurred with all EAW stories. Moreover, Hesiod's Watcher narratives also included an inversion, negating a parent-child relationship. How, then, did Second Temple authors establish authority concerning the topoi presented in this chapter? Much like the topos types in chapter 2, the authors of the passages concerning the topos types in chapter 3 borrowed from widely available concepts across the EAW and in the Tanakh, which were filtered through the milieu of Jewish Second Temple culture and history. As a result, the authority for these topos types lay in Second Temple Judaism, and through these authorities, the authors commended their readers to certain beliefs or practices.[194]

[194] It should also be noted the topos types in chapter 4 failed to exhibit the strong inversions that were present in chapter 3.

Chapter 6
POSSIBLE PRIMA FACIE DERIVATION OF AUTHORITATIVE TOPOI ACCORDING TO PRELIMINARY RESULTS: TANAKH LITERATURE

Writings from the Second Temple Period consistently invoked the Torah of Moses as authoritative sacred writing.
—Hindy Najman, *Interpretation as Primordial Writing*

6.1. Introduction

The focus of this chapter was the Short Quotation topos type derived from the Tanakh.[1] Short quotations designated any passage in Jewish apocalyptic literature quoted from the Tanakh and was intended to remind readers of the passage from which it was quoted. This definition delimited texts consisting of the Tanakh paired with textual expansion, such as Jubilees and the Testaments of Levi and Moses.[2]

The Short Quotation topos type built on this definition. For a short quote from the Tanakh to be considered a Short Quotation topos type in apocalyptic literature, a key phrase was used by the Second Temple apocalyptic author that helped the reader identify a narrative in the Tanakh from which the author then borrowed authority. In Qumran material, however, this topos type specifically referenced the protases of the Pesharim.[3]

---

[1] Because of the unique focus of this chapter and the single topos type examined here, the order of this chapter was extensively modified. Only certain substeps were applicable for examining the Short Quotation topos type. These steps are presented in the following subsections and varied by specific occurrence.

[2] In general, the concept of expanded scriptures (or textual expansion, as it was also known) was vast, and included several variables such as specifying rewritten scripture (rather than the broader term, expanded scriptures), methods of inner-biblical exegesis, and different scribal techniques concerning expansion. For a succinct explanation of these topics, see Crawford, *Rewriting Scripture*, 1–18. She presents a good overview in the introduction before examining several rewritten texts.

[3] Questions concerning the Pesharim and Qumran have created an enormous amount of scholarship; however, what concerned this research was specifically how

Underlying Short Quotation were two other topos types. The first was Scriptural Authority.[4] Although this authority supported the "Cross-Text: Possible Tanakh Sources" sections in the previous chapters of this study, the focus here was identifying how Jewish apocalyptic authors used Tanakh sources in short quotation or reference.[5] Where applicable, examination of possible EAW sources

---

the Teacher of Righteousness used the Short Quotation authoritative topos as it related to the Tanakh, which delimited the subsection specifically to that issue.

[4] Scriptural authority was defined here as authority deriving from a "generally accepted body of sacred literature that was considered by Jews to be uniquely authoritative, ancient in origin, and binding on the community for doctrine and practice" (Crawford, *Rewriting Scripture*, 6).

Note, this term, and the definition thereof, should not be confused with a modern understanding of canon nor understood as a canonical set of texts in the Second Temple period. The above definition, proposed by Crawford, was presented against Peter Flint's use of "canon" for Second Temple period material, which was a "closed list of books that was officially accepted retrospectively by a community as supremely authoritative and binding for religious practice and doctrine." Crawford, however, argued, "The Jewish community did not promulgate an official canon of Scripture until after the end of the Second Temple period. There was no Bible in Second Temple Judaism" (ibid.). Instead, she proposed "scripture," defined as presented here. Kurt Knoll went further in his doubt of authoritative Second Temple texts. He surveyed articles and research from Liz Fried, Karel van der Toorn, Reinhard Kratz, Arie van der Kooij, Martin Jaffee, Seth Schwartz, and James VanderKam and Eugene Ulrich to reach a conclusion that "the widespread idea that texts are able to exert religious authority, had reached only its earliest stages when the Second Temple was destroyed by the Romans" (see "Did 'Scripturalization' Take Place in Second Temple Judaism?" *SJOT* 25.2 [2011]: 206–08). In the opposite direction, Craig Evans argued for an awareness of authoritative writings by Jesus and in several Qumran texts (see "The Scriptures of Jesus and His Earliest Followers," in *The Canon Debate*, ed. Lee Martin McDonald and James A. Sanders [Peabody, MA: Hendrickson, 2002], 195), and Trebolle Barrera concluded several books existed as authoritative scripture based on the designations of Law and Prophets and later, Law, Prophets, and Psalms (see Julio C. Trebolle Barrera, "Origins of a Tripartite Old Testament Canon," in McDonald, *Canon Debate*, 144–45).

[5] Short quotation or reference delimited Jubilees from this chapter. The decision to do so stemmed from Najman's succinct statement of authority for Jubilees and other texts dealing with the material focused on the law or Moses "attempts to make Scripture relevant and accessible generated diverse views about how to interpret and apply this authoritative writing. As a result, distinctive interpretations and practices emerged. It became essential that writers justify their interpretations. One solution to this problem was to establish an authorizing link to the already accepted Torah of Moses." Najman's assessment highlighted the Second Temple authors' borrowing of

also occurred. Although the text, context, and cross-text methodology still lie at the heart of this work, this chapter follows a different organization: The text in question was presented first, followed by a discussion of the scriptural source and recensions of the short quotation as a gateway to understanding how redactors and copyists perceived the relationship between the short quotation and passage in the Tanakh.[6]

Thus defined, four passages and the Pesharim were presented here. The first two passages were in the Book of the Watchers. The third was the angelic declaration of God as thrice holy in reference to Isaiah 6, and the fourth was from the Apocalypse of Zephaniah.

6.2. Scriptural Authority: Short Quotation

In each of the following passages, a short reference to the Tanakh indicated the Jewish apocalyptic author borrowed authority. Each occurrence of topos type, however, authorized the author in a different manner. The work in this chapter began with the story of the beautiful daughters.[7]

6.2.1. The Beautiful Daughters

The Enochian author introduced the Watcher problem in 1 En. 6:1–2. The "Beautiful Daughters" occurred in the second verse:

---

authority from scripture in general, and in particular, from the Torah and Moses. The Testament of Levi and the Testament of Moses were both delimited as well because they were expansions of Tanakh text much like Jubilees. See Najman, "Interpretation as Primordial Writing," 379.

[6] The "Thrice Holy: The Heavenly Council's Cry" subsection defied any such organization; thus, it consisted only of the relationship between the quote and Tanakh passage.

[7] Although several Enochian texts have already been explored, the following work focused on specific texts that, prima facie, derived authority from the Tanakh. Several Tanakh references occurred by referencing concepts or ideas, rather than short direct quotation. These similar concepts or ideas were all delimited in the preliminary work because the quoted material received the highest scores possible in each category. For examples of these references, see Nickelsburg, *1 Enoch* vols. 1 and 2; Loren T. Stuckenbruck, *1 Enoch 91–108*, CEJL, ed. Loren T. Stuckenbruck et al (Berlin: de Gruyter, 2007); Isaac, "1 Enoch," in Charlesworth, *OTP* 1:1–89; Murphy, *Apocalypticism in the Bible*, 125–43.

> In those days, when the children of man had multiplied, it happened that there were born unto them handsome and beautiful daughters. And the angels, the children of heaven, saw them and desired them; and they said to one another, "Come, let us choose wives for ourselves from among the daughters of man and beget us children."

Reversing the order of steps from the previous chapters due to the material, step 4e was engaged first to examine the relationship between 1 En. 6:1–2 and Gen 6:1–2.

6.2.1.1. Step 4e: Cross-Text—Possible Tanakh Source

In Gen 6, the author introduced humanity's antediluvian growth and the subsequent corruption of the sons of God and daughters of man.[8] By connecting the Semyaz strain of the Watcher story to Gen 6, the Enochian author grounded it in an authoritative text.[9] Did the expanded passage negate borrowed authority? Exploring the variations of the text in the Second Temple period helped answer that question.

The exploration began with Gen 6:1–2 from the Tanakh, represented in the MT and LXX texts. Following these texts are translations used for comparative purposes:

> וַיְהִי֙ כִּֽי־הֵחֵ֣ל הָֽאָדָ֔ם לָרֹ֖ב עַל־פְּנֵ֣י הָֽאֲדָמָ֑ה וּבָנ֖וֹת יֻלְּד֥וּ לָהֶֽם׃
> וַיִּרְא֤וּ בְנֵי־הָֽאֱלֹהִים֙ אֶת־בְּנ֣וֹת הָֽאָדָ֔ם כִּ֥י טֹבֹ֖ת הֵ֑נָּה וַיִּקְח֤וּ
> לָהֶם֙ נָשִׁ֔ים מִכֹּ֖ל אֲשֶׁ֥ר בָּחָֽרוּ׃

> And it came about that humans began to multiply upon the face of the earth, and daughters were born to them. And then the

[8] This chapter followed the overall concept of text, context, and cross-text. However, it was organized differently here. The text in question was presented first, followed by the scriptural source (step 4e) and recensions of the short quotation as a gateway to understanding how redactors and copyists perceived the relationship between the quotation and the scriptural source. EAW material, where applicable, was then presented (step 4d). Organizing this chapter in this manner presented a clearer picture of the relationship between the passage of Second Temple apocalyptic literature being studied and the source of the quotation in the Tanakh.

[9] Named the Semyaz strain here because it referred to chapters 6–7 and the Watchers' sin concerning their interaction with the daughters of men. In contrast, the Azazel strain referred to chapter 8 and the presentation of the Watchers' sin concerning their revelation of several secrets to humanity.

> Sons of God saw the daughters of man, that they were beautiful, and they took for themselves wives, from whomever they chose.
>
> Καὶ ἐγένετο ἡνίκα ἤρξαντο οἱ ἄνθρωποι πολλοὶ γίνεσθαι ἐπὶ τῆς γῆς, καὶ θυγατέρες ἐγενήθησαν αὐτοῖς. ἰδόντες δὲ οἱ υἱοὶ τοῦ θεοῦ τὰς θυγατέρας τῶν ἀνθρώπων ὅτι καλαί εἰσιν, ἔλαβον ἑαυτοῖς γυναῖκας ἀπὸ πασῶν, ὧν ἐξελέξαντο.
>
> And it came about that many humans were born upon the earth, and daughters were born to them. And the Sons of God saw the daughters of men, that they were beautiful, [so] they took for themselves wives from whichever ones they chose.

The MT and LXX versions generally agreed, except for differences such as "multiply upon the face of the earth" versus "many humans born upon the earth." These differences were accepted as idiomatic variations and did not factor into this discussion.

In the Qumran Enochic text 4Q202 ar f1.ii:1–3, the extant parts of the fragment showed a shift to שפירן (pretty, beautiful) from the MT טֹבֹת הֵנָּה (good to behold). The text itself was minimally preserved, but a restoration provided by Martínez and Tigchelaar produced the word pair "pretty" and "attractive." If they were correct, this text evidenced the beginning of the word pair found in 1 En. 6:1–2.[10] Although small, this change followed (or occasioned) the shift in the Greek Enochic texts.

The problem, however, was in the restoration, which contains a compound phrase conjoined by the waw conjunction, but the waw itself was questionable.[11] A break in the text left very little of the letter. Moreover, the section holding the presumed waw was dissimilar to the previous waws in the text. Infrared imaging showed the light gray of the papyrus background surrounding the entire mark before the text breaks, negating it as a beginning of a waw. Consequently, 4Q202 most likely held one descriptive word, agreeing with the MT and LXX versions, as

---

[10] Martínez, *Dead Sea Scrolls Transcription*, 405.

[11] 4Q202 ar f1.ii:1–3 is available on Plate 380 Frg. 1 (B-361436) at the Leon Levy Dead Sea Scrolls digital library.

well as with the Enochic $\mathfrak{G}^{S}$ (Greek Syncelli) text.[12] Conversely, $\mathfrak{G}^{A}$ (Codex Panopolitanus) had ὡραῖαι καὶ καλαί, "beautiful and good," with which $\mathfrak{E}$ (Ethiopian Enoch) agreed. Yet, the $\mathfrak{E}$ translator or redactor inserted "beautiful" and "pretty," reversing the order as the first word carried the idea of "good" in its semantic domain. Thus, $\mathfrak{E}$ evidenced either a loose translation of $\mathfrak{G}^{S}$ or more likely, followed a different *vorlage*.[13] What resulted was the first half of a short quotation in which history evidenced one, and possibly two, variances from the MT and LXX, which creates a detracting dissimilarity and negates the first half of the passage as a verbal point of contact.[14]

The textual expansion in the second half of verse 2 also showed a variance. The MT and LXX provided a declarative statement: "They took for themselves wives from among the children of men from all whom they chose." Unfortunately, 4Q202 was unavailable for this half of verse 2, but the Greek and Syriac ($\mathfrak{S}$) texts had significant expansion. In $\mathfrak{G}^{A}$, $\mathfrak{G}^{S}$, and $\mathfrak{S}$, the Watchers lusted after the daughters of men; $\mathfrak{G}^{S}$ and $\mathfrak{S}$ added "went astray" before the Watchers enticed one another to take wives who would bear them children. Conversely, $\mathfrak{E}$ left out "went astray," evidencing a proclivity to the *vorlage* of $\mathfrak{G}^{A}$ over $\mathfrak{G}^{S}$. In $\mathfrak{G}^{A}$, $\mathfrak{S}$, and $\mathfrak{E}$, redactors added: "and they will beget children to us."[15] These expansions provided a detracting dissimilarity that negated the second half of verse two from any of the recensions as a point of verbal contact.

What, then, was the purpose of this expansion? Scholars have advanced assorted reasons for creating this text: an etiology of evil, a

---

[12] Nickelsburg also noted the Syriac text followed $\mathfrak{G}^{S}$. Nickelsburg, *1 Enoch* 1, 174. All references to the Syriac text in this chapter depended on Nickelsburg as noted here.

[13] Nickelsburg argued similarly that the extant Greek manuscripts were "not the *Vorlage* for the Ethiopic version." He noted that $\mathfrak{G}^{A}$ and $\mathfrak{E}$ "agreed with one another in common errors and thus reflected a common Greek archetype" (ibid., 18).

[14] In chapters 3 and 4 of this study, detracting dissimilarities were not considered when assessing the same word, cognates, or synonyms between texts as a point of verbal contact. However, in the Direct Quotation topos type, any shift or change in a quote had the potential to negate the authority drawn from the quoted text. In the above case, the variances negated the presence of synonyms from being a verbal point of contact.

[15] Thus, $\mathfrak{G}^{S}$ was peculiar, indicating a redactor lent little credence to the authority of 1 Enoch based on paraphrasing and the tendency to "habitually abridge redundant expressions" (F. Crawford Burkitt, *Jewish and Christian Apocalypses* [London: Oxford University Press, 1914], 53).

polemic against the priesthood, or (and) a condemnation of intermarriage between priestly and nonpriestly lines.[16] These teleological purposes, however, were meaningfully different from the Tanakh. There, the etiology of evil occurred in Gen 3 rather than Gen 6:1–2. Further highlighting this difference was the offspring of the union. In Genesis 6, the Nephilim were not given evil traits" However, in 1 Enoch, the offspring were giants who consumed the food and then turned to anthropophagy when the people detested feeding them (1 En. 7:2–5).

Further meaningful differences also existed. Reading the flood stories of Genesis and 1 Enoch together, the MT and LXX Sons of God became the 1 Enoch Watchers. Perhaps the first step in transition was the Aramaic Watchers account (Qumran document), which recorded the Gen 6:11 חָמָס, "fill[ed] out what sort of חָמָס occurred before the flood."[17] Authors then expanded the text of 1 Enoch to include a Revealed Secrets topos type concerning astrology and technology. As a result, not enough points of verbal contact and too many meaningful differences negated a parent-child relationship between this text and Gen 6:1–2.[18] Moreover, although scholars often attributed the Enochian passage to priestly sources for condemning marriage between priestly and nonpriestly lines, no borrowed authority came from ancient Hebraic movements.[19]

---

[16] Suter, "Fallen Angel, Fallen Priest," 124–35.

[17] Matthew Goff, "Warriors, Cannibals, and Teachers of Evil: The Sons of the Angels in Genesis 6, the Book of the Watchers and the Book of Jubilees," *SEÅ* 80 (2015): 88.

[18] This statement was not intended to deny Gen 6:1–2 was the story expanded by Jewish authors. Instead, it denied Gen 6:1–2 was used *authoritatively* by Jewish apocalyptic authors in their expansions.

[19] This text in 1 Enoch, however, likely became the source for other Second Temple apocalyptic material, but authority transfer was unlikely because of variants. In 2 En. 18:4, the author truncated the story, with the recensions introducing several variants. Two texts identified only three transgressors with the daughters of men, and a third blamed a pair of princes and two hundred followers, which "is known from 1 En. 6:6, along with several other substantial details of the episode" (F. I. Anderson, "2 (Slavonic Apocalypse of) Enoch: A New Translation and Introduction," in Charlesworth, *OTP* 1:132 n.*d*).

Further, the following verse in 2 Enoch repeated 1 En. 9:9 in the essentials, but with one distinct difference: women now bore much blame for the antediluvian "great evil" (18:5a). The 2 Enoch author had copied the story from 1 Enoch, but shifted blame for sin to woman, possibly for warning adherents of the supposed wily ways of women—a theme developed in pseudepigraphy mostly after the period studied here (but see Pss. Sol. 16:8). The Jubilean author worded the tale differently but followed the general idea in

6.2.1.2. Step 4c: Cross-Text—Germane Scholarship and Possible EAW Sources

Siam Bhayro searched for different sources of this passage. He identified three in particular: "Erra and Ishum," Absalom's rebellion in 2 Sam 15:7–12, and a generalized Mediterranean source for the name, Šemiḥazah. The problem, however, emerged in his conclusion:

> The above three cases demonstrate that the Noahic author was well versed in a variety of literary corpora and Near Eastern traditions. Moreover, our author was not shy when it came to integrating older Jewish sources into his narrative, or even borrowing from contemporary non-Jewish literature, for his own ends. His library contained an array of resources, and he was well able to integrate established narratives and motifs into the polemic he was constructing. If we can read the narrative with sensitivity to his use of these sources, then we can discern even more the genius of his composition.[20]

By assuming external sources in an otherwise well-written article, Bhayro had to conclude an author focused on non-Jewish reading material for cultic authority in an era so concerned with keeping Jewish things Jewish. Moreover, in his assessment of "Erra and Ishum," he argued for similarities between the Watchers and the relationship of Anu (heaven) and earth, which produced seven "agents of destruction." He wrote this passage "parallel[ed]...the giants of 1 Enoch 6–11, who were also the products of a union between the two realms of heaven and earth."[21]

The question, however, was why did this motif have to stem from "Erra and Ishum"? The phrase or concept of "heaven and earth" occurred throughout EAW material, often referring to a god and

---

Jub. 7:20–21, which was a brief overview of the Watcher story of 1 Enoch. There, however, authority was derived from righteousness, as noted in chapter 4 (above).

[20] Siam Bhayro, "Noah's Library: Sources for 1 Enoch 6–11," *JSP* 15.3 (2006): 177. Bhayro presented three cases of EAW sources: 1 Enoch 6–11 compared to "Erra and Ishum," 1 En. 6:6 and Absalom's Rebellion (2 Sam 15:7–12), and background texts for the name, Šemiḥazah. This section was focused on Bhayro's arguments because they affected the context of the Short Quotation topos type, which was more dependent on direct Tanakh context for borrowed authority.

[21] Ibid., 166.

goddess tied to cosmic beliefs in the EAW world.[22] In Hesiod's *Theogony* (lines 125–139), Gaea (earth) gave birth to Ouranos (heaven). They later produced the Titans, whom the youngest Titan, Kronos, successfully led in a war against Ouranos and the ancient gods. Kronos's son, Zeus, later deposed Kronos, which made way for the Olympians to take power. Thus, heaven and earth also bore children in the Greek narrative. Furthermore, the children were responsible for the parent's punishment and later were themselves deprived of power, which was a much closer resemblance to the Watcher story compared to that of "Erra and Ishum." Thus, Hesiod's *Theogony*, alongside other Greek tales such as *Prometheus Bound*, made a Hellenistic influence more likely (but see earlier sections on Greek tales). However, the widespread use of "heaven and earth" makes it difficult to confirm a parent-child relationship with a single text or culture.

In his last case, Bhayro attributed sources to the name Šemiḥazah by positing a Near Eastern deity, a linguistic morpheme, and geographic Mount Zaphon combined into one name. Consequently, the name translated to *Shem of Mount Ḫazzi*, "a north Syrian divine name equivalent to Ba'al Zaphon and Zeus Kassios."[23] According to Bhayro, Second Temple apocalyptic authors used these three elements to create a play on words that turned "Zaphon" into the Hebrew equivalent of "seeing," signifying the Watchers. Thus, he argued for a possible polemic against "those who watch[ed] for omens."[24]

This argument drew from possible roots across the EAW. However, the research evidenced not widespread roots but a concatenation of narratives that allowed the apocalyptic authors to draw from a rich tapestry of concurrent material in Second Temple Judaism. That material included both Tanakh and EAW literature, which denied three points of verbal contact with any single text or culture and therefore also denied a parent-child relationship between EAW texts and 1 En. 6:1–2.

---

[22] M. Hutter and M. de Jonge, "Heaven," *DDD*, 388.

[23] Bhayro, "Noah's Library," 176. Bhayro noted Mount Zaphon was locally known as Ḫazzi. Note: inclusion here does not equal acceptance of Bhayro's theory. Instead, it is included here so this research can interact with the idea.

[24] Ibid., 177.

6.2.2. Cries and Groans to Heaven

The cries and groans to heaven topos repeated three times in the Enochian Watchers narrative: 7:6; 8:4; and 9:10b. These three texts were in parallel, as noted by Reed: "It is striking…that all three summaries of angelic sin in this unit culminate with descriptions of the violence of the Giants against the creatures of the earth (7:3–5; 8:4a; 9:9) and the resulting outcry of either the earth itself (7:6) or humankind (8:4; 9:10)."[25]

Two of these texts, 8:1–4 and 9:10, may have been drawn from the Tanakh. In 1 En. 8, the author began with a list of sins from the Azazel strain, starting with Azazel teaching humanity to craft weapons, adornments, eye paint, dyes, and alchemy in verse 1. Others taught magic and astrology (verse 3). Between these lists, the redactor stated in 8:2, "There were many wicked ones and they committed adultery and erred, and all their conduct became corrupt."[26]

The author then restated the Watcher story (9:10) through the mouths of Michael, Surafel, and Gabriel, which in the narrative, then provoked God to action. Taken as one, these verses summarized the חָמָס in Gen 6 that was referenced in the previous subsection ("The Beautiful Daughters"). However, the Enochian passages also concluded with references to Exodus.

6.2.2.1. Step 4e: Cross-Text—Possible Tanakh Sources

The reference to Exod 2:23 occurred in 1 En. 8:4: "And (the people) cried and their voice reached unto heaven," and "Their groaning has ascended (into heaven), but they could not get out from before the face of the oppression that is being wrought on earth" (1 En. 9:10b). The Enochian author provided three connections to Exod 2: (1) oppression, (2) the words "cry" and "groan," and (3) a cognate between Hebrew and Ge'ez. These three connections looked to be three points of verbal contact. Further study of these contacts incorporated a study in the recensions.

The first point of verbal contact concerned oppression-caused suffering. For the Hebrews, the new pharaoh stripped them of their

[25] Reed, *Fallen Angels*, 30.

[26] The Syncelli variant for verses 1–2 made humanity responsible by precipitating the Watchers' fall. For more on this variant, see Coblentz Bautch, "Decoration, Destruction and Debauchery: Reflections on 1 Enoch 8 in Light of 4Qenb," *DSD* 15.1 (2008): 79–95.

security and put them to work making bricks for his building program; for antediluvian humanity, the Giants made humans feed them, and then, when the humans refused, the giants engaged in anthropophagy. In both circumstances, the oppressors treated the oppressed as slaves.

A second point of verbal contact was linguistic. The Exod 2:23b–24 passage read as follows in the LXX:

> καὶ κατεστέναξαν οἱ υἱοὶ Ισραηλ ἀπὸ τῶν ἔργων καὶ ἀνεβόησαν, καὶ ἀνέβη ἡ βοὴ αὐτῶν πρὸς τὸν θεὸν ἀπὸ τῶν ἔργων. καὶ εἰσήκουσεν ὁ θεὸς τὸν στεναγμὸν αὐτῶν, καὶ ἐμνήσθη ὁ θεὸς τῆς διαθήκης αὐτοῦ τῆς πρὸς Αβρααμ καὶ Ισαακ καὶ Ιακωβ.
>
> And the sons of Israel groaned from the work, and they cried out, and their cries went up to God from their labor. And God heard their groans, and God remembered his covenant with Abraham, Isaac, and Jacob.

"Cry" and "groan" translated the LXX βοὴ and στεναγμὸν, respectively. In 1 Enoch, the $\mathfrak{G}^{S}$ and $\mathfrak{G}^{A}$ redactors used βοὴ in 8:4, but in 9:10, the $\mathfrak{G}^{A}$ redactor included στενάζουσιν:

> καὶ νῦν ἰδοὺ βοῶσιν αἱ ψυχαὶ τῶν τετελευτηκότων καὶ ἐντυγχάνουσι μέχρι τῶν πυλῶν τοῦ οὐρανοῦ, καὶ ἀνέβη ὁ στεναγμὸς αὐτῶν.
>
> And now, behold the souls of the dead cry, and they appeal to the gates of heaven and their groans go up.

Creating this doublet drew a tighter connection to Exodus, although any date for its origin is conjecture.[27] Nevertheless, the variant provided a glimpse into the authorities from which redactors believed these texts derived again seen in $\mathfrak{G}^{S2}$ 8:4b–9:3:

---

[27] The Qumran text, 4Q201 ar iv:9 and 4Q202 ar iii.9 carried a doublet קלה(א) and זעק, outcry and wail—a pairing perhaps synonymous with cry and groan; however, נאק (or its derivations) were available in Jewish Aramaic, as presented in both the Galilean and Targum material, precipitating the question, why not follow the Exodus wording? Perhaps, the reason was they were not borrowing authority. Koehler, "נאק," *HALOT* 658.

> Οἱ δὲ λοιποὶ ἐβόησαν εἰς τὸν οὐρανὸν περὶ τῆς κακώσεως αὐτῶν, λέγοντες εἰσενεχθῆναι τὸ μνημόσυνον αὐτῶν ἐνώπιον Κυρίου. Καὶ ἀκούσαντες οἱ τέσσαρες μεγάλοι ἀρχάγγελοι, Μιχαὴλ καὶ Οὐριὴλ καὶ Ῥαφαὴλ καὶ Γαβριήλ, παρέκυψαν ἐπὶ τὴν γῆν ἐκ τῶν ἁγίων τοῦ οὐρανοῦ· καὶ θεασάμενοι αἷμα πολὺ ἐκκεχυμένον ἐπὶ τῆς γῆς καὶ πᾶσαν ἀσέβειαν καὶ ἀνομίαν γενομένην ἐπ᾽ αὐτῆς, εἰσελθόντες εἶπον πρὸς ἀλλήλους ὅτι Τὰ πνεύματα καὶ αἱ ψυχαὶ τῶν ἀνθρώπων στενάζουσιν ἐντυγχάνοντα καὶ λέγοντα ὅτι Εἰσαγάγετε τὴν κρίσιν ἡμῶν πρὸς τὸν ὕψιστον

The redactor followed the Exodus pattern of suffering, crying to heaven, and the occurrence of a memory. Note, however, the heavenly actors in this passage were angelic, rather than divine:

> But they remained, crying to heaven concerning their evil treatment, speaking to bring a memory of them before the Lord. And hearing, the four great archangels—Michael, Uriel, Rafael, and Gabriel—looked upon the earth out of the Sanctuary of heaven, and they saw for themselves much blood being shed upon the earth and all the lawlessness and impiety occurring on her, entering [a conversation] they said to one another, "the spirit and the soul of men groan, appealing and saying, 'take our case to the most high'"

Together, the $\mathfrak{G}^{S2}$ and $\mathfrak{G}^{A}$ texts pictured Exod 2:23b–24. Although this occurred in two different passages, those passages were in parallel, as noted by Reed. Moreover, in 𝔈 9:2 and 9:10, the translator clarified a connection to Exod 2:23 with the Ge'ez cognate, ʾänəqäṣä, for the Hebrew נַאֲקָתָם.[28] Further, the translator followed with Gəʿra, which translated as "cry," "cry out," "moan," or "sigh," distinguishing it from änəqäṣä, as the Hebrew and LXX did between "cry" and "groan."[29]

The third point of verbal contact related to the second. In the Enochic 𝔈 text, sämayä was a Ge'ez cognate of שָׁמַיִם. Although "heaven" replaced "God" in 𝔈 (and in every extant text including

[28] *CDG*, "ʾanaqa." Note, these were the only two occurrences of ʾänəqäṣä in 𝔈.
[29] Ibid., "Gəʿra."

Qumran), the metonymy still connected these verses.[30] The author, therefore, presented cries and groans ascending to God as in Exod 2:23. Their ascending cries (LXX—ἀνέβη ἡ βοὴ αὐτῶν πρὸς τὸν θεὸν) occurred in 4Q201 iv:6, 4Q202 iii:6, and $\mathfrak{G}^{A}$ (1 En. 8:4), while $\mathfrak{G}^{S}$ and $\mathfrak{G}^{S2}$ presented *how* they came before God, assuring the link to Exodus.

While dissimilarities existed, they were not dissimilar to the point of distracting the reader from the connection made to the passage in Exodus. Instead, the text read as a narrative reminding the reader of God's deliverance, whether it be from Egypt or from the Giants. The context of these verses was, therefore, complementary, which occasioned a fourth point of verbal contact. So, was this passage in a parent-child relationship with the Tanakh literature?

A question remained whether this relationship was an appeal to authority. The texts from which the Enochian P.authors drew posed a problem in terms of considering $\mathfrak{G}^{S2}$ and $\mathfrak{G}^{A.}$ The redactors responsible for $\mathfrak{G}^{S2}$ and $\mathfrak{G}^{A}$ clarified—or rewrote—the text for a stronger connection. Consequently, doing so evidenced an unclear or weak link in the redactor's eye, casting doubt on an author purposely borrowing authority. Although it could be posited $\mathfrak{E}$ proved dependence upon an original urtext based on a separate *vorlage*; the result of such an argument would still place the focus on $\mathfrak{G}^{S}$. Why was "groan" missing in $\mathfrak{G}^{S}$, and why were the two terms widely dispersed in $\mathfrak{G}^{S2}$? The Second Temple redactors most likely recognized the connection to Exodus but did not view the link as an authoritative topos. Thus, they felt free to edit or recast the passage as they thought necessary.

What, then, could be said about the Tanakh as a source? A probable relationship existed between the passage in Exodus and that in 1 Enoch based on the quote. The problem was that a study of the recensions evidenced the topos type did not carry authority. Moreover, even if it did carry authority, that authority was based in a found metanarrative; a story that provided definition for the community known as the Israelites. As such, the narrative was not tied to a single Hebraic movement.

[30] Over a century ago, scholars recognized this metonymy was already known, and thus, available for Jewish authors to use. See, for instance, Emil Schürer, *A History of the Jewish People in the Time of Jesus Christ, Second Division*, vol. 2 (Edinburgh: T&T Clark, 1890), 170; Ethelbert William Bullinger, *Figures of Speech Used in the Bible* (London: Eyre and Spottiswoode, 1898), 538.

6.2.2.2. Cross-Text—Possible EAW Sources

Might EAW sources have affected this topos? Two texts contained possible connections. The first text was Homer's *Iliad.* In it, two passages used the βοὴ and στεναγμὸν doublet. The second was a play, Aeschylus's *Persians.* In it, Xerxes recounted to the elders in Persia his military defeat against the Greeks.

6.2.2.2.1. Homer's Iliad

In Homer's *Iliad*, two passages used the same word pair for "cry" and "groan" as G^A; the stronger possible connection occurred in 2.95: "But the assembly is stirred up, and the earth under them groans; people seated them [again] but a din arose, and nine heralds, crying out, restrained them."[31] The context was an Achaean war council wherein the στεναχίζετο (groans) came from the earth rather than humanity seeking refuge. The heralds' βοόωντες (cries) occurred as they restrained the crowd. The author mentioned nothing of oppression, cries ascending to heaven, or a divine response; instead, the war council was a response to divine actions. This change of context and the concept of the earth groaning rather than the groans arising from the people seeking refuge created two meaningful differences. The same meaningful differences occurred in the second passage, found in 13.538. There, the groaning came from the city Troy amid war, and the shouts were a battle cry, a very different context from the 1 Enoch passage.[32]

6.2.2.2.2. Aeschylus's Persians

In Aeschylus's play, the couplet occurred between lines 1046 and 1059, beginning with Xerxes's exclamation, "Strike, Strike, and groan for my grace [for my sake]." The Chorus answered, "I, in fact, mourn with tears!" Xerxes then responded, "Now cry, re-echoing me!"[33] The context of this passage was Xerxes recounting the defeat of his forces by the Greeks. "Groan" and "cry" occurred not through

---

[31] "Τετρήχει δ' ἀγορή, ὑπὸ δὲ στεναχίζετο γαῖα λαῶν ἱζόντων, ὅμαδος δ' ἦν ἐννέα δέ σφεας κήρυκες βοόωντες ἐρήτυον."

[32] "Οἳ τόν γε προτὶ ἄστυ φέρον βαρέα στενάχοντα τειρόμενον κατὰ δ' αἷμα νεουτάτου ἔρρεε χειρός. Οἳ δ' ἄλλοι μάρναντο, βοὴ δ' ἄσβεστος ὀρώρει."

[33] "Ξέρξης: ἔρεσσ' ἔρεσσε καὶ στέναζ' ἐμὴν χάριν. Χορός: διαίνομαι γοεδνὸς ὤν. Ξέρξης; βόα νυν ἀντίδουπά μοι"—the colon separates speaker from the speech for clarification here. It was not original to the text.

oppression, but in losing a war he started. In addition, like in the *Iliad*, no mention of cries ascending to heaven or any divine action existed, which created three meaningful differences. Therefore, neither the *Iliad* nor *Persians* sat in a parent-child relationship with the topos in 1 Enoch.

6.2.3. Thrice Holy: The Heavenly Council's Cry

The phrase "holy, holy, holy" occurred in 1 En. 39:12, but it was not the only link in 1 En. 39 to Tanakh prophetic material. A second point of verbal contact was the phrase,"and it shall come to pass" (39:1a), and was the only use of this phrase in Second Temple apocalyptic literature. Therefore, exploring the trebled praise of 1 En. 39:12 had to begin with verse 1:

> And it shall come to pass in those days that the children of the elect and the holy ones [will descend] from the high heaven and their seed will become one with the children of the people. And in those days Enoch received the books of zeal and wrath as well as the books of haste and whirlwind. The Lord of the Spirits says that mercy shall not be upon them (39:1–2).

In this passage, "And it shall come to pass" referenced a future event. The phrase was similar to two Hebrew clauses. The first clause, וְהָיָה | בְּאַחֲרִית הַיָּמִים (and it will come to pass after those days) occurred only in the prophets: Isa 2:2; Jer 49:39; Mic 4:1.[34] Isaiah and Micah both referred to establishing the "mountain of the house (בֵּית) of YHWH," and Jer 49:39 concerned YHWH restoring Elam. All three passages, therefore, concerned restoration. The second phrase, וְהָיָה בַּיּוֹם (and in that day), occurred forty-one times in the Tanakh, with thirty-six of the occurrences in the prophets. All but one occurrence signaled a prophetic future.[35]

Arguably, any future-oriented discussion necessitated the Hebrew verb of being and resulted in the phrase "in those days." Yet, the

---

[34] Ezekiel 38:16 held a similar phrase, the context was too different to include here as בְּאַחֲרִית הַיָּמִים did not include the requisite וְהָיָה that began the phrase "and it will come to pass."

[35] Ezekiel 43:27 included a numeric adjective, "on the eighth day," and referred to instructions for purification. Note, however, while the phrase did not signify prophetic action, it fell within a divine journey concerning future events.

combination of "And it shall come to pass" with "in those days" (both being derivations of the verb of being) in 1 En. 39 evidenced an explicit link. The author also highlighted the future focus of the verse by repeating the phrase "forever and ever" in the following text (table 8).[36] Thus, the Enochian author clarified the message: The present turmoil was temporary, but future peace and righteousness were permanent. The author did so by incorporating phrasing that called to mind Tanakh prophetic texts. Therefore, although the "and it shall come to pass" and "in those days" clauses were used in various ways, the concept was a future point in time when YHWH would begin either judgment or restoration. This similarity created an overall complementary context, which made the context a third point of verbal contact.

Table 8. The Enoch Pattern

Passage	*Text*	*Significance*
39:1	And it shall come to pass in those days . . .	Opening line establishing prophesied future
39:2	And in those days . . .	Enoch received books establishing punishment of the Watchers
39:3-5	In those days . . . and thus [righteousness] is in their midst *forever and ever*	Beginning of a journey to the divine council
39:6	And in those days . . . and the righteous and elect ones shall be without number before him *forever and ever*	Enoch sees the "elect one" and his righteousness
39:9	In those days . . . "Blessed are you and blessed in the name of the Lord of the Spirits *forever and ever*"	Enoch in the divine council

The question, then, was whether this topos was authoritative? Did the author intentionally use a prophetic phrase to recall previous prophecies? The problem was that several other phrases in the Tanakh were stronger signals of prophetic material, such as "an oracle of…," "the word of YHWH came to…," or "thus says YHWH"; however, the lack of such statements did not deny "and it shall come to pass" and its derivation "in those days" was closely associated with Tanakh prophecy. Consequently, the question fell back to the first point of verbal contact between 1 En. 39:12 and Tanakh prophetic material; the heavenly court's cry of "holy, holy, holy."

The seraphim thrice declared God's holiness in 1 En. 39:12, reflecting the scene from Isa 6:1–3:

---

[36] Interestingly, "forever and ever" occurred only in places dealing with righteousness.

> They shall bless, praise, and extol (you), saying, "Holy, Holy, Holy, Lord of the Spirits; the spirits fill the earth." And at that place (under his wings) my eyes saw others who stood before him sleepless (and) blessed (him), saying, "Blessed are you and blessed is the name of the Lord of the Spirits forever and ever." And my face was changed on account of the fact that I could not withstand the sight (1 En. 39: 12b–14).

> In the year King Uzziah died, I saw the Lord sitting upon the throne, exalted and lifted up, and the train of his robe filled the temple. Seraphim stood above him with six wings each; with two they covered their face, and with two they covered their waist, and with two they flew. And they called this [one] to that [one] saying, "Holy, holy, holy" is YHWH of hosts, his glory fills all the earth" (Isa 6:1–3).[37]

Although similar, the Enochian author created several meaningful differences. First, the Isaiah account was a prophetic commissioning following a long-held tradition of prophets entering the heavenly council.[38] In the council, Isaiah heard the seraphim declaring God's holiness; but in 1 Enoch, the phrase was part of a narrated memory of Enoch praising God (verse 9). Second, in Isaiah, the trebled "holy" was the seraphim's declaration in God's presence; however, in 1 Enoch, the phrase fell in Enoch's declaration to God concerning what the angels would do: "They shall bless, praise and extol you, saying, 'holy, holy, holy, Lord of the Spirits, the spirits fill the earth'" (39:12). Third, the Enochian author stripped Isaiah's response from the passage. Following the seraphim crying "holy, holy, holy," Isaiah responded with "Woe is me because I am destroyed; I am a man of unclean lips, and I dwell amid a people of unclean lips, because the King, YHWH of Hosts, I have seen" (Isa 6:5). Isaiah recognized his and his

---

[37] Textual differences between Enochian recensions in this passage were of little importance as $\mathcal{E}^{2080}$ and $\mathcal{E}^{3}$ held only minor differences. These differences included changing "the spirits will fill the earth" with "He will fill the earth with spirits," or changing "Lord of the Spirits" to "Lord of Lords" (Isaac, "1 Enoch," in Charlesworth, *OTP* 1:31).

[38] Martti Nissinen, "Prophets and the Divine Council," in *Kein Land für sich allein: Studien Zum kulturkontakt in Kanaan, Israel/Palästina und Ebirnâri für Manfred Weippert Zum 65 Geburtstag*, ed. Ulrich Hübner and Ernst A. Knauf, OBO 186 (Göttingen: Vandenhoeck und Ruprecht, 2002), 16.

people's sins, but the Enochian author chose to write Enoch peering under an angel's wing to watch the chorus of praise.

Finally, 1 Enoch also included a connection to Moses. After observing the chorus of praise, the Enochian author wrote, "And my face was changed on account of the fact that I could not withstand the sight." This quote called to memory two passages with Moses as the main character. These passages came before and after the second set of stone tablets were provided to Moses by God in Exod 33:14 and 34:29–35. The first passage concerned God telling Moses, "No one is able to see my face, no man can see me and live." God then instructed him, "When my glory passes, I will put you in a rock crevice, and I will cover you with my hand until I pass." The second passage concerned Moses returning to the people after receiving the second set of tablets, as concluded in 34:35: "The Israelites saw the face of Moses, because the skin of Moses's face shined, so Moses returned a veil upon his face until he entered to speak with God." When compared with the Enochian passage, Enoch and Moses shared three characteristics: (1) both were in God's presence, (2) both had their faces physically changed, and (3) both had to look away because they could not withstand the sight.[39] The similarities linked the passage with the Exodus-Sinai story as well as Isaiah 6.

These three meaningful differences (Isaiah's commissioning, Enoch's use of the trebled "holy," and the 1 Enoch passage link to Exodus) moved the text outside of authority borrowed specifically from Isaiah. The Enochian author changed the commissioning text to a praise text wherein Enoch did not need to repent.[40] Moreover, the Enochian author diluted any possible prophetic authority by coupling the Isaiah reference with Exod 33 and 34, thus dividing authority between the prophetic movement and law or the priestly movement. Therefore, no parent-child relationship exists between 1 En. 39:1–9 and prophetic texts in the Tanakh. However, if the

---

[39] Isaiah's cry, "I am destroyed...because YHWH...my eyes have seen," paralleled Enoch's, "I could not withstand the sight," but the addition of a changed appearance linked the text to Moses. But, is it an early expression of the hermeneutical method later known as Hillel's second rule, *G'zerah Shavah*, or equivalence of expressions?

[40] Nickelsburg and VanderKam wrote that Enoch actually *joined* the heavenly council in praising God: "This is the first point in the Parables at which Enoch actually interacts with a scene to which he is witness; he joins the chorus of those who are praising the Lord of Spirits" (Nickelsburg-VanderKam, *1 Enoch 2*, 126). Enoch's role in the heavenly council in this passage also strengthened the claim that Enoch was only a go-between concerning the Watchers; or at least, understood that way by later Enochian authors.

connection to Exodus was accepted as a point of verbal contact, then this passage represented an appeal to the general topos of Scriptural Authority—the Law and the Prophets—as represented by the receiver of the law (Moses) and a very prominent prophet with prolific amounts of writing assigned to him.[41]

6.2.4. Neither Kept the Command…Nor Observed the Ordinances

The last passage considered for the Short Quotation topos type was Apoc. Zeph. 3:4: "These are the three sons of Joatham, the priest, who neither kept the commandment of their father nor observed the ordinances of the Lord." The authoritative topos occurred in the synonymous negative phrasing, neither kept…nor observed. This type of negative synonymous parallelism occurred in Tanakh poetry related to the Sinai covenant, such as Psa 78:10: "And they did not keep the covenant of God, and they refused to walk in his law," (לֹא שָׁמְרוּ בְּרִית אֱלֹהִים וּבְתוֹרָתוֹ מֵאֲנוּ לָלֶכֶת). Similar parallelism also occurred in the prophets, such as in Jer 11:8: "And they did not hear, nor did they stretch their ear" (וְלֹא שָׁמְעוּ וְלֹא־הִטּוּ אֶת־אָזְנָם). The problem was phrasing that was too general and a lack of three points of verbal contact to a single occurrence. Therefore, little evidence existed to show this phrase was used to call to mind specific Tanakh references.

6.3. Qumran

The Qumran community used a peculiar method of authority transfer identified by the Aramaic word פשר (*Pesher,* meaning "interpretation" or "solution"). Traditionally, scholars have understood Pesher as a hermeneutical approach to prophecy, but how did authority fit into this picture?

---

[41] Recognition of Isaiah existed throughout the Second Temple period, including the Qumran Isaiah scroll; the later Ascension of Isaiah; several references to Isaiah (for the connection of Isa 31:4 and 49:2 in 4 Ezra 13:10–11, see Flusser *Judaism* 2, 263); NT writings; and the Ethiopian eunuch in Acts 8:26–40 a probable Jew seeing as he came to Jerusalem to worship, as noted in 8:27–28; among others. Note, this topos occurred in 2 En. 21:1–2, recalling Isaiah's throne room commissioning scene. It had the tone of 1 Enoch—a scene of rehearsed praise—but lacked the Mosaic element nor was it found in the Dead Sea Scrolls.

6.3.1. Pesher at Qumran

A count of the occurrences of פשר in Qumran texts showed 106 out of 148 (72 percent) were interpretations of Tanakh prophetic passages.[42] Although many of these uses occurred within the same text, seventeen of twenty-five Pesher texts (68 percent) were interpretations of the Tanakh prophets. However, interpretations of Psalms had the second highest single set of occurrences (table 9).[43]

Table 9. Occurrences of פשר. Left, Occurrences of פשר among the OT book at Qumran. Right, occurrences of פשר by scroll.

	Total Occurrences of פשר	*Number of texts where* פשר *occurs**
OT Prophets	106	17
Psalms	36	5
Genesis	3	3
Deuteronomy	1	1
Other	2	2

*פשר occurs four times in 11Q13, each referring to a different section of the OT. As a result, this column totals twenty-eight texts rather than twenty-five texts.

Scroll	*OT Reference*	*Occurrences of* פשר
1QpHab	Habakkuk	31
4Q171	Psalms	29
4Q169	Nahum	18
4Q163	Isaiah	12
4Q161	Isaiah	8
4Q167	Hosea	7
1Q14	Micah	5
4Q166	Hosea	5
1Q16	Psalms	4
4Q165	Isaiah	4
4Q167	Hosea	4
11Q12	multiple	4

Were these statistics evidence of authority from the prophetic and wisdom movements in the Dead Sea Scroll community? A closer reading led to the conclusion the statistics only showed the community heavily used prophetic texts. The closer reading began with 1QpHab ii:1–9, which established the authority of the Teacher of Righteousness:

> It was reported [space] the interpretation of the word on the treacherous ones with the Man of the Lie because they did not believe in the words of the Teacher of Righteousness from the mouth of God, and against the treacherous ones of the new covenant because they did not believe in the covenant of God, and

[42] "Clear uses of Pesher" meant no textual corruption. García Martínez, *DSSSE*, 1.

[43] However, a tradition of Davidic material being prophetic existed, as seen in Qumran. Therefore, any Pesher from Psalms may also be considered prophetic—see Crawford, *Rewriting Scripture*, 137.

> they profaned the Holy Name. And likewise, [space] the interpretation of the word against the treacherous ones in the last days. They are violators of the covenant who will not believe when they hear all that is coming upon the final generation from the mouth of the priest whom God set in the midst of the congregation to interpret all the words of his servants, the prophets, by whom God wrote all that will happen to his people, Israel.[44]

Two critical points occurred here: (1) interpretations derived from God, not the Teacher of Righteousness; and (2) God set the Teacher among the congregation to interpret the prophets; but how, and what was the purpose?

6.3.2. Text and Context—Pesher and Germane Scholarship

John Collins argued "prophecy was not to be interpreted in its historical context but was assumed to refer to 'the last generation.' Scripture was a mysterious code and required further revelation for its true interpretation." Collins finished his paragraph indicating to whom the task of interpretation fell: "[It] was presumably attached to the office of interpreter of the law."[45] Similarly, Jassen noted the Qumran writers presented the Tanakh prophets in diverse ways, but one oft-repeated role involved declarations of future events. For the community, "the role of the classical prophets was clarified. [The prophets'] prophecies were not directed at their own time, but contained secrets concerning the end time, within which the sect envisaged its own existence."[46] Prophetic texts, then, held declarations of current events for Qumran, but as Jassen clarified, the authority fell not to the prophetic text, but to the Teacher of Righteousness.[47] The Pesharim were an "actualizing interpretation" of the Tanakh prophets

---

[44] Martínez, *DSSSE*, 2:1271.

[45] John J. Collins, "Dead Sea Scrolls," *ABD* 2:90.

[46] Alex Jassen, *Mediating the Divine: Prophecy and Revelation in the Dead Sea Scrolls and Second Temple Judaism*, STDJ 68 (Leiden: Brill, 2007), 29.

[47] Jassen made this point in his discussion of 1QpHab ii:5–10. Reflecting on line 8, he wrote, "[The Teacher of Righteousness] is portrayed as one to whom God has bestowed discernment in order to understand 'all the words of his servants, the prophets'" (ibid., 32–33).

focused on the "life and theology of the community."[48] Therefore, although a clear relationship existed between the prophetic material in the Tanakh and the Qumran Pesharim, it was not a relationship based on authority. Further support for this argument came from Armin Lange and his story of Pesher hermeneutics in EAW literature.

According to Lange, pesher hermeneutics stemmed from EAW omen interpretation. Lange described the likenesses between the presentation of the protasis, which "summarizes the omen," and following that, "an apodosis that interprets the omen."[49] He concluded, "This close relation between ancient Near Eastern omen interpretation and pesher hermeneutics demonstrate[d] that scriptural interpretation was an act of revelation for the pesherist."[50] Accordingly, the primary authority stemmed not from the prophetic movement, but from the Teacher of Righteousness, who interpreted texts by revelation.

6.4. Chapter Evaluation

The three passages in 1 Enoch and the single passage in the Apocalypse of Zephaniah appeared, on the surface, to be in a parent-child relationship with the Tanakh, but investigations exposed either dissimilarities or a nonauthoritative use of the Tanakh passage. At Qumran, the Pesharim first appeared dependent on Hebraic scriptures in general, and on the prophetic movement, specifically; however, a closer examination revealed the fallacy of this preliminary assessment. The authority was in the interpretive act. EAW material assisted in understanding the method, but texts from the EAW lent no authority to the texts. As such, all authority resided in the Teacher of Righteousness. From these findings, the Short Quotation authoritative topos type surprisingly lacked a parent-child relationship with the Tanakh.

How, then, did Second Temple apocalyptic authors use the Short Quotation topos type? The Tanakh provided a common foundation from which the Second Temple apocalyptic authors wove their narratives, and the prophetic texts provided a foundation from which the Teacher of Righteousness could introduce his teachings. These texts perhaps

[48] Jutta Jokiranta, "Pesharim: A Mirror of Self-Understanding," in *Reading the Present in the Qumran Library: The Perception of the Contemporary by Means of Scriptural Interpretations* [*RPQL*], ed. Kristen De Troyer and Armin Lange, SBLSS 30, ed. Christopher Matthews (Atlanta: Society of Biblical Literature, 2005), 24.

[49] Lange "Reading the Decline in Prophecy," in *RPQL*, 188.

[50] Ibid., 189.

depended on a general understanding of Scripture as authority, but the Second Temple apocalyptic authors did not depend upon that authority. Instead, they used the texts as background settings to clarify their own messages to their readers. Therefore, any authority deriving from these passages was grounded in Second Temple understanding of the larger narrative context, rather than the authority found in the Hebraic movements or EAW literature.

Chapter 7
CONCLUSION

7.1. Introduction

In the introduction to this research, a question was posed concerning how authoritative topoi in Second Temple apocalyptic literature compared to similar authorities or references to authority in other literature. A four-step process was used to identify nine topos types evidencing the strongest likelihood of a relationship with EAW or Tanakh material. The observations from those steps, and from the fourth step, in particular, were intended to form the foundation for understanding how Second Temple authors established authority in apocalyptic literature.

7.2. Assessing Established Authority in Apocalyptic Literature

In each of the topos types examined, the P.authors introduced changes to the topos type that made it unique to the Second Temple period. They drew from the literary milieu of their day from across the EAW but were not dependent on a specific outside culture or ancient movement. Instead, the authors depended on Second Temple understanding of Jewish historical and cultic realities.[1] This conclusion was drawn from three particular points. First, almost every inversion in the Second Temple material was situated against the Hellenistic and Egyptian gods, rulers, and cultures, which were threats to Second Temple Judaism.[2] Perhaps, the most dominant of these inversions was seen in the relationship between the Watchers and Prometheus. This inversion indicated Jewish thoughts on the appetite for war among the Hellenistic rulers rather than indicating Hellenistic roots of Jewish Apocalypticism.

Second, much of the material showed a generalization—that is, the ideas, references, and concepts within written language were found

[1] As seen in the waxing and waning of the popularity and beliefs concerning Enoch throughout Second Temple and early Rabbinical Judaism.

[2] The gods, temples, and priesthoods of ancient Egypt were still part of the Egyptian system under Ptolemy, as evidenced in "The Tradition of Seven Lean Years."

throughout several cultures. The history of the EAW, Hellenism, and Egypt supported this assessment. J. G. Manning wrote of the history and generalization of cultural distinctions in his book on Ptolemaic Egypt. Focusing on the scholarly discussion of Persian administration and Hellenism, he stated the discussion had resulted in "redraw[ing] Mediterranean cultural and chronological boundaries, and in some cases ...eliminat[ing] them altogether. In a sense, the many points of contact that existed between Greece and the Near East from the seventh to the third centuries BC[E] have been restored."[3] However, when Second Temple authors used generalized ideas, references, and concepts within written language, they most often employed them in ways that equally connected to the Tanakh.

Third, three of the topos types—Revelation of Secrets, Divinely Ordained Journeys, and Common Knowledge (the Watchers)—evidenced a trajectory or development in the Tanakh, but the conclusion of that development was not found there. Moreover, although EAW material existed that may have sat in a relationship with these topoi, that material could not fill in the literary or referential gaps between the Tanakh and Second Temple material.

What, then, was the overarching relationship with literature from cultures and movements considered sources by so many? The best term to describe the relationship was a "parallax gap."[4] A parallax gap, as applied here, occurs when two bodies of material look similar, and may even have the same origin, but are independent existing bodies. Knowledge of any one body would come only from studying that body, and such was true here. Second Temple apocalyptic literature was an independent body of literature that appeared to be—and in several cases, was—similar to EAW and Tanakh material; however,

---

[3] J. G. Manning, *The Last Pharaohs: Egypt under the Ptolemies, 305–30 BC* (Princeton, Princeton University Press, 2012), 2.

[4] Slavoj Žižek explained it as "the illusion on which [two stories sharing several links and thus, look to be related through similarity] rely, that of putting two incompatible phenomena on the same level, is strictly analogous to what Kant called 'transcendental illusion,' the illusion of being able to use the same language for phenomena which are mutually untranslatable and can be grasped only in a kind of parallax view, constantly shifting perspective between two points between which no synthesis or mediation is possible. Thus, there is no rapport between the two levels, no shared space—although they are closely connected, even identical in a way, they are, as it were, on the opposed sides of a Moebius strip" (*The Parallax View* [Cambridge: MIT Press, 2006], 3).

correlation does not imply causation; this causation fallacy of the History of Religions method drove an a priori assumption of literary roots outside of Second Temple Judaism and produced a fallacy that distracted Second Temple studies for well over one hundred years.

7.3. Observations on this Research

How did a modified postmodern method affect the research? To answer this question required a return to another element of postmodernity: wrestling with the false veil of objectivity, which included stepping into a first-person point of view. The following material was divided into two subsections. The first was an assessment of the challenges to using this method. The second was an assessment of the positive elements of this method.

7.3.1. Challenges

Perhaps, the greatest challenge to using a postmodern methodology was that of expectation. The traditional scientific method begins with a hypothesis from preliminary observations. This hypothesis was then tested or proven through a series of experimental tests. In literary work, this method changed to a presentation of the research question, followed by a step-by-step linear literary analysis that includes interaction with outside scholarship. In this present research, this step-by-step analysis led to a problem clarifying rigor and subsequent observations. To a traditional scholar, the loops used in this study could be interpreted as sloppy work that lacks controls. The irony, however, was that these loops were introduced precisely as a control against biases. They forced me to return to material previously dismissed (and in the step 3 loop, to additional material) in a continual effort to prove the earlier work produced proper observations.

A second challenge, representing more of a true critique of postmodern literary methods, was that of intertextuality. True intertextuality of all EAW material was excluded from this study at the outset because a synchronic approach reopened the door to inverted causality. Had controls to guarantee a diachronic focus not been introduced, any text could become a parent to any other text regardless of the date of origination. Therefore, an intentionally set control involved using possible source texts that dated at least one century before Second Temple apocalyptic literature.

A third challenge to using a postmodern methodology was another accurate critique of postmodernity. Any methodology based on true postmodernity is soon worthless for producing firm observations. A basic element of the postmodern method is to use an "author-is-dead" approach to textual studies. Based on this concept, meaning is located only in the interpretation, and therefore, the meaning of a text to one person is not the meaning of the text to the next. Each person then resides in his or her own hyperreality, and as such, no outside referents affect communication of any type of "truth." Therefore, the "truth" experienced by a reader is relevant only to the person experiencing the simulacrum. In this study, these postmodern elements were curbed by reintroducing the two-part concept of text and cross-text from the core of New Historicism. Moreover, while adhering to a text-first approach, textual direction allowed outside sources to be introduced, as was seen in the question of *ma'at* (Egyptian concept of order). These modifications allowed for a postmodern method while still producing results viable in an academic environment.

A fourth challenge, and perhaps, a derivative of the third challenge of using this method, involved another critique of postmodernism. This challenge was the inability of postmodern methods to produce concrete results. As mentioned in the first challenge, postmodernism (or more specifically, deconstruction) is always working to decenter language, and subsequently, any language-based work, observation, result, or philosophy. The result is an intellectual Ouroboros in which each step in a true postmodern method attempts to decenter the previous step. No result is therefore concrete as the very next step attempts to destabilize it. However, Scholars such as Hutcheon and Ankersmithave created modifications that made it possible to produce concrete results. The caveat to these modifications was a requirement to question continuously the referents used and results garnered. This caveat was at the heart of the loops I introduced in this study. However, even with this modification, the loops could have become infinite as the questioning would never cease. To stay away from infinite loops, step 3 (quantification) was introduced. Nevertheless, the challenges listed here were balanced by the positive elements encountered by using this method.

7.3.2. Positive Elements

As the material was analyzed, the patterns referenced in the above paragraphs soon became evident, which forced the implementation of other steps to avoid confirmation bias. The first step, found in chapter 1, was the secondary keyword search across a greater cross-section of material. Doing so forced a reassessment of the material already located and prompted processing of any new source material. A second step described in chapter 1 involved incorporating a count of all source material into the overall score for the topos type; this method was undertaken because any specific instance of a topos devalued by bias still contributed to the score totals.

Reflecting on the overall methodology, using a modified postmodern historical method created a flexible yet dependable framework for research. The purposed text-first approach enabled insights and observations without the noise of hundreds of voices debating a text. However, it also enabled me to include scholarly material. This approach strengthened my research by uncovering connections missed, by correcting previous understanding of events or philosophies (such as the *omphalos* myth), and by challenging working hypotheses throughout the research. Even more beneficial was the ability to use the method of quantification. Quantification allowed me to delimit copious amounts of material in ways that others can replicate to check for accuracy and examine for objectivity.

However, this approach did not allow quantification to become the final arbiter by which I could claim, "These are the objective results of quantified data" while still engaging in subjective organizing and scoring. Even more important, by not depending on quantification in the main body of work, I could redirect the focus away from so-called "facts" drawn from a narrative and focus instead on the larger context and interaction of each topos throughout the explored texts. That allowed an open-ended understanding without summary conclusions until completing the study of the topos. For these reasons, I am confident in my conclusions.

7.4. Future Considerations

The final question, then, was where to go from here? Several avenues were available, depending on the purpose. Because this present work was the first foray into using this methodology on a wide scale, the first avenue of future research should be conducting an in-depth study using a single apocalyptic book and researching all the possible authoritative topoi to verify or nuance the work here. A second (although easily combined with the first) avenue would be to repeat this project with several researchers involved in identifying, delimiting, and quantifying authoritative topoi, EAW sources, and material from the Tanakh. Such a study, spread among several researchers, may further temper biases and subjectivity, especially in the quantification step of the preliminary study.

Beyond re-examination and verification, a study of non-apocalyptic Second Temple material is necessary to understand the relationship of Apocalypticism with the greater Jewish culture in the Second Temple period. Do didactic texts share authoritative topoi, or is apocalyptic literature using authoritative topoi not relevant for the wider audience? Findings from such a study may help determine the sharpness of any distinction between communities represented by apocalyptic texts and those communities that were not represented by such material.

A fourth avenue lies in extending the study to Jewish canonical apocalyptic material, to post-Second Temple Jewish works, and to the book of Revelation for a much larger picture of the overall development of Apocalypticism. The purpose would be to follow the changes of authoritative topoi and from them, how communities accepted or rejected the inherent concepts located within the topoi types. Regardless of the specific avenue, such research into apocalyptic material could represent a new method for studying genres for which so much ink has already been spilled.

APPENDIX A
REASONING FOR DELIMITING SECOND TEMPLE APOCALYPTIC MATERIAL

The following list contains Second Temple apocalyptic books for which delimitation might be questioned. Other Second Temple apocalyptic literature not included in this study fell considerably outside the parameters set in the methodology.

Apocalypse of Abraham. Three issues excluded the Apocalypse of Abraham from this study. First, Christians and Gnostics introduced several interpolations into this text such as chapter 7; 9:7; 23:4–10; 29:3–17; 20:5, 7; 22:5—among others. Second, although some interpolations may have derived from Jewish sources, questions remained whether those sources were from Second Temple Judaism or Rabbinic Judaism. The second problem was perseveration—the extant text was Slavonic, and "may have been considerably altered by the Bogomils (a medieval dualist sect)"[1] The third problem was the date of the original composition, which was usually placed at the close of the first century CE or beginning of the second. Thus, the text "respond[ed] to the destruction of the Second Temple in 70 CE,"[2] and therefore originated outside the period designated for this study (538 BCE–70 CE). Rubinkiewicz also presented a late date for this material.

Apocalypse of Elijah. Although originally from the first century, too much Christian influence and interpolation existed to use the text in this study. For instance, Wintermute argued the Apocalypse of Elijah 4 was "strongly influenced by the account of the two martyrs in Rev 11:4–12."[3] In conclusion, he wrote, "Not only the

---

[1] Ryszard Rubinkiewicz, "Treatise of Shem: A New Translation and Introduction," in Charlesworth, *OTP* 1:681–83.

[2] Daniel C. Harlow, "Abraham, Apocalypse Of," *EDEJ* 297.

[3] Orval S. Wintermute, trans., "Apocalypse of Elijah: A New Translation and Introduction," in Charlesworth, *OTP* 1:721.

Christian editor who inserted the Enoch-Elijah martyrdom but also other early readers would have been aware of its [Apocalypse of Elijah 4] dependence on Revelation. Consequently, the final Christian edition of this text, which described the martyrdom of Elijah in an apocalyptic manner, came to be designated 'The Apocalypse of Elijah.'"[4] David Frankfurter argued for a later date: "the extant text, at least, and probably the composition as a whole (without vorlagen), may be confidently attributed to the second half of the third century, making it contemporaneous with a 'culture' of Christian martyrdom that arose with the edicts of Decius and Valerian."[5]

Testament of Abraham. The focus on Jewish Apocalyptic material delimits the Testament of Abraham. The extant narrative, according to Nickelsburg, was a Christian text that evidenced the influence of the New Testament on the longer recension.[6] While E. P. Sanders noted the origins within Judaism (and, perhaps, Egyptian Jews), he agreed the narrative along with two other writings together known as the Testaments of the Three Patriarchs "were Christianized and became the Exclusive property of the Church."[7]

Treatise of Shem. Although astrological signs were used in this text, there existed no authorities otherwise, nor was the text necessarily apocalyptic, but rather, consisted of straight forward prophetic accounts based on the aforementioned astrological signs. As such, this text was delimited from the study.

---

[4] Wintermute, trans., "Apocalypse of Elijah," 721.

[5] David Frankfurter, "The Cult of the Martyrs in Egypt before Constantine: The Evidence of the Coptic Apocalypse of Elijah," *VC* 48 (1994): 26.

[6] Nickelsburg, *Jewish Literature*, 327.

[7] E. P. Sanders, "Testament of Abraham: A New Translation and Introduction," in Charlesworth, *OTP* 1:85.

APPENDIX B

LIST OF EXTERNAL ANCIENT WORLD AND NON-CANONICAL HEBRAIC MATERIAL IN STAGE 2, STEPS 1–3 OF THIS STUDY

Akkadian

Anzu

Contracts

Marriage Customs; *Palace Receipt for the Return of a Marriage Gift*; *Purchase of Beer*; *Receipt for the Purchase of a Debt Slave*; *Sale of a Town*; *Security for a Loan*; *Seven years of Barrenness before a Second Wife*; *Transfer of Creditors*

Goring Ox at Nuzi

Inscription of

Narāmsîn, Campaign against Armānumand Ebla; *Narāmsîn, Deification of the King*; *Sargon, Foundation of the Akkadian Empire*

Laws

Lipit-Ishtar Lawcode (*see also: Sumerian*); *of Eshnunna*

Legal Documents

Old–*Amortization record*; *receipts* [3]

Nuzi—*Adoption* [3]; *Hebrew Slave Document* [2]; *Lawsuit*

Letters

Amarna—*from Tell El-Hesi*; *from Shechem*; *Taanach 1*

Archival—*Asking for the Return of Stolen Donkeys*; *concerning the Grain Tax of the Samarians*; *Murder of Sennacherib*; *of Enna-Dagan*; *of Takuhlina*; *Report on Work on Dūr-Šarrukin*; *Reporting Matters in Kalḫu*; *to Zalaia*

Other—*Agricultural Letters* [3]; *Boat Order*; *Boy to his Mother*; *concerning land* [2]; *concerning Legal affairs* [2]; *concerning Personnel* [4]; *concerning Slaves* [3]; *Distribution of Grain Rations* [6]; *Divine Revelations* [24]; *from Babi*; *from Eshnunna* [5]; *from Kish* [3]; *from Mugdan* [3]; *God of my Father*; *Happy Reign*; *Loan between Gentlemen*; *Mari Letters* [4]; *Order from Iddin-Erra*; *Punishment by Fire*; *Royal Decree of Equity*; *Substitute King*; *to a God*; *Treaties and Coalitions, a-b*

Myths and Epics—*Adapa*; *Atrahasis*; *Babylonian Theogony*; *Cosmological Incantation, The Worm and*

the Toothache; *Creation Epic*; *Creation of Man by the Mother Goddess*; *Descent of Ishtar to the Nether World*; *Epic of Gilgamesh*; *Etana*; *Legend of Sargon*; *Myth of Zu*; *Nergal and Ereshkigal*; *Vision of the Nether World*
Oracles and Prophecies
an Oracular Dream Concerning Ashurbanipal; *an Oracular Dream Concerning Ashurbanipal*; *Letter to Ashurbanipal*; *Old Babylonian Oracle from Uruk*; *Oracle of Ninlil Concerning Ashurbanipal*; *Oracles Concerning Esarhaddon*; *Prophecies*
Proverbs and Fables—*Counsels of Wisdom*; *Dispute between the Date Palm and the Tamarisk*; *Instructions of Shuruppak*; *Proverbs*
Ras Shamra Library
Rituals—*Daily Sacrifices to the Gods of the City of Uruk*; *for the New Year's Festival at Babylon*; *for the Repair of a Temple*; *for the Sixteenth and Seventeenth Days of an Unknown Month at Uruk*; *Program of the Pageant of the Statue of the God Anu at Uruk*; *to be Followed by the Kalū-Priest when Covering the Temple Kettle-Drum*
Treaties—*between Ashurnirari V of Assyria and Mati'ilu of Arpad*; *between Idrimi and Pilliya*; *between Niqmepa of Alalakh and Ir-dim of Tunip*; *of Esarhaddon with Baal of Tyre*
Will of Ammitaku Leader of Alalakh

Ammonite

ḤesbânOstracon A1, A2
Inscriptions—*Amman Citadel*; *Amman Theatre*; *Tell Sīrān*
Seal Impression

Aramaic

Contracts
Assyrian—*Loan Texts* [3]
Egyptian—*A Life Estate of Usufruct*; *Adoption*; *Apportionment of Slaves*; *Bequest in Contemplation of Death*; *Bequest of Apartment to Wife*; *Bequest of House to Daughter*; *Document of Wifehood* [3]; *Dowry Addendum*; *Grant of a Built Wall*; *Grant of House to Daughter*; *Grant of Usufruct to Son-in-law*; *Loan of Grain*; *Loan of Silver*; *Sale of Abandoned Property*; *Sale of Apartment to Son-in-law*; *Withdrawal from Goods* [2]; *Withdrawal from House*; *Withdrawal from Hyr'*; *Withdrawal from Land*
Hadad-yithʿi
Inscription (Seal)

Inscriptions—*Aswan Dedicatory*; *Bar-Ga'yahand*; *Bar-Rakib*; *Behistun*; *Hadad*; *Hazael Booty*; *Mati'el from Sefire*; *Panamuwa*; *Tomb of Si'Gabbar, Priest of Sahar*; *Tombstone* (*Greco-Roman Museum 18361*); *Zakkur, King of Hamath*
Letters—*Appeal of Adon King of Ekron to Pharaoh*; *Regarding Gift, Handmaiden, Allotment, and Pots*; *Report of Imprisonment of Jewish Leaders*
Manumission of a Female Slave and Her Daughter
Notice of Dispatch of Wood
Offer to Sew a Garment
Offering Table from the Memphis Serapeum
Ostraca—*Regarding Children and Inquiry Regarding Passover*; *Regarding Legumes and Barley, etc.*; *Regarding Silver for Marzeaḥ Regarding Tunic*; *to Aid Shepherd*; *to Shear Ewe*
Proverbs and Precepts
Request for Salt
Stelas (funerary)—*Brussels E. 4716*; *Carpentras*; *Saqqarah: Vatican Museum 10 Sala 22787*
Stelas (other)—*Bukān*; *Melqart Stela*; *Tell Dan Stele*
Story of Aḥiḳar (Aramaic)
Words of Aḥiḳar (Aramaic)
Tell Dan Bowl
Tell el-Maskhuṭa Libation Bowls [3]

Assyrian

Annals—*AššurClay Tablets*; *AššurClay Tablets*; *AššurClay Tablets*;
Aššur Charter
Black Obelisk
Black Stone Cylinder
Calaḫ Orthostat Slab
Contracts, Sales—*Debt Note*; *Estate*; *Land* [2]; *of Slaves* [3]; *Redemption of Slave*
Court Order from Samaria
Die (Pūru) of Yaḫali
Historical Documents of—*Adad-nirari III-Expedition to Palestine*; *Ashurbanipal*; *Ashurnasirpal II-Expedition to Carchemish and the Lebanon*; *Banquet of Ashurnasirpal II*; *Esarhaddon*; *Sargon II-The Fall of Samaria*; *Sennacherib*; *Shalmaneser III-Fight against the Aramean Coalition*; *Shamshi-Adad I-First Contact with the West*; *Tiglath-pileser I-Expeditions to Syria, the Lebanon, and the Mediterranean Sea*; *Tiglath-pileser III-Campaigns against Syria and Palestine*
Horse List

Inscriptions—*Cylinder Inscription*; *Esarhaddon–Babylonian Inscription*; *Great Summary*; *Nimrud Ivories*; *Nimrud*; *Pavement 4*; *Šamši-ilu–Stone Lions*; *Small Summary*; *Summary Inscription: 4, 7-10, 13*; *Tang-i Var*
Inscriptions (Sennacherib) *Azekah*; *Lachish Relief*
Kurkh Monolith
Legal Documents
Middle Assyrian—*Deed of Gift*; *Loan document*; *Receipt for Sale of House*
Neo-Assyrian—*Loan Interest*; *Punishment for Murder*
Old Assyrian—*Court Decisions* [2]; *Divorce Document*
Middle Assyrian Laws
Middle Assyrian Palace Decrees
Nimrud Prisms D and E
Orthostat Slab of Unknown Provenance
Sennacherib—*Capture and Destruction of Babylon*; *First Campaign against Merodach-baladan*; *Siege of Jerusalem* also see Inscriptions (Sennacherib)
Statues—*Aššur Basalt*; *Kurba'il*
Stelas—*Antakya*; *Borowski*; *Iran' Saba'a*; *Sammuramat (Semiramis)*; *Shalmaneser IV–Pazaricik/Maraş*
Story of Idrimi, King of Alalakh
Tell al Rimah text
Tell Sheik Hammad text
Tiglath-pileser III
Treaty between KTK and Arpad
Words of Ahiqar
Wine List

Babylonian

Courtcase, Slandered Bride
Historical Texts—*Dedication of the Shamash Temple by Yahdun-Lim*; *Gudea, e n s i of Lagash*; *Naram-Sin in the Cedar Mountain*; *Sargon Chronicle*; *Sargon of Agade*; *Sumerian King List*; *Text from the Accession Year of Nabonidus to the Fall of Babylon*; *Text from the First Year of Belibni to the Accession Year of Shamashshumukin*; *Text from the First Year of Esarhaddon to the First Year of Shamashshumukin*; *Text from the Tenth to the Seventeenth Year of Nabopolassar: Events Leading to the Fall of Nineveh*

(*Late*)

Inscriptions—*Ammi-ditana*; *Ekallatum–Shamshi-Addu*; *Hammu-rapi, 1-4*; *Iahdun-lim*; *Samsu-iluna*; *Zimri-lim*

(Middle Period)
Agreement Texts (Treaties?)—*Ir-Addu and Niqmepa*; *Legal Documents*; *Pillia and Idrimi*
Middle Babylonian—*Court Decisions* [2]
Neo Babylonian–*House Rental Agreement*; *Partnership Agreement*; *Receipts* [3]; *Sale of a Slave*
(Neo)
Dialogue Document
Laws of Neo-Babylon
Prayer of lamentation to Ishtar
Restoration Texts—*Nabonidus's Rebuilding of E-lugal-galga-sisa*; *Nabopolassar's Restoration of Imgur-Enlil*; *Nebuchadnezzar II's Restoration of Ebabbar Temple*; *Nebuchadnezzar II's Restoration of E-urimin-ankia*
Sippar Cylinder of Nabonidus
Sun Disk Tablet of Nabû-Apla-Iddina
(Old)
Abbael's Gift of Alalakh
Edict of Ammisaduqa
Historical Documents—*Conquest of Jerusalem*; *Mother of Nabonidus*; *Nabonidus and his God*; *Nabonidus* (*text*); *Nebuchadnezzar II*
Inheritance—*Estate of Ammurapi*; *of Ammitaku Leader of Alalakha*
Inscriptions—*Gungunum*; *Ipiq-Adad II*; *Ishbi-erra*; *Ishme-Dagan*; *Lipit-Eshtar*; *Nur-Adad*; *Rim-Sin 1-4*; *Shu-ilishu*; *Sin-iddinam*; *Ur-dukuga*; *Ur-Ninurta*; *Warad-Sin*
Laws—*of Eshnunna*; *of Hammurabi*
Legal Documents—*Division of Estate*; *House Rental*; *Lawsuit*; *Receipts* [2]
Offerings to the Temple Gates at Ur

Canaan/Palestine
Baal—*and Mot*; *and Yam*; *Palace of*
El Khadr Arrowheads
Fragments
Gezer Calendar
Hazor Lawsuit
Inscriptions—*Ben-Hadad of Damascus*; *Carthage Tariff*; *Ekron Inscription of Akhayus*; *Kilamuwa of Y'dy-Sam'al*; *King of Kedar*; *Marseilles Tariff*; *Punic* (*Ex-Voto*); *Seal Inscription*; *Siloam*; *Yehawmilk of Byblos*; *Zakir of Hamat and Lu'ath*
Letter from the Time of Josiah
Moabite Stone
Nikkal and the Kotharat
Ostraca—*Samarian*; *Arad* [3]

Tomb of Sekhemkare; *Turin Canon*
Legal Proceedings (Vizier)—*Appointment of*, *Installation of*, *Judicial Work of*
Legal Proceedings—*Lawsuit of Irinofret*; *Trial for Conspiracy*
Legends—*of Astarte and the Tribute of the Sea*; *of Isis and the Name of Re*; *of the Possessed Princess*
Letters—*Book of Kemit*; *Craft of the Scribe*; *Early Kingdom* [15]; *Eighteenth Dynasty* [7]; *from Queen Naptera of Egypt to Queen Puduḫepa of Ḫatti*; *Heqanakht Letters* [3]; *Later Middle Kingdom* [42]; *of Homage to Pharoah Merneptah*; *Praise of Pi-Ramessu*; *Ramesside* [26]; *Ramesside Community of Deir El-Medina* [130]; *Ramesside-Late* [43]; *to and from a Vizier* [21]; *to and from Royalty* [39]; *to Gods* [15]; *to the Dead* [2]; *Twenty-First Dynasty* [5]
Lists of Asiatic Countries under the Egyptian Empire
Lists of Ramses III—*Activity on the Mediterranean*; *Serfs of the Temples*; *Temple of Amun in Asia*; *Towns in Amon's Estate*
Litany in Praise of the Teacher
Litany of Rejoicing
Man and His Ba (Dispute over Suicide)
Megiddo Ivories
Memphite Theology
Middle Kingdom Egyptian Contacts with Asia [6]
Mythological Origin of Certain Unclean Animals
Old Kingdom Texts [3 notations from annals of reign of Snefru].
Oracles/Prophecy—*Admonitions of Ipuwer*; *Divine Nomination of an Ethiopian King*; *Divine Nomination of Thutmose III*; *Divine Oracle through a Dream*; *Divine Oracle through Visible Sign*; *Prophecy of Neferrohu*
Ostracon Gardiner 304
Palermo Stone
Papyrus—*Bremner-Rhind*; *Papyrus Chester Beatty I*; *Papyrus Harris 500*; *Papyrus Leiden I 350* (*concerning Amun*)
Peftjauawykhonsu Sells Self into Slavery
Pepi I—Asiatic Campaign Text
Pharaoh as a Sportsman
Praises—*of Amun*; *of Merenptah* [3]; *of Ramesses II as a Warrior*; *of the Delta Residence of Ramesses III*; *Praise of Amun-Rê*; *Praise of the City Ramses*

and Compassion; *God's Ownership of All Creation*; *Goddess Raiyt and Thebes*; *Great Cairo Hymn of Praise to Amun-Re*; *Great Hymn to Aten*; *Great Hymn to Osiris*; *Greatness of the King*; *His Protecting Power*; *Hymn and Prayer to Ptah*; *Hymn at Sunrise*; *Hymn from the Tomb of Ay*; *Hymn of Ascension to Rê*; *Hymn of King Unas* (*Ferrying across the Sky*); *Hymn of Triumph on the King's Ascension*; *Hymn of Victory of Thutmose III*; *Hymn to Amun-Rê* (*Credo of a High Priest of Thebes*); *Hymn to Geb*; *Hymn to Maat*; *Hymn to Ptah*; *Hymn to Ramesses II* (*On his First Jubilee*); *Hymn to Rê, Thoth, and Maat* [2]; *Hymn to the King* (*as a Flash of Lightning*); *Hymn to the King as a Primordial God*; *Hymn to the Nile*; *Hymn to the Risen King as Osiris*; *Hymn to the Rising Sun*; *Hymn to the Setting Sun* ; *Hymn to the Setting Sun*; *Hymn to the Setting Sun*; *Hymn to the Sun God, Rê*; *Hymn to Thoth and Maat*; *Hymn to Thoth*; *Hymn to Thoth*; *Hymns to the Gods as a Single God*; *Hymns to the Rising Sun* [6]; *Introductory Hymn to Osiris Wennefer* (*Papyrus of Ani*); *Introductory Hymn to Rê* [5]; *Khety's Hymn to the Nile*; *King as Conquering Hero*; *Leiden Hymns*; *Litany to Osiris*; *Love Song from Papyrus Harris 500*; *Memphis Ferry* ; *Metaphors for God's Nature*; *Morning Hymn to Amun-Rê as Horakhty*; *Ode to Senusert I*; *Pahery's Autobiography: His Claim of Rectitude*; *Power of God*; *Primacy of Thebes*; *Ramesside Hymn to the Nile*; *Resurrection of King Unas*; *Second Hymn: to Amun as Aton*; *Self-Creation of God*; *Song of the Royal Menial*; *Songs from the Tomb of King Intef*; *Songs from the Tomb of Neferhotep*; *Songs of Entertainment* [6]; *Songs of the Birdcatcher's Daughter, 2-4*; *Songs of the Common People* [2]; *Thebes, the Place of Truth*; *Theogony*; *to Amun as Sun God*; *to Pharaoh Coming to Thebes for His Jubilee*; *Trinity*; *Triumphal Hymn of Ascension*; *Two Hymns to the Rising and Setting Sun*; *Two Hymns to the Sun-god*; *Victory Song of Weni*

Stelas—*Abydos Stela* (*Royal Decree of Temple Privilege*); *Armant Stela of Thutmose III*;

Beth-Shan Stela 1-2; *Famine Stela*; *Gebel Barkal Stela of Thutmose III*; *Iikhernofret (12th dynasty, response to participation in passion play)*; *Memphis and Karnak Stelae of Amenhotep II*; *Merneptah Stela*; *Ramesside*; *Stele at Karnak, Elephantine, and Abu Simbel* (*Peace Between Egypt and Hatti under Ramses II*); *Victory Stela of King Piye* (*Piankhy*)
Story of Sinuhe
Syrian Captive Colony in Thebes
Syrian Interregnum
Taking of Joppa
Texts from Temples—*Block from the Mortuary Temple of Userkaf at Saqqara, Reused at Lisht* [3]; *Blocks from the Causeway of the Pyramid of Unas at Saqqara* [2]; *Building Inscriptions from Temples* [4]; *Festival Offerings Calendar for the Sun Temple of Niuserre at Abu Gurob*; *from the Temple of Sahure at Abusir* [8]; *from the Temples of Sneferu at Dahshur*; *of Pepy I and Teti from Tell Basta* [4]
Texts from the Tomb of General Horemheb
Thebes as the Place of Creation
Thutmose III, Campaigns—*against Qadesh and Amurru*; *against the Hittites*; *against the Libyans*; *biography of Amenemheb*; *from Sile to Pa-Canaan*; *to Irqata*; *to Yenoam and Lebanon* (*also see stelas*)
Tomb Biography of Ahmose of Nekheb
Tradition of Seven Lean Years in Egypt
Treaty, Egyptian (Hittite Treaty)
Trip to the Lebanon for Cedar
Tutankhamun's Restoration after the Amarna Revolution
Two Brothers
Vizier of Egypt (Text on)
War against the Peoples of the Sea
Writing Board from Giza
–*Note*: over two hundred records, inscriptions, and texts are delimited from this list due to limited space.

Greek

*Indicates source used only in Greek word searches
Aeschylus—*Agamemnon*; *Eumenides*; *Libation Bearers*; *Persians*; *Prometheus Bound*
Alcman—*Fragments*
Antiochus Soter (Reconstruction of Esagila and Ezida)
Apollodorus—*Library and Epitome*
Aristophanes—*Acharnians**; *Birds**; *Clouds*

Aristotle—*Athenian Constitution* Economics*; *Eudemian Ethics*; *Metaphysics*; *Nicomachean Ethics**; *Poetics*; *Politics*; *Rhetoric*; *Virtues and Vices**
Demosthenes—*Speeches 1-61*
Euripides—*Bacchae*; *Electra**; *Hecuba**; *Helen**; *Heracles**; *Ion**; *Iphigenia in Aulis*; *Iphigenia in Tauris**; *Orestes**; *Phoenissae**; *Rhesus*; *Suppliants**; *Trojan Women*
Herodotus—*The Histories—Books 1-9*
Hesiod—*Aegimius*; *Astronomy*; *Catalogues*; *Great Eoiai*; *Great Works*; *Idaean Works*; *Marriage of Ceyx*; *Melampodia*; *Precepts of Chiron*; *Shield of Heracles*; *Theogony*; *Various Fragments*; *Works and Days*
Homer—*Hymns to various gods* [34]; *Iliad*; *Odyssey*
Lysias—*Speeches*
Pindar—*Odes*
Plato—*Alcibiades 1, 2*; *Apology*; *Charmides*; *Cleitophon*; *Cratylus*; *Critias*; *Crito*; *Epinomis*; *Epistles**; *Euthydemus*; *Euthyphro*; *Gorgias*; *Hipparchus*; *Hippias Major*; *Hippias Minor*; *Ion*; *Laches*; *Laws*; *Lovers*; *Lysis*; *Menexenus*; *Meno*; *Minos*; *Parmenides*; *Phaedo*; *Phaedrus*; *Philebus*; *Protagoras*; *Republic*; *Symposium*; *Theages*; *Timaeus*
Sappho—*Fragments*; *Poems*;
Sophocles—*Ajax*; *Antigone*; *Electra*; *Ichneutae**; *Oedipus at Colonus*; *Oedipus Tyrannus*; *Philoctetes*; *Trachiniae*; *Tracking Satyrs*
Xenophon—*Agesilaus*; *Anabasis*; *Constitution of the Lacedaemonians*; *Cyropaedia*; *Hellenica*; *Hiero*; *Memorabilia*; *Minor Works*; *On Hunting*; *On the Art of Horsemanship*; *On the Cavalry Commander*; *Ways and Means*; *Works on Socrates*

Hittite

Appu and His Two Sons
Arbitration of Syrian Disputes by Mursili II of Hatti
Archival List from Büyükkale [4]
Azatiwata
Bilingual Edict of Ḫattušili I
Case against Ura-Tarḫunta and His Father Ukkura
Description of Cultic Image
Edicts of—*Hattusili III of Hatti concerning Fugitives from Ugarit*; *Hattusili III of Hatti concerning Merchants of Ura at Ugarit*; *Hattusili III of Hatti concerning Military*

Obligations of Kurunta of Tarhuntassa; *Ini-Teshshup of Carchemish concerning the Banishment of the Brothers of Ammistamru II of Ugarit*; *Ini-Teshshup of Carchemish concerning the Divorce of Ammistamru II of Ugarit*; *Mursili II of Hatti concerning the Frontiers of Ugarit*; *Mursili II of Hatti concerning the Tribute of Ugarit*; *Mursili II of Hatti recognizing the Status of Piyassili of Carchemish*; *Puduhepa of Hatti concerning Shipping Losses at Ugarit*; *Suppiluliuma I of Hatti concerning the Tribute of Ugarit*; *Talmi-Teshshup of Carchemish returning Dowry to Ehli-Nikkalu*; *Talmi-Teshshup of Carchemish returning Property to Ammurapi of Ugarit*; *Tudhaliya IV of Hatti concerning the Divorce of Ammistamru II of Ugarit*; *Tudhaliya IV of Hatti releasing Ammistamru II of Ugarit from Participation in War against Assyria*

Elkunirsa and Ashertu (der. Canaanite Myth)

Festival of the Warrior God

Historical Texts—*Hattusilis on Muwatallis' War against Egypt*; *Suppiluliumas and the Egyptian Queen*; *Suppiluliumas Destroys the Kingdom of Mitanni*

Hittite Laws

Hunter Kessi and His Beautiful Wife

Indictments—*Madduwatta by Arnuwanda I of Hatti*; *Mita of Pahhuwa and Treaty with the Elders of Several Anatolian Communities*

Instructions—*for Commander of the Border Guards*; *for Palaces Personnel*; *for Temple Officials*

Inventories of six Cities

Inventory of Ugaritic Tribute to Hatti

Investigation the Anger of the Gods (Omen)

Karkamiš

Kululu 4

Letters—*Hattusili III of Hatti to Adad-nirari I of Assyria*; *Hattusili III of Hatti to Kadashman-Enlil II of Babylon*; *King of Hanigalbat to a King of Hatti*; *King of Hatti to an Anatolian Ruler*; *Mashuiluwa of Mira-Kuwaliya to Mursili I of Hatti*; *Prince Piha-walwi of Hatti to Ibiranu of Ugarit*; *Prince Sutahapshap of Egypt to Hattusili III of Hatti*; *Queen Naptera of Egypt to Puduhepa of Hatti*; *Queen Puduhepa of Hatti to Ramses*

II of Egypt; *Ramses II of Egypt to Hattusili III of Hatti*; *Ramses II of Egypt to Kupanta-Kurunta of Mira-Kuwaliya*; *Ramses II of Egypt to Prince Tashmi-Sharrumma of Hatti*; *Ramses II of Egypt to Puduhepa of Hatti*; *Sharri-Kushuh of Carchemish to Niqmaddu II of Ugarit*; *Suppiluliuma I of Hatti to Niqmaddu II of Ugarit*; *Talmi-Teshshup of Carchemish to Ammurapi of Ugarit concerning His Divorce*; *to Kaššū and Pulli in Tapikka*; *to Kaššū and Zulapi in Tapikka* [2] *to Kaššūin Tapikka* [13]; *to Kaššū, Ḫulla and Zulapi in Tapikka*; *Tudhaliya IV of Hatti to an Assyrian Nobleman*; *Urhi-Teshshup*(*?*) *of Hatti to Adad-nirari I of Assyria*

Maraş 4

Myths and Epics—*Disappearance of Hannahanna*; *Disappearance of the Sun God*; *El, Ashertu and the Storm-god*; *Kamrusepa*; *Kingship in Heaven*; *Moon that Fell from Heaven*; *Myth fragments* [4]; *Myth of Illuyankaš, versions 1 and 2*; *Myths of the Goddess Inara* [6]; *Song of Ullikummis*; *other Storm God tales* [4]; *Telipinu, versions 1-3, Telipinu and the Daughter of the Sea God*; *Voyage of the Human Soul*

Prayers—*Daily Prayer of the King*; *Fragments of Prayers to the Storm-god of Nerik*; *Hattusili's Prayer of Exculpation to the Sun-goddess of Arinna*; *Hurrian Prayer of Taduhepa to Tessub for the Well-being of Tasmi-sarri*; *Invocation of the Sun Goddess of the Netherworld against Slander*; *Invocation of the Sun-goddess and the Storm-god against Slander*; *Invocation of the Sun-Goddess of Arinna for the Protection of the Royal Couple*; *Mursili's Accusations Against Tawannanna*; *Mursili's Exculpation for the Deposition of Tawannanna*; *Mursili's Prayer to Lelwani for the Recovery of Gassuliyawiya*; *Mursili's Prayer to the Sun-goddess of Arinna for the Recovery of Gassuliyawiya*; *Muwatalli's Model Prayer to the Assembly of Gods through the Storm-god of Lightning*; *Muwatalli's Prayer to the Storm-god Concerning the Cult of Kummanni*; *of a King*; *of a Mortal*; *of Arnuwanda*

and Asmunikal to the Sun-goddess of Arinna about the Ravages of the Kaska; *of Arnuwandas and Asmu-Nikkal Concerning the Ravages Inflicted on Hittite Cult-Centers*; *of Kantuzilis for Relief from his Sufferings*; *of Kantuzzili*; *of Pudu-hepas to the Sun-Goddess of Arinna and her Circle*; *Plague Prayers of Mursilis* [7]; *Puduhepa's Prayer to the Sun-goddess of Arinna and Her Circle for the Well-being of Hattusili*; *to be Spoken in an Emergency*; *to the Sun-god for Appeasing an Angry God*; *to the Sun-goddess of Arinna Concerning Plague and Enemies*; *Tudhaliya's Prayer to the Sun-goddess of Arinna for Military Success*

Rituals, Incantations, and Oaths—*against Domestic Quarrel*; *against Impotence*; *against Pestilence*; *before Battle*; *Counteract Sorcery*; *Evocatio*; *for the Erection of a House*; *for the Erection of a New Palace*; *Purification of God and Man*; *Purification Ritual Engaging the Help of Protective Demons*; *Removal of the Threat Implied in an Evil Omen*; *Soldiers' Oath*

Royal Grants—*Will of Ammitaku Leader of Alalakh, Land Grant AT 456*

Songs—*Hedammu*; *Kumarbi*; *Silver*; *the God LAMMA*; *the Song of Release*; *Ullikummi*

Tale of Two Cities: Kanesh and Zalpa

Ten-Year Annals of Great King Muršili II of Ḫatti

The Sun God, The Cow, and the Fisherman

Treaties—*Arnuwanda I of Hatti and the Men of Ismerika*; *God List, Blessings and Curses of the Treaty between Suppiluliumas and Mattiwaza*; *Hattusili III of Hatti and Benteshina of Amurru*; *Hattusili III of Hatti and Ramses II of Egypt*; *Hattusili III of Hatti and Ulmi-Teshshup of Tarhuntassa*; *King of Hatti and Paddatissu of Kizzuwatna*; *Muršili and Duppi-Tešub*; *Mursili II of Hatti and Kupanta-Kurunta of Mira-Kuwaliya*; *Mursili II of Hatti and Manapa-Tarhunta of the Land of the Seha River*; *Mursili II of Hatti and Niqmepa of Ugarit*; *Mursili II of Hatti and Targasnalli of Hapalla*; *Mursili II of Hatti and Tuppi-Teshshup of Amurru*; *Muwattalli II of Hatti and*

Other

Dates and King Lists—*Assyrian King List*; *Babylonian King List A, B*; *Excerpts from the Lists of Assyrian Eponyms*; *List of Date Formulae of the Reign of Hammurabi*; *List of Year Names: Samsuiluna, King of Babylon*; *Synchronistic Chronicle*

Letters—*from Mugdan in Akkadian and Sumerian*) [5]; *to and from a Man Named Mezi, written in Akkadian, Sumerian, or a mix* [4]

Phoenician Cebel Ires Daği (Contract)

Prophetic Letters, Texts, and Oracles from the ANE [142]

Seals—*Marduk-Zakir-Shumi*; *Nabu-Apla-Iddina*; *Rimut-iLani*

Sepulchral Inscriptions—*Agbar, Priest of the Moon-god in Nerab*; *Ahiram of Byblos*; *Eshmun'azar of Sidon*; *Tabnit of Sidon*

South Arabian Inscriptions—*Hadrami Inscriptions*; *Minaean Inscriptions*; *Qatabanian Inscriptions*; *Sabaean Inscriptions*

Weight Inscriptions [15]

Persian

Assignment to a New Lessor of Land

Cyrus Cylinder

Foundation Tablet of Xerxes

Seal Impression

Zend Avesta

Phoenician

Inscription of—*Azatiwada*; *Funerary from Pyrgi*; *King Yaḥimilk*; *King Yeḥawmilk*; *Kulamuwa*; *Seal Inscription*

Inscriptions (Sarcophagus)—*'Ahirom, King of Byblos*; *Eshmun ʿazor, King of Sidon*; *Tabnit, King of Sidon*

Roman

Cicero—*Divination*

Sumerian

Accounts—*Bala-Contribution*; *Calendar Text*; *Death of Shulgi*; *Functional Courtcase*; *Inheritance*; *Trail for Adultery*

Curse of Agade: Ekur Avenged

Deluge

Dumuzi and Enkimdu: Dispute between the Shepherd-God and the Farmer-God

Duties and Powers of the DEITIES: Inscription on the Statue of King Kurigalzu

Enki and Ninhursag: Paradise Myth

Gilgamesh—*and Agga*; *and the Land of the Living*; *Death of*

Gudea Cylinders [2]

Hymns and Psalms—*a Love Song*; *Hymnal Prayer of Enheduanna* (*the Adoration of Inanna in Ur*); *Ishkur and the Destruction of the*

Rebellious Land; *King of the Road: A Self-Laudatory Shulgi Hymn*; *Psalm to Marduk*; *Self-Laudatory Hymn of Inanna and Her Omnipotence*; *to Enlil as the Ruling Deity of the Universe*; *to Enlil, the All-Beneficent*; *to Ishtar*; *to Ninurta as a God of Wrath*; *to Ninurta as God of Vegetation*; *to the Ekur*; *to the Moon-God*; *to the Sun-God*; *Ur-Nammu Hymn: Building of the Ekur and Blessing by Enlil*

Inanna's Descent to the Nether World

Inscriptions—*Amar-Suena* [2]; *Babati*; *Ibbi-Sin* [2]; *Servants of the Kings*; *Shulgi* [4]; *Ur-Nammu* [4]

Lamentations—*Destruction of Sumer and Ur*; *Destruction of Ur*

Laws—*about Rented Oxen*; *Exercise Tablet*; *Handbook of Forms*; *Lipit-Ishtar Law code (see also, Akkad)*; *of Ur-Namma*; *of X*; *Reforms of Uru-inimgina*

Legal Documents—*Divorce Settlement*; *Labor Agreement*; *Lease of Land*; *Loan Agreements* [7]; *Manumission of Šarakam and Ur-guna'*; *Manumission of Umanigar*; *Marriage of Puzur-Haya and Ubartum*; *Marriage of Ur-Nanše and Šašunigin*; *Model Contract*; *Notation of Laborers*; *Real Estate Transaction* [2]; *Receipt*; *Record of Hire* [2]; *Shipping Contract*; *Slave Sale* [2]

Letters—*a Letter-Order*; *Affairs of Ishkun-Dagun* [2]; *concerning Legal Affairs and Real Estate* [9]; *concerning Personnel* [3]; *Death of a Messenger*; *Economic issues* [3] *from an Angry Housewife*; *from Namtare concerning a Donkey*; *from the Governor of Lagash*; *from Ur-Utu on Agade*; *Ilish-takal wants a Chariot*; *Petition to the King*; *Salt Concerns*; *to Enetarzi*

Marriage Texts

Dumuzi and Inanna—*Courting, Marriage, and Honeymoon*; *Ecstasy of Love*; *Love in the Gipar*; *Prayer for Water and Bread*; *Pride of Pedigree*; *Prosperity in the Palace*

Other—*Life is your Coming: King as Brother and Son-in-law*; *The Honey-man: Love-Song to a King*; *Inanna and the King: Blessing on the Wedding Night*; *Lettuce is my Hair: A Love-Song for Shu-Sin*; *Set me Free, my Sister: Sated Lover*

Matter of Arratta—narrative poems [4]
Petition to a King
Prayer of, or to—*Ashurbanipal to the Sun-God*; *Every God*; *the Gods of the Night*; *the Moon-God*
Ua-aua: A Sumerian Lullaby
Votive Inscriptions
Ibbi-Sin; Lugal-Murube Son of Zuzu
Wisdom Texts—*Akkadian Observations on Life and the World Order*; *Babylonian Theodicy*; *Dialogue about Human Misery*; *Dialogue of Pessimism*; *I Will Praise the Lord of Wisdom*; *Man and his God*

Ugarit

Accounts—*Land Grant along with Tithe Obligations*; *Village Tithe Payments*
Baal—*Anat's Consumption of*; *and his Son (fragment)*; *and Mot*; *and Yam*; *Devourers*; *Fathers a Bull*; *Palace of, the Heifer, and Anat*
Betrothal of Yarikh and Nikkal-Ib
Binding of a Monster
Birth
El—*Banquet for Rapiuma*; *Birth of the Gracious Gods Divine Feast*; *Wilderness*
Hymn to Anat
Land Sales and Grants—*Foreclosure and Redistribution of Land*; *Land Donation by the King*; *Land Donation for Service Rendered*; *Land Purchase Text* [2]; *Land Sale*; *Royal Land Grant* [2]
Letters—*ʾAbniya isn't happy*; *ʿAmmiṯtamru, King of Ugarit, to the King of Egypt*; *ʿAmmurāpiʾ to the King of Egypt*; *ʾAnantēnuto his Master Ḫiḏmiratu*; *Brother to Sister*; *Double Letter to Yabnīnu*; *Double letter, from ʿAzzīʾilt uto his Parents, from Same to his Sister*; *Double Letter: from the Queen to ʾUrtēnu and from ʾIlīmilku to the Same*; *Emergency Report from a City-commander*; *Getting one's Name Before the King*; *Governor to the Queen*; *Greetings that ʾAbniya Might Have Sent*; *King of Hatti to the King of Ugari*; *King of Tyre to the King of Ugarit in the Matter of Storm-damaged Ships*; *King of Ugarit to the Queen-mother in the Matter of his Meeting with the Hittite Sovereigns*; *King of Ugarit to the Queen-mother in the Matter of his Meeting with the Hittite Sovereign*; *King to Ḥayyaʾil Regarding an Allotment of Logs*; *King to the Queen-*

APPENDIX C
ENOCH AND MESOPOTAMIAN KING LISTS

Andrei Orlov devoted a section of his dissertation to similarities between Enoch and the Mesopotamian king list, beginning with a comparison of reported ages: "Mesopotamian kings, similar to the patriarchs from the Genesis account, had extraordinarily long reigns, ranging from 3,600 to 72,000 years"; but was this comparison proper? The Genesis account from which he makes this comparison placed the lifespans of Adam's antediluvian descendants between 895 and 969 years with two exceptions. Enoch was 365, and then he was "no more"; Lamech lived 777 years. The last two numbers were explained by Enoch's ascension (and possibly, the solar calendar if one accepts late redaction). Orlov argued for a Shamash cultic influence and 777 as symbolizing the fulfillment of the age. The rest of the ages, however, were fairly close together. Comparing the two lists, Jared, the longest living forefather in Jewish writing, lived 969 years, but Ubar-Tutu, the shortest-lived king of the King Lists, lived *almost twenty times* as long. How then, were they similar except for the fact both lists perpetuate narratives of lifespans beyond what was currently known?[1]

A greater question, however, concerned why the Genesis forefather list must depend on the Mesopotamian list when other accounts of extremely long lives exist in other cultures. In Jainism, Nābhirāja was reported to have lived 1 *crore pūrva*, or 70-plus billion years; Suvidhinātha lived 100 thousand *pūrva*, or 700 quintillion years; and Śreyāṅsanātha ruled 42 *Lakh* years, or 4.2 million years. In China, the legend of Peng Zu put him at seven hundred plus years, and Taoist stories echoed with emperors seeking longevity, many of whom lived over one hundred years. In the West, according to the Greek author, Lucian, Nester lived through three generations, and Teiresias, six generations (*Long Lives,* 6). He also wrote of Arganthonius, king of the Tartessians living 150 years, although he admits "some consider this a

[1] Orlov, "From Patriarch to Youth," 32–33.

fable" (8). He also listed several other centenarians. This fascination with long life did not cease with the ancient cultures.

Modern gerontologists have had to develop in-depth methods of age-validation to assess claims of extremely long lives (120 plus years). Thus, a concern with long life is both cross-cultural and diachronic. Consequently, there is little reason to assume a parent-child relationship between two ancient lists simply because both lists exhibited longevity of life.[2]

To be fair, however, Orlov included other reasons for accepting the Mesopotamian lists as sources for Genesis. He argued, "In other Mesopotamian sources Enmeduranki appears in many roles and situations which demonstrate remarkable similarities with the Enoch story." The problem was that Orlov compressed the Genesis account of Enoch with others found in the Pseudepigrapha, which created a synchronic vat of Enochian material from which he and other scholars pulled to produce dependence. Furthermore, this argument depended on varied traditions between fragments and the assumption that a final-form story was deliverable to apocalyptic writers in the third or second century BCE. Many scholars assumed a connection between these texts based on certain similarities but ignored both the distinctions and the traditions through which the Enochian stories developed. However, it would be incorrect to argue against *any* association between these lists.

Certain elements, such as similar placement and ascensions should spark interest, but such associations were as likely to be independent narratives with similarities based on similarly experienced life and concerns in the ancient world. Or, they also might have signified inverted narratives whereby Jewish authors were writing against the onslaught of cultural accretion (as seen in *Prometheus Bound*). In short, when the History of Religions method, which is still evident in scholarship, was removed, the differences between these texts stood as stark as their similarities.

---

[2] Vijay K. Jain, *Ācārya Samantabhadra's Svayambhūstotra—Adoration of the Twenty-Four TīRthaṅKara: Divine Blessings, Ācārya 108 Vidyanand Muni* (Uttarakhand: Vikalp Printers, 2015), 8, 191, 193; Eva Wong, *Tales of the Dancing Dragon: Stories of the Tao*, Eastern Philosophy and Taoism Series (Boston: Shambhala, 2007), 26; Robert D. Young et al., "Typologies of Extreme Longevity Myths," *Current Gerontology and Geriatrics Research* (2010).

BIBLIOGRAPHY

Abusch, Tzvi. "Ishtar," Pages 452–56 in *DDD*. 2nd extensively rev. ed. Edited by Karel van der Toorn, Bob Becking, and Pieter W. van der Horst. Leiden: Brill, 1999.

Adler, William. "Introduction." Pages 1–31 in *The Jewish Apocalyptic Heritage in Early Christianity*. Edited by James C. VanderKam and William Adler. Jewish Traditions in Early Christian Literature: Section 3 of Compendia Rerum Iudaicarum ad Novum Testamentum 4. Minneapolis: Fortress, 1996.

Alexander, Philip S. "From Son of Adam to Second God: Transformations of the Biblical Enoch." Pages 87–122 in *BFOB*. Edited by Michael E. Stone and Theodore A. Bergren. Harrisburg: Trinity Press, 1998.

Allen, James P. "Coffin Texts Spell 261." Pages 17–18 in vol. 1 of Hallo-Younger, *COS*.

Altman, Amnon. "Rethinking the Hittite System of Subordinate Countries from the Legal Point of View." *JAOS* 123.4 (2003): 741–56.

Amao, Albert. *The Birth of a New Consciousness and the Cycles of Time*. Bloomington: AuthorHouse, 2016.

Amiet, P. "Observations sur les 'Tabletter Magiques' d'Arslan Tash." *Aula Orientalis* 1 (1983): 109.

Anderson. F. I. "2 (Slavonic Apocalypse of) Enoch." Pages 91–221 in vol. 1 of Charlesworth, *OTP*.

Ankersmit, F. R. "Historiography and Postmodernism." *HistTh* 28.2 (1989): 137.

Arcari, Luca. "The Otherworldly Journey of the Book of Watchers as the Source of a Competitive Authority." *Asdiwal* 7.1 (2012): 41–53.

Arnold, Bill T., and David B. Weisberg. "Centennial Review of Delitzsch's 'Babel und Bibel' Lectures." *JBL* 121.3 (Autumn, 2002): 441–57.

Assefa, Daniel. "Dreams, Book of." Pages 552–53 in *EDEJ*.

Attridge, Harold W. "Greek Religions." Pages 699–701 in *EDEJ*.

Barkay, Gabriel. "The Divine Name Found in Jerusalem." *BAR* 9.2 (1983): 14–19.

Barker, Margaret. "Some Reflections Upon the Enoch Myth." *JSOT* 15 (1980): 7–29.

Barr, James. "Philo of Byblos and His 'Phoenician History.'" *BJRL* 57.1 (1974): 17–68.

Basser, Herbert W. "The Development of the Pharisaic Idea of Law as a Sacred Cosmos." *JSJ* 16.1 (1985): 104–16.

Baum, Armin D. "Revelatory Experience and Pseudepigraphical Attribution in Early Jewish Apocalypses." *BBRSup* 21.1 (2011): 65.

________. "A Theological Justification for the Canonical Status of Literary Forgeries: Jacob's Deceit (Genesis 27) and Petr Pokorný's Sola Gratia Argument." *JETS* 55.2 (2012): 273–90.

Baumgarten, Albert I. "Perception of the Past in the Damascus Document." Pages 1–15 in *The Damascus Document: A Centennial of Discovery: Proceedings of the Third International Symposium of the Orion Center for the Study of the Dead Sea Scrolls and Associated Literature*. Edited by Joseph M. Baumgarten, Esther G. Chazon, and Avital Pinnick. STDJ 44. Leiden: Brill, 1999.

________. *The Phoenician History of Philo of Byblos: A Commentary*. Ëtudes préliminaires aux religions orientales dans l'Empire 89. Leiden: E. J. Brill, 1981.

Baxter, Wayne. "Noachic Traditions and the Book of Noah." *JSP* 15.3 (2006): 179–94.

Beauchamp, Paul. "Le salut corporel des justes et la conclusion du livre de la Sagesse." *Bib* 45.4 (1964): 491.

Beckman, Gary M. *Hittite Diplomatic Texts*. 2nd ed. WAW 7. Atlanta: Scholars Press, 1999.

Bedard, Stephan J. "Hellenistic Influence on the Idea of Resurrection in Jewish Apocalyptic Literature." *JGRChJ* 5 (2008): 174.

Belcher-Rankin, Rebecca. "Narrative Authority in Hawthorne's 'the Ambitious Guest.'" *Tennessee Philological Bulletin* (2008): 17–25.

Bergsma, John S. "The Biblical Manumission Laws: Has the Literary Dependence of *H* on *D* Been Demonstrated?" Pages 65–69 in vol. 1 of *A Teacher for All Generations: Essays in Honor of James C. VanderKam*. SJSJ 153. Leiden: Brill, 2012.

Bernstein, Moshe J. "Pseudepigraphy in the Qumran Scrolls: Categories and Functions." Pages 1–26 in *Pseudepigraphic Perspectives: The Apocrypha and Pseudepigrapha in Light of the Dead Sea Scrolls; Proceedings of the International Symposium of the Orion Center for the Study of the Dead Sea Scrolls and Associated Literature, 12–14 January, 1997*. Edited by Esther G. Chazon, Michael E. Stone, and Avital Pinnick. STDJ 31. Leiden: Brill, 1999.

Best, Steven and Douglas Kellner. *Postmodern Theory: Critical Interrogations*. New York: Guilford Press, 1991.

Betz, H. D. "On the Problem of the Religio-Historical Understanding of Apocalypticism." *JTC* 6 (1969): 134.

Beyerle, Stefan. "'If You Preserve Carefully Faith': Hellenistic Attitudes Towards Religion in Pre-Maccabean Times." *ZAW* 118.2 (2006): 250.

Bhayro, Siam. "Noah's Library: Sources for 1 Enoch 6–11." *JSP* 15.3 (2006): 163–77.

Bickley, John T. "Dreams, Visions, and the Rhetoric of Authority." PhD diss., Florida State University, 2013. http://diginole.lib.fsu.edu/islandora/object/fsu:183664/datastream/PDF/view.

Bietenhard, Hans. *Die Himmlische Welt im Urchristentum und Spätjudentum*. Tübingen: Mohr, 1951.

Black, Matthew. *The Book of Enoch, or 1 Enoch: A New English Edition with Commentary and Textual Notes*. SVTP 7. Leiden: E. J. Brill, 1985.

Blenkinsopp, Joseph. *Judaism: The First Phase—the Place of Ezra and Nehemiah in the Origins of Judaism*. Grand Rapids: Eerdmans, 2009.

Bloch, René. "Pseudo-Orpheus." Pages 1008–9 in *EDEJ*.

Block, Daniel I. *Judges, Ruth*, NAC 6. Nashville: Broadman & Holman Publishers, 1999.

________. *The Gods of the Nations: Studies in Ancient near Eastern National Theology*. Evangelical Theological Society Studies. 2nd ed. Grand Rapids: Baker Academic, 2000.

Brand, Miryam T. *Evil within and Without: The Source of Sin and Its Nature as Portrayed in Second Temple Literature*. JAJSup 9. Göttingen: Vandenhoeck und Ruprecht, 2013.

Bréhier, Emile. *La Philosophie de Plotin*. Paris: Boivin, 1928.

Breslauer, S. Daniel. "Secrecy and Magic, Publicity and Torah: Unpacking a Talmudic Tale." Pages 263–82 In *Magic and Ritual in the Ancient World*. Edited by Paul Allan Mirecki and Marvin W. Meyer. RGRW 141. Leiden: Brill, 2002.

Brettler, Marc Z. *God Is King: Understanding an Israelite Metaphor*. JSOTSup 76. Sheffield: JSOT Press, 1989.

Briant, Pierre. *Historie de l'empire Perse: de Cyrus à Alexandre*. Paris: Fayard, 1996.

Bruce, F. F. *The Teacher of Righteousness in the Qumran Texts*. The Tyndale Lecture in Biblical Archaeology. London: Tyndale Press, 1957.

Brueggemann, Walter. "Of the Same Flesh and Bone, Gn 2:23a." *CBQ* 32.4 (1970): 532–42.

Bullinger, Ethelbert William. *Figures of Speech Used in the Bible*. London: Eyre and Spottiswoode, 1898.

Burkert, Walter. *Ancient Mystery Cults*. Carl Newell Jackson Lectures. Cambridge: Harvard University Press, 1987.

Burkitt, F. Crawford. *Jewish and Christian Apocalypses*. London: Oxford University Press, 1914.

Butler, Trent C. *Judges*. WBC 8. Nashville: Thomas Nelson, 2009.

Caquot, André. "La seconde tablette ou 'petite amulette' d'Arslan-Tash." *Syria* 48.3–4 (1971): 391–406.

Cartwright, Mark. "Eleusis." Cambridge University Press. January 14, 2015. http://www.ancient.eu /Eleusis.

Caspari, Carl P. "Jesajanische Studien." *Zeitschrift für die gesammte lutherische Theologie und Kirche* 4.2 (1843): 1–73.

Charles, Robert H. *Pseudepigrapha*. Vol. 2 of *APOP*. Oxford: Clarendon Press, 1913.

________. *A Critical History of the Doctrine of a Future Life in Israel, in Judaism, and in Christianity, or, Hebrew, Jewish, and Christian Eschatology from Pre-Prophetic Times till the Close of the New Testament Canon*. 2nd rev. ed. London: A. and C. Black, 1989.

Charlesworth, James H. ed. *Apocalyptic Literature and Testaments.* Vol. 1. of *OTP*. Peabody, MA: Hendrickson, 2010.
________. "Theodicy in Early Jewish Writings." Pages 470–508 in *Theodicy in the World of the Bible*. Edited by Antti Laato and Johannes C. de Moor. Leiden: Brill, 2003.
Charlesworth, James H., and D. L. Bock, eds. *Parables of Enoch: A Paradigm Shift*. London: Bloomsbury, 2013.
Chevalier, Jacques M. *A Postmodern Revelation: Signs of Astrology and the Apocalypse*. Toronto: University of Toronto Press, 1997.
Chwe, Michael *Rational Ritual: Culture, Coordination, and Common Knowledge*. Princeton: Princeton University Press, 2001.
Clauss, Manfred. *The Roman Cult of Mithras: The God and His Mysteries*. Translated by Richard Gordon. New York: Routledge, 2000.
Clifford, Richard J. "The Roots of Apocalypticism in near Eastern Myth." Pages 3–29 in *The Continuum History of Apocalypticism*. Edited by Bernard McGinn, John J. Collins, and Stephen J. Stein. New York: Continuum, 2003.
Coblentz Bautch, Kelley. "Decoration, Destruction and Debauchery: Reflections on 1 Enoch 8 in Light of 4Qenb." *DSD* 15.1 (2008): 79–95.
________. *A Study of the Geography of 1 Enoch 17–19: No One Has Seen What I Have Seen*. SJSJ 81. Leiden: Brill, 2003.
Coleman, James S. *Foundations of Social Theory*. Cambridge: Harvard University Press, 1994.
Collins, Billie J. "Ritual for the Infernal Deities." Pages 168–71 in vol. 1 of Hallo-Younger, *COS*.
Collins, Christopher. *Authority Figures: Metaphors of Mastery from the Iliad to the Apocalypse*. Lanham: Rowman and Littlefield Publishers, 1996.
Collins, John J. "Apocalypse Then." *AJS Perspectives: The Magazine of the Association of Jewish Studies*. Fall, 2012. http://www.bjpa.org/Publications/details.cfm?PublicationID=20997.
________. "Apocalyptic Eschatology in the Ancient World." Pages 40–55 in *The Oxford Handbook of Eschatology*. Edited by

Jerry L. Walls. OHS 40. Oxford: Oxford University Press, 2008.
________. “Introduction: Towards the Morphology of a Genre.” *Semeia* 14 (1979): 1–20.
________. *The Apocalyptic Imagination: An Introduction to Jewish Apocalyptic Literature*. Grand Rapids: Eerdmans, 1998.
________. “The Apocalyptic Technique: Setting and Function in the Book of the Watchers.” *CBQ* 44.4 (1982): 91–111.
________. “Apocrypha and Pseudepigrapha.” *EDSS*, 35–39.
________. “Dead Sea Scrolls.” *ABD* 2:85–100.
________. “Prophecy and History in the Pesharim.” Pages 209–26 in *Authoritative Scriptures in Ancient Judaism*. Edited by Mladen Popović. Leiden: Brill, 2010.
________. *Seers, Sibyls, and Sages in Hellenistic-Roman Judaism*. Boston: Brill Academic, 2001.
________. “Watchers.” *DDD*, 893–95.
________. “What Is Apocalyptic Literature?” Pages 1–16 in *Oxofrd Handbook of Apocalyptic Literature*. Edited by John J. Collins. OHS. Oxford: Oxford University Press, 2014.
Collins, John J. and Michael A. Fishbane. *Death, Ecstasy, and Other Worldly Journeys*. Albany: State University of New York Press, 1995.
Comfort, Philip. *Encountering the Manuscripts: An Introduction to New Testament Paleography and Textual Criticism*. Nashville: Broadman & Holman, 2005.
Cook, Stephen L. *The Apocalyptic Literature*. Interpreting Biblical Texts. Nashville: Abingdon, 2003.
Corbett, Glenn J. “Word Play: The Power of the Written Word in Ancient Israel.” *Bible History Daily: Biblical Archaeology Society*. May 15, 2015. http://www.biblicalarchaeology.org/daily/biblical-artifacts/artifacts-and-the-bible/word-play/.
Cornell, James. *The First Stargazers: An Introduction to the Origins of Astronomy*. New York: Scribner, 1981.
Cousland, J. R. C. “Philo of Byblos.” Page 513–14 in *The New Interpreter’s Dictionary of the Bible*. Vol. 4. Edited by Katharine Doob Sakenfeld and Marianne Blickenstaff. Nashville: Abingdon Press, 2006.
Craigie, Peter C. “Covenant.” *BEB* 1:530–36.

________. *The Book of Deuteronomy*. Grand Rapids: Eerdmans, 1976.

Crawford, Sidnie W. *Rewriting Scripture in Second Temple Times*. Studies in the Dead Sea Scrolls and Related Literature. Grand Rapids: Eerdmans, 2008.

Cross, Frank M. *Canaanite Myth and Hebrew Epic: Essays in the History of the Religion of Israel*. Cambridge: Harvard University Press, 1973.

Cross, Frank M., and Richard J. Saley. "Phoenician Incantations on a Plaque of the Seventh Century BC from Arslan Tash in Upper Syria." *BASOR* 197 (1970): 42–49.

Dandamaev, Muhammad. "Xerxes and the Esagila Temple in Babylon." *Bulletin of the Asia Institute* 7 (1993): 41–45.

Daubney, William H. *The Three Additions to Daniel: A Study*. Cambridge, Deighton Bell, 1906.

Davila, James R. *The Provenance of the Pseudepigrapha: Jewish, Christian, or Other?* SJSJ 105. Leiden: Brill, 2005.

de Souza Nogueira, Paul A. "Celestial Worship and Ecstatic-Visionary Experience." *JSNT* 25.2 (2002): 165–84.

Delcor, M. "L'immortalité de l'âme dans le livre de la Sagesse et dans les documents de Qumrân." *NRTh* 77 (1955): 614–30.

Delitzsch, Friedrich. *Babel und Bibel: ein Vortrag*. Leipzig: J. C. Hinrichs'sche Buchhandlung, 1902.

Deneef, A. Leigh. "The Poetics of Orpheus: The Text and a Study of Orpheus His Journey to Hell." *Studies in Philology* 89 (Winter, 1992): 20–70.

Derrida, Jacques. "Of an Apocalyptic Tone Recently Adopted in Philosophy." *The Oxford Literary Review* 6.2 (1984): 3–37.

Dimant, Devorah. "Ages of Creation." *EDSS*, 12–13.

________. *History, Ideology and Bible Interpretation in the Dead Sea Scrolls: Collected Studies*. FAT 90. Tübingen: Mohr Siebeck, 2014.

________. "Noah in Early Jewish Literature." Pages 123–50 in Stone, *BFOB*.

Dobroruka, Vicente. *Second Temple Pseudepigraphy: A Cross-Cultural Comparison of Apocalyptic Texts and Related Jewish Literature*. Ekstasis—Religious Experience from Antiquity to the Middle Ages. Edited by John R. Levison. Vol. 4. Berlin: de Gruyter, 2014.

Driver, Godfrey R. and John C. L. Gibson, eds. *Canaanite Myths and Legends*, London: T&T Clark, 2004

Durham, John I. *Exodus*. WBC 3. Dallas: Word, 1998.

Edmonds, Radcliffe G. "Sacred Scripture or Oracles for the Dead? The Semiotic Situation of the 'Orphic' Gold Tablets." Pages 257–70 in *The 'Orphic' Gold Tablets and Greek Religion: Further Along the Path*. Edited by Radcliffe G. Edmonds. Cambridge: Cambridge University Press, 2011.

Elliott, Mark Adam. *The Survivors of Israel: A Reconsideration of the Theology of Pre-Christian Judaism*. Grand Rapids: Eerdmans, 2000.

Ellis, E. Earle. Review of *Roots of Apocalyptic: The Mesopotamian Background of the Enoch Figure and of the Son of Man* by Helge S. Kvanvig. *SwJT* 34.1 (1991): 74.

Elwell, Walter A., and Philip W. Comfort. "Scythopolis." *Tyndale Bible Dictionary* 166–67. Wheaton, Tyndale House, 2001.

Eshel, Esther. "*Jubilees* 32 and the Bethel Cult Traditions in Second Temple Literature." Pages 21–36 in *Things Revealed: Studies in Early Jewish and Christian Literature in Honor of Michael E. Stone*. SJSJ 89. Leiden: Brill, 2004.

Eslinger, Lyle M. "Hosea 12:5a and Genesis 32:29: A Study in Inner Biblical Exegesis." *JSOT* 18 (1980): 91–99.

Espak, Peeter. "The Emergence of the Concept of Divine Warfare and Theology of War in the Ancient Near East." *ENDC Proceedings* 14 (2011): 115–29.

Evans, Craig. "The Scriptures of Jesus and His Earliest Followers." Pages 185–95 in *The Canon Debate*. Edited by Lee Martin McDonald and James A. Sanders. Peabody, MA: Hendrickson Publishers, 2002.

Facorellis, Yorgos, Marina Sofronidou, and Giorgos Hourmouziadis. "Radiocarbon Dating of the Neolithic Lakeside Settlement of Dispilio, Kastoria, Northern Greece." *Radiocarbon* 56.2 (2014): 511–28.

Faulkner, Paul. "On Telling and Trusting." *Mind* 116.464 (2007): 875–902.

Fitzmyer, Joseph A. "The Aramaic Suzerainty Treaty from Sefire in the Museum of Beirut." *CBQ* 20.4 (1958): 444–76.

Flusser, David. *Qumran and Apocalypticism*. Vol. 1 of *Judaism of the Second Temple Period*. Translated by Azzan Yadin. Grand Rapids: Eerdmans, 2007.

________. *Judaism of the Second Temple Period*. Vol. 2, *The Jewish Sages and Their Literature*. Translated by Azzan Yadin. Grand Rapids: Eerdmans, 2009.

Fontaine, Carole. "The Deceptive Goddess in Ancient near Eastern Myth: Inanna and Inaraš." *Semeia* 42 (1988): 84–102

Fossum, J. "Dove." *DDD* 263–64.

Foster, Benjamin R., trans. "Atrahasis." Pages 450–52 in vol. 1 of Hallo-Younger, *COS*.

Foster, John L., and Susan T. Hollis. *Hymns, Prayers, and Songs: An Anthology of Ancient Egyptian Lyric Poetry*. Vol. 8. Atlanta: Scholars Press, 1995.

Foucault, Michel. *The History of Sexuality*. Vols. 1–3. 1st Vintage Books ed. New York: Vintage Books, 1988.

Fraade, Steven D. "Enosh and His Generation Revisited." Pages 59–86 in Stone, *BFOB*.

Frankfurter, David. "The Cult of the Martyrs in Egypt before Constantine: The Evidence of the Coptic Apocalypse of Elijah." *VC* 48 (1994): 25–47.

Gager, John G. "Introduction." Pages 3–41 in *Curse Tablets and Binding Spells from the Ancient World*. Edited by John G. Gager. New York: Oxford University Press, 1999.

García Martínez, Florentino G. *Between Philology and Theology: Contributions to the Study of Ancient Jewish Interpretation*. Edited by Hindy Najman and Eibert C. Tigchelaar. SJSJ 162. Leiden: Brill, 2012.

García Martínez, Florentino G. and Eibert J. C. Tigchelaar. *Transcriptions*. Vol. 1 of *The Dead Sea Scrolls Study Edition*. Leiden: Brill, 1997.

________. *Translations*. Vol. 2 of *The Dead Sea Scrolls Study Edition*. Leiden: Brill, 1997.

George, A. R. "Sennacherib and the Tablet of Destinies." *Iraq* 48 (1986): 133–46.

Gignoux, Philippe. "Microcosm and Macrocosm in Pre-Islamic Iranian Thought: The Theory of the Correspondence between the Different Parts of the Human Being and those of the Cosmos."

Encylopaedia Iranica. New York: Encyclopaedia Iranica Foundation, 2004. http://www.iranicaonline.org/articles/microcosm-and-macrocosm

Glassner, Jean-Jacques. *Mesopotamian Chronicles*. Edited by Benjamin R. Foster. WAW 19. Atlanta: Society of Biblical Literature, 2004.

Glasson, Thomas F. *Greek Influence in Jewish Eschatology: With Special Reference to the Apocalypses and Pseudepigraphs*. Biblical Monographs 1. London: SPCK, 1961.

Goff, Matthew. "Recent Trends in the Study of Early Jewish Wisdom Literature: The Contribution of 4Qinstruction and Other Qumran Texts." *CurBR* 7.3 (2009): 376–416.

________. "Warriors, Cannibals, and Teachers of Evil: The Sons of the Angels in Genesis 6, the Book of the Watchers and the Book of Jubilees." *SEÅ* 80 (2015): 79–97.

________. "Wisdom and Apocalypticism." Pages 79–97 in Collins, *OHAL*.

Goldberg, Sanford. "Norms of Trust, *De Re* Trust, and the Epistemology of Testimony." Pages 229–55 in *Epistemology: Contexts, Values, Disagreement: Proceedings of the 34th International Ludwig Wittgenstein Symposium in Kirchberg, 2011*. Publications of the Austrian Ludwig Wittgenstein Society 19. Munchen: Walter de Gruyter, 2013.

Gotthard, Reinhold, ed. *Die Zahl Sieben Im Alten Orient: Studien Zur Zahlensymbolik in Der Bibel und Ihrer Altorientalischen Umwelt*, Frankfurt: Peter Lang, 2008.

Gowan, Donald E. *From Eden to Babel: A Commentary on the Book of Genesis 1–11*. Grand Rapids: Eerdmans, 1988.

Grabbe, Lester L. *An Introduction to Second Temple Judaism: History and Religion of the Jews in the Time of Nehemiah, the Maccabees, Hillel and Jesus*. London: T&T Clark, 2010.

________. *Judaic Religion in the Second Temple Period: Belief and Practice from the Exile to Yavneh*. London: Routledge, 2000.

Graff, Fritz. "Dionysus." *DDD* 252–258.

________. "The Bridge and the Ladder: Narrow Passages in Late Antique Visions." Pages 19–33 in *Heavenly Realms and Earthly Realities in Late Antique Religions*. Edited by Ra'anan

S. Boustan. Cambridge: Cambridge University Press, 2004. ProQuest Ebrary.

Green, Alberto. *The Storm-god in the Ancient Near east*. BJSUCSD 8. Winona Lake: Eisenbrauns, 2003.

Green, Yosef. "Who Knows Seven?" *JBQ* 41.4 (2013): 255–61.

Griffith, Mark. *The Authenticity of Prometheus Bound*. Cambridge Classical Studies. Cambridge: Cambridge University Press, 2007.

Grogan, Geoffrey W. "Isaiah." Pages 3–354 in *Isaiah, Jeremiah, Lamentations, Ezekiel*. Vol. 6 of *The Expositor's Bible Commentary*. Edited by Frank E. Gaebelein. Grand Rapids: Zondervan, 1986

Gruen, Erich S. *Heritage and Hellenism: The Reinvention of Jewish Tradition*. HCS 30. Berkeley: University of California Press, 1998.

Gunkel, Hermann. *Israel und Babylonien: Der Einfluss Babyloniens auf die israelitische Religion*. Göttingen: Vandenhoeck und Ruprecht, 1903.

Gunkel, Hermann and Heinrich Zimmern. *Schöpfung und Chaos in Urzeit und Endzeit: eine Religionsgeschichtliche Untersuchung über Gen 1 und Ap Joh 12*. Göttingen: Vandenhoeck und Ruprecht, 1895.

Häberl, Chuck G. "Unpublished Paper on the Arslan Tash Amulet No. 1." https://www.academia.edu/5074216/Arslan_Tash_Amulet_No._1_AT1.

Hallo, William W. and K. Lawson Younger, Jr., eds. *Context of Scripture*. 3 vols. Leiden: Brill, 1997–2002.

Hamilton, Victor P. *The Book of Genesis, Chapters 1–17*. NICOT. Grand Rapids: Eerdmans, 1990.

________. *The Book of Genesis, Chapters 18–50*. NICOT. Grand Rapids: Eerdmans, 1995.

Hanneken, Todd. *The Subversion of the Apocalypses in the Book of Jubilees*. Atlanta: Society of Biblical Literature, 2012.

Hanson, Paul D. *The Dawn of Apocalyptic: The Historical and Sociological Roots of Jewish Apocalyptic Eschatology*. Revised ed. Philadelphia: Fortress, 1975.

________. "The Matrix of Apocalypse." Pages 524–33 of *CHJ*. Vol. 2 of *The Hellenistic Age*. Edited by W. D. Davies and L. Finkelstein. Cambridge: Cambridge University Press, 1989.

Harlow, Daniel C. "Abraham, Apocalypse of." *EDEJ* 295–98.

________. "Ascent to Heaven." *EDEJ* 387–90.

Harrington, Hannah K. *The Purity Texts: Companion to the Dead Sea Scrolls*. New York: T&T Clark, 2004.

Hartley, John E. *The Book of Job*. Grand Rapids: Eerdmans, 1988.

Hasel, Gerhard F. "'New Moon and Sabbath' in Eighth Century Israelite Prophetic Writings." Pages 37–64 in *Wunschet Jerusalem Frieden: Collected Communications to the 12th Congress of the International Organization for the Study of the Old Testament*. BEATAJ 13. Frankfurt: Peter Lang, 1988.

Hayot, Eric. "Vanishing Horizons: Problems in Comparison of China and the West." Pages 88–107 in *A Companion to Comparative Literature*. Edited by Ali Behdad and Dominic Thomas. Chichester: John Wiley and Sons, 2011.

Hays, Richard B. *Echoes of Scripture in the Letters of Paul*. New Haven: Yale University Press, 1989.

Heiser, Michael S. "The Divine Council in Late Canonical and Non-Canonical Second Temple Jewish Literature." PhD diss., University of Wisconsin-Madison, 2004.

Hess, Richard S. *Israelite Religions: An Archaeological and Biblical Survey*. Grand Rapids: Baker Academic, 2007.

Hidding, K. A. H. "Der Hochgott und Der Mikrokosmische Mensch." *Numen* 18.2 (1971): 94–102.

Himmelfarb, Martha. *The Apocalypse: A Brief History*. Blackwell Brief Histories of Religion Series. Chichester: Wiley-Blackwell, 2010.

________. *Ascent to Heaven in Jewish and Christian Apocalypses*. New York: Oxford University Press, 1993.

________. "Torah, Testimony, and Tablets of Heaven: The Claim of Authority of the Book of Jubilees." Pages 19–29 in *A Multiform Heritage: Studies on Early Judaism and Christianity in Honor of Robert A. Kraft*. Edited by Robert A. Kraft and Benjamin G. Wright. Atlanta: Scholars Press, 1999.

________. *Tours of Hell: An Apocalyptic Form in Jewish and Christian Literature*. Philadelphia: University of Pennsylvania, 1983.

Hintikka, Jaakko. *Knowledge and Belief: An Introduction to the Logic of the Two Notions*. Texts in Philosophy. Edited by Vincent Hendricks and John Symons. Vol. 1. London: Kings College Publications, 2005.

Hoffner, Harry A. *Hittite Myths*. 2nd ed. Edited by Gary M. Beckman. WAW 2. Atlanta: Scholars Press, 1998.

Hogan, Karina M. *Theologies in Conflict in 4 Ezra: Wisdom Debate and Apocalyptic Solution*. SJSJ 130. Boston: Brill, 2008.

Hölbl, Günther. *A History of the Ptolemaic Empire*. London: Routledge, 2001.

Houtman, Cornelis. "What Did Jacob See in His Dream at Bethel: Some Remarks on Genesis 28:10–22." *VT* 27.3 (1977): 337–51.

Hultgren, Stephen. *From the Damascus Covenant to the Covenant of the Community: Literary, Historical, and Theological Studies in the Dead Sea Scrolls*. Edited by Florentino García Martínez. STDJ 66. Leiden: Brill, 2007.

Hutcheon, Linda. *A Poetics of Postmodernism: History, Theory, Fiction*. New York: Routledge, 2010.

Hutter, M. and M. de Jonge. "Heaven." *DDD* 389–90.

Isaac, E. "1 (Ethiopic Apocalypse of) Enoch: A New Translation and Introduction." Pages 5–89 in vol. 1 of Charlesworth, *OTP*.

Jäger, Christoph. "Epistemic Authority, Preemptive Reasons, and Understanding." *Episteme* (2016): 167–185.

Jain, Vijay K. *Ācārya Samantabhadra's Svayambhūstotra—Adoration of the Twenty-Four Tīrthaṅkara: Divine Blessings, Ācārya 108 Vidyanand Muni*. Uttarakhand: Vikalp Printers, 2015.

Jassen, Alex P. *Mediating the Divine: Prophecy and Revelation in the Dead Sea Scrolls and Second Temple Judaism*. Edited by Florentino García Martínez. STDJ 68. Leiden: Brill, 2007.

________. "Scriptural Interpretation in Early Jewish Apocalypses." Pages 69–84 in Collins, *OHAL*.

Jokiranta, Jutta. "Pesharim: A Mirror of Self-Understanding." Pages 23–34 in *Reading the Present in the Qumran Library: The Perception of the Contemporary by Means of Scriptural Interpretations*.

Edited Kristen De Troyer and Armin Lange. SBLSS 30. Atlanta: Society of Biblical Literature, 2005.

Kaiser, Walter C., Jr. "Exodus." Pages 285–498 in *Genesis, Exodus, Leviticus, Numbers*. Vol. 2 of *The Expositor's Bible Commentary*. Edited by Frank E. Gaebelein. Grand Rapids: Zondervan, 1990.

Karenga, Maulana. *Maat, the Moral Ideal in Ancient Egypt: A Study in Classical African Ethics*. African Studies. New York: Routledge, 2003.

Kassühlke, Rudolf and Barclay M. Newman, *Kleines Wörterbuch zum Neuen Testament: Griechisch-Deutsch.* Stuttgart: Deutsche Bibelgesellschaft, 1997.

Kee, H. C. "Testaments of the Twelve Patriarchs: A New Translation and Introduction." Pages 775–81 in vol. 1 of Charlesworth, *OTP*.

Keren, Arnon. "Trust and Belief: A Preemptive Reasons Account." *Synthese* 191.12 (August 1, 2014): 2593–615.

Kerényi, Karl. *Eleusis: Archetypal Image of Mother and Daughter*. Vol. 4 of *Archetypal Images in Greek Religion*. Translated by Ralph Manheim. Bollingen Series 64. New York: Bolligen Foundation, 1967. Reprint. Princeton: Princeton University Press, 1991.

Kim, Lawrence Y. *Homer between History and Fiction in Imperial Greek Literature*. Greek culture in the Roman World. Cambridge: Cambridge University Press, 2010. ACLS Humanities E-Book

Kissling, Paul J. *Genesis*. College Press NIV Commentary 1. Edited by Terry Briley and Paul Kissling. Joplin: College Press, 2004.

Kitchen, Kenneth. *On the Reliability of the Old Testament*. Revised ed. Grand Rapids: Eerdmans, 2003.

Kitchen, Kenneth, and Paul J. N. Lawrence. *TLC*. 3 vols. Wiesbaden: Harrassowitz Verlag, 2012.

Kline, Meredith G. *Treaty of the Great King: The Covenant Structure of Deuteronomy: Studies and Commentary*. Grand Rapids: Eerdmans, 1963.

Knibb, Michael A. "Apocalyptic and Wisdom in 4 Ezra." Pages 271–88 in *Essays on the Book of Enoch and Other Early Jewish Texts and Traditions*. Boston: Brill, 2008.

Koch, Klaus. "Daniel und Henoch: Apokalyptik im antiken Judentum." Pages 31–50 in *Apokalyptic und kein Ende?* Edited by Bernd U. Schipper and Georg Plasger. Biblische-Theologische Schwerpunkte 29. Göttingen: Vandenhoeck und Ruprecht, 2007.

Kreider, Glenn R. "The Flood Is as Bad as It Gets: Never Again Will God Destroy the Earth." *BSac* 171.684 (2014): 418–39.

Kugel, James L. *A Walk through Jubilees: Studies in the Book of Jubilees and the World of Its Creation*. Leiden: Brill, 2012.

Küper, Augustus. *Das Prophetenthum des Alten Bundes*. Leipzig Dörffling und Franke, 1870.

Kvanvig, Helge S. *Primeval History: Babylonian, Biblical, and Enochic: An Intertextual Reading*. SJSJ 149. Leiden: Brill, 2011.

________. *Roots of Apocalyptic: The Mesopotamian Background of the Enoch Figure and of the Son of Man*. WMANT 61. Neukirchen-Vluyn: Neukirchener Verlag, 1988.

Ladd, George Eldon. "Why Not Prophetic-Apocalyptic?" *JBL* 76.3 (1957): 192.

Lambert, Wilfred G. *The Background of Jewish Apocalyptic*. Ethel M. Wood Lecture Series. London: Athlone, 1978.

________. "Enmeduranki and Related Matters." *JCS* 21 (1967): 126–38.

Lange, Armin. "Reading the Decline in Prophecy." Pages 181–91 in *Reading the Present in the Qumran Library: The Perception of the Contemporary by Means of Scriptural Interpretations*. Edited by Kristen De Troyer and Armin Lange. SBLSS 30. Atlanta: Society of Biblical Literature, 2005.

Langer, Ruth. "Spiritual Practices: Mystical, Magical, and Apotropaic Prayer." Pages 211–22 in *Jewish Liturgy: A Guide to Research*. Illuminations: Guides to Research in Religion. Lanham: Rowman and Littlefield Publishers, 2015.

Larsen, Kasper. "Visdom Og Apokalyptik i Musar Lemevin (1Q/4Qinstruction)." *DTT* 65.1 (2002): 1–14.

Lauinger, Jacob. "Esarhaddon's Succession Treaty at Tell Tayinat." *JCS* 64 (2012): 87–123.

________. "Some Preliminary Thoughts on the Tablet Collection in Building XVI from Tell Tayinat." *Canadian Society for Mesopotamian Studies* 6 (fall, 2001): 5–12.

________. "The Neo-Assyrian *adê*: Treaty, Oath, or Something Else?" *Journal for Ancient Near East and Biblical Law* 19 (2003): 105–115.

Lempriére, J. *A Classical Dictionary, containing a Copious Account of All the Proper Names Mentioned in Ancient Authors, with the Value of Coins, Weights, and Measures among the Greeks and Romans, and a Chronological Table*. London: T. Cadell and W. Davies, 1820.

Leslau, Wolf, *Comparative Dictionary of Ge'ez: Classical Ethiopic; Ge'ez-English, English Ge'ez with an Index of the Semitic Roots*. Wiesbaden: Otto Harrassowitz, 1991.

Lesses, Rebecca. "Amulets and Angels: Visionary Experience in the Testament of Job and the Hekhalot Literature." Pages 49–74 in *Tablets of Heaven: Interpretation, Identity, and Tradition in Ancient Judaism*. Edited by Lynn R. LiDonnici and Andrea Lieber. SJSJ 119. Leiden: Brill, 2007.

Levine, Lee I. *Judaism and Hellenism in Antiquity: Conflict or Confluence?* Samuel and Althea Stroum Lectures in Jewish Studies. Seattle: University of Washington, 1998.

Lewis, Theodore J. "The Identity and Function of El/Baal Berith." *JBL* 115.3 (1996): 401–23.

Lichtheim, Miriam. *The Late* Period. Vol. 3 of *Ancient Egyptian* L*iterature*. Berkeley: University of California Press, 1973.

Lücke, Gottfried. *Versuch einer vollständigen Einleitung in die Offenbarung Johannis und in die gesamte apokalyptische Literatur*. Bonn: Weber, 1832.

Machinist, Peter, ed. *Prophets and Prophecy in the Ancient near East* (*Translations*). WAW 12. Atlanta: Society of Biblical Literature, 2003.

MacDonald, Dennis R. *Does the New Testament Imitate Homer? Four Cases from the Acts of the Apostles*. New Haven: Yale University Press, 2003.

Magness, Jodi. "Qumran." *EDEJ* 1126–32.

Mancini, Anna. *Maat, La Philosophie de la Justice de l'Ancienne Egypte*. 2nd ed. Paris: Buenos Books international, 2007.

Manning, J. G. *The Last Pharaohs: Egypt under the Ptolemies, 305–30 BC*. Princeton: Princeton University Press, 2012.

Martin, Wallace. *Recent Theories of Narrative*. Ithaca: Cornell University Press, 1986.

Mathews, Kenneth. A. *Genesis 1–11:26*. NAC 1A. Nashville: Broadman & Holman, 1996.

________. *Genesis 11:27–50:26*. NAC 1B. Nashville: Broadman & Holman, 2005.

McLeod, John. *Beginning Postcolonialism*. Beginnings. Manchester: Manchester University Press, 2012.

Meade, David G. *Pseudonymity and Canon: An Investigation into the Relationship of Authorship and Authority in Jewish and Earliest Christian Tradition*. Grand Rapids: Eerdmans, 1987.

Merlini, Marco. "Settling Discovery Circumstances, Dating, and Utilization of the Tărtăria Tablets." Pages in 111–96 in *Proceedings of the International Colloquium: The Carpathian Basin and Its Role in the Neolithisation of the Balkan Peninsula*. Edited by Sabin Andrian Luca. ATS 7. Sibiu: Lucian Blaga University, 2008.

Metzger, Bruce M. "Literary Forgeries and Canonical Pseudepigrapha." *JBL* 91.1 (1972): 3–24.

Millar, William R. *Priesthood in Ancient Israel*. Understanding Biblical Themes. St. Louis: Chalice, 2001.

Molenberg, C. "A Study of the Roles of Shemihaza and Asael in I Enoch 6–11." *JJS* 35.2 (1984): 136–46.

Mooney, D. Jeffrey. "Leviticus, Book of." In *Lexham Bible Dictionary*. Edited by John D. Barry, David Bomar, Derek R. Brown, Rachel Klippenstein, Douglas Mangum, Carrie Sinclair Wolcott, Lazarus Wentz, Elliot Ritzema, and Wendy Widder. Bellingham: Lexham Press, 2016.

Murphy, Frederick James *Apocalypticism in the Bible and Its World: A Comprehensive Introduction*. Grand Rapids: Baker Academic, 2012.

Murphy, Roland E. *Wisdom Literature: Job, Proverbs, Ruth, Canticles, Ecclesiastes, and Esther*. FOTL 13. Grand Rapids: Eerdmans, 1981.

Murray, Alexander S. *Manual of Mythology: Greek and Roman, Norse, and Old German, Hindoo and Egyptian Mythology*. New York: Charles Scribner's Sons, 1881.

Najman, Hindy. “The Inheritance of Prophecy in Apocalypse.” Pages 36–51 in Collins, *OHAL*, 36.

________. “Interpretation as Primordial Writing: Jubilees and Its Authority Conferring Strategies.” *JSJ* 30.4 (1999): 379–410.

________. “The Law of Nature and the Authority of Mosaic Law.” *SPhilo* 11 (1999): 55–73.

________. “Reconsidering Jubilees: Prophecy and Exemplarity.” Pages 229–43 in *Enoch and the Mosaic Torah: The Evidence of Jubilees*. Edited by Gabriele Boccaccini and Giovanni Ibba. Grand Rapids: Eerdmans, 2009.

________. *Seconding Sinai the Development of Mosaic Discourse in Second Temple Judaism*. Leiden: Brill, 2003.

________. “Torah of Moses: Pseudonymous Attribution in Second Temple Writings.” Pages 73–86 in *Past Renewals: Interpretive Authority, Renewed Revelation, and the Quest for Perfection in Jewish Antiquity*. Leiden: Brill, 2010.

Nel, Marius. “Daniel 9 as Part of an Apocalyptic Book?” *Verbum et Ecclesia* 34.1 (January, 2013): 1–8.

Neujahr, Matthew James. “Predicting the Past in the Ancient Near East: From Akkadian Ex Eventu Prophecies to Judean Historical Apocalypses.” PhD diss., Yale, 2001.

Neusner, Jacob. “Preface.” Pages ix–xiv in *Judaisms and Their Messiahs at the Turn of the Christian Era*. Edited by Jacob Neusner, William Scott Green, and Ernest S. Frerichs. Cambridge: Cambridge University Press, 1987.

Newsom, Carol A. “Mysticism,” *EDSS*, 588–94.

________. “Theodicy.” *EDEJ* 1303–05.

Nickelsburg, George W. E. *1 Enoch: Chapters 1–36, 81–108*. Vol. 1 of *A Commentary on the Book of 1 Enoch*. Hermeneia: A Critical and Historical Commentary on the Bible. Edited by Klaus Baltzer. Minneapolis: Fortress Press, 2001.

________. “Apocalyptic and Myth in 1 Enoch 6–11.” *JBL* 96.3 (1977): 383–405.

________. “Enochic Wisdom: An Alternative to the Mosaic Torah.” Pages 123–32 in *Hesed Ve-Emet: Studies in Honor of Ernest S. Frerichs*. Edited by Jodi Magness and Seymour Gitin. BJS 320. Atlanta: Scholars Press, 1998.

________. *Jewish Literature between the Bible and the Mishnah*. 2nd ed. Minneapolis, Fortress Press, 2005.

________. "Wisdom and Apocalypticism in Early Judaism: Some Points for Discussion." Pages 17–38 in *Conflicted Boundaries in Wisdom and Apocalypticism*. SBLSS 35. Leiden: Brill, 2003.

Nickelsburg, George W. E. and James C. VanderKam. *1 Enoch, Chapters 37–82*. Vol. 2 of *A Commentary on the Book of 1 Enoch*. Hermeneia: A Critical and Historical Commentary on the Bible. Edited by Klaus Baltzer. Minneapolis: Fortress, 2012.

Nicol, George G. "Isaiah's Vision and the Visions of Daniel." *VT* 29 (1979): 501–05.

Niditch, Susan. *Oral World and Written Word: Ancient Israelite Literature*. LAI. Edited by Douglas A. Knight. Louisville: Westminster John Knox Press, 1996.

Nissinen, Martti. "Prophets and the Divine Council." Pages 4–19 in *Kein Land für sich allein: Studien Zum kulturkontakt in Kanaan, Israel/Palästina und Ebirnâri für Manfred Weippert Zum 65 Geburtstag*. Edited by Ulrich Hübner and Ernst A. Knauf. OBO 186. Göttingen: Vandenhoeck und Ruprecht, 2002.

Noll, Kurt L. "Did 'Scripturalization' Take Place in Second Temple Judaism?" *SJOT* 25.2 (2011): 201–16.

Odeberg, Hugo. *3 Enoch or the Hebrew Book of Enoch*. New York: Ktav, 1973.

Oesterley, W. O. E. "Introduction." Pages vii–xxviii in *The Book of Enoch*. Robert H. Charles. London: SPCK, 1917.

Olson, Daniel C. "1 Enoch." Pages 904–41 in *Eerdmans Commentary on the Bible*. Edited by James D. G. Dunn and John W. Rogerson. Grand Rapids: Eerdmans, 2003.

Orlov, Andrei A. "Enoch, Slavonic Apocalypse of (2 Enoch)." *EDEJ* 587–90.

________. *The Enoch-Metatron Tradition*. TSAJ 107. Tübingen: Mohr Siebeck, 2005.

________. "From Patriarch to the Youth: The Metatron Tradition in '2 Enoch.'" PhD diss., Marquette University, 2004.

________. "The Learned Savant Who Guards the Secrets of the Great Gods: Evolution of Roles and Titles of the Seventh Antediluvian Hero in Mesopotamian and Enochic Traditions

(Part 1: Mesopotamian Traditions)." *Scrinium: Journal of Patrology and Critical Hagiography* 1.1 (2005): 248–64.
Oswalt, John N. *The Book of Isaiah, Chapters 1–39*. NICOT. Grand Rapids: Eerdmans, 1986.
Otto, Eckart. *Das Deuteronomium: politische Theologie und Rechtsreform in Juda und Assyrien*. BZAW 284. Reprint ed. Berlin: de Gruyter, 1999.
Parpola, Simo. "Neo-Assyrian Treaties from the Royal Archives of Nineveh." *JCS* 39.2 (1987): 161–89.
Peters, Dorothy M. *Noah Traditions in the Dead Sea Scrolls: Conversations and Controversies of Antiquity*. EJL 26. Atlanta: Society of Biblical Literature, 2008.
Pfann, Stephan. "Abducted by God? The Process of Heavenly Ascent in Jewish Tradition, from Enoch to Paul, from Paul to Akiva." *Hen* 33.1 (2011): 113–28.
Phillips, David B. W. "Center of the Land." In *Lexham Bible Dictionary*. Edited by John D. Barry, David Bomar, Derek R. Brown, Rachel Klippenstein, Douglas Mangum, Carrie Sinclair Wolcott, Lazarus Wentz, Elliot Ritzema, and Wendy Widder. Bellingham: Lexham Press, 2016.
Plöger, Otto. *Theokratie und Eschatologie*. Niedernberg: ReproPfeffer, 1990.
Pokorný, Petr and Ulrich Heckel. *Einleitung in das Neue Testament: Seine Literatur und Theologie im Überblick*. Uni-Taschenbücher 2798. Tübingen: Mohr Siebeck, 2007.
Pongratz-Leisten, Beate. *Religion and Ideology in Assyria*. Studies in Ancient near Eastern Records 6. Boston: de Gruyter, 2015.
Popović, Mladen. "Astronomy and Astrology." *EDEJ* 400–01.
________. "Networks of Scholars: The Transmission of Astronomical and Astrological Learning between Babylonians, Greeks, and Jews." Pages 153–93 in *Ancient Jewish Sciences and the History of Knowledge in Second Temple Literature*. Edited by Jonathan Ben-Dov and Seth L. Sanders. New York: New York University Press, 2014.
Portier-Young, Anathea E. *Apocalypse against Empire: Theologies of Resistance in Early Judaism*. Grand Rapids: Eerdmans, 2011.
Pritchard, James B., ed. *Ancient Near Eastern Texts Relating to the Old Testament*. Princeton: Princeton University Press, 1969.

Puech, Émile. "Apports des textes apocalyptiques et sapientiels de Qumrân à l'eschatologie du Judaïsme ancien." Pages 133–170 in *Wisdom and Apocalypticism in the Dead Sea Scrolls and in the Biblical Tradition.* Edited by Florentino García Martínez. BETL 168. Leuven: University, 2003.

Raz, Joseph. "Introduction." Pages 1–19 in *Authority.* Edited by Joseph Raz. Readings in Social and Political Theory. New York: NYU Press, 1990.

Reed, Annette Y. *Fallen Angels and the History of Judaism and Christianity: The Reception of Enochic Literature.* Cambridge: Cambridge University Press, 2005.

________. "Heavenly Ascent, Angelic Descent, and the Transmission of Knowledge in 1 Enoch 6–16." Pages 47–66 in *Heavenly Realms and Earthly Realities in Late Antique Religions.* Edited by Ra'anan S. Boustan. Cambridge: Cambridge University Press, 2004. ProQuest Ebrary.

Reeves, John C. "Noah," *EDSS* 612–13.

Rendtorff, Rolf. *The Covenant Formula: An Exegetical and Theological Investigation.* Edinburgh: T&T Clark, 1998.

Reyburn, William David and Euan Mcg Fry. *A Handbook on Genesis.* New York: United Bible Societies, 1998.

Roark, Kyle. "Iron Age Heroes and Enochic Giants." Pages 41–59 in *New Vistas on Early Judaism and Christianity: From Enoch to Montreal and Back.* Edited by Lorenzo DiTommaso and Gerbern S. Oegema. London: Bloombury T&T Clark, 2016.

Rogers, Robert W. *The Religion of Babylonia and Assyria, Especially in Its Relations to Israel: Five Lectures Delivered at Harvard University.* New York: Eaton and Mains, 1908.

Rowley, H. H. *The Relevance of Apocalyptic: A Study of Jewish and Christian Apocalypses from Daniel to the Revelation.* New York: Harper and Bros., 1943.

Rubinkiewicz, Ryszard. "Treatise of Shem: A New Translation and Introduction." Pages 681–88 in vol. 1 of Charlesworth, *OTP.*

Ruffell, Ian. *Aeschylus: Prometheus Bound.* Companions to Greek and Roman Tragedy. London: Bristol Classics Press, 2012.

Sacchi, Paolo. *The History of the Second Temple Period.* JSOTSup 285. Sheffield: Sheffield Academic Press, 2000.

________. *Jewish Apocalyptic and Its History*. Translated by William J Short. JSPSup 20. Sheffield: Sheffield Academic Press, 1996.
Sailhamer, John H. "*Genesis*." Pages 1–284 in *Genesis, Exodus, Leviticus, Numbers*. Vol. 1 of *The Expositor's Bible Commentary*. Edited by Frank E. Gaebelein. Grand Rapids: Zondervan, 1990.
Sanders, E. P. *Paul and Palestinian Judaism: A Comparison of Patterns of Religion*. Philadelphia: Fortress Press, 1977.
________. "Testament of Abraham: A New Translation and Introduction." Pages 871–82 in vol. 1 of Charlesworth, *OTP*.
Sanders, Seth. "'I Was Shown Another Calculation' (אחרן חשבון אחזית): The Language of Knowledge in Aramaic Enoch and Priestly Hebrew." Pages 69–101 in *Ancient Jewish Sciences and the History of Knowledge in Second Temple Literature*. Edited by Jonathan Ben-Dov and Seth Sanders. New York: NYU Press, 2014.
Sanft, Charles. *Communication and Cooperation in Early Imperial China: Publicizing the Qin Dynasty*. Suny Series in Chinese Philosophy and Culture. Albany: State University of New York Press, 2014.
Sarton, George. *Ancient Science through the Golden Age of Greece*. Dover ed. New York: Dover Publications, 1993.
Scanlon, Larry. *Narrative, Authority and Power: The Medieval Exemplum and the Chaucerian Tradition*. Cambridge Studies in Medieval Literature 20. New York: Cambridge University Press, 2007.
Schattner-Rieser, Ursula. "Levi in the Third Sky: On the `Ascent to Heaven' Legends within Their near Eastern Context and J. T. Milik's Unpublished Version of the Aramaic Levi Document." Pages 801–19 in *Dead Sea Scrolls in Context: Integrating the Dead Sea Scrolls in the Study of Ancient Texts, Languages and Cultures*. Vol. 2. Edited by Armin Lange, Emanuel Tov, and Matthias Weigold. VTSup 140. Leiden: Brill, 2011.
Scheftelowitz, Isidor. *Die Altpersische religion und das Judentum: Unterschiede, Übereinstimmungen und gegenseitige Beeinflussungen*. Giessen: Töpelmann, 1920.
Schiffman, Lawrence H. *Qumran and Jerusalem: Studies in the Dead Sea Scrolls and the History of Judaism*. Grand Rapids: Eerdmans, 2010.

Schipper, Bernd Ulrich and Andreas Blasius, eds. *Apokalyptik und Ägypten: Eine kritische Analyse der relevanten Texte aus dem griechisch-römischen Ägypten*. OLA 107. Leuven: Peeters, 2002.

Schofield, Alison. *From Qumran to the Yaḥad: A New Paradigm of Textual Development for "the Community Rule."* STJD 77. Leiden: Brill, 2009.

Schmidt, B. B. "Moon," *DDD* 585–93.

Schultz, Richard L. *The Search for Quotation: Verbal Parallels in the Prophets*. JSOTSup 180. Edited by David J. A. Clines, Philip R. Davies, and John Jarick. Sheffield: Sheffield Academic Press, 1999.

Schürer, Emil. *A History of the Jewish People in the Time of Jesus Christ, Second Division*. Vol. 2. Edinburgh: T&T Clark, 1890.

Scott, J. Julius. *Jewish Backgrounds of the New Testament*. Grand Rapids: Baker Books, 2000.

Sears, Elizabeth. "Orpheus." Pages 664–66 in *The Classical Tradition*. Edited by Anthony Grafton, Glenn W. Most, and Salvatore Settis. Harvard University Press Reference Library. Cambridge: Harvard University Press, 2010.

Seeman, Chris. "From Alexander to Pompey." *EDEJ* 25–39.

Selbie, J. A. "Recent Foreign Theology: The Babel-Bibel Controversy." *ExpTim* 14.12 (1903): 544–50.

Shaw, Ian. "Deir el-Bersha." Pages 196–97 in *A Dictionary of Archeology*. Edited by Ian Shaw and Robert Jameson. Malden: Blackwell Publishers, 1999.

Silverman, Jason M. "Iranian Details in the Book of Heavenly Luminaries (1 Enoch 72–82)." *JNES* 72.2 (2013): 195–208.

________. *Persepolis and Jerusalem: Iranian Influence on the Apocalyptic Hermeneutic*. LHBOTS 558. London: T&T Clark, 2014.

Skinner, Quentin. "Meaning and Understanding in the History of Ideas." *HistTh* 8.1 (1969): 3.

Smart, C. trans. *The Works of Horace*. Medford: Harper and Brothers, 1863.

Smelik, Klass A. D. "*Ma'at*." *DDD* 534–35.

Smith, Gary V. *Isaiah 1–39*. NAC 15A. Nashville: Broadman & Holman, 2007.

Smith, Jonathan Z. "Introduction." Pages ix–xxii in *The Myth of the Eternal Return: Cosmos and History*. Mircea Eliade. Bollingen Series 46. 2nd paperback ed. Princeton: Princeton University Press, 2005.

Smith, Richard G. *The Fate of Justice and Righteousness During David's Reign: Rereading the Court History and Its Ethics According to 2 Samuel 8:15–20:26*. LHBOTS 508. New York: T&T Clark, 2009.

Smith, William. "Zoroaster." Page 955 in *A New Classical Dictionary of Greek and Roman Biography Mythology and Geography Partly Based Upon the Dictionary of Greek and Roman Biography and Mythology*. Edited by Charles Anthon. New York: Harper and Brothers, 1878.

Smyth, Herber W. trans. *Aeschylus, with an English Translation by Herber Smyth.* Vol. 1 of *Prometheus Bound.* Cambridge: Harvard University Press, 1926.

Stausberg, Michael. "Zoroastrian Rituals." *Encyclopaedia Iranica.* New York: Encyclopaedia Iranica Foundation, 2014. http://www.iranicaonline.org/articles/zoroastrian-rituals.

Stokes, Ryan E. "The Throne Visions of Daniel 7, 1 Enoch 14 and the Qumran Book of Giants (4Q530): An Analysis of Their Literary Relationship." *DSD* 15.3 (2008): 340–58.

Stone, Michael E. "Enoch, Aramaic Levi and Sectarian Origins." *JSJ* 19.2 (1988): 159–70.

Stuckenbruck, Loren T. *1 Enoch 91–108*. CEJL. Berlin: de Gruyter, 2007.

________. "Apocrypha and Pseudepigrapha." *EDEJ* 143–62.

________. "Pseudepigraphy and First Person Discourse in the Dead Sea Documents: From the Aramaic Texts to Writings of the Yaḥad." Pages 295–326 in *Dead Sea Scrolls and Contemporary Culture: Proceedings of the International Conference Held at the Israel Museum, Jerusalem (July 6–8, 2008)*. Edited by Adolfo Roitman, Lawrence H. Schiffman and Shani Tzoref. STDJ 93. Leiden: Brill, 2011.

Suter, David W. "Fallen Angel, Fallen Priest: The Problem of Family Purity in 1 Enoch 6–16." *HUCA* 50 (1979): 115–35.

Sweeney, Marvin A. "Pardes Revisited Once Again: A Reassessment of the Rabbinic Legend Concerning the Four Who Entered Pardes." *Shofar* 22.4 (Summer, 2004): 43–56.

Terrien, Samuel. "The *Omphalos* Myth and Hebrew Religion." *VT* 20 (1970): 315–38.

Thomas, Samuel I. *The "Mysteries" of Qumran: Mystery, Secrecy, and Esotericism in the Dead Sea Scrolls*. EJL 25. Atlanta: Society of Biblical Literature, 2009.

Tigay, Jeffrey H. דברים; *Deuteronomy: The Traditional Hebrew Text with the New JPS Translation and Commentary*. The JPS Torah Commentary. Philadelphia: Jewish Publication Society, 1996.

Tigchelaar, Eibert. "Aramaic Texts from Qumran and the Authoritativeness of Hebrew Scriptures: Preliminary Observations." Pages 155–72 in *Authoritative Scriptures in Ancient Judaism*. Edited by Mladen Popović. Leiden: Brill, 2010.

Tirosh-Samuelson, Hava. "Jewish Mysticism." Pages 399–423 in *The Cambridge Guide to Jewish History, Religion, and Culture*. Edited by Judith R. Baskin and Kenneth Seeskin. Cambridge: Cambridge University Press, 2010.

Tov, Emanuel. *Textual Criticism of the Hebrew Bible*. 2nd rev. ed. Minneapolis: Fortress, 1992. 303.

Tong, Cheu Hock. "The Festival of the Nine Emperor Gods in Malaysia: Myth, Ritual, and Symbol." *Asian Folklore Studies* 55.1 (1996): 49–72.

Trebolle Barrera, Julio C. "Antiguo Testamento y helenismo: los últimos escritos del Antiguo Testamento y la influencia del helenismo." *EstBib* 61.2 (January 1, 2003): 277.

________. "Origins of a Tripartite Old Testament Canon." Pages 128–45 in *The Canon Debate*. Edited by Lee Martin McDonald and James A. Sanders. Peabody, MA: Hendrickson Publishers, 2002.

Ulanowski, Krzysztof. "Mesopotamian Divination: Some Historical, Religious, and Anthropological Remarks." *Miscellanea Anthropological et Sociologica* 15.4 (2014): 13–28.

Ulansey, David. *The Origins of the Mithraic Mysteries: Cosmology and Salvation in the Ancient World*. New York: Oxford University Press, 1991.

VanderKam, James C. *The Book of Jubilees*. Sheffield: Sheffield Academic, 2001.

________. *Enoch and the Growth of an Apocalyptic Tradition*. CBQMS 16. Washington: Catholic Biblical Association of America, 1984.

________. *An Introduction to Early Judaism*. Grand Rapids: Eerdmans, 2001.

VanGemeren, Willem. "Covenant." *BEB* 2:1860–62.

Vermes, Geza. "La communauté de la Nouvelle Alliances d'après ses écrits réemment découverts." *ETL* 27 (1951): 70–80.

von Rad, Gerhard. *The Theology of Israel's Prophetic Traditions*. Vol. 2 of *Old Testament Theology*. Translated by D. M. G. Stalker. New York: Harper and Row, 1965.

Wacholder, B. Z. "Jubilees as Super Canon: Torah-Admonition Versus Torah-Commandment." Pages 195–211 in *Legal Texts and Legal Issues: Proceedings of the Second Meeting of the International Organization for Qumran Studies, Cambridge, 1995, Published in Honour of Joseph M. Baumgarten*. Edited by M. J. Bernstein, García Martínez, and J. Kampen. STDJ 23 Leiden: Brill, 1997.

Waddell, Robby. "A Green Apocalypse: Coming Secular and Religious Eschatological Visions of Earth." Pages 133–50 in *Blood Cries Out: Pentecostals, Ecology, and the Groans of Creation*. Edited by A. J. Swoboda. Pentecostals, Peacemaking, and Social Justice 8. Eugene: Wipf & Stock, 2014.

Waldemer, Thomas P. "Hijacking Authority: Writing and Forgery in *Viva O Povo Brasileiro*." *Hispanofila* 146 (2006): 49–58.

Walzer, Michael. *In God's Shadow: Politics in the Hebrew Bible*. New Haven: Yale University Press, 2012.

Watts, John D. W. *Isaiah 1–33*. WBC 24. Rev. ed. Nashville: Thomas Nelson, 2005.

Weeks, Noel. *Admonition and Curse: The Ancient Near Eastern Treaty/Covenant Form as a Problem in Inter-Cultural Relationships*. LHBOTS 407. London: T&T Clark, 2004.

________. "The Bible and the 'Universal' Ancient World: A Critique of John Walton." *WTJ* 78.1 (2016): 1–28.

Weinfeld, Moshe. "God Versus Moses in the Temple Scroll: 'I Do Not Speak on My Own Authority, but on God's Authority.'" *RevQ* 15 (1992): 175–80.

Wenham, Gordon J. *Genesis 1–15*. WBC 1. Dallas: Word, 1998.

Wensinck, Arent J. "The Ideas of the Western Semites Concerning the Navel of the Earth." *Verhandelingen der Koninklijke Akademie van Wetenschappen: Nieuwe Reeks* 17.1 (1916): 10–70.

Werrett, Ian C. *Ritual Purity and the Dead Sea Scrolls*. Edited by Florentino García Martínez. STDJ 72. Leiden: Brill, 2007.

West, Martin L. *The Orphic Poems*. Oxford University Press Academic Monograph Reprints Series. Oxford: Clarendon Press, 1983.

Whitt, William D. "The Jacob Traditions in Hosea and Their Relation to Genesis." *ZAW* 103.1 (2009): 18–43.

Wildfang, Robin L. *Rome's Vestal Virgins: A Study of Rome's Vestal Priestesses in the Late Republic and Early Empire*. London: Routledge, 2006.

Williamson, Paul R. *Abraham, Israel, and the Nations: The Patriarchal Promise and Its Covenantal Development in Genesis*. LHBOTS 315. Sheffield: Sheffield Academic Press, 2000.

Wilson, Robert R. "From Prophecy to Apocalypticism." *Semeia* 21 (1981): 79.

________. *Prophecy and Society in Ancient Israel*. Philadelphia: Fortress, 2011.

Winckler, Hugo. *Himmels- und Weltenbild der Babylonier: Grundlage der Weltanschauung und Mythologie aller Völker*. AO 3.2/3. Leipzig: J. C. Hinrichs'sche Buchhandlung, 1903.

Wintermute, Orval S. "Apocalypse of Elijah: A New Translation and Introduction." Pages 721–35 in vol. 1 of Charlesworth, *OTP*.

Wolfson, Elliot R. "Unveiling the Veil: Apocalyptic, Secrecy, and the Jewish Mystical Imaginaire." *AJS Perspectives: The Magazine of the Association of Jewish Studies*, Fall 2012. http://www.bjpa.org/Publications/details.cfm?PublicationID=20997.

Wong, Eva. *Tales of the Dancing Dragon: Stories of the Tao*. Eastern Philosophy and Taoism Series. Boston: Shambhala, 2007.

Wright, Benjamin G. "Pseudonymous Authorship and Structures of Authority in the *Letter of Aristeas*." Pages 43–62 in *Scriptural Authority in Early Judaism and Ancient Christianity*. Edited by

Isaac Kalimi, Tobias Nicklas and Géza G. Xeravits. DCLS 15. Berlin: de Gruyter, 2013.
Wyatt, Nicholas. *Space and Time in the Religious Life of the Near East*. Sheffield: Sheffield Academic Press, 2001.
Xeravits, Géza G., ed. *Dualism in Qumran*. LSTS, New York: T&T Clark, 2010.
Yates, Frances A. *Giordano Bruno and the Hermetic Tradition*. Chicago: University of Chicago Press, 1964.
Yilmaz, Kaya. "Postmodernism and Its Challenge to the Discipline of History: Implications for History Education." *Educational Philosophy and Theory* 42.7 (2010): 779.
Young, Edward. *The Book of Isaiah*. Vol. 2: *Chapters 19–39*. Grand Rapids: Eerdmans, 1969.
Young, Robert D., Bertrand Desjardins, Kirsten Mclaughlin, Michel Poulain and Thomas T. Perls. "Typologies of Extreme Longevity Myths." *Current Gerontology and Geriatrics Research* (2010). http://dx.doi.org/10.1155/2010/423087
Zahn, Molly M. "Torah for 'the Age of Wickedness': The Authority of the Damascus and Serekh Texts in Light of Biblical and Rewritten Traditions." *DSD* 20.3 (2013): 410–32.
Zimmerli, Walther. *Ezekiel: A Commentary on the Book of the Prophet Ezekiel*. Translated by Ronald E. Clements. Vol. 2. Hermeneia: A Critical and Historical Commentary on the Bible. Edited by Frank Moore Cross, Klaus Baltzer, Paul D. Hanson, Leonard J. Greenspoon, and Walther Zimmerli. Philadelphia: Fortress, 1979.
Zimmern, Heinrich. *Biblische und Babylonische Urgeschichte*. AO 2.3. Leipzig: J. C. Hinrichs'sche Buchhandlung, 1903.
________. "Überblick über die babylonische Religion in bezug auf ihre Berührung it biblischen Vorstellungen." Pages 347–643 in *Die keilinschriften und das Alte Testament*. 3rd ed. Edited by Heinrich Zimmern and H. Winckler. Berlin: Verlag von Reuther and Reichard, 1903.
Zízěk, Slavoj. *The Parallax View*. Cambridge: MIT Press, 2006.

Index of Modern Authors

Index of Primary Sources

Subject Index